BEST PRACTICES IN EARLY LITERACY INSTRUCTION

Also from Diane M. Barone and Marla H. Mallette

Children's Literature in the Classroom: Engaging Lifelong Readers
Diane M. Barone

Literacy and Young Children: Research-Based Practices
Edited by Diane M. Barone and Lesley Mandel Morrow

Literacy Instruction for English Language Learners Pre-K–2
Diane M. Barone and Shelley Hong Xu

Literacy Research Methodologies, Second Edition
Edited by Nell K. Duke and Marla H. Mallette

Narrowing the Literacy Gap: What Works in High-Poverty Schools
Diane M. Barone

Teaching Early Literacy: Development, Assessment, and Instruction
Diane M. Barone, Marla H. Mallette, and Shelley Hong Xu

Best Practices in Early Literacy Instruction

Edited by
Diane M. Barone
Marla H. Mallette

THE GUILFORD PRESS
New York   London

© 2013 The Guilford Press
A Division of Guilford Publications, Inc.
72 Spring Street, New York, NY 10012
www.guilford.com

Printed in the United States of America

This book is printed on acid-free paper.

Last digit is print number: 9   8   7   6   5   4   3   2   1

Library of Congress Cataloging-in-Publication Data is available from the Publisher.

ISBN 978-1-4625-1156-3 (paperback)
ISBN 978-1-4625-1176-1 (hardcover)

About the Editors

Diane M. Barone, EdD, is Foundation Professor of Literacy Studies at the University of Nevada, Reno. Her research focuses on young children's literacy development and instruction in high-poverty schools. Dr. Barone served as the editor of *Reading Research Quarterly* and was a board member of the International Reading Association and the National Reading Conference. She is coeditor of *The Reading Teacher* with Marla H. Mallette.

Marla H. Mallette, PhD, is Associate Professor of Literacy Education at Binghamton University. Her research interests include literacy instruction and learning with students of culturally and linguistically diverse backgrounds, and early literacy. She is also interested in literacy research methodologies and has used various methodologies in her own work. Dr. Mallette is coeditor of *The Reading Teacher* with Diane M. Barone.

Contributors

Peter P. Afflerbach, PhD, is Professor in The Reading Center, University of Maryland, where he teaches graduate and undergraduate courses in reading assessment and reading comprehension. Dr. Afflerbach's research interests include reading assessment, reading comprehension, and the verbal reporting methodology. He is the author/editor of several books and has published in numerous theoretical and practical journals. He has served as Chair of the Literacy Assessment Committee, International Reading Association, and on the National Association of Educational Progress Reading Panel and Common Core Standards Review Panels. Dr. Afflerbach was elected to the Reading Hall of Fame in 2009.

Richard L. Allington, PhD, is Professor of Literacy Studies at the University of Tennessee and a past president of the International Reading Association and the Literacy Research Association. He has been twice corecipient of the Albert J. Harris Award in recognition of research contributing to the understanding of reading and learning disabilities, and has been named to the Reading Hall of Fame.

Kimberly L. Anderson, PhD, is Director of Professional Development for the Interactive Strategies Approach (ISA) Professional Development Project. She is jointly affiliated with the Child Research and Study Center and the Reading Department at the University at Albany. Her research interests include early literacy development and instruction and web-based professional development for teachers working with early literacy learners.

Diane M. Barone. See "About the Editors."

Monica T. Billen, MA, is a doctoral student at the University of Tennessee, Knoxville (UTK), in the Theory and Practice in Teacher Education Department. She is a graduate teaching assistant in the UTK Reading Center, where she teaches reading education undergraduate courses and a teacher education course for intern teachers. In addition, Ms. Billen supervises and mentors beginning teachers. Her research interests include reading instruction, preservice teacher identity, and the reciprocal relationship of reading and writing instruction. Before beginning her doctoral work, she was an elementary school teacher.

James Christie, PhD, is Professor of Social and Family Dynamics at Arizona State University. His research interests include early literacy development and children's play. He has published a number of books, chapters, and journal articles on these topics. Dr. Christie has been a member of the Early Literacy Development Committee of the International Reading Association and is a past president of the Association for the Study of Play. He has codirected Early Reading First (ERF) projects in Arizona (San Luis and Bullhead City) and Gallup, New Mexico. All three ERF projects have a heavy emphasis on literacy-enriched play settings. Dr. Christie also served as editorial advisor for *Sesame Street* magazine for many years.

Catherine Compton-Lilly, PhD, is Associate Professor in Curriculum and Instruction at the University of Wisconsin–Madison. She is the author of several articles and books, including *Reading Families: The Literate Lives of Urban Children* and *Reading Time.* Dr. Compton-Lilly engages in extended longitudinal research projects—in her most recent study, she followed a group of eight inner-city students from grades 1 through 11. Her interests include examining how time operates as a contextual factor in children's lives as they progress through school and construct their identities as students and readers.

Nell K. Duke, EdD, is Professor of Language, Literacy, and Culture at the University of Michigan. She focuses on early literacy development, particularly among children living in poverty. Among her books is *Literacy and the Youngest Learner: Best Practices for Educators of Children from Birth to 5.*

Tanya R. Flushman, PhD, is Assistant Professor in the School of Education at California Polytechnic State University at San Luis Obispo. Her research focuses on literacy and language development in early childhood and supporting practicing teachers with implementation of emergent literacy practices and content literacy instruction.

Kylie S. Flynn, PhD, is Associate in Research at Florida State University's Florida Center for Reading Research. Her research interests focus on improving early literacy skills for students living in poverty, as well as those at risk for or diagnosed with disabilities. Relatedly, she is interested in developing instructional interventions and methods of training teachers to effectively implement evidence-based practices.

Marcia Invernizzi, PhD, is the Henderson Professor of Reading Education at the University of Virginia's Curry School of Education, where she also serves as Director of the McGuffey Reading Center. She is Principal Investigator of Phonological Awareness Literacy Screening (PALS), a founder of the Book Buddies tutoring framework, and a coauthor of *Words Their Way.*

Smriti Jangra, MA, is a PhD student in Educational Psychology and Learning Systems at the College of Education at Florida State University and Graduate Research Assistant at National High Field Magnetic Laboratory. Her research interests include gender differences in curriculum and instruction at the preschool and elementary level.

Melanie R. Kuhn, PhD, is Associate Professor in Literacy Education at Boston University. She has taught in the Boston public schools, at an adult education program, and at an international school in England. She has authored or coauthored numerous articles, chapters, and the books *The Hows and Whys of Fluency Instruction* and *Fluency in the Classroom*. Her interests include literacy instruction for struggling readers and the importance of wide reading. She currently teaches courses on reading methods, assessment, and content-area literacy instruction.

Christopher J. Lonigan, PhD, is Distinguished Research Professor of Psychology and Associate Director of the Florida Center for Reading Research at Florida State University. His research interests include the development, assessment, and promotion of preschool early literacy skills and self-regulation.

Marla H. Mallette. See "About the Editors."

Jackie Marsh, PhD, is Professor of Education at the University of Sheffield, United Kingdom. Her research focuses on the role and nature of popular culture, media, and new technologies in young children's literacy development. Dr. Marsh is an editor of the *Journal of Early Childhood Literacy* and, with Joanne Larson, coeditor of the *Sage Handbook of Early Childhood Literacy* (2nd ed.).

Allyssa McCabe, PhD, is Professor of Psychology at the University of Massachusetts–Lowell. She researches how narrative develops with age, how parents and teachers can facilitate narrative development, and cultural differences in narration. She is coauthor of a theoretical approach to early literacy called the Comprehensive Language Approach, which looks at ways that various strands of oral and written language affect each other in the acquisition of full literacy.

Andrea Morency, MEd, is an elementary school teacher and a PhD student in Education at the University of Nevada, Reno. She is the program director for Reading Buddies, a literacy intervention program in three Reno elementary schools, and president of the Board of Directors for the Honors Academy of Literature in Reno.

Annie M. Moses, PhD, is Assistant Professor of Early Childhood/Teacher Education in the Department of Education and Allied Studies at John Carroll University. Her research focuses on early literacy development, media, and early childhood education. She has published on these topics in the *Journal of Children and Media*, the *Journal of Literacy Research*, *Young Children*, and more. She is also coauthor of the books *Literacy and the Youngest Learner: Best*

Practices for Educators of Children from Birth to 5 and *Beyond Bedtime Stories: A Parent's Guide to Promoting Reading, Writing and Other Literacy Skills from Birth to 5.*

Susan B. Neuman, EdD, is Professor in Teaching and Learning at the University of Michigan, specializing in early literacy development. She has served as the U.S. Assistant Secretary for Elementary and Secondary Education and is coeditor of *Reading Research Quarterly.* Her research and teaching interests include early childhood policy, curriculum, and early reading instruction, PreK–3, for children who live in poverty.

Kristina Zukauskas Phelan, MEd, is Reading Specialist at the Mahala F. Atchison School, a public elementary school in Tinton Falls, New Jersey, where she teaches K–3 students who need extra support in reading. She has over 15 years of experience as both a classroom teacher and reading interventionist working with individual students and small groups.

Beth M. Phillips, PhD, is Associate Professor of Educational Psychology and Learning Systems at the College of Education at Florida State University and Faculty Associate of the Florida Center for Reading Research. Her research interests and publication focus includes preschool curriculum and instruction, professional development, parental influences on learning, and overlap between literacy and behavioral development.

Shannon Riley-Ayers, PhD, is Assistant Research Professor at the National Institute for Early Education Research (NIEER) at Rutgers University. A former classroom teacher, she conducts research and provides technical assistance on issues related to early literacy, early childhood assessment, and professional development. She is the lead author of the Early Learning Scale, a comprehensive performance-based assessment system.

Kathleen A. Roskos, PhD, teaches courses in reading assessment and instruction at John Carroll University. Formerly an elementary classroom teacher, she has served in a variety of educational roles, including director of federal programs in the public schools, department chair in higher education, director of the Ohio Literacy Initiative at the Ohio Department of Education, and a coprincipal investigator of several ERF federal projects. Dr. Roskos studies early literacy development, teacher learning, and the instructional design of professional development for educators, and has published research articles, chapters, and books on these topics.

Deborah Wells Rowe, PhD, is Associate Professor in the Language, Literacy, and Culture Program at Peabody College, Vanderbilt University. Her research on social, cultural, and semiotic features of preschoolers' writing has been recognized with the International Reading Association's Dina Feitelson Research Award. She serves as coeditor for the *Journal of Early Childhood Literacy.*

Donna M. Scanlon, PhD, is Professor in the Reading Department at the University at Albany and is affiliated with the university's Child Research and Study Center. She has done extensive research focused on the causes and correlates of reading difficulties, approaches to preventing and remediating reading difficulties, and the relationships between instruction and success in learning to read. Dr. Scanlon's recent work focuses on teacher education and professional development for early literacy teachers.

Paula J. Schwanenflugel, PhD, is Professor of Educational Psychology and Adjunct Professor of Linguistics and Cognitive Science at the University of Georgia, where she teaches courses on educational psychology, child development, and applied psycholinguistics. Dr. Schwanenflugel has over 100 publications, most of which relate to the development of language and literacy. Her current work focuses on the development of reading fluency, particularly the development of reading expression and the instruction of reading fluency, and on effective instructional practices for enhancing oral language and early literacy in prekindergarten and kindergarten children. She has served on editorial boards of several journals over the course of her career.

Katherine A. Dougherty Stahl, EdD, is Associate Professor of Reading at New York University, where she teaches graduate courses and serves as Director of the Literacy Program and Director of the NYU Literacy Clinic. Her research focuses on reading acquisition, comprehension, and struggling readers. She taught in public elementary school classrooms for over 25 years.

Galiya A. Tabulda, MS, is currently pursuing her PhD in the Learning and Cognition Program at the Department of Educational Psychology and Learning Systems at Florida State University. Her research interests include first- and second-language acquisition among children and adult learners.

Laura S. Tortorelli, MEd, is Graduate Research Assistant with the PALS Español project at the Curry School of Education at the University of Virginia. A former reading teacher and curriculum developer for the Institute of Reading Development, she is now earning her PhD in Reading Education.

Frank R. Vellutino, PhD, is Distinguished Professor at the University at Albany, the State University of New York, where he holds joint appointments in the Department of Psychology and the Department of Educational and Counseling Psychology. Most of his research has been concerned with reading development, the cognitive underpinnings of reading, and the relationship between reading difficulties and various aspects of language and other cognitive functions.

Lynne M. Watanabe, MA, is a doctoral student in the Department of Educational Psychology and Educational Technology at Michigan State University. She is a former kindergarten teacher, and her research interests focus on the literacy learning and development of young children, particularly in relation to the reading and writing of specific genres.

Christine E. Wiggs, PhD, is a third/fourth-grade Title I and gifted teacher at an elementary school in Southern Illinois. Dr. Wiggs previously taught in a third-grade classroom and is a state-endorsed Reading Specialist. Her research interests include elementary literacy instruction, differentiated literacy instruction, and struggling readers' perceptions.

Tanya S. Wright, **PhD**, is Assistant Professor of Teacher Education at Michigan State University. She is a former kindergarten teacher whose research and teaching focuses on instruction in early language and literacy, with particular attention to improving educational outcomes for children living in poverty. Dr. Wright is the winner of the International Reading Association's Dissertation of the Year Award for 2012.

Dylan Yamada-Rice, PhD, is Lecturer in Early Years Education at the University of Sheffield, United Kingdom. Her research interests include early childhood literacy, multimodal communication practices, and visual and multimodal research methods. Ms. Yamada-Rice earned an Economic and Social Research Council (ESRC)-funded PhD that focuses on young children's interaction with and comprehension of the visual mode as one aspect of contemporary multimodality. Her previous research explored children's access to digital technologies that foreground the visual mode, the way in which family members support engagement with digital technologies, and differences in texts using the visual mode in the urban landscapes of Tokyo and London.

Preface

> The preschool classroom can be a significant source of early literacy learning for children. What is taught and how it is taught in this setting is a product of multiple influences: social, epistemological, and policy environments, teachers' beliefs and backgrounds, and—increasingly these days—research.
> —TEALE, HOFFMAN, and PACIGA (2010, p. 311)

Over the course of the past decade, the field of early literacy has become highly politicized, as evidenced in the National Early Literacy Panel Report (NELP, 2008), a report that identified and synthesized the research on early precursors to school success in literacy identified in experimental and predictive research, and a subsequent themed issue in *Educational Researcher* (2010), which featured theoretical and methodological critiques of the report by prominent early literacy scholars. The report found five variables that predicted future literacy skills: alphabet knowledge; phonological awareness; rapid naming of letters, objects, and colors; writing, including writing one's name; and phonological memory. The panel also found that concepts of print, print knowledge, reading readiness (e.g., combination of concepts or print, vocabulary, memory, and phonological awareness), oral language, and visual processing were predictors for future literacy achievement.

Research in early literacy is incredibly diverse and voluminous. Consider, for example, the *Handbook of Early Literacy Research* (Dickinson & Neuman, 2007; Neuman & Dickinson, 2003, 2010), which comprises three comprehensive volumes published in the course of just 7 years. These volumes include the more traditional phonological base for early literacy but move beyond this focus to include oral language, environment, home and school influences, and instructional materials and classroom practice, among other topics. The primary focus of these volumes is a comprehensive research review, large-scale studies, and theoretical overviews.

We considered this rich foundation of knowledge and instruction in early literacy as we created *Best Practices in Early Literacy Instruction*. We wanted this edited volume to address both research and resultant classroom practice. We asked each researcher to provide a research foundation for a topic in early literacy and then shift to showing this research in practice. We wanted teachers and researchers to acknowledge the links between research and practice so that these exemplary practices find their way to early childhood classrooms.

All the chapters are written by prominent early literacy scholars, and each provides practitioners, early childhood leaders, administrators, and university students with a comprehensive and concise overview of evidence-based best practices. Each author shares guiding questions, an overview of the topic, important theoretical background and research, and a classroom example of the practice(s). Moreover, the book is organized into four major parts. The first part targets influences on literacy development such as the home, cultural and linguistic diversity, language, and preschool effects. The second part centers on materials and text such as informational text, media, children's literature, and new literacies. The third part considers instruction with a look at phonological awareness and the alphabet, comprehension, vocabulary, fluency, writing, and play. The final part focuses on intervention and assessment in the primary grades and response to intervention (RTI).

Following is an overview of each of the chapters. We begin with Part I, "Influences on Literacy Development." In the first chapter, "Parent Involvement Supporting Early Literacy Achievement: Best Practices for Bridging the Home and School Environments," by Beth M. Phillips, Kylie S. Flynn, Galiya A. Tabulda, Smriti Jangra, and Christopher J. Lonigan, the authors tease out effective parental practices that support young children's literacy development. They offer specific practices that have a strong research base indicating success. Within their chapter are suggestions to bridge the school–home connection even when working with parents in high-poverty circumstances. In the second chapter, "A Comprehensive Approach to Building Oral Language in Preschool: Prerequisites for Literacy," by Allyssa McCabe, readers will explore how to support oral language development. The author shows exactly how preschool teachers can bring oral language practices to their classrooms. In the third chapter, "Working with Culturally and Linguistically Diverse Students: Lessons Learned from Reading Recovery," Catherine Compton-Lilly uses her experiences with Reading Recovery to offer suggestions for students with diverse backgrounds. Her student examples present readers with ways to observe, think about, and provide appropriate literacy strategies for young children. In the final chapter, "Supporting Language and Literacy Development in Quality Preschools," Shannon Riley-Ayers provides descriptions of high-quality preschools. For each quality she shares a real example from a preschool to showcase how these qualities work in practice and what students should be able to do. This first part of the volume offers numerous ways to support young learners both at home and at school in important literacy activities.

Part II, "Materials and Texts," shifts focus to materials and texts that are exemplary for young learners. This part begins with two chapters focusing on new literacies and media. In the first of these chapters, "Early Literacy Development in the Digital Age," Jackie Marsh and Dylan Yamada-Rice nudge teachers and researchers to consider the changes in literacy knowledge due to the digital age. They demonstrate how digital literacy can be interwoven into a preschool classroom. The second chapter, "What, When, and How Electronic Media Can Be Used in an Early Literacy Classroom," by Annie M. Moses, pairs nicely with the preceding chapter. The author examines the kinds of electronic media that young children use and their impact on early literacy skills, and highlights the decisions a teacher made as she brought electronic media into her classroom throughout a year. In the next chapter, "New Perspectives on Literature for Young Children," Diane M. Barone and Andrea Morency share the importance of understanding the visual in children's picture books and describe many new formats for children's books such as e-books and apps. In the final chapter, "Read All About I.T.!: Informational Text in the Early Childhood Classroom," Lynne M. Watanabe and Nell K. Duke highlight the definition, importance, types, and gender preferences of informational text in the early childhood classroom. Within their chapter are numerous ways for teachers to integrate informational text into their classrooms.

Part III, "Reconceptualizing Developmentally Appropriate Practice," considers traditional areas of literacy: phonological awareness, alphabet knowledge, comprehension, vocabulary, fluency, writing, and play. Each of these chapters offers the most current practices for young learners. In the first chapter, "Phonological Awareness and Alphabetic Knowledge: The Foundation of Early Reading," Marcia Invernizzi and Laura S. Tortorelli explain the importance of phonological awareness and alphabet knowledge. Moreover, they describe how these elements are woven together and how teachers can modify activities to support the learning of all students. In the next chapter, "Reading to Learn from the Beginning: Comprehension Instruction in the Primary Grades," Katherine A. Dougherty Stahl shares how even very young children can be taught to comprehend when listening to books and engaging in conversation about them. Further, she offers teachers the elements of a complete comprehension curriculum. In the next chapter, "Best Practices in Oral Vocabulary Instruction," Susan B. Neuman and Tanya S. Wright write about accelerating the vocabulary development of young children with recommendations for selecting words and then teaching them. In the following chapter, "Real Books, Real Reading: Effective Fluency Instruction for Striving Readers," Melanie R. Kuhn, Kristina Zukauskas Phelan, and Paula J. Schwanenflugel shift from vocabulary to fluency. These authors build connections among comprehension, vocabulary, and fluency. They offer research-based strategies to support fluency and describe their use within a classroom. In the next chapter, "Best Practices in Early Writing Instruction," Deborah Wells Rowe and Tanya R. Flushman provide a developmental continuum of early writing. They then illustrate this continuum in action as they provide examples of young children's writing. In the final chapter, "Strengthening Play in Early Literacy Teaching Practice," Kathleen A. Roskos and James Christie describe ways in which play and literacy are interrelated. They describe play settings that encourage literacy interactions with print.

Part IV targets "Intervention and Assessment." In the first chapter, " 'How Am I Doing?': Students' Perceptions of Literacy and Themselves," Marla H. Mallette, Peter P. Afflerbach, and Christine E. Wiggs offer readers an opportunity to explore reading through students' eyes. They suggest that students' perceptions can guide literacy instruction. In the second chapter, "The Interactive Strategies Approach to Early Literacy Intervention," Donna M. Scanlon, Kimberly L. Anderson, and Frank R. Vellutino share their research history and the resultant model for early literacy intervention. Readers may be surprised at how they focus on meaning as they simultaneously support students' word learning. In the final chapter, "An Evidence-Based Approach to Response to Intervention," Monica T. Billen and Richard L. Allington provide direction about RTI, including a complete description of the model and its intent, and an overview of instruction. From this theoretical grounding, the authors show how an exemplary teacher brings these practices to a classroom.

Each chapter within this volume offers important theoretical and practical knowledge. Collectively, the chapters offer a rich perspective of early childhood literacy education. We thank our authors for providing the links between theory and research and practice. We know that this volume will make a difference in the lives of young children as their teachers include these practices within their classroom instructional repertoire.

REFERENCES

Dickinson, D. K., & Neuman, S. B. (Eds.). (2007). *Handbook of early literacy research* (Vol. 2). New York: Guilford Press.

National Early Literacy Panel Report. (2008). *Developing early literacy.* Washington, DC: National Institute for Literacy.

Neuman, S. B., & Dickinson, D. K. (Eds.). (2003). *Handbook of early literacy research* (Vol. 1). New York: Guilford Press.

Neuman, S. B., & Dickinson, D. K. (Eds.). (2010). *Handbook of early literacy research* (Vol. 3). New York: Guilford Press.

Teale, W. H., Hoffman, J. L., & Paciga, K. A. (2010). Where is NELP leading preschool literacy instruction?: Potential positives and pitfalls. *Educational Researcher, 39*(4), 311–315.

Contents

PART III. RECONCEPTUALIZING DEVELOPMENTALLY APPROPRIATE PRACTICE

PART IV. INTERVENTION AND ASSESSMENT

PART I

INFLUENCES ON
LITERACY DEVELOPMENT

CHAPTER 1

❖

Parent Involvement Supporting Early Literacy Achievement

BEST PRACTICES FOR BRIDGING THE HOME AND SCHOOL ENVIRONMENTS

BETH M. PHILLIPS
KYLIE S. FLYNN
GALIYA A. TABULDA
SMRITI JANGRA
CHRISTOPHER J. LONIGAN

GUIDING QUESTIONS

A cornerstone of many educational models in the past 20 years, particularly those aiming to reduce achievement gaps, has been the importance of parent involvement (National Education Goals Panel, 1998; Epstein et al., 2008). Prototypical parent–child activities related to early literacy development may include labeling alphabet magnets on the refrigerator door, shared storybook reading at bedtime, and assisting children in sounding out words in beginning texts. Beyond these classic activities, numerous research studies give attention to parent involvement in early literacy development. Within various traditions, parent involvement has been defined as including practices engaged in by parents in both home and school settings. Other frameworks attend to whether the teacher or parent has initiated the involvement. Our model of parent involvement follows work by Epstein (2001), Hoover-Dempsey (e.g., Hoover-Dempsey et al., 2005), Bronfenbrenner (1986), and others in considering children to be colocated in overlapping environments, the home and the school, that influence their development and literacy achievement. These models emphasize the importance of the interpersonal relationship, built on bidirectional communication and trust, between teachers and parents so that children's experiences in the two environments are mutually supportive (Seginer, 2006). Given the focus on best practices for teachers, we give specific attention to practices that can be teacher initiated, although we also include home-based parent-initiated activities that mesh with the goal of building an infrastructure of parent–school partnerships in support of children's early literacy success.

Substantial research supports the idea that what parents do at home, and in the school setting, may influence their children's early language and literacy (Desforges & Abouchaar, 2003; Senéchal, 2006). Additional research suggests that how parents communicate their values, beliefs, and expectations regarding academic achievement and literacy also likely influences children's achievement. Much research also, however, identifies challenges to involvement that exist for parents from disenfranchised backgrounds and for parents of children at higher risk for literacy difficulties. Thus, a key theme throughout the chapter is that of improving accessibility: for families from all backgrounds and cultures, for children at high risk, and for schools in all communities. A second key theme is that of high-quality research. Our focus in this chapter is on parent-focused best practices in early literacy explicitly derived from the most rigorous research available. Our aim here is not only to provide teachers with suggested, research-based practices but to guide teachers and parents in how they too can select practices that have the most evidence supporting their effectiveness. Our guiding questions are focused on the two learning environments and on bridging the gap between them to better integrate learning opportunities at home and school. Specifically, our three overarching questions are:

❖ How can teachers facilitate parental engagement with research-based best practices that support the language and literacy development of their children at home?

❖ How can teachers facilitate parents' inclusion in activities in the school that support language and literacy development?

❖ How can teachers facilitate bridging the home and school settings to support language and literacy development?

KEY THEORETICAL MODELS

Epstein's categorical model of six types of parental involvement has been highly influential on both research and school policies. This model includes these types of behaviors: general parenting, communication, volunteering, learning at home, decision making, and collaborating with the community (Epstein, 2001). Here we focus specifically on communicating, volunteering, and learning at home; we refer readers to Rafferty and Griffin (2010) and Epstein et al. (2008) for information on practices related to the other three types of involvement. However, the style and emotional tone of general parenting and of many at-home practices does seem to influence the benefit of parental involvement practices (Pomerantz, Moorman, & Litwack, 2007; Tracey & Young, 2002). Another relevant organizing theory is that of Harris, Andrew-Power, and Goodall (2009) who divided parent involvement into that which is *for learning* (e.g., providing parents with home activities that align with the classroom instructional focus), *about learning* (e.g., increasing parents' under-standing about how young children learn to read and write), and *through learning* (e.g., parent education and training opportunities). Their model emphasizes the need to link school encouragement of parental engagement to behaviors most likely to have a direct impact on student learning. However, Harris et al. also stress the value of communication and access to the school for parents where they can gain insight into their children's learning processes.

OVERVIEW OF PARENT INVOLVEMENT AND EARLY LITERACY

There are two primary bodies of research that support the benefit of parental involve-ment in their children's education, including early literacy development. First, there is a very large correlational literature, including numerous longitudinal studies that take factors such as family socioeconomic status (SES) and child grade level into account, which demonstrates the unique relation between parent involvement and children's educational outcomes (e.g., Desforges & Abouchaar, 2003; Seginer, 2006). In particular, research suggests that parental communication of the value of educa-tion and of their expectations and aspirations for the child to progress far in their educational pursuits makes a substantial contribution to children's own motivation, aspirations, and ultimately achievement (Galindo & Sheldon, 2012; Pomerantz et al., 2007; Xu, Kushner Benson, Mudrey-Camino, & Steiner, 2010). Furthermore, some study results suggest that the influence of parental involvement on achievement may in part be indirect, through improvements in child behavior and social compe-tence (Dearing, McCartney, Weiss, Kreider, & Simpkins, 2004; El Nokali, Bachman, & Votruba-Drzal, 2010). Although generally positive, there are some studies indi-cating weak or nonsignificant direct relations for aspects of parental involvement on measures of children's academic skills; several of these studies have found that family ethnic background or SES might reduce the influence for some children (e.g., Graves & Wright, 2011; Lee & Bowen, 2006). Some mixed findings also exist within the research on whether at-home or at-school involvement may be of greater benefit (e.g., Zhang, Hsu, Kwok, Benz, & Bowman-Perrott, 2011).

One challenge within this research is that some studies show clear patterns of parental reactivity to poor prior achievement by their children (Pomerantz et al., 2007). That is, many parents are likely to increase their focus on assisting with homework, meeting with teachers, and monitoring when a child has already struggled in one or more areas of learning. These behavioral patterns can lead to negative relationships between parental involvement and child achievement outcomes in the statistical models. The appropriate conclusion, however, is not that parental involvement decreases children's success; rather, these types of findings point to some of the main challenges in extrapolating causal conclusions from this type of correlational research. In addition, even with family and child background characteristics considered, one cannot definitively conclude from these studies that higher frequencies of parental involvement cause the increases in student academic performance. This is because these studies cannot rule out the possibility that the families, or the children, were different from the start from those families less likely to enact parental involvement behaviors, in ways not represented in the research studies.

Fortunately, the second body of research indicating the benefits of parental involvement activities does allow for such causal conclusions. In these experimental studies, some families are provided with specific guidance and materials to use with their children while others are not. Findings from these research studies, many of which have focused specifically on early literacy achievement, show significant gains for children whose parents engaged in the targeted practices (e.g., Levin & Aram, 2012; Senéchal, 2006). Many of the practices investigated in these studies are discussed in more detail later and are represented in the tables. In general, the majority of these studies indicate that parents' adoption of a deliberately instructional role, rather than just monitoring or supporting child efforts, does seem to benefit their early language and literacy development. A further advantage of the experimental literature over the correlational literature is the clear description of the specific behaviors enacted by parents to derive the benefit, in contrast to many of the survey studies in which "helped with homework" or "read with child" likely represented myriad variations in actual practices. One question left unanswered by these experimental findings, however, is whether these benefits would generalize to parents who may be different from those who voluntarily participated in research studies.

CRITICAL TARGETS IN ADDITION TO LITERACY

Whereas the primary focus of this summary and guidance is on parent involvement practices related specifically to literacy, there are two other relevant areas in which parent involvement may be particularly important. First, foundational to any child's learning success is being present at school (Chang & Romero, 2008; Sheldon & Epstein, 2004). Recent studies report that a sizeable percentage of children, often overrepresenting children from lower-income and ethnic-minority households, are frequently not in attendance at school. For instance, Romero and Lee (2008) reported that roughly 25% of kindergarten children missed at least 12 school days, and approximately 11% were chronically absent. Research does suggest, however, that parental commitment to their children's school achievement and attendance, and outreach efforts by teachers and schools that inform parents about the importance of regular attendance are associated with significantly higher attendance rates. Successful outreach programs appear to motivate and reward attendance by children (e.g., free extracurricular activities after school), and provide parents with a specific contact at the school with whom to communicate about attendance (e.g., guidance counselor or truancy officer; Sheldon & Epstein, 2004). For example, Lehr, Sinclair, and Christenson (2004) provided preliminary evidence of impact (extending from stronger evidence with older students) for an attendance-promoting strategy in elementary schools called "check and connect" that includes personalized contact with each child and family, regular monitoring and communication regarding attendance, and promotion of achievement motivation and school affiliation.

Second, a growing body of research suggests that the difference in environments experienced during the summer months by children from distinct socioeconomic backgrounds may help explain why the achievement gaps between children do not seem to close over time even after numerous years of comparable schooling (Borman, Benson, & Overman, 2005; Burkam, Ready, Lee, & LoGerfo, 2004). Other research has investigated whether school outreach programs during the summer, primarily involving sending books home for summer reading, have an impact on children's literacy achievement (Allington et al., 2010; Kim & White, 2008; Wilkins et al., 2012). At present, results indicate that whereas there is little evidence for benefit from just sending books for a single summer, programs that actively involve teachers or parents in discussing the books or in monitoring and encouraging reading may provide significant learning opportunities for participating children.

SELECTING BEST PRACTICES FOR PARENT INVOLVEMENT: USING RESEARCH AS A GUIDE

Teachers, particularly those in early childhood education, may often hear recommendations or suggestions for using "developmentally appropriate" and/or "best" practices. However, sifting through those ideas to choose the instructional activities that are truly "best" practices can seem daunting. To streamline this process, researchers have developed criteria for determining various levels of effectiveness for educational strategies, interventions, and curricula. We discuss three levels of criteria for educators to use in determining best practices: (1) likely influential, (2) probably efficacious, and (3) effective.

Strong correlational studies often help us to determine how particular skills may relate to one another. For example, researchers have observed that oral language skills seem to correlate with later reading ability (Whitehurst & Lonigan, 1998) making them "likely influential" on children's literacy development. But do we know how to best develop children's oral language skills? To determine if and to what extent a specific intervention or activity results in measurable growth, researchers have to conduct studies with tightly controlled conditions. These procedures allow researchers to know with the highest degree of certainty that it is the targeted intervention itself and not something else (such as the children's ongoing maturation or another activity) that caused the growth. Typically, an intervention is considered "probably efficacious" if it has been evaluated in two or more well-conducted randomized trials that indicate that the intervention is more effective than not receiving intervention. But how do we know that this same intervention will also work in less controlled environments? To determine if the intervention outcomes can also be obtained outside of a research lab, researchers then need to conduct studies in general settings such as classrooms or homes. An intervention is generally considered "effective" if it has been studied in two or more well-conducted randomized control trials by independent research teams that find the intervention is superior to alternative or established interventions for the general population (Lonigan, Elbert, & Johnson, 1998).

The federal government has recently taken a vested interest in making research findings more accessible to educators. A National Reading Panel (NRP) of scholars convened by Congress assessed the effectiveness of different approaches used to teach children to read (National Institute of Child Health and Human Development, 2000). Similarly, a National Early Literacy Panel (NELP), also convened by government agencies, conducted a synthesis of the scientific research on the development of early literacy skills in children ages 0 to 5 (Lonigan, Schatschneider, & Westberg, 2008). Reports and executive summaries from the NRP and NELP are easily accessible on the Internet. Furthermore, in 2002 the U.S. Department of Education's Institute of Education Sciences created the What Works Clearinghouse (2012) to be a central and trusted online resource of scientific evidence for what works in education (*http://ies.ed.gov/ncee/wwc*). As administrators and teachers become well versed in effective practice for developing children's literacy skills, it will become part of their responsibility to share this knowledge with parents in ways that support parent involvement in children's literacy development.

USING THE TABLES IN THIS CHAPTER

There are two tables in this chapter, each focused on how early childhood teachers can facilitate parents' engagement with research-based best practices for language and literacy (1) in school, (2) at home, and (3) by bridging the home and school settings. Table 1.1 provides suggestions and adaptations that can make at-school involvement more accessible for all parents. Table 1.2 represents the at-home and bridge contexts and contains suggestions for each of the five scientifically based reading components (i.e., phonological awareness, phonics, fluency, vocabulary, and comprehension). For each suggested activity, we have indicated the ideal age/ grade level and accommodations for children with disabilities. Also, in the "Scaling it up," "Scaling it down," and "Bridging and feedback" columns there are recommendations for a range of facilitation based on teacher and parent resources

TABLE 1.1. Teacher Facilitation of Parents' Engagement with Research-Based Best Practices for Language and Literacy in the Classroom

Activity	Strategies for increasing parent participation for diverse families
Invite parents in for parent–teacher conferences and/or IEP (individualized education plan) meetings.	Accommodate meeting times beyond school hours. Personally invite parents either in-person or via the phone.
Invite parents to visit the classroom.	Keep the purpose of the classroom visit open (i.e., just let them observe). Personally invite parents either in person or via the phone. Create virtual tours and post them to the school's website.
Invite parents to help in the classroom with small groups or individual children.	Provide clear, explicit directions and translations as needed. Personally invite parents either in person or via the phone.
Invite parents to share about their career, culture, or home.	Provide clear, explicit directions and translations as needed. Allow them to cook a dish or create a poster to send in with their child.
Invite parents to attend school events	Accommodate times beyond school hours. Personally invite parents either in person or via the phone.
Invite parents to attend/chaperone field trips.	When possible, schedule field trips beyond school hours. Personally invite parents either in person or via the phone.
Invite parents to participate in extracurricular activities with their child.	Accommodate times beyond school hours. Personally invite parents either in person or via the phone.
Invite parents to prepare classroom materials.	Provide clear, explicit directions and translations as needed. Allow parents to prep materials in the classroom or at home.
Invite parents to record read-alouds for paired home reading.	Encourage parents to do this in their native language or to create translations of English books. Allow parents to create recordings in the classroom or at home.

TABLE 1.2. How Teachers Can Facilitate Bridging the Home and School Settings to Promote Language and Literacy

Skill area	Grade	Suggestions/activity	Accommodations for students with disabilities	Range of facilitation		Level of effectiveness	Bridging and feedback
				Scaling it up	Scaling it down		
Phonological awareness	PreK–1	Word games. Teacher encourages parents to play word games with their child, such as forming and recognizing rhymes, breaking apart compound words, clapping out syllables, reciting alliterations, and identifying the first sound in words.	Begin with larger units of sounds (e.g., counting words in sentences or breaking apart compound words) before moving on to smaller units of sound (e.g., syllables, onset–rime, phonemes).	Teacher prescribes specific activities based on child's performance in the classroom. Teacher provides a specific script for specific activities.	Teacher provides parents with general handouts or information about the benefits of developing children's phonological awareness.	Effective	For the bridge, teachers should use words from a current theme or topic being studied in the classroom. These words could be a word family or topical (e.g., words associated with the rainforest, solar system, geometry)
Phonics	K–2	Word-family reading. Teacher sends home a word list that has already been taught and practiced at school. Parents listen to child read.	List can be shortened or individualized to child's specific level.	Provide parents with a script for providing error corrections. Parents return to teacher with the number of words child can comfortably read.	Limit the number of words that go home.	Effective	Feedback loop: It will be important for teachers to use words provided in the reading curriculum and that have already been introduced and practiced at school.
Fluency	PreK	Letter-naming fluency. Teachers encourage parents to have children label letters and their sounds as they appear in text	Teachers can also send home letters in the form of flash cards, magnet letters, or stencils. For children with disabilities, limit	Provide parents with specific letters that child is struggling with.	Teacher sends home all 26 letters and lets parents make decision about what letters to practice and	Effective	Feedback loop: Have parents return mastered letters to get more. Keep track of this progress.

(continued from previous page)		within the natural environment and in supported writing and play activities.	the number of letters or just send the letters in child's name.		how often to rotate.		
Fluency	K–2	Word-naming fluency. Teachers encourage parents to have children read high-frequency (e.g., *the, was, there*) and common environmental words (e.g., *juice, cereal,* street names in their neighborhood) in isolation.	Parents may choose to focus on helping their child to identify pictures and words from a picture-exchange system or communication device.	Provide parents with specific words that the child is struggling with.	Help parents select words at the child's level to reduce frustration and increase autonomy.	Probably efficacious	Feedback loop: Have parents return mastered words to get more. Keep track of this progress.
Fluency	K–2	Decodable books. After books have been introduced and practiced in class, teacher sends them home for parents to listen to their child read.	Make sure book is at child's reading level.	Provide parents with script for providing error corrections. Have parents circle children's "tricky" words before returning book.	No additional parent monitoring.	Effective	Feedback loop: The teacher could monitor the "tricky" words as indicated by parents and continue to send home books focusing on specific word families.
Vocabulary	PreK–2	Talking with children. Teachers should encourage parents to talk frequently with their children about their environment by asking questions and asking children to label items.	Children with disabilities benefit from these types of purposeful conversations, but may require more frequent opportunities to talk.	Provide parents with specific scripts or vocabulary words for them to focus on with their children.	Send home more general information about the benefits of exposing children to a wide range of vocabulary.	Likely influential	Feedback loop: Teachers could ask parents to send back the list of vocabulary words with stars next to words that parents observe their child using.

(continued)

TABLE 1.2. (*continued*)

Skill area	Grade	Suggestions/activity	Accommodations for students with disabilities	Range of facilitation		Level of effectiveness	Bridging and feedback
				Scaling it up	Scaling it down		
Vocabulary	PreK–K	Dialogic reading, levels 1 and 2.	Nonverbal children can respond by pointing. Props or objects can be used to reinforce vocabulary development.	Provide parents with suggestions for questions and/or bookmarks.	No additional parent monitoring.	Effective	Feedback loop: Teachers can provide a list of vocabulary words that were previously introduced in class. Parents can circle any "tricky" words for their child and return to teacher.
Vocabulary and Comprehension	PreK–2	Additional reading activities: Parents should be encouraged to read to their child, listen to their child read, participate in paired reading with their child, encourage independent frequent reading, and allow their child to read along to a recorded book.	Children with disabilities benefit from these types of literacy activities, but may require more frequent participation.	Provide parents with specific activities to do with books, such as comprehension questions or discussion topics.	Assist parents in helping their child select books at an independent reading level to reduce frustration and increase autonomy.	Probably efficacious	Feedback loop: As parents return books and request new books, teachers can monitor the amount of reading opportunities parents are engaging in with their child.

Comprehension	PreK–K	Dialogic reading, level 3.	Parents may need to spend more time on levels 1 and 2 developing their child's vocabulary before moving on to level 3.	Provide parents with suggestions for questions and/or bookmarks.	No additional parent monitoring.	Effective	Feedback loop: Teachers can provide a list of comprehension questions that were previously introduced in class. Parents can circle any "tricky" questions for their child and return to teacher.
Comprehension	PreK–2	Educational programming. Parents should be encouraged to have conversations with their child during and after educational TV programs.	For children with disabilities, parents can cowatch and guide their child through stories as he or she progresses though the narrative. Parents should model narrative comprehension to their child. Or, they can continue to focus on vocabulary as needed.	Provide parents with sample scripts and specific examples of questions.	No additional parent monitoring.	Probably efficacious	Feedback loop: Teachers can provide a list of comprehension questions or concepts related to a particular theme that were previously introduced in class. Parents can circle any "tricky" questions for their child and return to teacher.

and availability. Finally, criteria level of effectiveness (i.e., likely influential, probably efficacious, and effective) are provided for each suggested activity based on our analysis of the quality and quantity of the existing research literature. These tables are not intended to be exhaustive lists of every possible strategy for facilitating home literacy practices. Rather, they are intended to highlight those practices with the strongest current evidence base and to be a guide and a template for how teachers might make decisions for choosing literacy activities and facilitating parent involvement.

In each section below, we provide a brief example of a teacher working with parents to overcome one or more of the challenges to parent involvement and sustaining a best practice with their children. Specifically, for school, home, and bridging we pursue our theme of accessibility by discussing what some challenges may be to engaging parents in these suggested practices, and offering some suggested solutions for these challenges.

KNOWLEDGE TO PRACTICE: A TEACHER MODEL

Ms. Thomas was a second-year prekindergarten teacher in a large urban school district where over 50 different languages were spoken. In her particular school, the majority of families came from Chinese, Russian, African American, and Hispanic cultures. As such, her school had a designated ESOL (English for speakers of other languages) program. None of the teachers spoke Chinese or Russian and just a few spoke Spanish. Ms. Thomas did not speak a second language and was overwhelmed by the cultural diversity, particularly as a new teacher who had grown up in a white-majority Midwestern town.

Encouraging Parent Involvement in the School Setting

In keeping with our theoretical framework of viewing children to be colocated in the home and school environments (e.g., Epstein, 2001) and the importance for these environments to be mutually supportive (Seginer, 2006), it naturally follows that parental involvement in the school setting would both facilitate the development of parent–school partnerships and provide direct benefits to children (Galindo & Sheldon, 2012). A considerable number of the correlational studies mentioned earlier have investigated aspects of family characteristics to help explain why some parents participate more in school-based educational involvement practices. However, one cautionary finding relates to some educators' belief that less visibly involved parents, often those from lower SES or minority backgrounds, value education less. In fact, repeated investigation has indicated that many times the opposite holds true— many ethnic-minority families reportedly give higher ratings to the importance of educational success and have higher educational goals for their children than do some white parents (Ryan, Casas, Kelly-Vance, Ryalls, & Nero, 2010). Similarly, although numerous studies suggest that family background may influence the frequency of particular types of involvement for some families, there is considerable variation for involvement practices within any given SES or ethnic subgroup (Durand, 2011; Ryan et al., 2010).

Another important area of study has been the relevance of parental beliefs about their parental role and its inclusion or exclusion of academic, instructional behaviors (Hoover-Dempsey et al., 2005; Lareau & Shumar, 1996; Ryan et al., 2010). Studies indicate that parents whose role construction includes supporting academic achievement and who have greater self-efficacy for their practices in this area are more likely to demonstrate greater levels of involvement (Green, Walker, Hoover-Dempsey, & Sandler, 2007). Unfortunately, some parents may have a history of low academic self-efficacy and feel incompetent or doubtful about engaging in literacy- and language-promotion activities with their children (Neuman, Caperelli, & Kee, 1998). Some parents' own historical discomfort with or lack of success within educational settings also may play a role in making them feel either unwelcome or unwilling to attend school-based functions (Bruckman & Branton, 2003; Kaplan, Liu, & Kaplan, 2004).

Research suggests that the amount of social capital a parent possesses (e.g., knowledge about the workings and expectations of the school system and familiarity with other parents) contributes uniquely to predicting levels of parental involvement, particularly in the school setting (Baker, 2003; Durand, 2011; Lee & Bowen, 2006). For example, a parent who attended elementary school in a different state or country may not understand the standards and expectations of their child's school district. Likewise, a parent who has contact with many other parents of comparably aged children may know which second-grade teacher to request for his or her own child. Additionally, more pragmatic influences on parental involvement often involve barriers such as language, transportation, child care for younger children, and the capacity to be available during school hours (Hoover-Dempsey et al., 2005; Lareau & Shumar, 1996). Finally, parents' mental health and stress levels, including concerns with depression and financial insecurity, can affect the energy and attention parents are able to devote to supporting their child's educational development (Castro, Bryant, Peisner-Feinberg, & Skinner, 2004; Waanders, Mendez, & Downer, 2007).

> Ms. Thomas faced many of the challenges and obstacles mentioned above in getting her students' parents involved at the school level. However, in one way, her lack of any preconceived notions about the various cultural backgrounds of her students aided her in coping with these challenges. In her enthusiasm, she sought to create a classroom community that was open and inviting to parents. During the

first month of school, she worked with the school district's translation services to create very simple invitations in the families' native languages requesting parents to attend her open house scheduled in the evening. She even included a photograph of their child with a personal message dictated by their child. Ms. Thomas's willingness to go beyond sending home the schoolwide flyer by sending something more personal was an excellent strategic move.

Invitations from children and teachers appear to mitigate some of the concerns related to parents' reluctance to participate in school-based functions (Desforges & Abouchaar, 2003; Hoover-Dempsey et al., 2005) and could thereby increase their social capital as they become more comfortable in the school setting. Notably, many authors suggest that teacher invitations may be particularly powerful if they encompass specifics on what parents should do; our comments below build on this to provide detailed suggestions for teachers about what they could request of parents.

Although Ms. Thomas's open house was well attended, she still had to grapple with a second challenge—she didn't speak any of the additional languages spoken by her students' families and was unsure how many of them spoke or understood English. Thus, she created a multimedia presentation to show during her open house. She included pictures and videos of her students participating in a variety of learning activities in her classroom and then included pictures from the Internet of families engaging in similar activities in their homes and communities (e.g., at the public library and park). In this way, she was able to communicate her desire for the parents to support their students as learners in the home setting. She followed this up with a tour of the school, including the cafeteria, library, kindergarten classrooms, and playground.

In fact, broadening the scope and purpose of parent visits to schools beyond more active volunteering roles to include observations and/or tours may help parents become more familiar and comfortable in the school setting and with the school's expectations. Additionally, accommodating meetings and school visits beyond school hours may help parents with time constraints due to their employment and/or transportation needs. In addition to Ms. Thomas's strategy above, technology may aid in parents' accessibility to the school environment by providing web-based virtual tours and uploading information regarding instruction and school events to the school website. See Table 1.1 for additional suggestions for increasing parental involvement in the school context.

Encouraging Parental Involvement with Literacy Development at Home

At-home involvement typically includes three primary aspects of creating a physical and motivational context for learning, monitoring and setting rules for children's school attendance and homework completion, and direct involvement in the form of reading, tutoring, or playing educational games with children (Patall, Cooper, & Robinson, 2008; Pomerantz et al., 2007; Seginer, 2006). Evidence suggests that children benefit when parents set rules for homework completion; more pragmatically, parents can be encouraged to establish a regular routine and location in the home where children can work. With young children, both correlational and experimental evidence supports the benefits of shared reading for language and vocabulary development (Lonigan et al., 2008; Senéchal, 2006). There is also compelling evidence that parental reading, tutoring, and listening to their child read aloud can be effective in supporting early decoding and fluency skills, particularly using practices such as explicit instruction, paired reading, repeated readings, and specific corrective feedback (Erion, 2006; Senéchal, 2006).

Despite the evidence supporting parental involvement, much research also indicates that parents vary widely in how frequently they engage in home language and literacy activities (Phillips & Lonigan, 2009; Pomerantz et al., 2007). Parents have many different reasons for their decisions regarding how they spend time with their children, including knowledge, resources, and competing demands for their attention. A further pivotal contributor to the parents' role construction related to at-home engagement is the family's cultural background. Some cultures' belief systems and typical practices reserve the specific instructional responsibilities for educational personnel, whereas the parental role is focused more on character development and behavior management. These parents may frequently monitor children's classroom behavior and homework completion but not feel that it is their place to act as an at-home instructor and engage in more hands-on reading practices (Durand, 2011; Hoover-Dempsey et al., 2005). Although we focus in this chapter on the home activities that fall under the more active role, as noted above, the most critical aspect of parents' involvement does appear to be conveying the value of education, which can take many outward forms. Teachers can convey respect for, and encourage more participation from, parents of all cultural backgrounds and belief systems by clearly communicating the full range of behaviors in which parents can engage to support their child's literacy achievement, including both more and less instructive roles.

> Simply by unlocking some of the "mystery" of the educational setting and what she did there, Ms. Thomas provided a model of some of the options that parents could generalize to the home setting. She conveyed her respect for parents' varying models of involvement by asking families to share with her examples of literacy-related activities they enjoyed with their children and then developing a bulletin board of home-literacy activities based on their contributions. Ms. Thomas wants to encourage the parents to play phonological awareness games with their children at home. During the time period in which she teaches compound word manipulation with her students she asks each parent to create a book page of photographs

or drawings of compound words found in their home environment (e.g., *popcorn, oatmeal, skateboard*). She then assembles the book, makes a copy for each family, and asks the parents to review it with their child to practice blending and separating the words within the compound words.

Creating a Bridge between School and Home

There are numerous ways in which educators can raise parents' awareness of the importance that their at-home involvement in literacy and language development activities has for their child. Teachers can repeatedly remind parents of the value of education and ask them to transmit this value to their children. They can provide specific educational activities for parents to do at home with their child. Parents should also be informed why they are doing a particular activity and how it will help in enhancing their child's literacy skills, as some findings suggest that parents are more likely to engage in activities that have clear goals and structure (Baker, 2003; Epstein & Van Voorhis, 2001).

> Ms. Thomas wanted to do more than provide parents with information about their students' progress—she wanted to engage them as full partners in their child's education. Thus, she focused on a specific, simple, and universal literacy activity to connect the school and home environments—shared book reading. To encourage parents to read with their students, she went to local thrift stores to find children's books in English and in her students' native languages and created a lending library. She also personally invited parents in for their conferences and included a brief "training" on how to use the lending library and how to support their children's literacy development by making the book readings interactive. These trainings were tailored to the specific needs of the family and included a translator when appropriate.

In this way, Ms. Thomas was sensitive to parents' financial limitations and was consistent with researchers' suggestions that parents should be made aware of different ways in which they can be involved in interactive readings or other activities with their children that do not require expenditures (Levin & Aram, 2012). She could also have solicited donations from parents of greater means to support other families in the school.

Table 1.2 provides suggestions for bridging the home and school settings to promote language and literacy in young children. One of the unique features of this table is our notion of a feedback loop. When teachers make recommendations for language and literacy activities for parents to engage in with their child, they should consider making those activities connect to their classroom instruction. Ideally, parents can provide feedback to teachers about how their child is performing at home, thereby giving teachers valuable information about how students may or may not be generalizing their literacy skills beyond the classroom. In the bridging and feedback column of the table there are specific suggestions for facilitating this feedback loop.

Of course there may be challenges in creating this bridge between home and school related to diversity, SES, parent availability, English learners, and children with disabilities. According to the U.S. government, the percentage of nonwhite public school children increased by 2008 to 44% (Aud, Fox, & KewalRamani, 2010). This statistic has wide-ranging political, economic, and cultural implications for a variety of governmental entities, especially the U.S. public school system. Educational leaders face a unique set of challenges when they attempt to accommodate needs of students and their parents who come from a variety of racial and ethnic backgrounds. Overcoming communication difficulties that stem from racial/ethnic and cultural differences is one of those challenges. Ideally, more teachers would be able to communicate in languages additional to English (Tang, Dearing, & Weiss, 2012). Yet, as discussed in one recent study (Howard & Lipinoga, 2010) it is not always the linguistic barrier per se but rather the teachers' use of complicated "pedagogical" terminology and inaccurate assumptions about the families and about their knowledge regarding school procedures that creates communication difficulties between teachers and parents from disparate backgrounds.

Practices that create, rather than bridge, the distance with families may be improved if schools become more flexible in their approaches to communication with parents. Many of these strategies have the advantage of universal design, in that they are applicable to any group of families that may be unaccustomed to the school context or to the predominantly middle-class, educated culture that most teachers bring to these interactions. Suggestions include access to knowledgeable interpreters, face-to-face contact with parents rather than mail or technology-based contact, communication in jargon-free, accessible language, extension of time allotted for parent–teacher contact, and most importantly, awareness and dexterity within the communicative role assumed by the teachers. In describing ways to involve immigrant parents of students with disabilities in the educational process, Al-Hassan and Gardner (2002) suggest that parents need frequent and precise information about their child's progress beyond a few progress reports a year. In doing so, teachers should have a good understanding of the language needs of their families and provide information, written and oral, in a very clear way that enable parents to understand. Beyond using interpreters, Al-Hassan and Gardner recommend making school reports simple by avoiding educational or psychological jargon and using icons (e.g., happy and sad faces) when possible. These types of communications may fit nicely with our notion of a feedback loop. For example, when the teacher sends home tricky words for students to practice reading, he or she could include two envelopes, one with a green light and one with a red light. The parent could return to the teacher the words their child is still struggling with in the "red-light" envelope.

Additionally, as appropriate, teachers should encourage parents to conduct at-home activities in their native language (Roberts, 2008). However, teachers should also not presume that parents are highly literate in their native language and be mindful of that in selecting activities to go home. Fortunately, in early childhood education, there are still many appropriate literacy activities that are not dependent upon the parents having a specific level of literacy. For example, in dialogic reading, parents only need to talk about the pictures in the book with their child; they do not need to read the text.

Finally, parents of children with disabilities need to be encouraged to engage their child in these same types of activities that promote language and literacy skills in typically developing children. Although a growing body of evidence lends support to the premise that *all* children can benefit from having literacy experiences, children with disabilities appear to receive fewer literacy opportunities, particularly at home (Weikle & Hadadian, 2004). As parents of children with disabilities may not fully understand the importance of their role in providing literacy experiences for their children, teachers play a critical role in encouraging parents to engage their children in such activities. Technologies, such as communication devices and picture exchange systems, as well as simple audiobooks, can be used with children with disabilities as well as with English learners (Koskinen et al., 2000).

Limited time availability is yet another barrier faced by parents on the way to greater involvement in children's education-related activities at home (Harris et al., 2009). Time constraints, low levels of energy, and parents' own history of low academic self-efficacy are often intertwined with other parent factors, such as SES, parental education, belongingness to racial/ethnic minority, and occupation status (Edin & Lein, 1997; Lareau, 2003). Parents' limited emotional availability is often associated with stressful life events, mental illnesses, anxiety, and depression, raising multiple children and/or being a single parent (Gutman, Sameroff, & Cole, 2003). When parents can only devote a limited amount of emotional resources to interaction with their children, opportunities for engagement in activities that promote literacy and language development diminish. Thus it becomes even more important to provide parents with clear guidance regarding how to best use their limited time.

When working with parents who struggle with availability issues, teachers and school administrators should focus on relevant, research-based practices with documented evidence of effectiveness, such as those highlighted in Table 1.2. Rather than suggesting a large number of activities with variable impact, encouraging parental engagement in specific activities with a likelihood of impacting children's literacy development is also a way to build the parent's own self-efficacy and motivation for further involvement. Parents can also benefit from discussions and demonstrations of how at-home literacy and language development activities are best implemented, such as through workshops, individual training opportunities, and video models for independent review (Baker, 2003; Judkins et al., 2008). The suggested at-home practices should be relatively brief, enjoyable, and easy to learn and implement (Padak & Rasinski, 2006). In addition, teachers should attempt to raise parents' awareness about the importance of maintaining a warm and positive relationship with their children, and of showing sensitivity and encouragement, which are related to higher academic achievement of children (Caspe, Lopez, & Wolos, 2007) and to children's greater benefit from parent involvement (Baker, 2003; Tracey & Young, 2002).

CONCLUSION

At the end of the school year, Ms. Thomas reflected on the benefits she, the students, and their parents received from participating in school- and home-based involvement activities. She recognized that her instruction was enriched by her bidirectional communication with parents. By providing parents with specific, individualized at-home activity ideas, the parents were then able to provide specific, individualized feedback on their child's skill development. This feedback allowed her to better pace lessons and match each child's instructional needs during the year. For instance, for children learning English, she was able to learn more about their vocabulary knowledge in their home languages from parent feedback. As well, parents who played the at-home letter-matching games with their children were able to provide feedback regarding children's letter–sound learning that informed how quickly she moved through teaching the alphabet. Ms. Thomas also reviewed the portfolios she assembled of children's home-based projects as part of her end-of-year child evaluations to pass on to the kindergarten teachers and to share with the parents in conferences. She felt that her understanding of each child was more comprehensive and detailed from having these additional sources of information on the children's performance.

Ideally, teachers such as Ms. Thomas may increase the effectiveness of their classroom instruction through thoughtfully selected and meaningfully integrated parent involvement. For example, teachers who recruit and provide training to parent volunteers in the classroom are better able to manage small-group and individual instruction during the week. Teachers also can use the feedback loop of carefully crafted, even differentiated, at-home activity suggestions as additional formative assessment opportunities to support their instructional decision making. From the parents' perspective, receiving regular messages regarding their child's classroom instruction and learning goals can support their desire to engage in aligned interactions with their child at home, and to feel relevant to, informed by, and knowledgeable about the school their child attends. Ultimately, this can strengthen children's feelings of consistency in goals and attitudes between the school and home environments, and further build their motivation to succeed in early literacy.

REFERENCES

Al-Hassan, S., & Gardner, R. (2002). Involving immigrant parents of students with disabilities in the educational process. *Teaching Exceptional Children, 34*(5), 52–58.

Allington, R. L., McGill-Franzen, A., Camilli, G., Williams, L., Graff, J., Zeig, J., et al. (2010). Addressing summer reading setback among economically disadvantaged elementary students. *Reading Psychology, 31*(5), 411–427.

Aud, S., Fox, M., & KewalRamani, A. (2010). *Status and trends in the education of racial and ethnic groups* (NCES 2010-015). Washington, DC: U.S. Government Printing Office.

Baker, L. (2003). The role of parents in motivating struggling readers. *Reading and Writing Quarterly: Overcoming Learning Difficulties, 19*(1), 87–106.

Borman, G. D., Benson, J., & Overman, L. T. (2005). Families, schools, and summer learning. *Elementary School Journal, 106*(2), 131–150.

Bronfenbrenner, U. (1986). Ecology of the family as a context for human development: Research perspectives. *Developmental Psychology, 22,* 723–742.

Bruckman, M., & Blanton, P. W. (2003). Welfare-to-work single mothers' perspectives on parent involvement in Head Start: Implications for parent–teacher collaboration. *Early Childhood Education Journal, 30*(3), 145–150.

Burkam, D. T., Ready, D. D., Lee, V. E., & LoGerfo, L. F. (2004). Social-class differences in summer learning between kindergarten and first grade: Model specification and estimation. *Sociology of Education, 77*(1), 1–31. Retrieved from *www.jstor.org/stable/3649401.*

Caspe, M., Lopez, M. E., & Wolos, C. (2007). *Family involvement in elementary school children's education. Family involvement makes a difference: Evidence that family involvement promotes school success for every child of every age.* Cambridge, MA: Harvard Family Research Project.

Castro, D. C., Bryant, D. M., Peisner-Feinberg, E., & Skinner, M. L. (2004). Parent involvement in Head Start programs: The role of parent, teacher and classroom characteristics. *Early Childhood Research Quarterly, 19*(3), 413–430.

Chang, H. N., & Romero, M. (2008). *Present, engaged, and accounted for: The critical importance of addressing chronic absence in the early grades. Executive Summary.* New York: National Center for Children in Poverty.

Dearing, E., McCartney, K., Weiss, H. B., Kreider, H., & Simpkins, S. (2004). The promotive effects of family educational involvement for low-income children's literacy. *Journal of School Psychology, 42*(6), 445–460.

Desforges, C., & Abouchaar, A. (2003). *The impact of parental involvement, parental support and family education on pupil achievement and adjustment.* Nottingham, UK: Department for Education and Skills.

Durand, T. M. (2011). Latino parental involvement in kindergarten: Findings from the Early Childhood Longitudinal Study. *Hispanic Journal of Behavioral Sciences, 33*(4), 469–489.

Edin, K., & Lein, L. (1997). *Making ends meet: How single mothers survive welfare and low-wage work.* New York: Russell Sage Foundation.

El Nokali, N. E., Bachman, H. J., & Votruba-Drzal, E. (2010). Parent involvement and children's academic and social development in elementary school. *Child Development, 81*(3), 988–1005.

Epstein, J. L. (2001). *School, family, and community partnerships: Preparing educators and improving schools.* Boulder, CO: Westview Press.

Epstein, J. L., Sanders, M. G., Sheldon, S., Simon, B. S., Salinas, K. C., Jansorn, N. R., et al. (2008). *School, family and community partnerships: Your handbook for action* (3rd ed.). New York: Corwin.

Epstein, J. L., & Van Voorhis, F. L. (2001). More than minutes: Teachers' roles in designing homework. *Educational Psychologist, 36*, 181–193.

Erion, J. (2006). Parent tutoring: A meta-analysis. *Education and Treatment of Children, 29*(1), 79–106. Retrieved from *www.educationandtreatmentofchildren.net*.

Galindo, C., & Sheldon, S. B. (2012). School and home connections and children's kindergarten achievement gains: The mediating role of family involvement. *Early Childhood Research Quarterly, 27*(1), 90–103.

Graves, S. L., & Wright, L. B. (2011). Parent involvement at school entry: A national examination of group differences and achievement. *School Psychology International, 32*(1), 35–48.

Green, C. L., Walker, J. M. T., Hoover-Dempsey, K., & Sandler, H. M. (2007). Parents' motivations for involvement in children's education: An empirical test of a theoretical model of parental involvement. *Journal of Educational Psychology, 99*(3), 532–544.

Gutman, L. M., Sameroff, A. J. & Cole, R. (2003). Academic growth curve trajectories from 1st grade to 12th grade: Effects of multiple social risk factors and preschool child factors. *Developmental Psychology, 39*(4), 777–790.

Harris, A., Andrew-Power, K., & Goodall, J. (2009). *Do parents know they matter?: Raising achievement through parental engagement.* London: Network Continuum.

Hoover-Dempsey, K. V., Walker, J. M. T., Sandler, H. M., Whetsel, D., Green, C. L., Wilkins, A. S., et al. (2005). Why do parents become involved?: Research findings and implications. *Elementary School Journal, 106*(2), 105–105.

Howard, K., & Lipinoga, S. (2010). Closing down openings: Pretextuality and misunderstanding in parent–teacher conferences with Mexican immigrant families. *Language and Communication, 30*(1), 33–47.

Judkins, D., St. Pierre, R., Gutmann, B., Goodson, B., von Glatz, A., Hamilton, J., et al. (2008). *A study of classroom literacy interventions and outcomes in Even Start* (NCEE 2008-4028). Washington, DC: National Center for Education Evaluation and Regional Assistance, Institute of Education Sciences, U.S. Department of Education.

Kaplan, D. S., Liu, R. X., & Kaplan, H.B. (2004). Explaining intergenerational parallelism in adverse school experiences: Mediating influence of young and middle adulthood experiences. *Journal of Experimental Education, 72*(2), 117–159.

Kim, J. S., & White, T. G. (2008). Scaffolding voluntary summer reading for children in grades 3 to 5: An experimental study. *Scientific Studies of Reading, 12*(1), 1–23.

Koskinen, P. S., Blum, I. H., Bisson, S. A., Phillips, S. A., Creamer, T. S., & Baker, T. K. (2000). Book access, shared reading, and audio models: The effects of supporting the literacy learning of linguistically diverse students in school and at home. *Journal of Educational Psychology, 92*, 23–36.

Lareau, A. (2003). *Unequal childhoods: Class, race, and family life.* Berkeley: University of California Press.

Lareau, A., & Shumar, W. (1996). The problem of individualism in family–school policies. *Sociology of Education*, 24–39.

Lee, J., & Bowen, N. K. (2006). Parent involvement, cultural capital, and the achievement gap among elementary school children. *American Educational Research Journal, 43*(2), 193–215.

Lehr, C. A., Sinclair, M. F., & Christenson, S. L. (2004). Addressing student engagement and truancy prevention during the elementary school years: A replication study of the check and connect model. *Journal of Education for Students Placed at Risk, 9*(3), 279–301.

Levin, I., & Aram, D. (2012). Mother–child joint writing and storybook reading and their effects on kindergartners' literacy: An intervention study. *Reading and Writing: An Interdisciplinary Journal, 25*(1), 217–249.

Lonigan, C. J., Elbert J. C., & Johnson, S. B. (1998). Empirically supported psychosocial interventions for children: An overview. *Journal of Clinical Child Psychology, 27*, 138–145.

Lonigan, C. J., Schatschneider, C., & Westberg, L. (2008). Impact of code-focused interventions on young children's early literacy skills. In *Developing early literacy: Report of the National Early Literacy Panel* (pp. 107–151). Washington, DC: National Institute for Literacy.

National Education Goals Panel. (1998). *Ready Schools*. Washington, DC: Author.

National Institute of Child Health and Human Development. (2000). *Report of the National Reading Panel. Teaching children to read: An evidence-based assessment of the scientific research literature on reading and its implications for reading instruction* (NIH Publication No. 00–4769). Washington, DC: U.S. Government Printing Office.

Neuman, S. B., Caperelli, B. J., & Kee, C. (1998). Literacy learning, a family matter. *The Reading Teacher, 52*(3), 244–252.

Padak, N., & Rasinski, T. (2006). Home–school partnerships in literacy education: From rhetoric to reality. *The Reading Teacher, 60*(3), 292–296.

Patall, E. A., Cooper, H., & Robinson, J. C. (2008). Parent involvement in homework: A research synthesis. *Review of Educational Research, 78*(4), 1039–1101.

Phillips, B. M., & Lonigan, C. J. (2009). Home literacy environments for preschool children: A cluster analytic perspective. *Scientific Studies of Reading, 13*, 146–174.

Pomerantz, E. M., Moorman, E. A., & Litwack, S. D. (2007). The how, whom, and why of parents' involvement in children's academic lives: More is not always better. *Review of Educational Research, 77*(3), 373–410.

Rafferty, Y., & Griffin, K. W. (2010). Parenting behaviours among low-income mothers of preschool age children in the USA: Implications for parenting programmes. *International Journal of Early Years Education, 18*(2), 143–157.

Roberts, T. A. (2008). Home storybook reading in primary or second language with preschool children: Evidence of equal effectiveness for second-language vocabulary acquisition. *Reading Research Quarterly, 43*, 103–130.

Romero, M., & Lee, Y. (2008). *The influence of maternal and family risk on chronic absenteeism in early schooling.* New York: National Center for Children in Poverty.

Ryan, C. S., Casas, J. F., Kelly-Vance, L., Ryalls, B. O., & Nero, C. (2010). Parent involvement and views of school success: The role of parents' Latino and white American cultural orientations. *Psychology in the Schools, 47*(4), 391–405.

Seginer, R. (2006). Parents' educational involvement: A developmental ecology perspective. *Parenting: Science and Practice, 6*(1), 1–48.

Senéchal, M. (2006). *The effect of family literacy interventions on children's acquisition of reading: From kindergarten to grade 3.* Washington, DC: National Institute for Literacy.

Sheldon, S., & Epstein, J. L. (2004). Getting students to school: Using family and community involvement to reduce chronic absenteeism. *School Community Journal, 14*, 39–56.

Tang, S., Dearing, E., & Weiss, H. B. (2012). Spanish-speaking Mexican-American families' involvement in school-based activities and their children's literacy: The implications of having teachers who speak Spanish and English. *Early Childhood Research Quarterly, 27*(2), 177–187.

Tracey, D. H., & Young, J. W. (2002). Mothers' helping behaviors during children's at-home oral-reading practice: Effects of children's reading ability, children's gender, and mothers' educational level. *Journal of Educational Psychology, 94*(4), 729–737.

Waanders, C., Mendez, J. L., & Downer, J. T. (2007). Parent characteristics, economic stress and neighborhood context as predictors of parent involvement in preschool children's education. *Journal of School Psychology, 45*(6), 619–636.

Weikle, B., & Hadadian, A. (2004). Literacy, development and disabilities: Are we moving in the right direction? *Early Child Development and Care, 174*(7–8), 651–666.

What Works Clearinghouse. (2012). *Find what works.* Washington, DC: U.S. Department of Education and Institute of Education Sciences. Retrieved February 10, 2012, from *http://ies.ed.gov/ncee/wwc.*

Whitehurst, G. J., & Lonigan, C. J. (1998). Child development and emergent literacy. *Child Development, 69*(3), 848–872.

Wilkins, C., Gersten, R., Decker, L., Grunden, L., Brasiel, S., Brunnert, K., et al. (2012). *Does a summer reading program based on Lexiles affect reading comprehension?* (NCEE 2012-4006). Washington, DC: National Center for Education Evaluation and Regional Assistance, Institute of Education Sciences, U.S. Department of Education.

Xu, M., Kushner Benson, S. N., Mudrey-Camino, R., & Steiner, R. P. (2010). The relationship between parental involvement, self-regulated learning, and reading achievement of fifth graders: A path analysis using the ECLS-K database. *Social Psychology of Education: An International Journal, 13*(2), 237–269.

Zhang, D., Hsu, H. Y., Kwok, O., Benz, M., & Bowman-Perrott, L. (2011). The impact of basic-level parent engagements on student achievement: Patterns associated with race/ethnicity and socioeconomic status (SES). *Journal of Disability Policy Studies, 22*, 28–39.

CHAPTER 2

❖

A Comprehensive Approach to Building Oral Language in Preschool

PREREQUISITES FOR LITERACY

Allyssa McCabe

GUIDING QUESTIONS

❖ How can teachers facilitate preschool children's language development?

❖ More specifically, how can teachers build children's vocabulary and sense of story, both of which will aid in later reading comprehension?

❖ How can teachers get parents involved in their children's acquisition of literacy if those parents are not necessarily very advanced in their own literacy skills?

OVERVIEW OF THE TOPIC

Preschool classrooms present a crucial opportunity for children to develop their oral language skills, especially those children coming from an impoverished background. A child's receptive vocabulary and ability to produce a narrative, among other oral skills, upon entrance to kindergarten predicts their fourth-, seventh-, and 10th-grade reading comprehension (Snow, Porche, Tabors, & Harris, 2007). Because of such documented stability, preschool teachers are uniquely poised to change the trajectory of a child's academic success. Fortunately, we are in a position to offer research-based suggestions about how this can be achieved.

IMPORTANT THEORETICAL BACKGROUND AND RESEARCH BASE

Children begin literacy by developing oral language (Dickinson & Tabors, 2001). Numerous aspects of oral language development have been found to predict literacy skill (Snow, Burns, & Griffin, 1998). Children acquire language by exposure to child-directed talk, and the more of this they receive, the larger their vocabularies (Hart & Risley, 1995; Hurtado, Marchman, & Fernald, 2008; Huttenlocher, Haight, Bryk, Seltzer, & Lyons, 1991; Huttenlocher, Waterfall, Vasilyeva, Vevea, & Hedges, 2010). Other aspects of oral language also are acquired by children interacting one-on-one with adults; in particular the extent to which a child's narration is elaborated by parents predicts the quality of children's narratives (Fivush, Reese, & Haden, 2006).

What children need is input that is responsive to them (Tamis-LeMonda, Bornstein, & Baumwell, 2001). That is, children will not learn very much, if any, language from watching even supposedly educational television. Instead, they need to hear positive discussion of real objects or events that interest them. They benefit from hearing various kinds of talk, especially when that talk is contingent upon something they themselves say or indicate (McCabe, Tamis-LeMonda, Bornstein, Cates, Golinkoff, et al., 2013/under review). In America, children whose parents speak a language other than English benefit from having their parents speak the language that the parents are most comfortable with and fluent in, as well as from exposure to English in the first several years of life (Kovelman, Baker, & Petitto, 2008).

Unfortunately, not all children have parents who converse with them in such a positive, nurturing way (Hart & Risley, 1995); children from impoverished backgrounds hear a great deal less talk directed to them, as well as proportionately more negatively tinged commands—kinds of input that are less than optimal for language development.

And despite the promise of preschool—a place where oral language can be bolstered for less fortunate children so that they will enter kindergarten equipped to successfully begin to learn how to read (Snow et al., 1998)—many studies have documented what can only be termed missed opportunities in classrooms (see Dickinson, McCabe, & Clark-Chiarelli, 2004; McCabe, Boccia, Bennett, Lyman, & Hagen, 2010, for review). The importance of talking individually to children about things that interest them gets put aside in the interest of maintaining order in the classroom or more formal instruction in the alphabet or numbers or no talk at all.

To bring children up to speed verbally is no simple task. The truth is that there are many aspects of oral language that are critical prerequisites for literacy acquisition: phonological awareness, vocabulary, syntax, and narrative discourse; the notion that all these facets of oral language should be attended to is a tenet of the Comprehensive Language Approach (CLA) to early literacy (Dickinson, McCabe, Anastasopoulos, Peisner-Feingerg, & Poe, 2003). The CLA believes that too many researchers and practitioners have focused on fostering phonological awareness in preschoolers to the exclusion of other equally important aspects of oral language such as vocabulary and narrative and that such unequal emphasis does not serve children well. The CLA has been supported by a large national study (National Institute of Child Health and Human Development Early Child Care Research Network, 2005). Ideally, teachers will focus on all these oral skills in addition to print-related skills more typically associated with literacy. Adding to this challenge is the additional fact that even under optimal circumstances, there are more children than adults in the classroom. This imbalance of children and adults means that for each child to receive enough input responsive to his or her interests, a clear and consistent focus on the importance of such talk needs to be implemented.

A number of programs have had documented success in building aspects of children's language and literacy skills. When adults read interactively with children while asking and inviting questions, a practice known as *dialogic reading*, children's expressive and receptive vocabulary are significantly expanded (Arnold & Whitehurst, 1994; Whitehurst & Lonigan, 2001). Dialogic reading is listed as the most effective intervention for building oral language in early childhood education by the What Works Clearinghouse (*http://ies.ed.gov/ncee/wwc/reports/topic.aspx?tid=13*).

Another study found that *joint writing* significantly outperforms joint reading and control instruction in facilitating phonological awareness, word writing, orthographic awareness, and letter knowledge even in children as young as 3 to 4 years of age (Aram & Biron, 2004). The joint writing program involved a variety of games and creative activities that encouraged letter knowledge, phonological awareness, and emergent writing activities with children ages 3 to 5 years. Children were taught to recognize their own written names and written names of friends, word segmentation, letter names, and letter–sound correspondences. For example, in a lesson about a month into the program, children were alternately asked to do such things as pick out the first letters of their names from stickers or magnetic letters or to write the first letter of their name with crayons. That session ended with each child saying his or her name, the first syllable of the name, the first letter, and goodbye (e.g., "My name is Maria, my name starts with *ma*, with the letter *M*, goodbye"). In the present intervention—which involves slightly older children (4 years instead of 3)—teachers would say things like, "See *S* makes the /s/ sound (in memory story, Appendix 2.1). *S* begins the words *ssso, ssshiny*, and *ssstory* right here and here and here [pointing to the words in question]."

Elaborating a child's narrative by asking a child more questions improves the ability to tell a narrative. That is, in past research, we randomly assigned low-income mothers to a condition in which we explained the importance of following up on what children talked about. Children whose mothers received this intervention improved their receptive vocabulary and narrative ability compared to a control group of children whose mothers did not receive the intervention (Peterson, Jesso,

& McCabe, 1999). In fact, a review of extensive research has documented the considerable positive impact elaborating a child's narrative has on a wide variety of linguistic, cognitive, and socioemotional development (Fivush et al., 2006). Elaborating narrative, like joint writing, has been found by one group of researchers to be even more effective than dialogic reading in improving children's narrative ability and reading comprehension (Reese, Leyva, Sparks, & Grolnick, 2006). When 4- to 5-year-old children *recounted educational activities*, their expressive and receptive language improved (Riley, Burrell, & McCallum, 2004).

Having 6- to 7-year-old children *dictate a story* in response to a picture prompt significantly increased the level of development of their story structure and use of spatial–temporal-setting elements (Pontecorvo & Zuccermaglio, 1989). Sulzby (1981) analyzed the dictated stories of kindergartners and found that these varied from stories they told in a number of ways; dictated stories can be an important aspect of developing emergent literacy such that children learn the link between their own words and print. Justice, Pullen, and Pence (2008) found that although preschool children seldom pay attention to print in various types of storybook reading, *explicit referencing of print* is one way to significantly increase such attention. In the course of taking dictation of a child's narrative, it is very natural to refer to print (e.g., "See, this is where I wrote your name. And this is where I wrote *jewelry*").

BRINGING THIS KNOWLEDGE TO THE EARLY LITERACY CLASSROOM

Description of the Preschool Program

To meet the challenges of facilitating children's oral language development, as well as their emergent literacy skills, I developed a method of talking with children that combined all of the aspects of oral language found to effectively predict children's literacy accomplishments with print-related skills: The Remembering, Writing, Reading program (RWR).

Congruent with the CLA, our RWR intervention combined aspects of numerous effective programs: (1) dialogic reading; (2) joint writing; (3) elaborating personal narratives; (4) recounting educational and other activities; (5) taking dictation of a narrative while explicitly referencing print related to children's own words ("Slow down, I need more time to write down all you said—see?"); (6) bolstering receptive vocabulary; and (7) engaging in emergent literacy skills such as letter recognition, directionality of writing, and the relationship of speech to text. The RWR approach builds on the Language Experience Approach (LEA) to reading instruction (Stauffer, 1970). Despite many variations, the essential LEA concept remains: to teach a child with limited language effectively, one should use the student's own vocabulary and narrative structure to create reading materials that that student can comprehend

(Dixon & Nessel, 1983). The LEA has been particularly recommended for ELL (English language learning) students (e.g., Peregoy & Boyle, 2001), as it makes use of the English vocabulary the students have already acquired in order to ensure that they will understand a passage after working to decode it.

The form for implementing RWR is in Appendix 2.1 at the end of the chapter. At the first session, a teacher tells a child a brief personal narrative (e.g., "See this Band-Aid? I was peeling an apple last night, and I slipped, and I cut my finger. Did anything like that ever happen to you?"). This narrative sets the exchange up as a conversation rather than a testlike situation and has been found to be very effective in getting children to narrate (Peterson & McCabe, 1983). Children are encouraged to draw or look at photos of various locations in the area (e.g., a park) that might trigger a memory.

Oral into Written Language: Emergent Literacy Skills

When the child begins to narrate, the teacher begins to write down what the child is saying, repeating the child's words in the process. This echoing ensures that the child understands he or she is being listened to and buys the teacher time to print the child's words. While teachers are advised to use the exact words that the child said, some changes will invariably occur (e.g., pronunciations get clarified, words are sometimes forgotten). Such minor changes are not important and did not, will not compromise the efficacy of RWR. In fact, correcting a child's grammar is sometimes advisable: For example, a teacher might say, "You wented outside? OK, I'll write 'I went outside.'"

Elaborating Narrative

If the child stops narrating, teachers are encouraged to ask open-ended follow-up questions such as *"Who* else was there?" *"What* did you order at the restaurant?" *"When* did this happen?" *"Where* does your grandma live?" *"How* fast did you run yesterday?" *"Why* do you think that little boy hit his sister?" *"What* do you think your brother felt when you said he couldn't play with you?" The goal is to get the child to extend his or her narrative.

While it is good practice to ask such open-ended questions to begin with, children with relatively little language and/or relatively little English may need more structured questions. If the child can't answer a general question, then follow up with specific, yes/no questions such as "Was your father with you too?"

Introducing Vocabulary

Sometimes a child will struggle in the midst of reminiscing, saying something like "I almost drowned but I was wearing the orange thing." That would be an optimal time to introduce a vocabulary word related to what the child is interested in discussing: "Oh, you almost drowned but you were wearing a *life jacket*?" Other times, as in the example in Appendix 2.1, teachers may find that the best time to introduce a word to a child is at the end of the narrative. In Appendix 2.1, the teacher said, "Your parents were generous, weren't they? Do you know what *generous* means? No? It means *giving*. Your parents gave you lots of things." Teachers should note the vocabulary item they introduced on the form.

Interactive (or Dialogic) Reading (or Rereading) of Child's Narrative

After the child has finished the narrative, the teacher proceeds to read what he or she wrote aloud to the child. The teacher can make corrections if the child desires. The teacher can also ask some more elaborative questions and add to the written narrative if the child responds.

In future sessions, teachers reread the child's narrative, noting the date of the rereading, reminding the child of the vocabulary word, and asking additional elaborative questions. The goal is to have a total of four rereadings (five readings in all) of the narrative, five repetitions of the vocabulary word.

Emergent Literacy: The Alphabet

Teachers can also extend the session by pointing out a couple of letters (e.g., *J* and *S* in the example in Appendix 2.1). The teacher can say something like "See this word here—it is *jewelry*. *Jewelry* begins with a *J*. The letter *J* makes the /j/ sound." To cover the complete alphabet for each child requires that teachers keep track of what letters they introduce. To simplify this process, teachers may well want to call attention to letters in sequence and simply keep track by looking at the child's previous dictation sheets. If there is no word that begins with the letter in question, teachers may want to introduce a vocabulary word appropriate to the child's dictation that begins with the letter in question—for example: "Did the pink jacket Barbie was wearing have a zipper? *Zipper* starts with Z—see [teacher points to where he or she has written *zipper* on the page] the Z right here in the word *zipper*?"

Results of a Study Implementing RWR

This program was implemented in a public preschool that served low-income, primarily English ELL children. Children were pretested in the fall and posttested in the spring on the Peabody Picture Vocabulary Test (Dunn & Dunn, 1997) and oral narrative skill. The progress of these children after a year of RWR was compared with that of comparable children in other public preschools who simply received the standard preschool curriculum of the school district. In the course of the school year (roughly October through May), children received on average of twenty-six 20-minute one-on-one RWR dictation sessions.

Children in the RWR intervention gained significantly more in terms of receptive vocabulary and narrative skill over the course of their preschool year compared to nonintervention children. What is more, vocabulary scores of intervention children at the outset of the RWR intervention were significantly below those of the normative population, but by the end of the intervention year, children's vocabulary scores were not significantly different from the normative average. That is, the high-risk children in this study were set to succeed in literacy skill in kindergarten and thereafter.

Tracking Progress

Teachers are encouraged to include narratives in a portfolio folder for each child. In Figure 2.1, I offer the system we use to assess narratives (adapted from McCabe & Rollins, 1994). The narrative in Appendix 2.1 is classified as a chronological narrative. Knowing that, a teacher would know that what is missing is a main point; a good follow-up question on a future rereading would be "What was your favorite part of the fair?" By the end of their fourth year, children should be telling narratives that consist of more than three events, as does the narrative in Appendix 2.1.

Appendix 2.2 at the end of the chapter gives a more detailed description of different forms of narrative. Research (Peterson & McCabe, 1983) has established that by age 4, children typically tell a leapfrog narrative, consisting of at least three actions, but often jumping around in chronology and leaving out important actions. By 5, children should be telling end-at-the-high-point narratives, which chronologically sequence several actions but end prematurely at the climax, or emotional high point. By 6, children should tell a classic narrative that is like an end-at-the-high-point narrative but goes on to resolve the situation.

Teachers can easily determine the structure of a child's narrative by asking a series of questions (see Figure 2.1), continuing down to the next question if they answer yes, or right to find the structure of the narrative if they answer no. A portfolio of dictated stories from each child could document that the child went from telling a two-event narrative in September to, say, a leapfrog narrative in March— clear progress.

Figure 2.2 is a dictated narrative produced by a child to a volunteer university student who was an art major. This was part of a project done at a homeless shelter. The art student, in addition to asking the elaborative questions recommended above, superimposed the drawing the child did while hearing her prior narrative read aloud to her. (The art student combined pictures and narratives by a number of

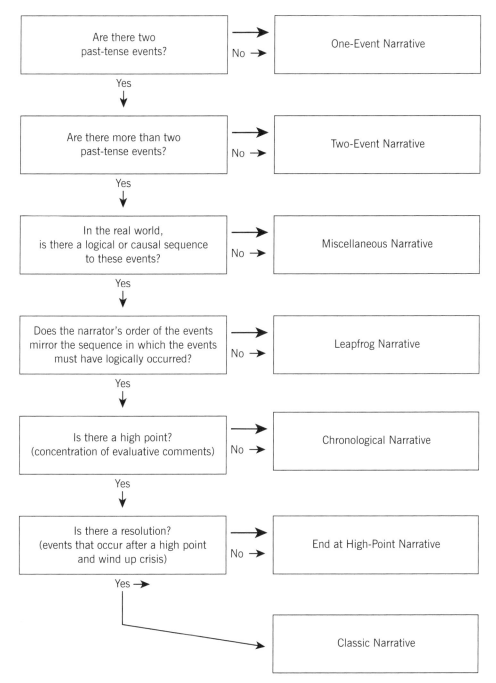

FIGURE 2.1. High-point analysis. Reprinted with permission from Figure 2, Questions for scoring narrative structure: The North-American–Caucasian–English-speaking model, from the article "Assessment of Preschool Narrative Skills," by A. McCabe and P. R. Rollins, published in *American Journal of Speech–Language Pathology, 3*, 45–56. © Copyright 1994. American Speech–Language–Hearing Association. All rights reserved.

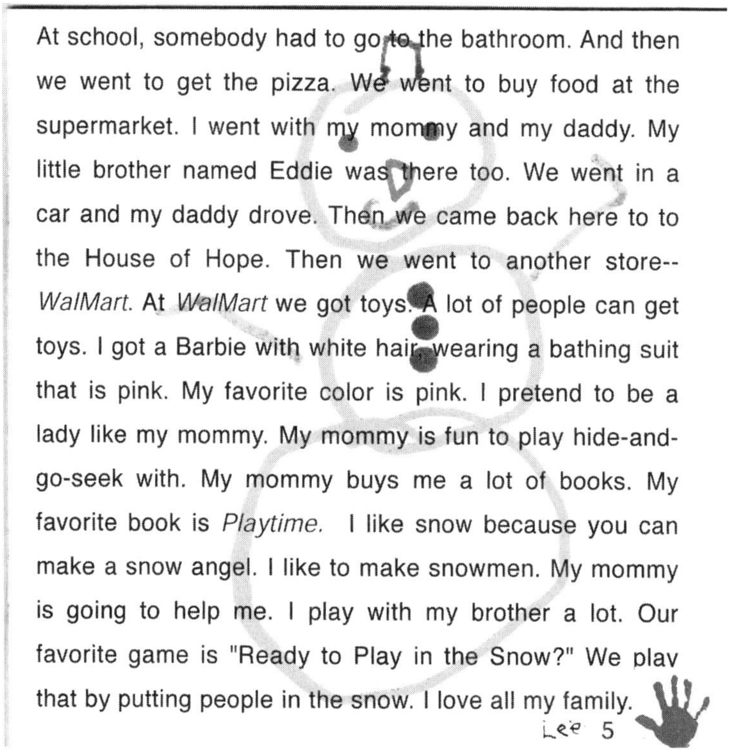

> At school, somebody had to go to the bathroom. And then we went to get the pizza. We went to buy food at the supermarket. I went with my mommy and my daddy. My little brother named Eddie was there too. We went in a car and my daddy drove. Then we came back here to to the House of Hope. Then we went to another store-- *WalMart*. At *WalMart* we got toys. A lot of people can get toys. I got a Barbie with white hair wearing a bathing suit that is pink. My favorite color is pink. I pretend to be a lady like my mommy. My mommy is fun to play hide-and-go-seek with. My mommy buys me a lot of books. My favorite book is *Playtime.* I like snow because you can make a snow angel. I like to make snowmen. My mommy is going to help me. I play with my brother a lot. Our favorite game is "Ready to Play in the Snow?" We play that by putting people in the snow. I love all my family.
>
> Lee 5

FIGURE 2.2. Sample dictation of child's narrative.

other children in the homeless shelter into a book that was given to each contributing child.) In the course of several sessions with the art student, the child elaborated her narrative and the result is a chronological narrative in that it consists of more than two events that mirrored a possibly logical sequence of events. No one event in that sequence of 10—(1) going to the bathroom, (2) going for pizza, (3) went to buy food, (4) went with parents, (5) went in car, (6) daddy drove, (7) came back to HOH, (8) went to another store, (9) got toys, and (10) got a Barbie—was more heavily evaluated than another. Instead, future elaborative interactions with the art student resulted in the child talking about some of her favorite things.

The Rich Get Richer

One challenge for teachers who commit to a classroom rich in oral language is that the more verbal children often are able to grab the conversation and get even more interactive feedback. Teachers need to notice the too-quiet children and single them out for perhaps even more dictations than their more talkative peers.

Parent Outreach Program

Many educators recommend trying to increase parent involvement in their child's education. Almost everyone tries to increase the frequency of parents reading to children. When parents are educated, this works wonderfully. However, many low-income and/or immigrant parents struggle with literacy themselves and/or cannot find many books in the language they are most comfortable reading. One mother I know, a Portuguese–English bilingual with minimum education and literacy skills, dutifully tried to read books with her child as the child's first-grade teacher had recommended. She confessed to me, however, that this was very stressful, that she and her daughter wound up shouting at each other every time. Such fraught literacy experiences quite probably do more harm than good. Thus, a program that simply attempts to increase the frequency and quality of parent–child *talk* to improve the child's abilities has important potential.

Fortunately, we have a program that has been demonstrated to improve children's receptive vocabulary and narrative production skills (Peterson et al., 1999). Low-income mothers of preschoolers (average age 3 years, 7 months) were randomly assigned to either an intervention or a control condition. Mothers who were involved in the intervention were shown transcripts of exemplary narrative conversations that we had collected from parents of excellent narrators in a prior project (McCabe & Peterson, 1991). Mothers in the intervention project took turns reading these exemplary conversations aloud to a partner who read the child's part. We emphasized the following points (Peterson et al., 1999):

1. Talk to your child frequently and consistently about past experiences.
2. Spend a lot of time talking about each topic.
3. Ask plenty of "wh" questions (*who, what, when, where, how, why*) and fewer "yes/no" questions (e.g., "Was Grandpa wearing a red coat?"). As part of this, ask questions about the context or setting of the events, especially where and when they took place.
4. Listen carefully to what your child is saying, and encourage elaboration.
5. Encourage your child to say more than one sentence at a time by using back-channel responses (e.g., "I see" or "Really?") or simply repeating what your child has just said.
6. Follow your child's lead. That is, talk about what your child wants to talk about.

Finally, we reminded parents every month of the importance of reminiscing with their children about past events.

At the end of 1 year, children in the comparison group had significantly greater increases in their receptive vocabulary compared with those in the control group. A year later, their children's narrative skills had increased significantly more than the control group children's skills.

EXEMPLARY PRACTICE

Naomi Simpson is a teacher in a Head Start classroom in a working-class neighborhood in the Northeast. She attended a workshop in which I presented some of the ideas we have discussed here. When I returned to her classroom 2 weeks later, I was delighted to see dozens of dictated narratives hanging at child eye level from the bathroom all the way to the door. That way, she said, she could read a child's narrative when they were waiting in line for any reason. The children had already started to anticipate this ritual and to enjoy listening to each other's narratives.

Naomi said that she had become so interested in the way children talked about the things that had happened to them, that she had taken to engaging them in conversations during lunch. She would often get ideas from those conversations about what the children saw as newsworthy happenings in their lives, things she would ask them to elaborate on when they sat down at the "Memory" table to do dictation.

How could she pull off 20-minute one-on-one conversations with children? She thought of several times that would work for her classroom. One was early drop-off times or late pickup times, when there would be just one child present. Also, about twice a week another aide would lead children in exercise time in the gym. Because she reasoned that the children got plenty of exercise every day at recess, she decided that occasionally missing this time in the cause of furthering literacy was acceptable. She also trained her aide and parent volunteers to take dictation at the Memory table, so that that could be a choice and she could supervise other choice times.

Naomi kept careful records of each child's times at the Memory table, so that each child was ensured of access to this rich opportunity. She also implemented the parent outreach program by talking about it on Parents' Night. She followed up by sending home a list of the instructions given above, which she also repeated in the monthly parent newsletter. In every newsletter thereafter, she reminded parents of the importance of talking with their children at length about what happened to them. Every day, she sent home a slip of paper with several events that had happened during the school day: "Today, ask your child about the storyteller who came in. And about the snowman we all built." Finally, when she saw parents at drop-off or pickup, she would think of individual prompts: "Alice had an interesting experience at lunch today. You should ask her about it." Parents' curiosity was piqued, which increased their participation in the program.

CONCLUSION

This chapter has described two methods of building a child's sense of story and vocabulary, among other oral language skills, that have been found to be effective in past research. By implementing RWR at school and engaging parents in reminiscing with their children about past experiences, teachers can facilitate all aspects of oral language and print knowledge that have been found to predict literacy acquisition and eventual reading comprehension. Recall that children's oral language skills *upon entrance to kindergarten*—especially their narrative skill and vocabulary—predict Head Start children's fourth-, seventh-, and 10th-grade reading comprehension (Snow et al., 2007) and that children's skills remained constant from kindergarten throughout high school (Dickinson et al., 2004). By focusing consistently and emphatically on enriching all of the oral language skills that predict subsequent literacy skill, preschool teachers are poised to enable even high-risk children to succeed.

REFERENCES

Aram, D., & Biron, S. (2004). Joint storybook reading and joint writing interventions among low SES preschoolers: Differential contributions to early literacy. *Early Childhood Research Quarterly, 19*(4), 588–610.

Arnold, D. S., & Whitehurst, G. J. (1994). Accelerating language development through picture book reading: A summary of dialogic reading and its effects. In D. K. Dickinson (Ed.), *Bridges to literacy: Approaches to supporting child and family literacy* (pp. 103–128). Cambridge, MA: Blackwell.

Dickinson, D. K., McCabe, A., Anastasopoulos, L., Peisner-Feinberg, E. S., & Poe, M. D. (2003). The comprehensive language approach to early literacy: The interrelationships among vocabulary, phonological sensitivity, and print knowledge among preschool-aged children. *Journal of Educational Psychology, 95,* 465–481.

Dickinson, D. K., McCabe, A., & Clark-Chiarelli, N. (2004). Preschool-based prevention of reading disability: Realities versus possibilities. In C. A. Stone, E. R. Silliman, B. J. Ehren, & K. Apel (Eds.), *Handbook of language and literacy: Development and disorders* (pp. 209–227). New York: Guilford Press.

Dickinson, D. K., & Tabors, P. O. (2001). *Beginning language with literacy.* Baltimore: Brookes.

Dixon, C. N., & Nessel, D. (1983). *Language experience approach to reading (and writing): Language-experience reading for second language learners.* Englewood Cliffs, NJ: Prentice-Hall.

Dunn, L. M., & Dunn, L. M. (1997). *Peabody Picture Vocabulary Test–III.* Circle Pines, MN: American Guidance Service.

Fivush, R., Reese, E., & Haden, C. A. (2006). Elaborating on elaboration: Role of maternal reminiscing style in cognitive and socioemotional development. *Child Development, 77,* 1568–1588.

Hart, B., & Risley, T. R. (1995). *Meaningful differences in the everyday experience of young American children*. Baltimore: Brookes.

Hurtado, N., Marchman, V. A., & Fernald, A. (2008). Does input influence uptake? Links between maternal talk, processing speed and vocabulary size in Spanish-learning children. *Developmental Science, 11*(6), F31–F39.

Huttenlocher, J., Haight, W., Bryk, A., Seltzer, M., & Lyons, T. (1991). Early vocabulary growth: Relation to language input and gender. *Developmental Psychology, 27*, 236–248.

Huttenlocher, J., Waterfall, H., Vasilyeva, M., Vevea, J., & Hedges, L. V. (2010). Sources of variability in children's language growth. *Cognitive Psychology, 61*, 343–365.

Justice, L. M., Pullen, P. C., & Pence, K. (2008). Influence of verbal and nonverbal references to print on preschoolers' visual attention to print during storybook reading. *Developmental Psychology, 44*(3), 855–866.

Kovelman, I., Baker, S. A., & Petitto, L. A. (2008). Age of first bilingual language exposure as a new window into bilingual reading development. *Bilingualism: Language and Cognition, 11*(2), 203–223.

McCabe, A., Tamis-LeMonda, C. S., Bornstein, M. H., Cates, C. B., Golinkoff, R., Hirfsh-Pasek, K., et al. (2013/under review). *Multilingual children: Beyond myths and towards best practices*.

McCabe, A., Boccia, J., Bennett, M., Lyman, N., & Hagen, R. (2010). Improving oral language skills in preschool children from disadvantaged backgrounds: Remembering, writing, reading (RWR). *Imagination, Cognition and Personality, 29*(4), 363–391.

McCabe, A., & Peterson, C. (1991). Getting the story: A longitudinal study of parental styles in eliciting narratives and developing narrative skill. In A. McCabe & C. Peterson (Eds.), *Developing narrative structure* (pp. 217–253). Hillsdale, NJ: Erlbaum.

McCabe, A., & Rollins, P. (1994). Assessment of preschool narrative skills. *American Journal of Speech–Language Pathology, 3*(1), 45–56.

National Institute of Child Health and Human Development Early Child Care Research Network. (2005). Pathways to reading: The role of oral language in the transition to reading. *Developmental Psychology, 41*, 428–442.

Peregoy, S. F., & Boyle, O. F. (2001). *Reading, writing, and learning in ELL. A resource book for K–12 teachers*. New York: Longman.

Peterson, C., Jesso, B., & McCabe, A. (1999). Encouraging narratives in preschoolers: An intervention study. *Journal of Child Language, 26*, 49–67.

Peterson, C., & McCabe, A. (1983). *Developmental psycholinguistics: Three ways of looking at a child's narrative*. New York: Plenum.

Pontecorvo, C., & Zucchermaglio, C. (1989). From oral to written language: Preschool children dictating stories. *Journal of Reading Behavior, 21*, 109–126.

Reese, E., Leyva, D., Sparks, A., & Grolnick, W. (2010). Maternal elaborative reminiscing increases low-income children's narrative skills relative to dialogic reading. *Early Education and Development, 2*(3), 318–342.

Riley, J., Burrell, A., & McCallum, B. (2004). Developing the spoken language skills of reception class children in two multicultural, inner-city primary schools. *British Educational Research Journal, 30*(5), 658–672.

Snow, C. E., Burns, S., & Griffin, P. (Eds.). (1998). *Preventing reading difficulties in young children*. Washington, DC: National Academy Press.

Snow, C. E., Porche, M. V., Tabors, P. O., & Harris, S. R. (2007). *Is literacy enough: Pathways to academic success for adolescents*. Baltimore: Brookes.

Stauffer, R. G. (1970). *The language–experience approach to the teaching of reading*. New York: Harper & Row.

Sulzby, E. (1981). *Kindergarteners begin to read their own compositions: Beginning readers' developing knowledges about written language project*. Final report to the Research Committee of the National Council of Teachers of English. Evanston, IL: Northwestern University.

Tamis-LeMonda, C. S., Bornstein, M. H., & Baumwell, L. (2001). Maternal responsiveness and children's achievement of language milestones. *Child Development, 72*(3), 748–767.

What Works Clearinghouse. (2012). *Find what works*. Washington, DC: U.S. Department of Education and the Institute of Education Sciences. Retrieved February 10, 2012, from *http://ies.ed.gov/ncee/wwc/reports/topic.aspx?tid=13*.

Whitehurst, G. J., & Lonigan, C. J. (2001). Emergent literacy: Development from pre- readers to readers. In S. B. Neuman & D. K. Dickinson (Eds.), *Handbook of early literacy research* (Vol. 1, pp. 11–29). New York: Guilford Press.

APPENDIX 2.1. Example of Dictated Memory
(RWR Intervention)

Child's name _____   Voc. Rereading 1 date _____

Child's date of birth _____   Voc. Rereading 2 date _____

Date narrative recorded _____   Voc. Rereading 3 date _____

Researcher's name _____   Voc. Rereading 4 date _____

Letter(s) pointed out:

A B C D E F G H I **J** K L M N O P Q R **S** T U V W X Y Z

a b c d e f g h i **j** k l m n o p q r **s** t u v w x y z

Vocabulary word introduced: generous = giving

Narrative:

"Tell me about the fair?"

It was **s**o nice. It had so many real fairs and so many rides. And **j**ewelry and they gave us **j**ewelry. They just let us play. "Get the Pepsi and drink it and then throw it and then fist it and then get another one." And then we get to go to get tickets and then go to get money for my games I wanted, and my mom's going to bring me my games. And then we will go to the mall. And then we'll go get **s**ome food and then go to the train.

"Then?"

We went to Mickey Mouse upstairs to buy my collection and buy pink and blue dresses. **S**hiny and light. And that's the **s**tory.

"Your parents were generous, weren't they? Do you know what *generous* means? No? It means giving. Your parents gave you lots of things."

Time it took to write down narrative: 5 minutes; session = 20 minutes with rereading
of old narrative and this one

APPENDIX 2.2. Structural Patterns of Narratives in High-Point Analysis

CLASSIC PATTERN

The narrator may begin with an abstract ("Did I ever tell you about when I broke my arm?") or attention-getter ("You know what?"). The narrator then provides orientation information about who, what, when, and where some experience occurred, followed by a series of complicating actions that build to a high point ("You can't believe the worst part"), and then give additional series of events that resolve the problem ("I had to go to the hospital and get a cast on").

ENDING-AT-THE-HIGH-POINT PATTERN

The narrator gives a chronological sequence of events, as in the classic pattern above, but simply builds to a high point and ends the narrative. There is not resolution in this pattern.

CHRONOLOGICAL PATTERN

The narrative is a simple description of successive, but not causally related events (e.g., "We went to Disney World. We rode on roller coasters and ate ice cream. We saw Mickey Mouse").

LEAPFROGGING PATTERN

The narrator gives more than two complicating actions that are components of a single experience, but does not give them in chronological order and/or omits key events. That is, the narrator jumps around and leaves events out.

TWO-EVENT PATTERN

The narrator only tells us two events that constituted an experience (e.g., "One time I tripped and fell").

ONE-EVENT PATTERN

The narrator only tells us a single event that constituted an experience (e.g., "I got stung on a trampoline, not on my foot, right here").

Based on Peterson and McCabe (1983).

CHAPTER 3

❖

Working with Culturally and Linguistically Diverse Students

LESSONS LEARNED FROM READING RECOVERY

CATHERINE COMPTON-LILLY

GUIDING QUESTION

Teachers are familiar with the achievement gap in reading for children from diverse backgrounds. We also recognize that children from diverse backgrounds are often overrepresented among our struggling readers. While many educators have worked hard to support these readers, in some cases our attempts have resulted in frustration as student progress remained stagnant and student text reading level plateaued. In this chapter, I ask a question that I suspect is shared by many of my colleagues and that continues to drive my work:

❖ How can teachers support literacy development for young children from diverse backgrounds?

I use the term *diverse backgrounds* to highlight the vast range of abilities, practices, and experiences that children bring to school that are often different from practices and experiences that they encounter in school. We have all learned a great deal about teaching from our own schooling background and from our teacher education experiences. These experiences have taught us messages about what children should be able to do at particular points in time, about the types of experiences that we assume are most helpful to young literacy learners, and about the ways children learn literacy. Unfortunately, our own experiences can prevent us from recognizing alternative ways of being and becoming literate that children bring to school. If we expect children to be able to write their names when they enter kindergarten, we might identify children who cannot do this as less capable without recognizing the rich storytelling experiences that these same children might bring.

This became clear to me when I moved from teaching in a middle-class suburban school to a high-poverty inner-city school. In our suburban school, I worked with a talented team of first-grade teachers, who used nursery rhymes as the first texts their students encountered in first grade. Because the children in this community already knew these familiar texts, these experienced teachers used the rhymes to help their students acquire and solidify concepts about reading, such as pointing to words with one-to-one correspondence, tracking print from left to right, and locating familiar words in text. Familiarity with the rhymes allowed the students to focus on learning literacy concepts and behaviors without attending to the actual decoding of the texts.

The following year, I moved to an inner-city school located in a high-poverty community. The school population was comprised of African American and Puerto Rican students. Prior to the start of the school year, I mentioned to one of my first-grade colleagues that I planned to begin the year with the nursery rhymes as we had done in my prior school. My new colleague shook her head and lamented:

> "These kids don't know the nursery rhymes. Their parents don't spend time with them and teach them things like that. You have to know that these kids are not like the ones you taught in the suburbs. They are very low. They really don't know anything."

As a relatively novice teacher with limited experiences, but great hopes, I was concerned by this comment. I knew that this teacher had been at my new school for several years, and I did not want to discount her experiences, but I was also not willing to accept her assessment that my students did "not know anything."

As I left my school that afternoon, I noticed a cluster of young girls gathered on the concrete outside the community center that was attached to our school. They were jumping rope—performing complicated double-Dutch steps accompanied by verses and rhymes. Unfamiliar with their game, I stopped and watched. As I drove home that evening, I reflected on what I had observed. On Monday, I visited the community center with my handheld tape recorder and with the permission of the community center staff and the girls—who were excited to share their skills—I collected over a dozen jump rope and hand-clapping rhymes that I transcribed and photocopied on sheets of paper. In a few cases, I made minor changes in the lyrics—revising words and concepts that were not acceptable in school. Despite these changes, the children in my class were excited as they recited the familiar playground rhymes. We read the poems in class and used them to acquire and solidify the same skills I had addressed in the suburbs—pointing to words with one-to-one correspondence, tracking print from left to right, and locating familiar words.

I realized that while I expected children to know their nursery rhymes and could have considered my new students deficit for not knowing these texts, they did possess rich literate knowledge. The girls at the community center taught me an important lesson. While my new students did not know the nursery rhymes, they did know many texts that were equally as useful in the classroom.

In this chapter, I review research and instructional practices that hold promise for working with diverse learners around literacy. I argue that recognizing the knowledge that children bring is key to helping young children become readers and writers. In particular, like McNaughton (2002), I argue that diversity takes two forms. First, children vary significantly in what they know about written text. Some children enter school knowing the letters of the alphabet, the sounds the letters make, and are able to write simple messages. Other children can sing the alphabet song, write their names, or spell a few words. Children may or may not recognize the one-to-one correspondence between spoken words and text or the left-to-right directionality that is characteristic of English. All children do not bring these same literacy "skills" to school.

A second form of literacy knowledge involves the various types of literacy experiences that children engage with or witness. Some children live in homes where families read newspapers in multiple languages, participate in various religious literacy practices, or visit cultural websites that feature films, cartoons, and texts in languages other than English. Other children have vast experiences with oral storytelling, music lyrics, environmental print, and/or storybook reading. As McNaughton (2002) maintained, there are two domains of knowledge and skills related to reading. The first set "includes those processes that help a reader to decode print into sound and sound into language" (p. 167). The second set operates in the "domain of language and knowledge—those concepts a child comes to have about the world, including their experiences in familiar events" (p. 167).

I argue that teachers must be cognizant and consciously consider both of these forms of diversity—which I characterize as differences in literacy knowledge and literacy practices—as they work in linguistically and culturally diverse classrooms. Like all authors, I draw on my own experiences when I write. For the greater part of the past 20 years, I have been involved with Reading Recovery—first, as a teacher in a high-poverty urban school and later as a Reading Recovery trainer who was responsible for training Reading Recovery teacher leaders for school districts and sites in the Midwest. I draw on Reading Recovery not only because it is the reading intervention that is most familiar to me but also because it offers enormous potential for thinking about diversity as well as for documenting the micro interactions between students and teachers that accompany learning to read.

In this chapter, I draw on my experiences as a Reading Recovery teacher, trainer, and researcher to illustrate some of the lessons Reading Recovery students have taught me about student diversity and the effects diversity can have on learning to read. Prior to introducing the reader to some of the children I have taught, I briefly review Reading Recovery and some of the research that I have drawn on to help me to think about diversity and the teaching of reading. In the following sections, I explore what Reading Recovery offers to discussions of diversity in literacy knowledge. I then draw on the work of Clay (2005b, 2005c) and others to explore diversity in literacy practices.

TWO FORMS OF DIVERSITY: LITERACY KNOWLEDGE AND LITERACY PRACTICES

While my over 25 years of teaching at the elementary and college levels has been accompanied by reading many articles and conducting many of my own research projects, I present a small sampling of ideas and theories that have helped me to think about diversity alongside literacy learning. I begin briefly providing information about the Reading Recovery program and diversity in literacy knowledge. I then explore research that is directly related to diversity in the literacy practices and experiences that children bring to classrooms.

Reading Recovery and Diversity in Literacy Knowledge

The most highly ranked reading intervention on the What Works Clearinghouse website (2012) is Reading Recovery (Clay 2005b, 2005c). The effectiveness of Reading Recovery is demonstrated by a set of five empirical quantitative studies. These studies indicate the "extent of evidence for *Reading Recovery*® to be medium to large for alphabetics, small for fluency and comprehension, and medium to large for general reading achievement." Reading Recovery brings a set of significant practices that have been identified as contributing to its effectiveness. Three of these are (1) a theoretical base grounded in observations of children working with connected texts, (2) an emphasis on ongoing assessment of children, and (3) extensive teacher professional development.

A Theoretical Base Grounded in the Observation of Children

Reading Recovery is a 12- to 20-week individualized reading intervention that is grounded on a theoretical base that privileges close observations of children as they interact with connected texts—reading books and writing sentences and short stories. The instructional strategies described in Clay's books, *Literacy Lessons Parts One and Two* (2005b, 2005c), have been refined and revised based on close observations of thousands of children over 30 years and continue to be revisited by practicing Reading Recovery professionals. The theoretical premises that underlie Reading

Recovery are not treated as a priori models of literacy learning that direct literacy instruction but are considered to contribute to dynamic and evolving theories that lead to individualized lessons for students.

Ongoing Assessment

Developing theories based on observation and individualizing instruction requires careful and ongoing assessment. Clay's *Observation Survey* (2005a) explores a vast range of the dimensions of reading and writing to help teachers craft rich understandings of young children as literacy learners. The *Observation Survey* can provide teachers with information about the letter–sound knowledge that children bring, their understandings of various concepts about print, known letters and words, and their ability to hear and record the sounds children hear in words, as well as their processing of connected text. In addition, Reading Recovery teachers take daily running records of their students' reading to identify the strategies that students use. The *Observation Survey* and ongoing running records (Clay, 2005a) provide teachers with significant information about the literacy strengths and weakness of their students. Reading Recovery teachers use this information to create individualized lessons that target the strengths and challenges for each student.

Ongoing Professional Development

Finally, ongoing professional development including collaborative teacher problem solving is a required component for all Reading Recovery professionals. Reading Recovery teachers participate in regularly scheduled "behind-the-glass" lessons. During these lessons groups of teachers watch and discuss ongoing lessons being taught by their peers. The objective is not to critique each other's teaching but to use these shared examples as opportunities to discuss dimensions of reading processing, teacher/student interactions, teaching–learning opportunities, and the ways young children strategize with texts.

Diversity in Literate Practices

While often unacknowledged, I argue that Reading Recovery has the potential to be equally attentive to the cultural and linguistic diversity that children bring to school. In particular, Marie Clay's most recent treatises on Reading Recovery theory and methods—*Literacy Lessons Parts One and Two* (Clay, 2005b, 2005c)—feature multiple references to the diversity that children bring and highlight the need to teachers to attend to that diversity. As Clay explains:

> Some children will transition into school from homes or preschools that emphasize speaking and oral language. While this is a great preparation for literacy

learning, it might be that an emphasis on oral traditions in some cultures has severely reduced exposure to printed language. If this is the case, the school needs to deliver extra opportunities for engaging with print, approaching this with due sensitivity. Other children entering school may have had great experiences with books in another language that is not the language of school. Bridges need to be built for both these groups of new entrants to engage with books in another language. Too few schools build those bridges and too few schools plan for make-up opportunities. (2005b, p. 6)

Clay clearly places the onus of responsibility for dealing with the differences in what children bring on schools and teachers. Teachers are responsible for recognizing and building on oral traditions while providing students with rich opportunities to engage with text. Schools and teachers must build bridges between home and school knowledge and provide opportunities for children to acquire school-sanctioned forms of literacy. Clay closes the first volume of *Literacy Lessons* by highlighting teacher expertise:

> *And in the end it is the individual adaptation made by the expert teacher to that child's idiosyncratic competencies and history of past experiences that starts him on the upward climb to effective literacy performances.* (2005b, p. 63, italics in the original)

Building on Clay's interest in both literacy knowledge and diverse literacy practices, Reading Recovery provides a magnificent microcosm of teacher–student actions and interactions that have allowed me to attend closely to the ways diversity in literacy knowledge and literacy diversity matter in the teaching of reading. The challenge for teachers is to find ways to do this. In the following paragraphs, I review some of the research that has informed my thinking about teaching reading to students from diverse backgrounds.

I am much indebted to the work of González, Moll, and Amanti (2005). These researchers have argued for over 20 years that all children bring multiple funds of knowledge to classrooms. They define funds of knowledge as "historically accumulated and culturally developed bodies of knowledge and skills essential for household or individual well-being" (p. 72). Rather than viewing children from diverse communities as lacking, this perspective highlights what children bring. In the Latino(a) communities they have studied, González and her colleagues have identified knowledge about farming, ranching, mining, construction, business, medicine, and religion as among the many funds of knowledge that children and families possess. Awareness of these forms of knowledge invites literacy educators to incorporate these types of knowledge into reading, writing, speaking, and listening activities at school.

Genishi and Dyson (2009) highlight not only the diversity of students' literacy and language practices but also the various speeds at which children learn language and become literate. Focusing on diverse learners, they worry that few classrooms and curricular materials "allow children either the time or space to learn about or through language in a way that they choose or that enables them to utilize what they already know" (p. 7). Like Clay (2005b, 2005c), they argue that literacy and language instruction must be based on close observation of children that attends to what they bring while helping them to use what they know to extend the range and scope of their literacy abilities and practices in ways that honor their identities and how they learn.

As Genishi and Dyson (2009) note, understandings about language are central to working with children from diverse backgrounds. Drawing on claims that differences should be conceptualized as strengths, Escamilla (2006) worries that teachers often misinterpret bilingual writers' attempts as problems: "linguistic rules for the first language . . . are often misinterpreted as a language problem rather than as a natural progression of second-language literacy development" (p. 2332). In particular, Escamilla argues that teachers need to develop an appreciation for the complexities that accompany learning to read and write in two languages. She highlights the challenges that emerging Spanish writers face as they learn to use accent marks to denote past tense and problems with the use of writing rubrics that have been translated from English to Spanish to evaluate student writing. When children apply Spanish writing practices to their early attempts to write in English, these children should be viewed as strategic rather deficit and Spanish should be treated as a resource rather than as a problem. Teaching linguistically diverse students requires that teachers have knowledge of the language systems students bring and understand how these systems map on to varieties of English privileged in schools. This is true for children who enter classrooms speaking languages other than English, as well as children who also speak various forms of English.

Gregory (2008) laments that "young new language learners are largely absent from research on reading" (p. 14). She argues that children who are learning English as a second language approach the tasks of learning to read and write differently than monolingual children. Her careful observations of second-language learners suggest that due to their familiarity with other oral and written languages that second-language learners apply graphophonic, lexical, syntactical, and semantic cues differently than monolingual children. For example, some sound–symbol relationships in Spanish are different in English, some languages are read from right to left rather than from left to right, and the meanings of some words—but not others—are related across some languages. Thus, children who are becoming biliterate have important lessons to learn not only about how to read in one language but also about how reading in one language is related to reading in another language. By becoming knowledgeable about the languages students bring to classrooms, teachers can help children to negotiate these differences and to use the knowledge they bring about reading in one language to support them as they become biliterate.

This bringing together of diversity in literacy abilities with a diversity of literacy practices echoes arguments made by Purcell-Gates and her colleagues (Purcell-Gates, Jacobson, & Degener, 2004) about the ways cognitive and social practices perspectives in literacy overlap. They note "the majority of cognitive researchers do not discount the existence and relevance of sociocultural contexts of learning. Nor do sociocultural researchers deny the role of cognition in learning to read and write" (p. 82). In the examples below, I draw upon my own teaching as a Reading Recovery professional to think about intersections between learning about print and the wealth of experiences that all children bring to literacy learning.

LESSONS TAUGHT:
LEARNING FROM READING RECOVERY STUDENTS

In the remainder of this chapter, I present a series of lessons that I learned by either teaching or observing Reading Recovery lessons. During Reading Recovery lessons, educators can focus on the actions of one student and his or her teacher as he or she engages in interactions around literacy, without the distractions that accompany teaching groups of students.

Case 1: "Hey! I can write in Spanish."

It was Rosa's first week of Reading Recovery lessons. I had completed the *Observation Survey* (Clay, 2005a) with her a few days earlier. Despite the many struggles she had with reading, I had been impressed by her ability to hear and record the sounds she heard in a sentence that I read aloud. When I asked her to write the sounds she heard, she recorded almost all of the consonants in the correct sequence and was even successful with a few of the vowels. Thus when I asked her to draw a picture and write about it during her lesson, I was not surprised that she completed this task with relative ease.

I was still getting to know Rosa, but I remembered that on the way to our lesson that morning she had mentioned that she liked *Dora the Explorer* (Gifford, Walsh, & Weiner, 2000). When I asked why she liked Dora, she explained that "Dora speaks Spanish just like me." Later in that lesson, Rosa drew a picture of a cat. She easily wrote, "I lk cat" under her picture. As she wrote, she articulated each word slowly, listening for the sounds she needed to record. I asked Rosa how you would say "cat" in Spanish and she replied "gato." I then asked Rosa to write "gato" on her paper. Rosa looked up and shook her head sadly saying, "I don't know how to write in Spanish." Apparently, Rosa had never considered the possibility that writing in Spanish was similar to writing words in English. I assured her that she certainly could write "gato." I directed her say the word slowly, which she did. Rosa aptly wrote every letter of the word and then looked up at me with pride saying "Hey! I can write in Spanish."

Despite Rosa being halfway through her first-grade year, she did not realize that the skills that she was developing in English would serve her as a writer of Spanish. In her mind, Spanish and English were totally separate and school reading and writing, which was all in English, were unconnected to the language that she spoke at home with her family. Rosa clearly had knowledge about writing that transferred across languages, but it took explicit conversation instruction for her to make that connection.

Case 2: Negotiating Home and Book Languages

In a very different way, Lashanda, an African American student, also learned to navigate between languages. When Lashanda started Reading Recovery, it was not unusual for her reading of texts to reflect the African American language patterns she brought from home. Speakers in Lashanda's home often drew upon a sophisticated and rule-governed linguistic system that included not only elements of Southern English but also some structural dimensions of the African languages that her ancestors brought to America (Adger, Christian, & Taylor, 1999; Baugh, 1999). African American English is not an inferior dialect of English. It is a viable and powerful communicative system that is used effectively to convey sophisticated ideas.

> During one of our early Reading Recovery lessons when reading a book about rain, Lashanda read "It rain on my head" rather than "It falls on my head." In this example, Lashanda—who was not yet attending to the first letters in the words—substituted the word *rain* for *falls*. In addition to reading the wrong word, she also applied a syntactical pattern that is common in African American English. She deleted the *s* for a third-person singular verb. During her early attempts with reading, Lashanda also displayed other language patterns that reflected African American English—she omitted *ed* endings from past-tense verbs and often dropped the possessive *s* on nouns. However, over time, Lashanda read fluently and soon began to attend to the first letters in words. In addition, the sentences she read generally made sense and sounded right to her although they often reflected her home language syntactical patterns rather than the language of books.
>
> To help Lashanda learn the language structures that are common in books, whenever I introduced Lashanda to a new book, I was careful to have her practice saying language structures that I predicted would be tricky for her. We discussed how books sounded different than regular speech and we explored different ways of talking by role playing the characters from the books we were reading by having them "try on" different types of talk. Over time, Lashanda not only become adept at using visual cues, especially word endings, to monitor her reading, but she was also able to monitor her reading to make sure that what she read sounded like a book. Although there were times when she became engrossed in stories and her home language practices emerged, by the end of her 20-week program, Lashanda

was generally able to monitor her reading and match her reading to the book language of the texts and was on her way to being an accomplished code switcher who could move between texts and talk.

The microcosm of the Reading Recovery lesson provided me with an opportunity to observe changes related to both language and reading that are often invisible in classroom settings where the number of students makes these observations difficult. While my first inclination with students who bring language differences to schools was to prompt them to check the ends of words, students like Lashanda have taught me about the amazing and flexible language resources that children bring and have alerted me to the importance of helping children to master the language conventions found in texts while respecting the language systems that children bring.

Case 3: "I almost wrote an h!"

In the next example, Devon drew on dimensions of childhood and popular cultures as he attempted to write during a Reading Recovery lesson. Childhood culture involves activities, artifacts, and multimedia texts that are valued by children and often less familiar to adults. Popular culture overlaps with childhood culture; Disney films and characters, cartoons, and some types of video games are examples of popular culture products that explicitly target young children.

> During a Reading Recovery lesson Devon was writing in his journal. He wanted to write the sentence "My bed has Hot Wheels on it." Hot Wheels are small toy cars that are popular with 6-year-old boys. Like many toys, these cars have inspired a range of products including the bedspread and sheets on Devon's bed at home. Although Devon wrote the first part of the sentence easily, he paused when he came to the word *wheels*. I sketched a series of six boxes on the workspace area of his journal (Clay, 2005c).

w					

It was mid-November and Devon had become adept at sequentially recording the sounds that he heard in words. To make the task more challenging, I purposely drew a box for every letter in the word, even those letters that are not voiced. Before Devon began to sound through the word, I reminded him that he had probably seen that word many times on the cars and on the packaging and that he should think about what the word "looked like." Devon said the word *wheels* and easily recorded the *w* in the first box. As he spoke the word slowly he was readily able to hear the /e/ and reported, "It's an *e*." I concurred; I pointed and instructed him to record the *e* in the third box. To our surprise, Devon drew a straight perpendicular line in the third box and remarked with a tone of amazement, "I almost wrote an *h*."

w				l	

I praised Devon for remembering what the word "looked like" as I tore off a piece of correction tape and helped him to relocate the *h* to the second box and then record the *e, l,* and final *s*.

w	h	e		l	s

Devon was again able to access his visual memory of the word *wheels* to record the second *e*. I suspect that his success is attributable to the text that surrounds his many meaningful interactions with the toy cars (i.e., trademarks on toys, packaging, bedspread).

In this example, Devon drew on what was important to him—Hot Wheels—and his experiences with those toy cars to assist him with his writing. He brought together his skills in saying words slowly and listening for the sounds (phonemic awareness) with his visual memory of a word (spelling) that was important to him. Children in the United States grow up in communities that are saturated with print. While each child might bring a different set of experiences with words that relate to childhood and popular culture, many children bring knowledge of words that they have learned outside of schools from signs, cereal boxes, toys, light switches, and video games. Learning about these words and seeking opportunities to use these words in school can be critical for students who struggle with learning to read.

Case 4: "You know about Little Willie?"

My fourth case study relates to gender and race. Kevin was an African American child who often misbehaved in class and was uncooperative during his Reading Recovery lessons. At the time, I was a Reading Recovery trainer and was often called in to help with children who were struggling in the program. I had just completed a series of lessons with another child at Kevin's school when his Reading Recovery teacher came to me. She was concerned because Kevin had become increasingly less cooperative during lessons and eventually refused to leave his class for his lessons. I offered to teach Kevin for a few days to see what I could do to help get Kevin back on course.

Perhaps due to the novelty of the situation, Kevin willingly accompanied me for a Reading Recovery lesson. When we arrived at the room, I placed some of the books he had been reading on the table and asked him to choose one to read. He did, but after a few minutes his head was down on the table and he refused to read despite my cajoling. I put the books away, looked him in the eye, and tried to engage him in conversation. I asked him about the things he liked to do. He answered:

> KEVIN: I like going places.
>
> CCL: Oh, where do you like to go?
>
> KEVIN: To the park.
>
> CCL: Good. Where else?
>
> KEVIN: Chuck E. Cheese.

It was clear that Kevin was giving me generic answers. While he may enjoy going to the park and Chuck E. Cheese, these destinations are safe answers that tell me nothing about Kevin as an individual. I tried a new line of questioning:

> CCL: Hey, Kevin, what kind of music do you like to listen to?
>
> KEVIN: Um . . . um, instruments.

Confused by this response, I asked, "Is that what you listen to at home?" Kevin looked down at his shoes and a smile emerged on his face as he shook his head. I asked him what kind of music he really liked. Kevin spoke tentatively and whispered, "rap." I then asked him if he liked Little Willie the rapper. Kevin's eyes lit up as he asked "You know about Little Willie?" That broke the ice. In the days that followed, Kevin revealed that he liked basketball, race cars, and wrestling. In particular, Kevin was a huge fan of WWE (World Wrestling Entertainment). He knew all the wrestlers and their moves.

As I thought about Kevin and his interests, two things became clear. First, Kevin was initially hesitant to reveal his true interests. Going to the park and Chuck E. Cheese are generic answers that children often provide to appease teachers. It wasn't until I revealed that I knew a little bit about his world that Kevin began to trust me and disclosed more about himself. As we know, classrooms privilege particular ways of being that do not generally celebrate rap music and wrestling. Second, all of Kevin's passions were decidedly masculine. Unfortunately, many of the books used in Reading Recovery, even those with male protagonists, present sweet stories of children and animals engaged in idyllic adventures—a far cry from the competitive and "tough" characters that interested Kevin.

For the next 2 months, I worked hard to find books that reflected Kevin's masculine interests. With his mother's approval, I regularly downloaded pictures of his favorite wrestlers from the Internet and he wrote a book describing the various wrestlers and their moves. Kevin was teaching me about the wrestlers he loved. Once I identified his passions, Kevin readily attended Reading Recovery lessons;

however, valuable time had been lost. Despite notable gains during his final few weeks of instruction, at the end of the 20-week Reading Recovery program Kevin was still behind in reading. While he did not successfully complete the program and continued to qualify for reading intervention, Kevin left the program with a sense that reading and writing were tools that he could use to pursue his interests and he had begun to view himself as a reader and as a writer.

Case 5: "I won't read like that."

The final case I offer involves an African American boy who I observed as he worked with another teacher. My prior experiences with Reading Recovery suggested that Reading Recovery served as a microcosm for observing interactions between children and their teachers. Thus, I designed a study that involved observing four African American students over the course of their Reading Recovery program. In some of these cases, the children and their teachers worked together fluently and appeared to develop close relationships. In other cases, particularly those involving African American boys, tensions became apparent as I watched the lesson series unfold across the 20 weeks.

Linguists interested in infant language acquisition have identified talk that they refer to as *parentese*. Parentese refers to the ways middle-class, White adults, and others, tend to talk to babies. It is characterized by high-pitched glissando intonations that often involve simplified sentence structures. In this chapter, I suggest that teachers often use a parallel system of talk when they address young children. In the examples below, Ms. Camp used exaggerated language when she introduced new books to Martin. Like parentese, Ms. Camp's *teacherese* involved high-pitched talk that exaggerated the exciting elements of the texts that she wanted to share with Martin. However, Martin actively resisted this way of talking and reading.

> Martin was an African American 6-year-old student. When I visited his home, it was clear that Martin was a responsible young man. His mother was a single mother of three and Martin was the oldest. At home, Martin juggled multiple responsibilities—completing his homework, helping his mother with the babies, and assisting with household tasks. He was clearly competent and acted as a valued assistant. However, my observations of Martin at home were very different from what I observed in the Reading Recovery situation.
>
> Martin's Reading Recovery teacher, Ms. Camp, was an accomplished educator who had received national honors for her teaching. She was among the most successful Reading Recovery teachers in the school district and the majority of her students were consistently successful in Reading Recovery. Despite this history of success, teaching Martin frustrated Ms. Camp.
>
> The following examples reflect interactions that were repeated many times over the course of the lesson series. The first book was about two cats and Ms.

Camp used an exaggerated, high-pitched tone as she excitedly invited Martin to think about the story he was about to read:

> Ms. Camp: Ohhhh! So what does the big cat do? Let's find out!!!
>
> Martin: What?
>
> Ms. Camp: Let's find out what the big cat does!!!
>
> Martin: You going to make me laugh. (*Starts making singsong sounds imitating Ms. Camp's intonation patterns.*)

A few pages later, Ms. Camp continues with her introduction to the book.

> Ms. Camp: Uh-oh!!! (*spoken with exaggerated intonation*) What just happened here???
>
> Martin: You making me laugh!

On another day, Ms. Camp was again introducing a book using her teacherese voice. Martin laughs at her antics.

> Ms. Camp: What's wrong?
>
> Martin: You act funny when you do that.
>
> Ms. Camp: I know I do.
>
> Martin: I can't read like that.

Martin's closing comment summed up the import of this interaction. Martin, a young man with significant adult responsibilities at home, was not going to buy into an activity that positioned him as infantile. While Ms. Camp was drawing on her cultural knowledge of what engaged 6-year-old boys, that positioning was not acceptable to Martin and the ways he viewed himself. He was not going to read like that. As teachers, we must often move beyond habitual ways of being, step back, and consider how our students interpret our actions. However, this is not easy and it takes continual monitoring and questioning of our actions, interactions, and assumptions.

CONCLUSION

It is my hope that the stories presented above provide educators with examples of the types of things that can help them in supporting students from diverse backgrounds. Just as the children in my first-grade classroom may not have known their nursery rhymes, they did possess a rich set of oral texts that were equally useful in the classroom. As researchers (Clay, 2005b, 2005c; Escamilla, 2006; Genishi &

Dyson, 2009; González et al., 2005; Gregory, 2008) have demonstrated, all children bring linguistic and literate abilities to classrooms; it is the responsibility of educators to determine how to develop those experiences and abilities in ways that help children succeed with school literacy.

McNaughton (2002) and Purcell-Gates et al. (2004) maintain that this requires educators to attend not only to the literacy abilities that children bring but also the literacy practices that are familiar and important to children. Each of the cases presented offered a glimpse into the strengths that diverse students brought. Rosa's case highlighted the ways literate abilities in one language could be accessed to write another language. Lashanda reminded us that language differences could not be reduced to decoding and that learning to read was easier when children were supported in learning the language of books. Devon taught us how valued experiences with environmental print outside of school could be a tool for helping children to solve tasks in school. Kevin's case highlighted the significance of getting to know students and helping them to enter literacy through texts that mattered to them. Finally, Martin reminded us that the interactional styles that we routinely bring to teaching might not be equally helpful to all children. We must be sensitive to the ways our interactions position children and the models of reading and writing that we provide to children.

In this chapter, I drew on my own experiences as a Reading Recovery professional. While Reading Recovery teachers have a huge advantage in that they are able to work closely with individual children—monitoring children's reading and writing behaviors as well as their responses to their teaching, I argue that mismatches between teachers and children occur all the time in all classrooms and propose that Reading Recovery can be viewed as a microcosm for thinking about the teaching of diverse students. These cautionary tales can provide all teachers with ways of thinking about their students and strategies for meeting the needs of the children who struggle with reading.

REFERENCES

Adger, C. T., Christian, D., & Taylor, O. (1999). *Making the connection: Language and academic achievement among African American students*. McHenry, IL: Center for Applied Linguistics and Delta Systems.

Baugh, J. (1999). *Out of the mouths of slaves*. Austin: University of Texas Press.

Clay, M. M. (2005a). *An observation survey of early literacy achievement*. Portsmouth, NH: Heinemann.

Clay, M. M. (2005b). *Literacy lessons: Designed for individuals, part one: Why? When? And how?* Portsmouth, NH: Heinemann.

Clay, M. M. (2005c). *Literacy lessons: Designed for individuals, part two: Teaching procedures*. Portsmouth, NH: Heinemann.

Escamilla, K. (2006). Semilingualism applied to the literacy behaviors of Spanish-speaking emergent bilinguals: Bi-illiteracy or emerging bi-literacy? *Teachers College Record, 108*(11), 2329–2353.

Genishi, C., & Dyson, A. (2009). *Children, language, and literacy: Diverse learners in diverse times.* New York: Teachers College Press.

Gifford, C., Walsh, V., & Weiner, E. (2000). *Dora the explorer.* Orlando, FL: Nickelodeon Cable Television Network.

Gonzalez, N., Moll, L. C., & Amanti, C. (2005). *Funds of knowledge: Theorizing practices in households, communities, and classrooms.* New York: Teachers College Press.

Gregory, E. (2008). *Learning to read in a new language.* Los Angeles: Sage.

McNaughton, S. (2002). *Meeting of minds.* Wellington, NZ: Learning Media.

Purcell-Gates, V., Jacobson, E., & Degener, S. (2004). *Print literacy development: Uniting cognitive and social practice theories.* Cambridge, MA: Harvard University Press.

What Works Clearinghouse. (2012). *Reading Recovery report summary.* Washington, DC: U.S. Department of Education and the Institute of Education Sciences. Retrieved June 7, 2012, from *http://ies.ed.gov/ncee/wwc/interventionreport.aspx?sid=420.*

CHAPTER 4

❖

Supporting Language and Literacy Development in Quality Preschools

SHANNON RILEY-AYERS

In the United States, preschool attendance has been increasing for more than 2 decades (Barnett & Yarosz, 2007). Currently, roughly 75% of young children attend preschool at age 4 and 50% attend at age 3 (Barnett, 2011). The varieties of programs that these children attend differ in too many ways to list, but several variable characteristics include length of school day and year, age range in the classroom, teacher qualifications, and cost to the family to attend.

Preschool or school entrance does not signal the beginning of learning. Children learn from the start of life, and the home environment plays a role in this learning (Duncan et al., 2007; Melhuish et al., 2008; Zimmerman et al., 2009). More important, there are differences in literacy experiences in the home, such as book ownership and frequency of reading together, and these differences are related to social class differences (Burchinal et al., 2011; Duncan & Magnuson, 2005). These early experiences are directly related to cognitive differences at kindergarten and the economic-related differences persist well beyond school entry (Burchinal et al., 2011; Dickinson, 2011; Hart & Risley, 1995). Preschool has been shown to have a positive effect on early cognitive development and thus minimize these notable early differences.

GUIDING QUESTIONS

❖ What are the effects of preschool on language and literacy development?

❖ What are the necessary content areas to teach in preschool to provide a positive effect on language and literacy development?

❖ What are the instructional behaviors/strategies of effective teachers in each of these content areas?

SUPPORTING RESEARCH

Early literacy skills, those found at preschool-age, have been shown to have a moderate to strong relationships with later literacy skills such as decoding, comprehension, and spelling. Both a meta-analysis of close to 300 correlational studies (National Early Literacy Panel [NELP], 2008) and an analysis of large-scale extant data (Duncan et al., 2007) provide strong evidence that early precursors to literacy such as alphabetic knowledge, phonological awareness, concepts about print, and writing are highly related to later literacy proficiency in kindergarten and beyond. Although important, the relationship of these "code skills" with later literacy learning should not overshadow the importance of language development in the early years. There is strong evidence that language ability at ages 3 and 4 has strong predictive power for literacy skills in the early grades through high school (Camilli, Vargas, Ryan, & Barnett, 2010; Dickinson & Porche, 2011; National Institute of Child Health and Human Development Early Child Care Research Network [NICHD], 2005; Verhoeven, van Leeuwe, & Vermeer, 2011).

The brain develops rapidly in early childhood creating a specific "window of opportunity" that is sensitive to experiences to establish certain capabilities. Preschool interventions have been shown to make an impact that can produce moderate to large effects on early literacy skills and later achievement (NELP, 2008). The flip side to this sensitive period, where interventions provide the most substantial impact, is that it is also the time where the brain is most highly susceptible to the absence of these critical experiences. This absence can have lasting detrimental effects as children who enter school substantially behind are unlikely to catch up (Duncan et al., 2007; Heckman, 2006). Furthermore, this early skill development provides the foundation for later conceptual knowledge and therefore creates an interdependency of early learning that magnifies the importance of providing a strong foundation before kindergarten entry (Dickinson, McCabe, & Essex, 2006; NICHD, 2005; Shonkoff & Phillips, 2000). These factors establish the need for high-quality preschool programs for young children.

The Effects of Preschool on Language and Literacy Development

Studies of specific state preschool programs have demonstrated strong effects of preschool at kindergarten entry on language and literacy skills (Gormley, Gayer, Phillips, & Dawson, 2005; Hustedt, Barnett, Jung, & Friedman, 2010; Lipsey, Farran, Bilbrey, Hofer, & Dong, 2011). A recent study looking at data from eight state preschool programs in combination demonstrated that high-quality preschool can have uniformly large effects on emergent literacy and vocabulary (Barnett, Jung, Frede, Hustedt, & Howes, 2011). In addition, several well-known longitudinal studies of the effects of early intervention demonstrate a relationship between preschool experiences and later achievement. The HighScope Perry Preschool Study (Schweinhart et al., 2005) looked at the effects of a 2-year half-day preschool program (with home visits by the teachers) and found moderate effects on reading and language achievement through adolescence. The Chicago Child–Parent Center Program Study (Reynolds, 2000) found effects of comprehensive educational and family support services for economically disadvantaged children's reading achievement in kindergarten through high school. The Abecedarian Study (Campbell, Ramey, Pungello, Sparling, & Miller-Johnson, 2002) examined the effect of a time-intensive education program and found large effects on reading achievement through age 21. A recent meta-analysis (Camilli et al., 2010) found an effect size that would equal approximately 70% of the achievement gap closed for initial effects of intervention for the most rigorous studies with the highest quality. Although this effect decreased over time, it was still quite notable later on, perhaps, in part, due to the substantial size of the initial effects.

It should be noted that not all interventions have been shown to be as equally effective as those described above. The National Impact Study of Head Start (Puma et al., 2010) and the evaluation of Early Head Start (Vogel, Xue, Moiduddin, Lepidus, Carlson, et al., 2010) found little to no initial effect on language and literacy. It is of no surprise that these small initial impacts for these interventions disappeared over time as we have seen that the effects of the initial impact often decrease over time.

There may be several possible rationales for the conflicting findings. One, program features such as teacher qualifications and compensation may have some impact. However, this is unlikely to alone have an effect on outcomes (Barnett, 2011). Two, the decrease of the initial impact may be the effect of compensatory efforts of high-quality public school experiences focused on children entering school with lower skills and thus what is observed is "catch-up" rather than "fade out" (Barnett, 2011). Three, and arguably the most important, it has been demonstrated that the attributes and quality of the intervention are a factor in determining the effect of early education and care on cognitive outcomes (Sylva et al., 2011; Vandell et al., 2010). And, unfortunately, most programs are not of high quality (Karoly, Ghosh-Dastidar, Zellman, Perlman, & Fernyhough, 2008; Justice, Mashburn, Hamre, & Pianta, 2008).

DEFINING HIGH-QUALITY PRESCHOOL

Young children's development encompasses physical, social, emotional, cognitive, and language domains and these domains are dynamic and interrelated (Shonkoff & Phillips, 2000; Strickland, 2004). The main focus for the description of preschool quality for this chapter is on young children's language development and cognitive learning in the area of literacy. However, teachers are reminded that these language and literacy skills do not develop in isolation without the nurturing of other cognitive content areas as well as social and emotional development and physical development (Strickland & Riley-Ayers, 2007).

There is strong research support for key areas of development that have direct links to children's later success in early reading (NELP, 2008; Snow, Burns, & Griffin, 1998; Strickland & Riley-Ayers, 2006). Oral language, phonological awareness, alphabetic knowledge, print concepts, and writing have all been shown to correlate to and be predictive of later reading outcomes. Effective preschool teachers focus their literacy interactions and developmentally appropriate instruction around these key principles.

Case Example

The following illustration provides an example of an effective high-quality preschool classroom that is rich in language and literacy learning. This teacher promotes early literacy with a developmentally appropriate approach for preschool children.

> At snack one morning, Ms. Lea sat with her preschool children and discussed what was on the menu for the day, two graham crackers and half a banana. The children chimed in with "likes" and "dislikes" for these two foods. Ms. Lea took the opportunity to make a graph of favorite foods that the children reported, asking children to write and draw their favorite foods. Although macaroni and cheese and spaghetti were on the list, pizza was the overwhelming leader. Shortly following the results of the poll, the group decided to create a pizza restaurant in the dramatic play area. Ms. Lea set several items in the play area and the next day, interested children began creating the pizzeria. They used construction paper to create several of the necessary ingredients for the pizza. Ms. Lea added in examples of various menus from local pizzerias and scaffolded the children as they created their own. She also added several Italian cookbooks to the area for reference and assisted the children as they created a sign for their restaurant. As she guided the children's play, the teacher intentionally used various vocabulary words such as *waiter* and *waitress, menu, order, slice,* and so on. The children utilized clipboards and notepaper to record orders from "customers."

In addition to teaching through play, Ms. Lea conducted shared writing lessons so that the class created a pizza recipe. Here she introduced vocabulary such as ingredients and temporal words (*first, second, next*). Ms. Lea then worked in small groups throughout the week with the children to create their own recipes for various foods and collated them into a class cookbook. She valued each child's contribution that included various forms of communication based on the child's capabilities. This ranged from dictation, where the teacher wrote the child's words for the recipe to the child drawing pictures or independently writing to communicate the recipe. Some children wrote letters or letterlike forms, and others matched and wrote letters corresponding to the beginning sounds in the words. Ms. Lea also read books such as *The Little Red Hen (Makes a Pizza)* (Sturges, 1999) (fiction text) and *Making Pizza* (Dufresne, 2007) (informational text). The class engaged in discussions about the content in the book and made personal connections to what they had heard. Ms. Lea also placed several books in the accessible library area of the classroom around this theme (although not all the books in the library area were exclusive to this theme). Last, to bring the learning alive (and because of limited access to area restaurants as a class), Ms. Lea used media as she and the children took a virtual field trip online to view how a pizza is made and then worked collaboratively to generate a pizza lunch for the class.

Oral Language

Oral language is the foundation for learning. It encompasses listening comprehension, verbal expression, and vocabulary development (Strickland & Riley-Ayers, 2006). Listening comprehension is the act of listening on purpose and responding with understanding. Verbal expression is the act of using language to communicate. Vocabulary development can be separated into two distinct categories. Expressive vocabulary is the language that the children can use themselves, whereas receptive vocabulary is the amount of words that children can understand when heard in context. Early oral language development has been shown to be related to later literacy learning (Camilli et al., 2010; Dickinson & Porche, 2011; NICHD, 2005; Verhoeven et al., 2011) and thus should be considered important for preschool children.

Language experiences have been shown to differ for young children before the start of the school experience. The landmark study conducted by Hart and Risley (1995) examined the effects of home experiences on young children's language development from 10 months to 36 months for 42 American children. They found that children from professional families heard over 11 million words per year, children in working-class families heard approximately 6 million words, and children in low-income families heard approximately 3 million words annually. Therefore, it is critical for teachers to be planful, thoughtful, and purposeful in their teaching of oral language skills during the preschool years as there are already large gaps in language learning before schooling begins.

Intentional teaching means that teachers act with specific outcomes or goals in mind for children's development and learning (Epstein, 2007). Data have shown that much of the communication teachers have with young children in the classroom is focused on controlling and correcting behavior (Perry, Colman, & Cross, 1986) and that the directedness of the teacher's language impacts the amount of language production by the children (Girolametto, Weitzman, van Lieshout, & Duff, 2000). On the other hand, effective teachers engage children in meaningful conversations where they intentionally model communication skills. Teachers expand and extend children's language by using complex language including articles (e.g., *the, a, an*) and adjectives (e.g., *big, happy, fast*) before nouns, prepositional phrases (e.g., *on the table*), and by putting two thoughts together into one sentence (e.g., *If it is raining, then we will play inside.*).

Children make higher gains when teachers use explicit methods of vocabulary introduction or a combination of explicit and implicit methods rather than using implicit methods of exposure to vocabulary alone (Marulis & Neuman, 2010). Explicit instruction includes providing detailed definitions and explanations or examples of the word before reading as well as a follow-up discussion about the particular vocabulary after reading. In addition to this introduction of novel words, teachers should engage in repeated reading of stories to enhance vocabulary development (Penno, Wilkinson, & Moore, 2002; Sénéchal, 1997).

Expanding vocabulary within one category so that children distinguish the differences among nouns in a single category is another important approach for preschool teachers (Bridges, Justice, Hogan, & Gray, 2011). Teachers incorporate synonyms into conversations to expand the children's vocabulary banks and to teach small variations of words. Such examples include *drowsy* and *tired, happy* and *thrilled*, and *walk* and *stroll*. Teachers are intentional about the introduction of key vocabulary words throughout the day. Often this is related to the topic of study such as the pizzeria theme in the case example earlier. During those few weeks of study, in the dramatic play area, the teacher purposefully commented that the pizza was scorching when it came out of the oven and that she had to wait for it to cool before eating it. Later that week, the children experimented with the new word, "Be careful, the pizza is *scorch*."

Reading aloud with young children is an important component of the preschool curriculum. However, just reading the story is not enough to impact children's development to the fullest extent. Rather, interactive experiences with books show more effect on children's oral language development. Engaging in discussions of characters' actions, events in the story, and the meaning of words has been shown to relate both to vocabulary skills in kindergarten (Dickinson & Smith, 1994) and later in fourth grade (Dickinson & Porche, 2011). Retelling stories and summarizing information learned in expository text provides children the opportunity to monitor comprehension and demonstrate their level of understanding of the text.

In general, preschool teachers have been shown to ask more literal questions following text reading rather than inferential questions (Scheiner & Gorsetman, 2009). Inference questions include those that ask children to infer, predict, reason, and/or explain and these skills are the very skills fluent readers use to self-question and improve comprehension (van Kleeck, 2006). Teachers should be sure to pose questions so that children utilize their background knowledge and reasoning skills to provide answers (Bridges et al., 2011). This type of questioning includes asking children to infer how a character is feeling at certain points of the story, asking children to consider what the character might do next, and asking questions for informational text such as why a particular event occurs (e.g., the chameleon changes color, the adult gets a ticket for a train ride).

Phonological Awareness

Phonological awareness is the awareness of the constituent sounds of words in learning to read and spell. Phonological awareness involves the detection and manipulation of sounds at three levels of sound structure: syllables (e.g., *ro-bot, o-pen*, and *rec-tan-gle*), onset and rime (separating the first sound from the rest of the word; e.g., /c/ /at/ and /sh/ /ip/), and phonemes (individual sounds; e.g., /t/ /ŭ/ /b/ and /s/ /ŏ/ /k/). The development of phonological awareness begins with children detecting or manipulating syllables before they can detect or manipulate onset and rime, followed by, generally after the preschool years, the ability to discriminate and manipulate individual phonemes in words (Anthony & Francis, 2005).

Phonological awareness forms the basis of early decoding and spelling ability, which are correlated with later reading and spelling achievement. It makes sense that the subsets of phonological awareness, phonemic awareness (the ability to hear, identify, and manipulate sounds in words), and phonics (connecting sounds to the letters that represent them) are key precursors to word identification and reading. Children will struggle with learning to read without a strong sense of how phonemes (represented by letters) are blended to form words.

Few young children spontaneously acquire phonological understanding, but with planned activities to draw children's attention to the phonemes in words teachers increase children's understanding of the sounds of language. For example, teachers expose children to the rhythm and rhymes of language through stories, nursery rhymes, and other chants and songs. At times, the teacher reads or recites familiar rhyming stories or poems, pausing so children can fill in the rhyme. As children's understanding progresses, they can begin to substitute new rhymes for the familiar ones. Clapping or stomping out syllables, separating and blending onsets and rimes, and playing rhyming games are all excellent activities for teachers to use as transitions from one activity to the next. For example, to transition children to the sink to wash hands before snack, the teacher sings "Willoughby Wallaby Woo." This song replaces the first sound in the child's name with /w/ (see Figure 4.1 for lyrics). Children are involved in singing along and actively listening for the rhyme with their name.

Alphabetic Knowledge

Letter knowledge, which includes letter identification and letter–sound connections, is one of the best predictors of later reading and spelling abilities (Hammill, 2004; Schatschneider, Fletcher, Francis, Carlson, & Foorman, 2004). A recent meta-analysis demonstrated that the effects of instruction on alphabet outcomes differed by content and context of instruction (Piasta & Wagner, 2010). In addition, some researchers note that it is possible that alphabetic knowledge is a by-product of other rich early literacy experiences (Strickland, 2004) rather than a direct reflection of what has been taught.

Teachers of preschool children, although intentional in their teaching, should not provide instruction that mimics the "skill and drill" approach when teaching children letters. Research reports that rapid letter naming, the speed at which one names letters, is a skill that is related to literacy outcomes later for young children (NELP, 2008). However, although it may be tempting to translate this finding into practice that provides repetitive and increasingly faster teaching of letters, this would be developmentally inappropriate for young learners. Alphabetic instruction should occur within a larger literacy context with teachers providing multiple opportunities to discuss letter names and sounds within rich literacy and oral language experiences.

Children need plentiful exposure to the alphabet letters throughout the school day. This exposure can take several different forms. One strategy is to provide

Willoughby wallaby woo,

An elephant sat on you!

Willoughby wallaby wee,

An elephant sat on me!

Willoughby wallaby Weyton,

An elephant sat on Peyton!

Willoughby wallaby Wenry,

An elephant sat on Henry!

FIGURE 4.1. Phonological awareness song for transitions.

children letters in several different forms—magnetic letters, stamps, and sten-cils—to explore and use independently and with guidance. Children's names offer a great opportunity to identify letters, noting whose names begin with the same letters and how many letters are in each name. Teachers point out letters in the environment such as those on labels in the classroom, they find items indoors and outside that resemble letters (e.g., a stick that looks like the letter *y*, a pretzel that looks like the letter *p*), and they talk about letter names while reading and writing.

Concepts of Print

Concepts of print refers to what emergent readers need to understand about how printed language works and how it represents language (Clay, 1979). These con-cepts include knowing how to hold a book the appropriate way, differentiating between print and pictures, turning pages properly, and being able to tell the front of the book from the back. Additional concepts include identifying the title of the book, understanding that we read left to right and top to bottom, that letters are individual units, and that letters make up words.

All emergent readers are expected to master the concepts of print in order to become successful at reading. Most children do so by first or second grade (Paris, 2011). Thus, the focus for this content is on the children's rate of mastery not neces-sarily their final knowledge (Paris, 2011). Researchers have noted that this develop-ment may be a product of early literacy experiences (Lonigan, Burgess, & Anthony, 2000) and that through intentional exposure to and experiences with text, children can become adept with these skills.

In particular, shared reading experiences can work well to foster several early literacy skills such as concepts about print (Teale & Sulzby, 1989). This occurs when a teacher or adult reads a book with large print to multiple students in a small or large group. This is a great time to interact with children by asking them questions about book concepts and by introducing or highlighting print concepts that might be new to the students. Similar activities can take place with a read-aloud by an adult one-on-one with a child.

Books should be strategically placed throughout the classroom not just in the library area. Ms. Lea, in the case example presented earlier, placed cookbooks and menus into the dramatic play area as part of the pizzeria. This provided spontane-ous opportunities for the teacher to provide guidance on concepts of print and for the children to explore the books in a meaningful manner during play. Note that the Common Core State Standards (CCSS; National Governors Association Center for Best Practices, Council of Chief State School Officers, 2010) calls for a balance of narrative text and informational text in kindergarten and beyond. Thus, preschool teachers should be sure to include both narrative and informational types of texts, among others (e.g., cookbooks, comics, poetry) into their shared reading, read-alouds, and classroom libraries.

Preschool classroom environments have visible print displaying various functions. For example, there are meaningful labels in the classroom that the teacher references as children clean up toys or ask questions about a procedure ("This sign says we wash hands before eating"). Teachers take the opportunities to use the children's names in print for various activities such as noticing the first letter of the children's names and sorting

them. Teachers model writing and write collectively as a group on a regular basis. When writing, teachers make the thought processes transparent to assist children in understanding the procedures of writing. Noting that "I'm going to start writing over here and then I'll go this way" provides students another exposure to the directionality of print through a concrete experience.

Writing

Writing is a combination of several early literacy skills. Children demonstrate their understanding of concepts of print, alphabetic knowledge, phonological awareness, and communication capabilities. Writing development begins long before children's writing resembles true print. Development starts with children putting marks on a page. Children begin combining drawing, mock letters, and letter strings together. This is the production of writing. However, the composing of writing is the attachment of meaning to the marks on the page. A child who writes three lines and identifies it as "my name" or provides a three-sentence "story" of what the lines "say" is demonstrating an understanding that print communicates a message.

Teachers respond positively to all attempts at writing that the children produce. They ask questions about the writing and often record the child's dictation of the story. Encouraging children to write their name on their work will provide ownership of the piece and offer practice in producing the letters. Teachers value all attempts at writing from the children and prominently display their writing in the classroom.

Providing opportunities for children to write in a writing center filled with materials such as paper, stencils, name tags, and various writing implements is an excellent way for teachers to incorporate writing in the classroom. However, it is equally important for teachers to provide writing supplies throughout the classroom so that children can spontaneously construct a written piece. Children's writing played a prominent role in the dramatic play area as it was transformed into the pizzeria described in the case example in this chapter. The teacher talked with the children about how potential customers would know to come to the pizzeria. This led to the development of the pizzeria sign and the creation of pizzeria menus. In addition, children took on the role of waiter or waitress and recorded "customers'" orders at the pizzeria.

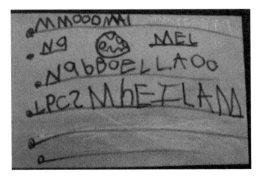

THE ROLE OF PLAY IN EARLY LANGUAGE AND LITERACY LEARNING

Language and literacy learning in the preschool classroom occurs through play and playful learning. As demonstrated above, language-rich environments, where the teacher actively engages in conversations and takes an active role in the children's play, can provide the models and practice that children need with language. Children demonstrate their most advanced language skills during play and this talk during play has consistently been shown to relate to later literacy outcomes (Dickinson & Tabors, 2001). When provided the opportunity, young children incorporate literacy props into their play and engage in increased amounts of narrative, emergent reading, and writing. This can be seen as children write shopping lists, play with language, and read stories to stuffed animals. Children's narrative structure of sociodramatic play mirrors the narratives of storybooks, which provide practice with and understanding of the structure of stories that will aid in later comprehension.

CONCLUSION

Key characteristics of the preschool classroom and effective instructional strategies that are necessary for early literacy development have been outlined in this chapter. Figure 4.2 (on pages 70–71) summarizes the research on the five critical areas for preschool education. This provides teachers an "at-a-glance" look at the research and the translation of that research into classroom practice. It additionally provides teachers with insight into what the expectations are for children's development in these areas by the end of preschool. This understanding of child development and standards for preschool instruction is becoming even more critical as we, as a nation, move to a more accountable system of early education including high-stakes assessments.

Content	Research: What we know	Practice: What we should do	Outcomes: What we can expect
Oral Language	Oral language is the foundation for literacy development and is related to later reading outcomes. A rich vocabulary facilitates early reading. Children begin preschool with vast differences in oral language development. Children whose language skills are behind in kindergarten tend to stay behind. Children need repeated exposure to words to begin to use the word in their expressive vocabulary.	Engage children in meaningful conversations. Extend children's talk by enriching their productions—for example: A child says, "Milk!" A teacher responds, "Yes, Jesse, I will get you some more of this cold, white milk." Introduce new vocabulary and build background knowledge on a regular basis by guiding children's play, and through experiences and story reading. Engage in multiple readings of books and ask open-ended and inferential questions when discussing books and at other times.	*By the end of preschool, children:* Actively participate in conversations with peers and adults. Use language to express ideas and needs. Respond to questions about stories and events. Retell familiar stories with some accuracy and details. Use new vocabulary in their play and discussions.
Phonological Awareness	Phonological awareness is a precursor to early reading success. Phonological awareness is a listening skill. Phonological awareness forms the basis of early decoding and spelling ability, which are correlated with later reading and spelling achievement.	Plan playful, but intentional manipulation with words (alliteration, rhyming). Incorporate phonological awareness into transition activities. Read poems, nursery rhymes, and storybooks with rhyming language. Clap or stomp out syllables in words (especially children's names). Connect phonemes (sounds) with letters.	*By the end of preschool, children:* Recite chants and rhymes. Separate words into syllables. Create own rhymes and/or alliteration. Begin to attend to beginning and ending sounds of words. Recognize when words begin with or end with the same sound.
Concepts of Print	What young children know about print is a key predictor of later reading achievement.	Print is visible throughout the classroom (e.g., children's names, classroom labels, children's writing, shared writing).	*By the end of preschool, children:* Understand that print holds meaning and can be used for different functions.

	Learning about print should be done in a way that connects to multiple literacy areas. Children are better advantaged to learn to read when they start reading instruction with the precursor skills of a well-developed knowledge about print.	Read books (multiple readings) to children to model book handling, tracking the print, while commenting on print conventions. Ask children to "read" to an adult. Provide materials and a comfortable place to read to allow for opportunities for children to independently explore books.	Hold a book correctly and turns pages properly. Begin to recognize that print moves from left to right and top to bottom. Identify environmental print. Recognize that letters forms words. Actively engage in "reading."
Alphabetic Knowledge	One of the strongest individual predictors of later reading achievement is letter identification. This letter learning should be provided within a larger literacy-rich context.	Point out letters/words in the environment and while reading or writing. Model writing and offer transparency to your thought process (think aloud). Provide various letter-related materials (e.g., magnetic letters, letter stamps, alphabet puzzles).	*By the end of preschool, children:* Identify several letters, including those in their names. Recognize that letters form words. Notice letters in the environment. Recognize that letters represent sounds.
Writing	Reading and writing develop together. Children begin to bridge their oral and written worlds through drawing, scribbling, making lines, mock letters, actual letters, and various combinations of these in purposeful ways.	Encourage writing by providing a variety of writing materials and include these writing materials around the room, not just in a writing center. Value children's writing and write down their stories. Model writing for different functions and in different forms (e.g., letters, recipes, lists). Incorporate writing into children's play.	*By the end of preschool, children:* Experiment with a variety of writing tools and materials. Attach meaning to their "writing." Write some letters and/or letterlike forms.

FIGURE 4.2. Summary of critical preschool language and literacy content.

REFERENCES

Anthony, J. L., & Francis, D. (2005). Development of phonological awareness. *Current Directions in Psychological Science, 14*, 255–259.

Barnett, W. S. (2011). Effectiveness of early educational intervention. *Science, 333*, 975–978.

Barnett, W. S., Jung, K., Frede, E., Hustedt, J., & Howes, C. (2011). *Effects of eight state prekindergarten programs on early learning.* New Brunswick, NJ: Rutgers University, National Institute for Early Education.

Barnett, W. S., & Yarosz, D. J. (2007). *Who goes to preschool and why does it matter?* (Preschool Policy Brief No. 15). New Brunswick, NJ: Rutgers University, National Institute for Early Education.

Bridges, M. S., Justice, J. M., Hogan, T. P., & Gray, S. (2011). Promoting lower- and higher-level language skills in early education classrooms. In R. Pianta (Ed.), *Handbook of early education* (pp. 177–193). New York: Guilford Press.

Burchinal, M., McCartney, K., Steinberg, L., Crosnoe, R., Friedman, S. L., McLoyd, V., et al., and National Institute of Child Health and Human Development Early Child Care Research Network. (2011). Examining the black–white achievement gap among low-income children using the National Institute of Child Health and Human Development Study of Early Child Care and Youth Development. *Child Development, 82*(5), 1404–1420.

Camilli, G., Vargas, S., Ryan, S., & Barnett, W. S. (2010). Meta-analysis of the effects of early education interventions on cognitive and social development. *Teachers College Record, 112*(3), 579–620.

Campbell, F. A., Ramey, C. T., Pungello, E. P., Sparling, J. J., & Miller-Johnson, S. (2002). Early childhood education: Young adult outcomes from the Abecedarian project. *Applied Developmental Science, 6*, 42–57.

Clay, M. (1979). *Reading: The patterning of complex behavior* (2nd ed.). Auckland, NZ: Heinemann.

Dickinson, D., McCabe, A., & Essex, M. (2006). A window of opportunity we must open to all: The case for high-quality support for language and literacy. In D. K. Dickinson & S. B. Neuman (Eds.), *Handbook of early literacy research* (pp. 11–28). New York: Guilford Press.

Dickinson, D. K. (2011). Teachers' language practices and academic outcomes of preschool children. *Science, 333*, 964–967.

Dickinson, D. K., & Porche, M. V. (2011). Relation between language experiences in preschool classrooms and children's kindergarten and fourth-grade language and reading abilities. *Child Development, 82*(3), 870–886.

Dickinson, D. K., & Smith, M. W. (1994). Long-term effects of preschool teachers' book readings on low-income children's vocabulary and story comprehension. *Reading Research Quarterly, 29*(2), 104–122.

Dickinson, D. K., & Tabors, P. O. (Eds.). (2001). *Beginning literacy with language: Young children learning at home and school.* Baltimore: Brookes.

Dufresne, M. (2007). *Making pizza.* Northampton, MA: Pioneer Valley Books.

Duncan, G. J., Dowsett, C., Claessens, A., Magnuson, K., Huston, A., Klebanov, P., et al. (2007). School readiness and later achievement. *Developmental Psychology, 43,* 1428–1446.

Duncan, G. J., & Magnuson, K. (2005). Can family socioeconomic resources account for racial and ethnic test score gaps? *The Future of Children, 15,* 35–52.

Epstein, A. S. (2007). *The intentional teacher: Choosing the best strategies for young children's learning.* Washington, DC: National Association for the Education of Young Children.

Girolametto, L., Weitzman, E., van Lieshout, R., & Duff, D. (2000). Directiveness in teachers' language input to toddlers and preschoolers in day care. *Journal of Speech, Language, and Hearing Research, 43,* 1101–1114.

Gormley, W. T., Jr., Gayer, T., Phillips, D., & Dawson, B. (2005). The effects of universal pre-K on cognitive development. *Developmental Psychology, 41*(6), 872–884.

Hammill, D. D. (2004). What we know about correlates of reading. *Exceptional Children, 70,* 453–468.

Hart, B., & Risley, T. (1995). *Meaningful differences in the everyday experience of young American children.* York, PA: Maple Press.

Heckman, J. J. (2006). Skill formation and the economics of investing in disadvantaged children. *Science, 312,* 1900–1902.

Hustedt, J. T., Barnett, W. S., Jung, K., & Friedman, A. (2010). *The New Mexico preK evaluation: Impacts from the fourth year (2008–2009) of New Mexico's state-funded preK program.* New Brunswick, NJ: Rutgers University, National Institute of Early Education.

Justice, L. M., Mashburn, A. J., Hamre, B. K., & Pianta, R. C. (2008). Quality of language and literacy instruction in preschool classrooms serving at-risk pupils. *Early Childhood Research Quarterly, 23,* 51–68.

Karoly, L. A., Ghosh-Dastidar, B., Zellman, G. L., Perlman, M., & Fernyhough, L. (2008). *Prepared to learn: The nature and quality of early care and education for preschool-age children in California.* Santa Monica, CA: RAND Corporation.

Lipsey, M. W., Farran, D. C., Bilbrey, C., Hofer, K. G., & Dong, N. (2011). *Initial results of the evaluation of the Tennessee voluntary pre-K program.* Nashville, TN: Vanderbilt University, Peabody Research Institute.

Lonigan, C. J., Burgess, S. R., & Anthony, J. L. (2000). Development of emergent literacy and early reading skills in preschool children: Evidence from a latent variable longitudinal study. *Developmental Psychology, 36,* 596–613.

Marulis, L. M., & Neuman, S. B. (2010). The effects of vocabulary intervention on young children's word learning: A meta-analysis. *Review of Educational Research, 80,* 300–335.

Melhuish, E. C., Phan, M. B., Sylva, K., Sammons, P., Siraj-Blatchford, I., & Taggart, B. (2008). Effects of home learning environment and preschool center experience upon literacy and numeracy development in early primary school. *Journal of Social Issues, 64*(1), 95–114.

National Early Literacy Panel. (2008). *Developing early literacy: Report of the National Early Literacy Panel.* Washington, DC: National Institute for Literacy.

National Governors Association Center for Best Practices, Council of Chief State School Officers. (2010). *Common Core State Standards.* Washington, DC: Author.

National Institute of Child Health and Human Development Early Child Care Research

Network. (2005). Pathways to reading: The role of oral language in the transition to reading. *Developmental Psychology, 41*(2), 428–442.

Paris, S. G. (2011). Developmental differences in early reading skills. In S. B. Neuman & D. K. Dickinson (Eds.), *Handbook of early literacy research* (Vol. 3, pp. 228–241). New York: Guilford Press.

Penno, J. F., Wilkinson, I. A. G., & Moore, D. W. (2002). Vocabulary acquisition from teacher explanation and repeated listening to stories: Do they overcome the Matthew effect? *Journal of Educational Psychology, 94*(1), 23–33.

Perry, F., Colman, M., & Cross, T. G. (1986). Conversations with children in kindergartens. In T. G. Cross & L. M. Riach (Eds.), *Aspects of child development* (pp. 66–76). Melbourne, Australia: AE Press.

Piasta, S. B., & Wagner, R. K. (2010). Developing early literacy skills: A meta-analysis of alphabet learning and instruction. *Reading Research Quarterly, 45*, 8–38.

Puma, M., Bell, S., Cook, R., Heid, C., Shapiro, G., Broene, P., et al. (2010). *Head Start impact study: Final report.* Washington, DC: U.S. Department of Health and Human Services, Administration for Children and Families.

Reynolds, A. J. (2000). *Success in early intervention: The Chicago child–parent centers.* Lincoln: University of Nebraska Press.

Schatschneider, C., Fletcher, J. M., Francis, D. J., Carlson, C. D., & Foorman, B. R. (2004). Kindergarten prediction of reading skills: A longitudinal comparative analysis. *Journal of Educational Psychology, 96*(2), 265–282.

Scheiner, Y., & Gorsetman, C. (2009). Do preschool teachers consider inferences for book discussions? *Early Child Development and Care, 179*(5), 595–608.

Schweinhart, L., Monti, J., Xiang, Z., Barnett, W. S., Belfield, C., & Nores, M. (2005). *Lifetime effects: The High/Scope Perry preschool study through age 40. Monographs of the High/Scope Educational Research Foundation, 14.* Ypsilanti, MI: High/Scope Press.

Sénéchal, M. (1997). The differential effect of storybook reading on preschoolers' acquisition of expressive and receptive vocabulary. *Journal of Child Language, 24*, 123–138.

Shonkoff, J. P., & Phillips, D. A. (Eds.). (2000). *From neurons to neighborhoods: The science of early childhood development.* Washington, DC: National Academy Press.

Snow, C., Burns, M., & Griffin, P. (1998). *Preventing reading difficulties in young children.* Washington, DC: National Academy Press.

Strickland, D. S. (2004). The search for balance. *Children and Families: The Magazine of the National Head Start Association, 18*, 24–31.

Strickland, D. S., & Riley-Ayers, S. (2006). *Early literacy: Policy and practice in the preschool years (Preschool Policy Brief No. 10).* New Brunswick, NJ: Rutgers University, National Institute for Early Education.

Strickland, D. S., & Riley-Ayers, S. (2007). *Literacy leadership in early childhood: An essential guide.* New York: Teachers College Press.

Sturges, P. (1999). *The little red hen (makes a pizza).* New York: Puffin.

Sylva, K., Chan, L., Melhuish, E., Sammons, P., Siraj-Blatchford, I., & Taggart, B. (2011). Emergent literacy environments: Home and pre-school influences on children's literacy development. In S. B. Neuman & D. K. Dickinson (Eds.), *Handbook of early literacy research* (Vol. 3, pp. 97–118). New York: Guilford Press.

Teale, W., & Sulzby, E. (1989). Emerging literacy: New perspectives. In D. Strickland & L. Morrow (Eds.), *Emerging literacy: Young children learn to read and write* (pp. 1–15). Newark, DE: International Reading Association.

Vandell, D. L., Belsky, J., Burchinal, M., Steinberg, L., Vandergrift, N., & National Institute of Child Health and Human Development Early Child Care Research Network. (2010). Do effects of early child care extend to age 15 years?: Results from the National Institute of Child Health and Human Development Study of Early Child Care and Youth Development. *Child Development, 81*(3), 737–756.

van Kleeck, A. (2006). Fostering inferential language during book sharing with preschoolers: A foundation for later text comprehension strategies. In A. van Kleeck (Ed.), *Sharing books and stories to promote language and literacy* (pp. 269–318). San Diego, CA: Plural.

Verhoeven, L., van Leeuwe, J., & Vermeer, A. (2011). Vocabulary growth and reading development across the elementary school years. *Scientific Studies of Reading, 15*, 8–25.

Vogel, C. A., Xue, Y., Moiduddin, E. M., Lepidus Carlson, B., & Eliason Kisker, E. (2010). *Early Head Start children in grade 5: Long-term follow-up of the Early Head Start research and evaluation study sample* (OPRE Report No. 2011-8). Washington, DC: Office of Planning, Research, and Evaluation, Administration for Children and Families, U.S. Department of Health and Human Services.

Zimmerman, F. J., Gilkerson, J., Richards, J. A., Christakis, D. A., Xu, D., Gray, S., et al. (2009). Teaching by listening: The importance of adult–child conversations to language development. *Pediatrics, 124*(1), 342–349.

PART II

MATERIALS AND TEXTS

CHAPTER 5

❖

Early Literacy Development
in the Digital Age

Jackie Marsh
Dylan Yamada-Rice

GUIDING QUESTIONS

❖ How is literacy changing in the digital age?

❖ How can teachers develop children's literacy and multimodal communication skills using technology?

❖ How can the skills, knowledge, and understanding that children develop through these activities be assessed?

OVERVIEW OF THE TOPIC

In this chapter, we consider how teachers in kindergartens and elementary classrooms might face the challenge of offering curricula and pedagogy appropriate for the digital age. Drawing on a case study conducted in a nursery (preschool) in Sheffield in the United Kingdom, we identify best practice that can inform future developments in this area. This topic is important because of the way that literacy is changing in the digital age. Young children have access to a range of technologies from birth and develop a variety of skills, knowledge, and understanding as a result of this use (Blanchard & Moore, 2010; Marsh, Brooks, Hughes, Ritchie, & Roberts, 2005). When they attend kindergarten and school, therefore, we need to build on these early experiences and ensure that children extend their competencies if they are to navigate the digital world and its related multimodal communication practices effectively. In the first part of this chapter, we provide an overview of the key theory underpinning this area in order to inform our understanding of practice. In the second part of the chapter, we outline a case study of a project undertaken in Sharrow Nursery, Sheffield, England, in order to provide an illustrative example of how such important work might be addressed by early years teachers.

THEORETICAL BACKGROUND AND RESEARCH BASE

This chapter is framed within the understanding that social, economic and digital technologies have brought about significant changes in communication practices (Kress, 2003). Specifically, communication practices have evolved so that modes (means of communication) such as image, writing, music, gesture, and speech are increasingly combined in the dissemination of texts. As Kress outlines, "Mode is a socially shaped and culturally given semiotic resource for making meaning" (2010, p. 79). Focusing on the social and cultural emphasis of modal use aids understanding of how contemporary communication practices have evolved. Within a Western context, modal preferences have evolved alongside media and social advances, with the most noticeable change being a shift from the previous centuries-long dominance of written texts in books and documents (Kress & van Leeuwen, 2001) to those that revolve around digital technologies, which foreground screens as the new site for communication and meaning making (Bezemer & Kress, 2008; Kress, 2003). The implications of this shift from books to screen impacts on the use of modes in communication, such as the extent to which particular modes are foregrounded. It also changes the dynamics between producers and interpreters of texts. These two areas are considered next.

CONTEMPORARY MULTIMODAL COMMUNICATION PRACTICES

The history of Western communication provides an understanding of how present practices in this context have emerged. As described above, the move from the dominance of the book to screen-based media illustrates how meaning making is now reliant on multiple rather than singular (predominately written) modes of communication. This relatively recent emergence of digital technologies in relation to the West's extensive communication history often leads to academic and educational focus on the "new," such as in the use of "new media," "new literacies," and "digital literacies." However, this can be confusing because many digital media are more likely a radical "repackaging" of traditional media than anything specifically new (Kress & van Leeuwen, 2001, p. 90). Nevertheless, there are new aspects of literacy in the digital world that we review in this chapter, such as the potential for reaching out to new audiences (Lankshear & Knobel, 2011).

By considering digital technologies in relation to communication history, it is possible to see how the development of writing over the last 20 years has accelerated due to computing. The most recent evolution of technology such as smart phones and tablets combine cameras, video recorders, telephones, face-to-face chat options, Internet, and 3G access. In this way, computing propels the use of multiple modes for communicating. Additionally, the newest technologies are highly portable, allowing increasingly easy means by which texts can be broadcast. Further, the dominance of screens and lenses in new technologies has brought about an intensified foregrounding of the visual mode. Put simply, digital technologies increasingly rely on the "logics" of visual rules (Kress, 2003). Foregrounding modes beyond the written, and in particular the visual mode, has a twofold impact on communication practices. First, it means that communication practices center more strongly on the affordances of the visual mode, which utilizes the properties of "space, size, colour, shape [and] icons of various kinds" (Bezemer & Kress, 2008, p. 171).

Second, the visual mode conveys information and meaning, like all modes, in unique ways. For example, the success of photography has been based on the way in which it radically accelerated the process of visual reproduction to allow the visual mode to keep pace with speech (Benjamin, 1936). The aforementioned digital technologies take this desire for instantaneous visual communication to a new level, allowing photographs and videos to move beyond offering a simple means of recording memories (Van Dijck, 2008) to being used increasingly to share and record information (Davies, 2006; Okabe & Ito, 2006; Van Dijck, 2008). In this way, being able to access camera technology and the Internet via a portable device such as a smart phone or tablet allows social interaction to be recorded in new ways. As an example, Kress (2010) states that smart-phone technology makes "representing reality by selecting and 'capturing' a 'naturalized' activity so that 'present reality is conceived in terms of possible future needs of representations . . . rather than of living experience'" (p. 189). This means that such technologies allow "reality" to be recorded visually in photographs or multimodally in videos and disseminated through social networking sites and blogs. Further, often these means of disseminating texts are more strongly foregrounded in the authors' minds than just living the experience in the present moment. Kress continues to describe how, through these processes, digital media allow an easy transition between online and off-line worlds and related communication practices.

There are considerable epistemological implications in these changes to communication practices. If meaning making can now be made and disseminated through a range of modes and digital media, it allows messages to be fine-tuned to define and convey knowledge in new ways. While such processes have always existed, the use of modes other than the written has until recently primarily been confined to specialist producers, such as artists, designers, and musicians. Nowadays, the design process has become an important part of contemporary communication practices, as when creating a text in contemporary societies the producer must both perceive the audience and select the most suitable media and mode(s) for them and the text (Bezemer & Kress, 2008; Kress, 2005, 2008). Simultaneously, they must produce a "competitive" message that can stand out in an information-saturated society (Mackey, 2002). As a result, design and creativity as "selection, arrangement, foregrounding and social repositioning" (Bezemer & Kress, 2008, p. 184) become important parts of the production process. This differs from the past, where texts were largely unidirectional and monomodal. It makes sense, therefore, that in the past, teaching writing and reading in order to decode and encode texts created using the dominant written mode would have been most essential. These newfound means of allowing nonspecialists to produce and receive messages through the process of design by media selection, modal choice, and arrangement change the constraints on how knowledge is defined. Perhaps it is better to conceive of the impact of this change on young children by viewing them as emerging specialists in designing and communicating through a range of modes with a variety of tools, both traditional and digital. Indeed, the case study discussed later in this chapter illustrates how acknowledging contemporary communication practices in education means allowing children to make meaning in a range of modes with a range of tools and this process changes how knowledge is constructed. Additionally, multimodal communication across media involves transformations in the relationship between author and audience in the making and dissemination of texts.

THE CONTEMPORARY RELATIONSHIP BETWEEN AUTHOR AND AUDIENCE

Traditionally, the author–reader relationship was governed by authors who were privileged figures of authority communicating with a collective, known audience (Kress, 2010). In the every day, but particularly in education, this meant that

> schooled literacy was an assimilating business . . . few individuals ever got to voice abstract authority through writing; most were included by exclusion, included to the extent that they were readers of the texts of command and the mass media, but excluded from forms of creation of the written word through which they might themselves have been one of the voiceless voices and thus have a real impact on their social environment. (Kalantzis & Cope, 2000, pp. 142–143)

By contrast, digital technologies allow anyone with access to the appropriate hardware and software to be an author of a text that can be widely disseminated both to known and unknown audiences. Additionally, "the interconnectivity of the Internet [has] changed modes of distribution, the nature and availability of audiences, and created incredible new opportunities for collaboration" (Woolsey, 2005, p. 5). Contemporary multimodal communication practices, therefore, allow individuals to be "the remakers, transformers, of sets of representational resources" (Kress, 2000, p. 160), which happens as a collaborative process usually through digital media that emphasise user-created content. Chandler-Olcott and Mahar (2003) suggest that not only are meaning-making practices collaborative but that learning how to use digital media and software is widely influenced by online mentors who teach and share information. Thus, practice, teaching, and learning are all collaborative practices that are focused more on distributed expertise and intelligence than on commercial production and consumption (Lankshear & Knobel, 2007, p. 227). These changes represent a new social relationship with regard to communication, production, and interpretation. However, like most of the processes described in this chapter, collaborative practices are not new (Cope & Kalantzis, 2000; Kress, 1987). The process of communication has always been a two-way collaborative process between producer and interpreter of messages (Halliday, 1978; Kress, 1987); digital media have simply extended the collaborative process.

The implications of these changes in the relationship between authors and interpreters of text is that the traditional, hierarchical power structures of teacher and student relationships have also been undermined by new communication processes. Given education budgets, if children are already aware (or will become knowledgeable) of how to share knowledge on software and related applications, the most immediate gain that formal education can aim to achieve is the teaching of design and creativity. Research to date has provided some specific examples of how curricula could benefit from the inclusion of design. Mackey (2002) argues that multimodal texts require the ability of producers to be alert to the connections that exist between modes. Mackey suggests further that many classrooms do not provide any space to think cross-modally. This is in spite of the fact that previous research illustrates that much classroom teaching is already highly multimodal (Franks, 2003; Jaipal, 2009; Jewitt, Kress, Ogborn, & Tsatsarelis, 2001; Kress & van Leeuwen, 2001; Marquez, Izquierdo, & Espinet, 2006; Prain & Waldrip, 2006) and that there are marked differences in the ability of children who can and cannot make links and understanding across modes (Jaipal, 2009; Prain & Waldrip, 2006). Ideally, all children should have the ability to design messages so that it becomes

> a means of projecting an individual's interest into their world with the intent of effect in the future. It is the position taken by those who have become accustomed to produce . . . and who disseminate their messages in and to a world which they address confidently. (Kress, 2010, p. 23)

Understanding the changes in communication practices outlined in this section sets the context for the case study, outlined below. While the landscape of communication has changed, as previously argued, these changes have not always been reflected in early literacy curricula and pedagogy, as suggested in a review of this area conducted by Burnett and Merchant (2013). It is important, therefore, to document best practice in order to outline how teachers might attend to the digital turn in literacy and multimodal communication.

BRINGING THIS KNOWLEDGE TO THE EARLY LITERACY CLASSROOM

The following case study was undertaken as part of a larger-scale study, the Digital Futures in Teacher Education (DeFT) project conducted by Sheffield Hallam University and the University of Sheffield, in collaboration with a range of partners. Sharrow Primary School in Sheffield, a city in the north of England, was one of 10 schools participating in the project. The study was undertaken in the nursery (preschool), attended by children ages 3 and 4.

Sharrow Nursery serves a diverse community, which includes families with Pakistani, Yemeni, and Somalian heritages, in addition to African Caribbean and White English and Irish families. This rich multilingual environment offers opportunities for children to learn about each other's cultural backgrounds. The nursery and school occupy a new building, which provides a stimulating context for the students and the community.

The teachers involved in the case study, Alice and Zubeda, worked together on this project. Alice has been teaching for 5 years and has worked in Sharrow nursery for 2 years. Zubeda trained 2 years ago and has been employed in the nursery for 2 years. She is currently completing a master's program in education. Alice and Zubeda participated in this project because they wished to use digital technologies to promote oral language, reading, and writing, with a particular focus on talk, because of the needs of the bilingual students in their nursery. The aims of the project, therefore, were to use digital technologies imaginatively in order to (1) promote young children's oral language and (2) encourage children's participation in reading and writing activities.

The project focused on a topic about farms. Children attending the nursery live in the inner city and rarely have opportunities to see farm animals. One of the central activities in the project, therefore, was a visit to a local inner-city farm in which children had an opportunity to see goats, horses, pigs, and a range of other small animals. Alice and Zubeda planned the topic and chose a range of appropriate picturebooks to read to the children throughout it, such as *Mrs. Wishy Washy* (Cowley, 2005), which focuses on the story of a farming woman who is dismayed to find a group of animals that have become dirty through their playful antics in mud. She washes all of the animals in a bath. The language is simple and repetitive, ideal for young bilingual learners.

The two teachers decided on the target language that they wanted to promote through the project, which included key words such as the names of specific animals. Alice and Zubeda also identified the digital technologies that they wished the children to use in the project, which were digital cameras, iPads, and desktop computers. Although the children had access to computers on a daily basis in the nursery, they had not used digital cameras or iPads in the curriculum previously. The teachers felt that the use of these technologies would promote oral language and that the visual and intuitive tactile nature of the iPad might work particularly well with bilingual learners.

Alica and Zubeda set up a blog for the project (see Figure 5.1). Blogs are now used in a widespread fashion in schools, given their ease of use. They enable a range of texts, including photographs, videos, and written texts, to be posted online and made available to external audiences. A key audience for this blog was the parents of children in the nursery. Alice and Zubeda therefore ensured that all entries posted onto the blog were tagged with the names of individual children in the nursery, which would enable parents to click on their child's name in order to access his or her work (see Figure 5.2). The teachers decided that photographs that included the faces of children would not be placed on the blog, in order to protect anonymity.

The project began with children having plenty of opportunities to play with toy farm animals in the nursery. During some of these play episodes, the children were

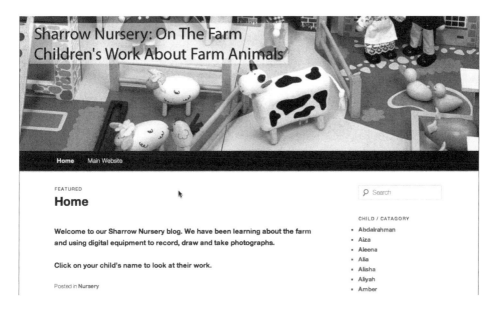

FIGURE 5.1. Sharrow Nursery blog.

FIGURE 5.2. Children's names on the blog.

given digital cameras in order to take photographs and digital films of their play with toy animals. The teachers then uploaded these photographs and films onto the blog, with the children having the opportunity to view their uploaded texts (see Figure 5.3).

The competence that these 3- and 4-year-old children demonstrated in using digital cameras will be of no surprise to those who are aware of how children have extensive access to digital technologies in homes and communities. From a very young age, children have opportunities to use the still and video camera features on their parents' mobile phones, for example (Blanchard & Moore, 2010; Marsh et al., 2005). In this project, the placing of the photographs on the blog enabled children to extend their understanding of how they might communicate with external audiences through technology. One of the researchers on the DeFT project, Nicky, left a message for the children using the comments feature on the blog (see Figure 5.4).

In this example, the affordances of social networking sites such as blogs can be seen. They enable children to engage in dissemination of their work to external audiences, both known and unknown, and to receive comments on this work. In a previous project using blogs undertaken in this nursery, the children and teachers were delighted to find comments posted by the children's families in distant places, such as London and Bangladesh.

Midway through the project, children and parents visited Heeley City Farm, which was in walking distance to the school. The children spent a very exciting day, recording their observations of the farm animals using digital cameras. A further

Our farm small world photos

The children enjoyed taking these photos.

FIGURE 5.3. Small-world photographs.

affordance of blogs is the opportunity to post podcasts. Alice and Zubeda worked with the children to create a range of podcasts that found them retelling the story of *Mrs. Wishy Washy* (Cowley, 2005), and adding commentary to photographs that the children had taken on their visit to the farm. This included children making podcasts in their first language. In those cases in which children did not choose to make an oral podcast, the teachers recorded the children's comments in writing (see Figure 5.5).

Finally, Alice and Zubeda decided to introduce the children to iPads, to be used as a drawing tool. They chose the app "Brushes" for its ease of use. The children spent time both in the nursery and on the trip to the farm drawing pictures of animals. Examples of the children's iPad drawings can be seen in Figures 5.6, 5.7, and 5.8.

This entry was posted in **Nursery** by **nursery**. Bookmark the **permalink**.

ONE THOUGHT ON "OUR FARM SMALL WORLD PHOTOS"

Nicky on **May 14, 2012 at 12:03 pm** said:
Thesse are lovely photoes! It looks like a very busy farm.

Reply ↓

FIGURE 5.4. Comment on the blog.

This case illustrates a number of successful strategies that were employed by Alice and Zubeda to achieve their aims. Their pedagogical approaches were underpinned by what can be conceptualized as the "six C's":

1. *Collaboration.* This is important in any approach to learning and teaching that is based on social-constructivist principles. Pedagogical approaches should enable students to collaborate in dyads, small groups, and large groups that are both mixed ability and same ability; in friendship groups and mixed-friendship groups; and mixed-gender and same-gender groups. Utilizing these various group structures across contexts and being flexible in approach to suit different purposes will enable teachers to address specific learning outcomes. In the case study, children worked individually and in small groups to complete tasks, depending on the activity and its goals. With a particular focus on language, collaboration is key to learning for young bilingual students. Further, the use of social networking sites such as Blogger can offer exciting opportunities for collaboration in the digital age (Chandler-Olcott & Mahar, 2003; Lankshear & Knobel, 2011).

2. *Co-construction.* Linked to having opportunities to collaborate, co-construction of learning enables students to engage in situations in which they are cognitively stretched and in which teachers can offer the kind of "just-in-time" scaffolding and intersubjectivity that leads to effective learning. Alice and Zubeda

Humaira said "Ducks running in the water. They would go in the water because they dirty. Black and white. I like white one. I got duck in my house. It was in the attic. Toy one."

Posted in **Humaira, Nursery** | **Leave a reply**

FIGURE 5.5. Children's comments on their digital photographs.

intervened as necessary to extend children's understanding of the multimodal texts they encountered.

3. *Choice.* Enabling students to choose the direction in which they want their work to go provides them with opportunities to make informed decisions and deploy skills such as the ability to prioritize, sequence tasks effectively, and solve problems. Children in Sharrow preschool were free to choose whether they wished to participate in various activities and many demonstrated enthusiasm for working with new technologies in the choices they made.

4. *Control.* This is linked to the previous category, so that when children have more choice and control over the pace and content of their learning, they are more

FIGURE 5.6. iPad drawing of a dog.

FIGURE 5.7. iPad drawing of a goat.

FIGURE 5.8. iPad drawing of a cat.

engaged and motivated as learners. Children in the case study had opportunities to experiment with the digital cameras and iPads and were thus able to develop confidence in their use.

5. *Creativity.* If students have choice and control with regard to their learning, they are more likely to take risks and experiment, which can promote in the development of literacy skills, knowledge, and understanding. As Bezemer and Kress (2008) suggested, creative decision making is embedded into the multimodal design process.

6. *Community engagement.* Opening the classroom to the external community is a powerful means of developing authentic purposes for reading and writing. The advances in social networking now mean that it is much easier to engage outside audiences within the curriculum, using sites such as Blogger and Twitter. Through publishing children's work on the blog, Alice and Zubeda enabled the children to communicate directly with an audience external to the nursery, providing an authentic context for reading and writing. This provides opportunities for students to become involved in the kinds of communicative practices that are well established in the world outside of schools.

One of the key questions that must inform future developments in this field is how to assess this kind of work. We need to develop new criteria for literacy assessment, given that criteria based on written language are no longer sufficient in the digital age. Before considering *what* is to be assessed, however, the *how* of assessment needs to be considered. As Murphy argues:

> Warrants for assessment should recognize the possibilities as well as the limitations of design in relation to the situation or circumstances of any one assessment activity. In particular, the representational possibilities for knowing offered by assessment designs should be acknowledged as limiting some representations while enabling others. Reasoned and reasonable warrants form the basis for thinking about the consequences of an assessment. (Murphy, 2013, p. 563)

This would suggest that we need a broad portfolio of tools to draw on in assessing students' literacy learning including diagnostic tests, observation, analysis of products, questioning, the use of diaries and portfolios, and techniques such as recall. In considering reading and writing in the digital age, we also require approaches to assessment that capture and enable teachers to analyze multimodal interactions across media and so, to the above list, we could add electronic portfolios and the use of screen-capture software, for example. In terms of identifying the knowledge, skills, and understanding that should be assessed, we are in the early stages of developing a full understanding. In England, the following list constitutes elements of assessment in communication, language, and literacy for the Statutory Framework for the Early Years Foundation Stage Framework (Department of Education, 2012, pp. 7–9), for children ages birth to 5. Children are expected to demonstrate attainment of these criteria at the end of the Foundation Stage:

Communication and Language

Listening and attention: Children listen attentively in a range of situations. They listen to stories, accurately anticipating key events, and respond to what they hear with relevant comments, questions, or actions. They give their attention to what others say and respond appropriately, while engaged in another activity.

Understanding: Children follow instructions involving several ideas or actions. They answer "how" and "why" questions about their experiences and in response to stories or events.

Speaking: Children express themselves effectively, showing awareness of listeners' needs. They use past, present, and future forms accurately when talking about events that have happened or are to happen in the future. They develop their own narratives and explanations by connecting ideas or events.

Literacy

Reading: Children read and understand simple sentences. They use phonic knowledge to decode regular words and read them aloud accurately. They also read some common irregular words. They demonstrate understanding when talking with others about what they have read.

Writing: Children use their phonic knowledge to write words in ways which match their spoken sounds. They also write some irregular common words. They write simple sentences which can be read by themselves and others. Some words are spelled correctly and others are phonetically plausible.

These criteria pay little attention to the kinds of multimodal communicative practices that children in the Sharrow Nursery case study demonstrated. To the above, we would, therefore, suggest adding the following:

Multimodal communication: Children enjoy interacting with and responding to multimodal texts. They know that modes can carry meaning and are able to distinguish between different modes (e.g., image, writing, sound) in texts. They use their knowledge of different modes to construct multimodal texts across a range of media and attempt to construct multimodal texts for different purposes and audiences.

This is not intended to be an exhaustive list but offers a starting point for considering the kinds of skills, knowledge, and understanding that children are now developing in the digital age. There needs to be further research in the years ahead that will enable progression frameworks in the analysis and production of multimodal texts to be developed.

CONCLUSION

The case study above illustrates how one nursery has developed its practice in relation to the teaching and learning of digital literacies. Through this work the teachers, Alice and Zubeda, have developed their own understanding of ways in which children's digital competences can be developed and how the production of digital texts can extend speaking and listening, and reading and writing. The work undertaken by Sharrow Nursery also enabled the staff to reach out to parents and the community, engaging them in these developments and allowing the parents to celebrate the children's achievements.

In the years ahead, there will be inexorable progress in the range of technologies available and, correspondingly, what they will enable their users to do. The implication for teachers, therefore, is not to focus on enabling children to develop a narrow set of skills that relate to specific technologies but instead to help them to acquire a wide range of competence that can be transferred across modes and media. The aim should be to enable children, through the use of digital technologies, to develop skills such as problem solving and resilience in order to promote creativity. The children in Sharrow Nursery, through their participation in the digital literacy activities offered in the curriculum, are thus acquiring the skills and knowledge that will enable them to participate actively as digital citizens in the decades ahead.

REFERENCES

Benjamin, W. (1936). *The work of art in the age of mechanical reproduction*. Available from *www. marxists.org/reference/subject/philosophy/works/ge/benjamin.htm*.

Bezemer, J., & Kress, G. (2008). Writing in multimodal texts: A social semiotic account of designs for learning. *Written Communication, 25*, 166–195.

Blanchard, J., & Moore, T. (2010). *The digital world of young children: Impact on emergent literacy* (Pearson Foundation White Paper). Retrieved from *www.pearsonfoundation.org/PDF/ EmergentLiteracy-WhitePaper.pdf*.

Burnett, C., & Merchant, G. (2013). Learning, literacies and new technologies: The current context and future possibilities. In J. Larson & J. Marsh (Eds.), *Handbook of early childhood literacy* (2nd ed., pp. 575–586). Thousand Oaks, CA: Sage.

Chandler-Olcott, K., & Mahar, D. (2003). Tech-savviness meets multiliteracies: Exploring adolescent girls' technology-mediated literacy practices. *Reading Research Quarterly, 38*, 356–385.

Cope, B., & Kalantzis, M. (2000). Designs for social futures. In B. Cope & M. Kalantzis (Eds.), *Multiliteracies: Literacy learning and the design of social futures* (pp. 203–238). London: Routledge.

Cowley, J. (2005). *Mrs. Wishy Washy*. Berkshire, UK: Kingscourt/McGraw-Hill.

Davies, J. (2006). Affinities and beyond!: Developing ways of seeing in online spaces. *E-Learning, 3*(2), 217–234.

Department for Education. (2012). *Statutory framework for the Early Years Foundation Stage Framework*. Retrieved from *http://media.education.gov.uk/assets/files/pdf/e/eyfs%20statutory%20framework%20march%202012.pdf*.

Franks, A. (2003). Palmers' kiss: Shakespeare, school drama and semiotics. In C. Jewitt & G. Kress (Eds.), *Multimodal literacy* (pp. 155–172). New York: Lang.

Halliday, M. A. K. (1978). *Language as a social semiotic*. London: Arnold.

Jaipal, K. (2009). Meaning making through multiple modalities in a biology classroom: A multimodal semiotics discourse analysis. *Science Education, 94*(1), 48–72.

Jewitt, C., Kress, G., Ogborn, J., & Tsatsarelis, C. (2001). Exploring learning through visual, actional and linguistic communication: The multimodal environment of a science classroom. *Educational Review, 53*(1), 5–18.

Kalantzis, M., & Cope, B. (2000). Changing the role of schools. In B. Cope & M. Kalantzis (Eds.), *Multiliteracies: Literacy learning and the design of social futures* (pp. 121–148). London: Routledge.

Kress, G. (1987). *Before writing: Rethinking the paths to literacy*. London: Routledge.

Kress, G. (2000). Design and transformation: New theories of meaning. In B. Cope & M. Kalantzis (Eds.), *Multiliteracies: Literacy learning and the design of social futures* (pp. 153–161). London: Routledge.

Kress, G. (2003). *Literacy in the new media age*. London: Routledge.

Kress, G. (2005). Gains and losses: New forms of texts, knowledge, and learning. *Computers and Composition, 22*, 5–22.

Kress, G. (2008). So what *is* learning, actually? Social change, technological change and a continuing place for the school? In *The educational and social impact of new technologies on young people in Britain*. Report of the ESRC seminar held on October 21, 2008, Graduate School of Education, University of Bristol (Paper 2, pp. 16–22).

Kress, G. (2010). *Multimodality: A social semiotic approach to contemporary communication*. London: Routledge.

Kress, G., & van Leeuwen, T. (2001). *Multimodal discourse: The modes and media of contemporary communication*. New York: Oxford University Press.

Lankshear, C., & Knobel, M. (2007). Researching new literacies: Web 2.0 practices and insider perspectives. *E-Learning, 4*(3), 224–240.

Lankshear, C., & Knobel, M. (2011). *New literacies: Everyday practices and classroom learning* (3rd ed.). Maidenhead, Berkshire, UK: Open University Press.

Mackey, M. (2002). *Literacies across media*. London: Routledge.

Marquez, C., Izquierdo, M., & Espinet, M. (2006). Multimodal science teachers' discourse in modelling the water cycle. *Science Education, 90*(2), 202–226.

Marsh, J., Brooks, G., Hughes, J., Ritchie, L., & Roberts, S. (2005). *Digital beginnings: Young children's use of popular culture, media and new technologies.* Sheffield, UK: University of Sheffield. Retrieved from *www.digitalbeginings.shef.ac.uk.*

Murphy, S. (2013). Finding literacy: A review of the research on literacy assessment in early childhood education. In N. Hall, J. Larson, & J. Marsh (Eds.), *Handbook of early childhood literacy* (2nd ed., pp. 561–574). London: Sage.

Okabe, D., & Ito, M. (2006). *Everyday contexts of camera phone use: Steps toward technosocial ethnographic frameworks.* Retrieved from *www.itofisher.com/mito/publications/everyday_contex.html.*

Prain, V., & Waldrip, B. (2006). An exploratory study of teachers' and students' use of multimodal representations of concepts in primary science. *International Journal of Science Education, 28*(15), 1843–1866.

Van Dijck, J. (2008). Digital photography: Communication, identity, memory. *Visual Communication, 7*(1), 57–76.

Woolsey, K. (2005). *New media literacies: A language revolution.* Retrieved from *http://archive2.nmc.org/summit/Language_Revolution.pdf.*

CHAPTER 6

❖

What, When, and How Electronic Media Can Be Used in an Early Literacy Classroom

Annie M. Moses

GUIDING QUESTIONS

❖ Which electronic media do young children regularly use and for how much time?

❖ What is the impact of regularly used electronic media on young children's early literacy skills?

❖ How can electronic media be integrated successfully into an early literacy classroom?

Electronic media are commonplace in many homes as well as school settings, and children seem to grow quite comfortable with television, videos/DVDs, and computers, as well as tablets and cell phones. Often they do so to the amazement of the adults around them. Because young children's daily lives are immersed with media, in this chapter, I first highlight which electronic media young children (birth to 8 years) typically use and for how much time during a typical day. Then, I review what research has shown about the effects of media on children's early literacy skills. Finally, I discuss strategies that teachers can use to integrate electronic media into an early literacy classroom.

CASE EXAMPLE

Mrs. Piper, a teacher entering her 34th year of teaching, is beginning her first year with an interactive whiteboard (IWB) in her kindergarten classroom. After an initial 2-day training and some individual assistance, Mrs. Piper is excited to use the IWB to incorporate more media and to do so more seamlessly. Her years of experience and education have equipped her with an extensive set of effective teaching strategies, a deep knowledge of students' development and learning, and a flexibility to achieve her curricular goals. However, with so many media materials, Mrs. Piper revisits her thinking about selecting and using media to help her students acquire critical early literacy skills. She wonders, too, whether and how children will make connections between what they learn with and what they learn without electronic media.

WHICH ELECTRONIC MEDIA DO YOUNG CHILDREN REGULARLY USE AND FOR HOW MUCH TIME?

Compared to previous generations, children's options have expanded greatly in how they access media content, in the content that they can choose from, and in how they interact with it. They are often introduced to electronic media as infants and become regular users at young ages. National surveys within, as well as outside of, the United States detail young children's media use at home (e.g., Common Sense Media, 2011; Marsh, Brooks, Hughes, Ritchie, & Roberts, 2005; Rideout & Hamel, 2006). For example, Common Sense Media (2011) reports that "Children [ages birth to 8 years] spend an average of 1:44 watching TV or videos in a typical day, compared to :29 reading, :29 listening to music, and :25 playing computer or video games" (p. 11). Others have reported upward of 3.6 hours of just television and video/DVD viewing by children during an average day at home (Tandon, Zhou, Lozano, & Christakis, 2011). Surveys consistently show that young children engage with media early on and often and that television viewing, in particular, is a priority.

Children engage with electronic media, too, in child care and school settings. This adds to their total media consumption, but the amount of additional time varies. Differences stem from the type of early education setting. K-12 teachers have reported access to a broader range of electronic media than prekindergarten (PreK) teachers, and access may explain why approximately 75% of K–12 teachers reported using some form of media regularly whereas only 33% of PreK teachers reported regular use (PBS and Grunwald Associates, LCC, 2009). Greater access to television and video/DVD players may also account for the many hours that child care settings use this particular medium. In a survey of licensed child care settings from across four states, researchers found that "when television is viewed at all, infants and children spend 2 to 3 hours watching in home-based programs and ~1.5 hours watching in center-based programs" (Christakis & Garrison, 2009, p. 1631).

Rarely have studies examined media habits across a child's full day, though. One exception is a study conducted by Tandon et al. (2011), which established that preschool-age children averaged 4.1 hours watching television and videos/DVDs (other media were not reported). Here, too, home-based facilities reported more hours with television than center-based settings. Thus, purely by number of hours, electronic media, especially television, are central in young children's daily lives.

WHAT IS THE IMPACT OF REGULARLY USED ELECTRONIC MEDIA ON YOUNG CHILDREN'S EARLY LITERACY SKILLS?

The quantity of electronic media consumption can be unsettling to adults, and three main concerns usually revolve around (1) displacement, that is, the belief that time

with media takes away from children's time in nonmedia activities (e.g., socializing with family and friends, reading books, playing outside); (2) exposure to inappropriate content; and/or (3) passive consumption. These concerns have led to many studies of media's influence on nearly all aspects of children's development. A consistent message is that electronic media can influence what children think, how they feel, and what they do, and young children can learn positive as well as negative things from their time with media. Learning literacy is no exception.

Some researchers have gone beyond the question of time, though, and discovered that differences exist between the effects of educational media and the effects of noneducational media (Anderson, Huston, Schmitt, Linebarger, & Wright, 2001; Ennemoser & Schneider, 2007; Wright et al., 2001). While each medium has its own particular features that allow for learning and can contribute distinctively to literacy growth (e.g., Neuman, 2009), common findings have emerged from across studies of television- and computer-based media. In this section, I review the small, but growing, body of research looking at electronic media and early literacy, and I highlight factors that matter with regard to media's impact on early literacy. These factors include (1) time, revisited; (2) content and features; (3) level of involvement; (4) child characteristics; and (5) context.

Time Matters, Revisited

Concern and disagreement over media's influence on young children persist, in part, because of relationships that have been found between media consumption and negative outcomes, such as higher instances of obesity, lower physical activity, lower math achievement (e.g., Pagani, Fitzpatrick, Barnett, & Dubow, 2010), and greater aggression (after viewing much violent content; Murray, 2007). The more hours that children use media, the more likely they are to display these outcomes. Because of these findings, the American Academy of Pediatrics "discourages media use by children younger than 2 years" (2011, p. 4) and recommends "limit[ing] children's total media time (with entertainment media) to no more than 1 to 2 hours of quality programming per day" thereafter (2001, p. 424).

Content and Features Matter

However, when children use media in moderation few negative—and even some positive—outcomes emerge (e.g., Ennemoser & Schneider, 2007). First, engaging with educational media does not relate to displacement of other important activities (Huston, Wright, Marquis, & Green, 1999). Second, engaging with educational media can increase children's early literacy skills (see Bus, Verhallen, & de Jong, 2009; Moses, 2008; Shamir & Korat, 2009; Uchikoshi, 2009). Viewing educational programming has been linked to positive literacy outcomes during the early childhood years (Wright et al., 2001), as well as in relationship to long-term reading achievement, habits, and attitudes (Anderson et al., 2001). Table 6.1 includes a list of educational television programs that have been shown to positively impact a range of early literacy skills without adult mediation. Other programs exist that aim to promote and influence early literacy skills, but have not, to my knowledge, been evaluated or results made available (see Moses, 2009).

Engaging with electronic books (e-books), as well as other computer programs (e.g., Labbo & Reinking, 2003), can also promote early literacy. Not all e-books do so (e.g., Korat & Shamir, 2004), but those that specifically focus on literacy skills can. These e-books also contain content and features that are relevant to the central story or topic, and they provide cues for understanding the main content. By doing so, they can improve word recognition, understanding of word meanings, phonological awareness, story comprehension, and/or concepts about print (see Bus et al., 2009; Shamir & Korat, 2009). Notably, Segers, Takke, and Verhoeven (2004) demonstrated that children's comprehension and vocabulary scores were comparable after hearing a story read by a computer and hearing a story read by a teacher. Much of the time, children interact with the e-books on their own, so these findings are promising, but adult guidance can also help to advance early literacy skills, especially when children need extra support (e.g., Korat, Segal-Drori, & Klien, 2009).

Level of Involvement

Some believe that media, such as television, requires less mental effort than other activities, including reading books (Salomon, 1984), and others assume that exposure to media leads to mindless consumption and passivity (Healy, 1990; Winn, 2002). However, when children are gazing at a screen, their minds can be hard at work (e.g., Bickham, Wright, & Huston, 2001; Mayer, 2005; Neuman, 1995). Studies examining children's attention to—and understanding of — media demonstrate that children are capable of actively engaging with the images, sounds, and language presented on screens.

Certain features are particularly effective in promoting active participation (see the section "Strategies Related to Level of Involvement"; Huston, Bickham, Lee, & Wright, 2007). In fact, in their 2012 position statement, the National Association for the Education of Young Children and the Fred Rogers Center distinguished between "interactive media" and "noninteractive media." Interactive media includes "software programs, applications (apps), broadcast and streaming media, some children's television programming, e-books, the Internet, and other forms of content designed to facilitate active and creative use by young children and to encourage social engagement with other children and adults" (2012, p. 1). In contrast, noninteractive media do not possess these qualities. E-books on a computer or tablet, for instance, encourage interaction as children use a mouse or touch

TABLE 6.1. Educational Television Programs (All Available on PBS) That Have Been Evaluated for Impact on Early Literacy Skills (without Adult Mediation)

Program title	Ages targeted by program	Skills positively impacted and for whom	Peer reviewed?
Arthur	4- to 8-year-olds	• Kindergarten Spanish-speaking English language learners: narrative skills (story structure and story evaluation) (Uchikoshi, 2005)	• Yes
Between the Lions	3- to 7-year-olds	• Kindergarten and first graders: word recognition, phonemic awareness, letter–sound correspondences, and test of reading abilities, especially for young children (K) and moderately- or not-at-risk viewers (Linebarger, Kosanic, Greenwood, & Doku, 2004)	• Yes
		• Kindergarten Spanish-speaking ELLs: phonological awareness (Uchikoshi, 2006)	• Yes
Sesame Street	2- to 4-year-olds	• 3- to 5-year-olds and 4- to 6-year-olds from "disadvantaged backgrounds and advantaged" backgrounds from rural, suburban, and urban areas, especially children who watched the program more: letter recognition, naming letters, matching letters in words, and reading words (Ball & Bogatz, 1970; Bogatz & Ball, 1971)	• No
		• 3- to 5-year-olds (watching *Plaza Sésamo*): letter recognition, word recognition, and word reading (Díaz-Guerrero & Holtzman, 1974)	• Yes
		• 3- to 3½-year-olds: general receptive vocabulary (Rice, Huston, Truglio, & Wright, 1990)	• Yes
Super WHY!	3- to 6-year-olds	• Preschoolers: program-specific symbolic representation and phonemic awareness, (standardized) letter recognition, and nonprogram speech to print matching (Linebarger, McMenamin, & Wainwright, 2009)	• No
Word World	3- to 5-year-olds	• Preschoolers: program-specific vocabulary words (receptive) and program-specific word recognition for all participants, and phonemic awareness for children with parents who had low education levels or had low initial receptive vocabulary scores (Michael Cohen Group, n.d.)	• No

screen to complete a story or game. Some television programs encourage participation when characters "look" at viewers, ask viewers questions, wait for responses, and encourage viewers to join them in singing and dancing, find letters or words, and solve problems. Interactive features can prompt children's interactions with literacy content. However, learning from it depends not just upon characteristics of the medium but also of the children who use it.

Child Characteristics Matter

Some evidence suggests that electronic media can be particularly helpful for certain children: children who are 2½ years and older, children who have lower literacy skills and/or lower language proficiency, and children who come from low-income backgrounds.

Age

Across the early childhood years, children enjoy both educational and noneducational media; as reviewed earlier, educational content can lead to literacy learning. This has been the case especially for children age 2½ years and older (see Wartella & Richert, 2009, for a review). For children under 2½ years, results from the small amount of work have been mixed, even with educationally oriented programs (e.g.,

Linebarger & Walker, 2005). Although infants and young toddlers may pick up new words (e.g., Lemish & Rice, 1986) or learn to copy new actions (Meltzoff, 1988), learning is less certain for them in comparison to live interactions.

Language and Literacy Levels

Some evidence suggests that young children who lag behind their peers in language proficiency (e.g., second-language learners) or early literacy skills can make important gains through media intervention. This has been found after watching certain educational programming without teacher mediation (Linebarger, Kosanic, Greenwood, & Doku, 2004) and with teacher mediation (Golos & Moses, 2011; Penuel et al., 2012; Silverman & Hines, 2009), as well as after using e-books with moving images and narration (e.g., Verhallen, Bus, & de Jong 2006) and literacy games on the computer (Segers & Verhoeven, 2002). The thinking is that educational media provides practice with literacy skills and may motivate children who are otherwise reluctant to engage in literacy (e.g., McKenna & Zucker, 2009).

Income Level

National surveys have revealed noticeable differences in media access and usage by socioeconomic status. The Common Sense Media's (2011) survey found that birth to 8-year-olds from lower-income backgrounds used media almost an hour more, on average, than children from higher-income homes. Children from lower-income backgrounds watched educational television programs more often than their higher-income peers. In addition, they used educational games and programs on computers and mobile or tablet devices less often than their higher-income peers.

When Zill (2001) looked at the relationships between viewing *Sesame Street* by socioeconomic status (SES), he found that it was "more strongly associated with signs of emergent literacy . . . among 4-year-olds from low-income families than among more 'advanced' children from higher-income families" (p. 121). Because some media content is available for free, there has always been great hope that it would help children, especially those from low-income backgrounds. Some evidence suggests that certain educational programs can.

Context Matters

In addition to media and child characteristics, contextual factors come into play too. Contextual factors include whether adults mediate children's media interactions and whether media experiences connect with a broader literacy curriculum. On the one hand, children can benefit from educational television programs without adult guidance (see Table 6.1). On the other hand, adults' facilitation can enhance literacy learning (e.g., Korat et al., 2009; Reiser, Tessmer, & Phelps, 1984). In addition, adults can embed effective strategies during media-based interactions to support learning (e.g., Fisch, Shulman, Akerman, & Levin, 2002; Labbo, 2009).

Related to adult mediation, electronic media can be integrated into classrooms in ways that develop children's early literacy. It is important to note that, when studied, teachers received training and ongoing assistance around the media materials. This occurred when *Between the Lions* episodes were integrated into preschool classrooms. Several studies found that preschoolers' early literacy skills and the classroom literacy environment improved as a result (Linebarger, 2009; Prince, Grace, Linebarger, Atkinson, & Huffman, 2002). In another study, experimental preschool classrooms utilized literacy-related PBS Kids videos and online games over the course of 10 weeks. This led to significantly higher scores on letter naming, letter–sound correspondence, and concepts of print measures when compared to scores in the control classrooms that implemented science-related media materials (Penuel et al., 2012).

As noted in the "Child Characteristics Matter" section, educational media may be particularly helpful for children who struggle in language and early literacy. When video segments were added to a research-tested literacy program (Success for All), first graders at risk for reading problems made more gains in measures of nonsense-word reading, word recognition, passage comprehension, and fluency than their peers who did not view the video segments (but did receive the same literacy instruction; Chambers, Cheung, Madden, Slavin, & Gifford, 2006). Finally, Silverman and Hines (2009) examined the effects of adding informational video segments (e.g., from the *National Geographic* Really Wild Animal Series) to vocabulary-focused read-alouds. Their sample included English language learners (ELLs) as well as non-ELLs between PreK and grade 2. Whereas the videos did not further non-ELLs' vocabulary knowledge, it did increase ELLs'. In fact, they noted that "the gap between non-ELL and ELL children in knowledge of words targeted during the intervention was closed, and the gap in general vocabulary knowledge was narrowed" (p. 311) as a result of experiencing the media-enhanced read-alouds.

Taking all of these factors into account suggests that the most powerful scenario likely involves skilled teachers using effective, educational media that connect with the classroom's literacy curriculum. Rather than seeing electronic media as a solution on its own, teachers should consider it one part of their overall curriculum.

Why Do Children Learn from Media?

One remaining question pertains to how children learn from media. Two prominent theories have been proposed: dual coding theory (Paivio, 1986) and the theory of media synergy (Neuman, 1995, 2009). First, dual coding theory posits that individuals can take in information through a "verbal route" and through a "nonverbal route." Paivio (2006) provides two examples to illustrate the difference between them: a crossword puzzle (verbal) versus a jigsaw puzzle (nonverbal). One can imagine a similar parallel to children's book—a print-only book versus a wordless picturebook. Although extreme as examples, young children who are emerging in literacy rely heavily on nonverbal information (e.g., pictures) but need extensive experience with verbal information (e.g., words) in order to become conventional readers and writers. Both routes provide critical information, but dual coding theory argues that presenting the same concepts and skills both verbally and nonverbally will lead to better understanding and remembering later.

Here is where electronic media can have an advantage. E-books, for instance, can contain either static or moving images to go along with the text on-screen. Movement might distract children and lower story comprehension, or it might increase children's understanding through richer visual information. In fact, when moving images are consistent with the text, children's comprehension has been shown to increase. For example, second-language learners' understanding of an e-story was better with moving images and narration than with static images and narration, particularly after repeated encounters with the e-book (e.g., Verhallen et al., 2006). A similar assumption has been made about effective television programming; that is, television can bring together moving images and language in ways that promote, rather than take away from, literacy learning (Neuman, 1995; Uchikoshi, 2009).

Neuman's theory of synergy complements and expands on dual coding theory by pointing out that the same visual and verbal content pops up in different media, and children often seek out common content across media (2009). For example, a child's favorite character on television may spark his or her interest in exploring games on the program's website, which will allow him or her additional practice with program-related letters, sounds, and words. Liking a particular program may also prompt a child to ask for program-related books (as well as toys, games, and clothing), which can add to his or her literacy experiences (Marsh, 2005; Marsh & Thompson, 2001). In addition, the theory of synergy also proposes that "each medium's physical features, its structure, its method of handling material, may add a new dimension to children's knowledge and the means they employ to attain new knowledge" (Neuman, 2009, p. 52). When content overlaps across media, children should experience even greater growth than from one medium alone.

In looking across the literature on media's effects, the main messages are (1) children spend a great deal of time with media, (2) certain educational media can positively impact children's early literacy skills, and (3) effects may be enhanced when content is presented visually and verbally and is connected across media. This sets the stage for teachers who want to make the most of electronic media to foster children's early literacy skills.

HOW CAN ELECTRONIC MEDIA BE INTEGRATED SUCCESSFULLY INTO AN EARLY LITERACY CLASSROOM?

Mrs. Piper's Class Learns about Fairytales

With the beginning of the school year under way, Mrs. Piper's focus is on fairytales, so she has prepared different experiences for her kindergarteners to learn about that genre. After using the new IWB as a whole class to play an online game focused on the letters *P* and *W* and /ig/ words, Mrs. Piper reads aloud "The Three Little Pigs" (Parkes & Smith, 1985). As she reads, she points out focal letters and sounds, key story elements, and instances of cause and effect. At the end, she and the children review and expand upon the targeted skills and information. Then, Mrs. Piper transitions them into writing a journal entry about the fairytale.

Later, during afternoon whole-class time, Mrs. Piper tells her students that they will be watching an episode of *Super WHY!*, "The Three Little Pigs," to revisit the ideas and skills from earlier in the day. *Super WHY!* is an educational program targeting early literacy skills that includes characters from well-known fairytales, that live in a place called Storybook Village, and use fairytales to solve their problems. Each of the four main characters represents one set of skills (e.g., Wonder Red has "word power," Super Why has "the power to read") and the viewer is considered the fifth main character with the "power to help." In the episode, Pig has a problem—Jill (of "Jack and Jill") repeatedly knocks down his blocks, even when he asks her to stop. So, Pig asks his friends for help, and the Super Readers come together to solve his problem. They fly into "The Three Little Pigs" fairytale to find out why the wolf destroys others' property; they want to use that information to solve Pig's problem with Jill. As the episode unfolds, Mrs. Piper's kindergarteners sing along with Alpha Pig's version of the "ABCs," spot the "super letters" that

pop up throughout, and make guesses about the "super story answer" (based on the super letters they've found). Today's answer to the problem is "friend" (i.e., by being a friend and offering to play with her, Pig can stop Jill from knocking down his blocks). After viewing, Mrs. Piper and her class discuss the main events, instance of cause and effect, and specific letters and sounds presented on-screen.

Mrs. Piper was intentional in integrating electronic media into her early literacy classroom. She selected, planned for, and implemented media for specific reasons, and those reasons stemmed from an understanding of her students, her curriculum, and the available media materials. I present strategies employed by Mrs. Piper, as well as others from the research literature, for incorporating electronic media into an early literacy classroom, and I connect these back to the factors of time, content and features, level of involvement, child characteristics, and context.

Strategies Involving Time

Simply adding media to the children's school day may delight them, but it will not guarantee literacy learning. In addition, the significant number of hours that children spend with media remains a concern. Therefore, teachers must assess the amount of time students engage with media as it compares to time with manipulatives, print and writing materials, and engaged in pretend, construction, and free play. Moderation in the classroom is most conducive to learning, as is moderation outside of the classroom. Mrs. Piper found that parents were enthusiastic about her use of media in the classroom, and they often shared about their child's media use at home. This provided her with a good place to start when considering time with media in her classroom.

Strategies Involving Content and Features

The range of electronic programs and products can be daunting, but a second strategy is to choose high-quality media to implement in the classroom. Thinking about quality means examining content itself as well as the ways in which it is presented (features). When evaluating for quality, teachers should consider the following.

Content Is Educational and, Here, Focused on Early Literacy

Teachers can first determine whether the media content is educational. Generally, does it have educational goals or curriculum supporting it? If so, do the goals specifically concentrate on early literacy? Teachers, like Mrs. Piper, can often find this information online. For example, the PBS Teachers website (*www.pbs.org/teachers*) includes descriptions of children's programming, along with resources and recommendations for using materials in classrooms by grade and content area. Details about a particular program may also be reported in evaluation studies, if available. Ultimately, though, teachers are the best judge as to whether the program aims are worthwhile for their students.

In addition, teachers should listen and look closely at the messages about literacy within media. Not many popular television programs, even educational ones, include characters interacting with print, and a few may even present negative messages about reading, writing, or listening to print being read (Mates & Strommen, 1995/1996; Moses & Duke, 2008). Very recently, more literacy-orientated programs have been created; they likely include much more print and positive messages (e.g., Moses et al., 2013) than programs focused on other domains. But teachers can check not just for appropriate literacy goals but also positive literacy messages.

Content Is Connected and Relevant

The main content should have a connected thread, whether it involves a story or information on a specific topic. In addition, any other sights, sounds, and activities should directly relate to that story or topic and provide clarification or additional background information. For instance, e-book "hot spots" can include kid-friendly definitions of key words to support comprehension. Whereas relevant content facilitates learning, irrelevant content or features can distract from understanding and learning (e.g., Shamir & Korat, 2009).

Content Is Presented in a Way That Will Facilitate Dual Coding

Teachers can examine media to see whether key content and skills are presented visually and verbally and do so at (approximately) the same time. For instance, during an episode of *Martha Speaks*, which aims to promote 4- to 7-year-olds' oral vocabulary, one character witnesses another character dumping pieces of aluminum on a sidewalk (visual). The first character responds by saying, "When people pollute that means they make things dirty or dangerous to live in." Then, he goes on to say that "Pollution can be in the air, it can be in the water, it can be on the ground. Like that big pile of aluminum you just dropped." Images are shown of smog in the air, trash in a body of water, and the pile of aluminum on the sidewalk, respectively. This provides the viewer with visual and verbal information about the meaning of the target word *pollute*, and its variant *pollution*. Providing new information in both ways will help children process and remember it.

Content Is Repeated

Generally, children learn through repetition. While some may think that repetition will decrease their level of interest or involvement, children have been found to attend to and take an increasingly active role over repeated encounters (e.g., Labbo, 2009), which can further their learning (e.g., Bus et al., 2009; Crawley, Anderson, Wilder, Williams, & Santomero, 1999).

The Television- or Computer-Based Program Has Been Evaluated for Effectiveness

Teachers can look especially for research-tested media materials. Being research tested provides greater confidence about the materials' quality and effectiveness related to literacy. However, some media have been evaluated by the companies that make them (thus, the potential for conflict of interest), and many others have not been evaluated at all with respect to literacy outcomes. Teachers should review such media more carefully with regard to use in the classroom.

Strategies Related to Level of Involvement

Media typically include a multitude of features related to sights, sounds, and pacing that attempt to gain and keep children's attention and encourage their active participation. Effective features should focus children on important content. One way to do so is to present key content in the middle of the screen. For example, print appears centrally during episodes of *Between the Lions* and *Super WHY!*, especially when characters say the corresponding sounds, letters, or words. Another effective strategy is to highlight on-screen print whenever a character reads it. This helps emerging readers (start to) attend to the print and make connections between sounds and their representation in print.

Additional effective features for e-books and other computer-based programs include separating instructional content from games and offering different modes for reading (with and without narration; Shamir & Korat, 2009). Separation allows children to concentrate solely on the story and then practice targeted skills and information at a different time. Having different reading modes provides varying degrees of support for a child and gives adults the option to read the text to the child themselves.

Finally, effective features permit users control over navigation and pacing (Labbo, 2009; Shamir & Korat, 2009). For example, an e-book user should be able to choose when to start, stop, advance, and go back, as well as choose hot spots, and prerecorded television and videos/DVDs allow more control of what and when content is viewed. In addition, a few educational television programs attempt to provide appropriate pacing by having characters pause and wait for viewer participation, but will continue either way. Teachers can look for these features as they consider which media will promote children's interactions with important content.

Child Characteristics

When children have sufficient background knowledge and skill level, they will respond to and learn from media. Based on child characteristics, teachers can gauge the amount and type of language used and the topics addressed in media. (Certainly, media with stereotypical, aggressive, or other negative messages will be avoided.) Teachers can also weigh the amount of print and illustrations provided on-screen with regard to child characteristics. In addition, media should target literacy skills that children will find neither too easy nor too difficult. For example, at the group level, Mrs. Piper thought about her students as beginning-of-the-year kindergarteners when she selected media that focused on letter recognition and letter–sound correspondence. Later in the year, she selected media that focused on word recognition and putting words together to form sentences. The same can be said of selecting media at the individual level; certain children will benefit more, for instance, from a video clip or an online game concentrating on initial sounds in words than others.

Strategies Related to Context

The previously mentioned strategies can guide teachers' choice of electronic media. Once selected, teachers should consider when and in what ways to use media within their classroom. To do so, teachers should consider the following.

Content Connects with an Overarching Theme or Unit of Study

In addition to having coherent content within a program, content should fit with instruction and activities outside of the program. Mrs. Piper selected videos and other media materials that aligned with her current topic and instructional goals. This occurred when she chose a *Super WHY!* episode directly related to "The Three Little Pigs" (Parkes & Smith, 1985). It also occurred when her class studied ocean life. Prior to visiting a local aquarium, Mrs. Piper's class viewed video clips to research about sea animals, and they also researched more about the topic online. After their visit, students reviewed and selected photographs of sea animals taken during their field trip. Then, they reviewed and pulled together all of the information they learned in the video clips, online, and during their firsthand experience to write about one sea animal. This strategy exemplifies Neuman's (2009) theory of synergy and how media experiences can build upon each other to promote learning.

Content Includes Information or Skills Not Otherwise Accessible

Firsthand experiences are essential in young children's learning. However, certain concepts or skills are challenging for teachers to address through firsthand experiences owing to distance, expense, and/or classroom space. Dramatic play is one way for children to simulate occupations, space travel, camping, and other complex concepts and skills. So, too, can electronic media vividly show more abstract ideas, such as the solar system, the concept of time, and faraway locations, to name a few. In doing so, electronic media can increase students' vocabulary and background knowledge and can be coupled with literacy instruction and activities.

Content Is Presented in a Variety of Structures

Teachers should also consider how to utilize electronic media during whole-class, small-group, and individual work. A teacher can conduct a read-aloud with an e-book presented through an IWB, which can enlarge images and print for the whole class. Then, s/he can provide the e-book, and print versions if possible, in a center for children to reread at their own pace and choosing. Finally, individual and pairs of children can use games and other interactive features in the e-book to practice targeted literacy skills. This enables repeated exposure to the critical content and offers varying levels of support for children.

Content and Features Allow Teachers to Take on a Variety of Roles

Whatever the structure, teachers have to decide their role in using media in an early literacy classroom. In a series of shared e-book experiences with her young grandson,

Labbo (2009) documented what an adult can do to mediate young children's inter-actions with electronic media. Initially, her roles included "(1) Focuser, (2) Ques-tioner, (3) Connector, (4) Navigator, (5) Pacer, and (6) Relationship Builder" (p. 204). After repeated experiences with the same e-book, she became "Co-Questioner, Co-Answerer, Co-Connector, Co-Navigator, Co-Pacer, Relationship Builder, and Cel-ebrator" (p. 206). That is, Labbo employed a number of roles, and they changed over time as her grandson gained familiarity with the story and the technology. Although used in a one-on-one structure, teachers can adapt these roles for whole-class and small-group time. Similar to effective (print) shared-reading strategies, teachers can choose when and how to question, clarify, reread, make connections, and encourage as they use electronic media with children.

Also, as active participants, teachers will have many opportunities to demon-strate the educational, not just entertainment, uses of media. In addition, they can help children begin to develop critical thinking skills in order to evaluate media content for accuracy and appropriateness (see Rogow, 2002, for suggestions when working with preschoolers). Children should begin to see media as having the abil-ity to teach them new things, but they should also start to recognize that not all of it is true or good for them. Teachers can provide safe and reliable websites to visit and programs to watch in school, and they can offer recommendations for interested families to utilize at home. Teachers can also encourage children to ask questions about who created the media content, what reasons they may have had in doing so, and whether the information matches other, reliable sources (i.e., books, teacher instruction).

Challenges Related to Media and Its Integration into an Early Literacy Classroom

With all of the potential that exists, challenges do too. First, as noted earlier, teachers may not have access to certain hardware or software that will allow them to promote students' early literacy. Knowing the range of resources, though, will help teachers make the most of what resources they do have. Another challenge is teachers' com-fort with the technical aspects of electronic media. More teachers are using electronic media for personal use (Wartella, Schomburg, Lauricella, Robb, & Flynn, 2010), and growing familiarity will give them greater confidence when using it in their class-room. Professional development opportunities and experienced colleagues can also assist teachers in how to use new media and technology in their classroom.

In addition, the research literature is limited. New media materials arrive regu-larly, and studies are continually needed to examine what children use and how it affects their learning. In addition, characteristics of children and the contexts within which they learn must be investigated more, especially with regard to how teachers can utilize electronic media to foster literacy learning.

CONCLUSION

Reasons abound for why teachers may—and may not—incorporate media in their early literacy classroom. Hopefully, the information presented in this chapter will assist teachers in making decisions about what, when, and how to use electronic media to promote young children's early literacy development.

REFERENCES

American Academy of Pediatrics. (2001). Child, adolescents and television. *Pediatrics, 107*(2), 423–426.

American Academy of Pediatrics. (2011). Media use by children younger than 2 years. *Pediatrics, 128*(5), 1–6.

Anderson, D. R., Huston, A. C., Schmitt, K., Linebarger, D. L., & Wright, J. C. (2001). Early childhood television viewing and adolescent behavior: The recontact study. *Monographs of the Society for Research in Child Development, 66*(1, Serial No. 264).

Ball, S., & Bogatz, G. A. (1970). *The first year of Sesame Street: An evaluation.* Princeton, NJ: Educational Testing Service.

Bickham, D. S., Wright, J. C., & Huston, A. C. (2001). Attention, comprehension, and the educational influence of television. In D. G. Singer & J. L. Singer (Eds.), *Handbook of children and media* (pp. 101–119). Thousand Oaks, CA: Sage.

Bogatz, G. A., & Ball, S. (1971). *The second year of Sesame Street: A continuing evaluation.* Princeton, NJ: Educational Testing Service.

Bus, A. G., Verhallen, M. J. A., & de Jong, M. T. (2009). How onscreen storybooks contribute to early literacy. In A. Bus & S. Neuman (Eds.), *Multimedia and literacy development: Improving achievement for young learners* (pp. 153–167). New York: Routledge.

Chambers, B., Cheung, A., Madden, N. A., Slavin, R. E., & Gifford, G. (2006). Achievement effects of embedded multimedia in a Success for All reading program. *Journal of Educational Psychology, 98*(1), 232–237.

Christakis, D. A., & Garrison, M. M. (2009). Preschool-aged children's television viewing in child care settings. *Pediatrics, 124*(6), 1627–1632.

Michael Cohen Group. (n.d.). *The effects of Word World viewing on pre-school children's acquisition of pre-literacy and emergent literacy: A cluster-randomized controlled trial.* Retrieved from *http://extranet.mcgrc.com/Ready_To_Learn_Files/Final%20Word%20World%20Summative.pdf.*

Common Sense Media. (2011). *Zero to eight: Children's media use in America.* Retrieved from *www.commonsensemedia.org/research/zero-eight-childrens-media-use-america.*

Crawley, A. M., Anderson, D. R., Wilder, A., Williams, M., & Santomero, A. (1999). Effects of repeated exposures to a single episode of the television program *Blue's Clues* on the viewing behaviors and comprehension of preschool children. *Journal of Educational Psychology, 91*(4), 630–637.

Diaz-Guerrero, R., & Holtzman, W. H. (1974). Learning by televised *Plaza Sesamo* in Mexico. *Journal of Educational Psychology, 66*(5), 632–643.

Ennemoser, M., & Schneider, W. (2007). Relations of television viewing and reading: Findings from a 4–year longitudinal study. *Journal of Educational Psychology, 99*(2), 349–368.

Fisch, S. M., Shulman, J. S., Akerman, A., & Levin, G. A. (2002). Reading between the pixels: Parent–child interaction while reading online storybooks. *Early Education & Development, 13*(4), 435–451.

Golos, D. B., & Moses, A. M. (2011). How teacher mediation during video viewing facilitates literacy behaviors. *Sign Language Studies, 12*(1), 98–118.

Healy, J. M. (1990). *Endangered minds: Why our children don't think*. New York: Simon & Schuster.

Huston, A. C., Bickham, D. S., Lee, J. H., & Wright, J. C. (2007). From attention to comprehension: How children watch and learn from television. In N. Pecora, J. Murray, & E. Wartella (Eds.), *Children and television: Fifty years of research* (pp. 41–63). Mahwah, NJ: Erlbaum.

Huston, A. C., Wright, J. C., Marquis, J., & Green, S. B. (1999). How children spend their time. *Developmental Psychology, 35*(4), 912–925.

Korat, O., Segal-Drori, O., & Klien, P. (2009). Electronic and printed books with and without adult support as sustaining early literacy. *Journal of Educational Computing Research, 41*(4), 453–475.

Korat, O., & Shamir, A. (2004). Do Hebrew electronic books differ from Dutch electronic books?: A replication study of a Dutch content analysis. *Journal of Computer Assisted Learning, 20*(4), 257–268.

Labbo, L. D. (2009). "Let's do it again, Nana": A case study of how a 2–year-old and his grandmother shared thinking spaces during multiple shared readings of an electronic story. In A. Bus & S. Neuman (Eds.), *Multimedia and literacy development: Improving achievement for young learners* (pp. 153–167). New York: Routledge.

Labbo, L. D., & Reinking, D. (2003). Computers and early literacy education. In N. Hall, J. Larson, & J. Marsh (Eds.), *Handbook of early childhood literacy* (pp. 338–354). London: Sage.

Lemish, D., & Rice, M. L. (1986). Television as a talking picture book: A prop for language acquisition. *Journal of Child Language, 13*(2), 251–274.

Linebarger, D. L. (2009). *Evaluation of the Between the Lions Mississippi Literacy Initiative*. Retrieved from *http://pbskids.org/lions/parentsteachers/pdf/Linebarger_2009.pdf*.

Linebarger, D. L., Kosanic, A. Z., Greenwood, C. R., & Doku, N. S. (2004). Effects of viewing the television program *Between the Lions* on the emergent literacy skills of young children. *Journal of Educational Psychology, 96*(2), 297–308.

Linebarger, D. L., McMenamin, K., & Wainwright, D. K. (2009). *Summative evaluation of Super Why!: Outcomes, dose and appeal*. Retrieved from *http://pbskids.org/read/files/SuperWHY_Research_View.pdf*.

Linebarger, D. L., & Walker, D. (2005). Infants' and toddlers' television viewing and language outcomes. *American Behavioral Scientist, 48*(5), 624–645.

Marsh, J. (2005). Ritual, performance and identity construction: Young children's engagement with popular cultural and media texts. In J. Marsh (Ed.), *Popular culture, new media and digital literacy in early childhood* (pp. 28–50). London: Routledge Falmer.

Marsh, J., Brooks, G., Hughes, J., Ritchie, L., & Roberts, S. (2005). *Digital beginnings: Young children's use of popular culture, media and new technologies.* Sheffield, UK: University of Sheffield. Retrieved from *www.digitalbeginnings.shef.ac.uk.*

Marsh, J., & Thompson, P. (2001). Parental involvement in literacy development: Using media texts. *Journal of Research in Reading, 24*(3), 266–278.

Mates, B. F., & Strommen, L. (1995/1996). Why Ernie can't read: *Sesame Street* and literacy. *The Reading Teacher, 49*(4), 300–306.

Mayer, R. E. (2005). Cognitive theory of multimedia learning. In R. Mayer (Ed.), *The Cambridge handbook of multimedia learning* (pp. 31–48). New York: Cambridge University Press.

McKenna, M. C., & Zucker, T. A. (2009). Use of electronic storybooks in reading instruction: From theory to practice. In A. Bus & S. Neuman (Eds.), *Multimedia and literacy development: Improving achievement for young learners* (pp. 255–272). New York: Routledge.

Meltzoff, A. N. (1988). Imitation of televised models by infants. *Child Development, 59*(5), 1221–1229.

Moses, A. M. (2008). Impacts of television viewing on young children's literacy development in the USA: A review of the literature. *Journal of Early Childhood Literacy, 8*(1), 67–102.

Moses, A. M. (2009). What television can (and can't) do to promote early literacy development. *Young Children, 64*(2), 80–89.

Moses, A. M., & Duke, N. K. (2008). Portrayals of print literacy in children's television programming. *Journal of Literacy Research, 40*(3), 251–289.

Moses, A. M., Jennings, N. A., Brod, R., Hooker, S. D., Cordell, B., & Sallee, T. (2013). *"With the Power to Read": The effects of consistent, positive literacy messages in an educational television program.* Manuscript submitted for publication.

Murray, J. P. (2007). TV violence: Research and controversy. In N. Pecora, J. Murray, & E. Wartella (Eds.), *Children and television: Fifty years of research* (pp. 183–203). Mahwah, NJ: Erlbaum.

National Association for the Education of Young Children and the Fred Rogers Center for Early Learning and Children's Media. (2012). *Technology and interactive media as tools in early childhood programs serving children from birth through age 8.* Retrieved from *www.naeyc.org/files/naeyc/file/positions/PS_technology_WEB2.pdf.*

Neuman, S. B. (1995). *Literacy in the television age: The myth of the TV effect.* Norwood, NJ: Ablex.

Neuman, S. B. (2009). The case for multimedia presentations in learning: A theory of synergy. In A. Bus & S. Neuman (Eds.), *Multimedia and literacy development: Improving achievement for young learners* (pp. 44–56). New York: Routledge.

Pagani, L. S., Fitzpatrick, C., Barnett, T. A., & Dubow, E. (2010). Prospective associations between early childhood television exposure and academic, psychosocial, and physical well-being by middle childhood. *Archives of Pediatric and Adolescent Medicine, 164*(5), 425–431.

Paivio, A. (1986). *Mental representations: A dual coding approach.* Oxford, UK: Oxford University Press.

Paivio, A. (2006). *Dual coding theory and education*. Retrieved from *www.umich.edu/~rdytolrn/ pathwaysconference/presentations/paivio.pdf*.

Parkes, B., & Smith, J. (1985). *The three little pigs*. Crystal Lake, IL: Rigby.

PBS and Grunwald Associates, LCC. (2009). *Digitally inclined*. Retrieved from *www.pbs.org/ teachers/_files/pdf/annual-pbs-survey-report.pdf*.

Penuel, W. R., Bates, L., Gallagher, L. P., Pasnik, S., Llorente, C., Townsend, E., et al. (2012). Supplementing literacy instruction with a media-rich intervention: Results of a randomized controlled trial. *Early Childhood Research Quarterly, 27*(1), 115–127.

Prince, D. L., Grace, C., Linebarger, D. L., Atkinson, R., & Huffman, J. D. (2002). *Between the Lions: Mississippi literacy initiative*. Retrieved from *www.pbs.org/parents/lions/educators/ research.html*.

Reiser, R. A., Tessmer, M. A., & Phelps, P. C. (1984). Adult–child interaction in children's learning from *Sesame Street*. *Educational Communication and Technology Journal, 32*(4), 217–223.

Rice, M. L., Huston, A. C., Truglio, R., & Wright, J. C. (1990). Words from *Sesame Street*: Learning vocabulary while viewing television. *Developmental Psychology, 26*(3), 421–428.

Rideout, V. J., & Hamel, E. (2006). *The media family: Electronic media in the lives of infants, toddlers, preschoolers and their parents*. Menlo Park, CA: Kaiser Family Foundation.

Rogow, F. (2002). *ABC's of media literacy: What can preschoolers learn?* Retrieved from *www. medialit.org/reading-room/abcs-media-literacy-what-can-pre-schooolers-learn*.

Salomon, G. (1984). Television is "easy" and print is "tough": The differential investment of mental effort as a function of perceptions and attributions. *Journal of Educational Psychology, 76*(4), 647–658.

Segers, E., Takke, L., & Verhoeven, L. (2004). Teacher-mediated versus computer-mediated storybook reading to children in native and multicultural classrooms. *School Effectiveness and School Improvement, 15*(2), 215–226.

Segers, E., & Verhoeven, L. (2002). Multimedia support of early literacy learning. *Computers & Education, 39*(3), 207–221.

Shamir, A., & Korat, O. (2009). The educational electronic book as a tool for supporting children's emergent literacy. In A. Bus & S. Neuman (Eds.), *Multimedia and literacy development: Improving achievement for young learners* (pp. 168–181). New York: Routledge.

Silverman, R., & Hines, S. (2009). The effects of multimedia-enhanced instruction on the vocabulary of English-language learners and non-English-language learners in prekindergarten through second grade. *Journal of Educational Psychology, 101*(2), 305–314.

Tandon, P. S., Zhou, C., Lozano, P., & Christakis, D. A. (2011). Preschoolers' total daily screen time at home and by type of child care. *Journal of Pediatrics, 158*(2), 297–300.

Uchikoshi, Y. (2005). Narrative development in bilingual kindergarteners: Can educational television help? *Developmental Psychology, 41*(3), 464–478.

Uchikoshi, Y. (2006). Early reading development in bilingual kindergarteners: Can educational television help? *Scientific Studies of Reading, 10*(1), 89–120.

Uchikoshi, Y. (2009). Effects of television on language and literacy development. In A. Bus & S. Neuman (Eds.), *Multimedia and literacy development: Improving achievement for young learners* (pp. 182–195). New York: Routledge.

Verhallen, M. J. A. J., Bus, A. G., & de Jong, M. T. (2006). The promise of multimedia stories for kindergarten children at risk. *Journal of Educational Psychology, 98*(2), 410–419.

Wartella, E., & Richert, R. A. (2009). Special audience, special concerns: Children and the media. In A. Bus & S. Neuman (Eds.), *Multimedia and literacy development: Improving achievement for young learners* (pp. 15–27). New York: Routledge.

Wartella, E., Schomburg, R. L., Lauricella, A. R., Robb, M., & Flynn, R. (2010). *Technology in the lives of teachers and classrooms: Survey of classroom teachers and family child care providers.* Retrieved from *www.fredrogerscenter.org/media/resources/TechInTheLivesofTeachers.pdf.*

Winn, M. (2002). *The plug-in drug: Television, computers, and family life.* New York: Penguin.

Wright, J. C., Huston, A. C., Murphy, K. C., St. Peters, M., Pinon, M., Scantlin, R., et al. (2001). The relations of early television viewing to school readiness and vocabulary of children from low-income families: The early window project. *Child Development, 72*(5), 1347–1366.

Zill, N. (2001). Does *Sesame Street* enhance school readiness?: Evidence from a national survey of children. In S. M. Fisch & R. T. Truglio (Eds.), *G is for growing: Thirty years of research on children and Sesame Street* (pp. 115–30). Mahwah, NJ: Erlbaum.

CHAPTER 7

❖

New Perspectives on Literature
for Young Children

DIANE M. BARONE
ANDREA MORENCY

GUIDING QUESTIONS

❖ As you engage with this chapter consider how might you focus children to interpret both the text and visual aspects of picturebooks?

❖ Once you have explored postmodern picturebooks, how will you share their unique characteristics with young students? How will you support students with the ambiguity present in these books?

❖ How might you bring e-books or apps to your class for student use?

OVERVIEW OF THE TOPIC

When most teachers of young children think about children's literature they often focus on picturebooks. Frequently, they share the work of Eric Carle, Bill Martin, or Dr. Seuss with their young students. While these picturebook authors and illustrators are exemplary, the purpose of this chapter is to encourage teachers to branch out and share some of the newer authors and illustrators and to consider the more complex attributes of children's books in both print and electronic formats.

Simultaneously, this chapter nudges teachers to spend as much time with the visual elements of picturebooks as they do with the text, or story line. Serafini (2010) wrote about the two sign systems used in picturebooks—written language and image. He observed that the overreliance of teachers to focus on text limits children's visual development at a time when visual image is dominant in their lives. For instance, teachers frequently conduct picture walks focused on using the illustrations as a guide to the plot of a book where the quality of the illustration or interpretation is never targeted. Further, Kress (2003) identified current shifts in literacy and language as used in communication, describing the increased use of images as children interact with the screen. He also hypothesized that visual images, used in screen reading and communication, are more critical in a young child's literacy learning than alphabetic writing seen in a book. He indicated that the screen would become the principal form of text. Certainly, early informal experiences with print text and the screen structure the basis of knowledge that children rely on as they develop reading skills in more formal contexts (Lave & Wenger, 1991).

Often, teachers expect that the illustrations will be directly connected to text; however, this is not always the reality. For example, Nikolajeva (2005) identified several ways that text and illustrations relate. She observed that the text and illustrations might be symmetrical where the text and illustration are redundant (e.g., *The Dot* by Reynolds, 2003). Illustrations and text can be complementary where each is needed for a full interpretation (e.g., *Thump, Quack, Moo* by Cronin & Lewin, 2008). Illustrations might also enhance a text (e.g., *All God's Critters* by Staines, 2009) or they may tell different stories (e.g., *How to Be a Good Dog* by Page, 2006). Finally, text and illustrations might be contradictory with ambiguity left open to a viewer's interpretation (e.g., *Voices in the Park* by Browne, 1998).

In addition to the relationship between text and image, visual images are important and require interpretation to determine meaning. Most teachers are not very familiar with the visual elements of color, line, shape, texture, or perspective and how they influence a viewer (Sipe, 2008). For instance, diagonal lines usually indicate instability, whereas red might mean danger. Following is a brief overview of the influence of each of these elements:

Color

White backgrounds are safer than dark.
Red is the color of excitement and gains attention.
Black is associated with darkness.
Blue is connected to the sea and sky and is restful.

Line

Wavy lines—movement.
Horizontal lines—peace.
Circular lines—safety.
Thin lines—fragility.
Thick lines—emphasis.

Shape

Horizontal shapes—stability and calmness.
Vertical shapes—active.
Diagonal shapes—motion or tension.

Location of Shape

Upper half—freedom or happiness.
Bottom half—heavier or sadder.
Center—center of attention.

Texture

Allows an image to feel soft, hard, rough, or smooth.

Perspective

Bird's-eye view—looking down on illustration.
Worm's-eye view—looking up at illustration.

Each of these elements contributes to the composition of the image on a page or two-page layout and begs the viewer to use the visual qualities for interpretation (Barone, 2011; Kress & van Leeuwen, 1996; Serafini & Giorgis, 2003). For students, this means that they view the image and determine an interpretation based on its elements. They might say, "I see the black all around the characters and that makes me know they are in trouble." Or they might comment, "I am viewing this image from the back of the boy. I am entering the park with him. I feel like I get to experience it too."

THEORETICAL BASE

Within this section we provide an overview of newer children's literature, both paper and electronic, for teachers to consider. Although we don't address more familiar children's picturebooks, we hope that teachers take time to revisit these books and interpret the visual as well as the textual components to enrich students' understandings and interpretations.

Postmodern Picturebooks

Teachers and students will find postmodern picturebooks a challenge visually and textually. Frequently these books are not structured with a linear plot that encourages a reader/viewer to co-create the plot with the author (Wolfenbarger & Sipe, 2007). For instance, when originally presented with Macaulay's *Black and White* (1990), many teachers did not know how to share it with students. How would they read the four stories, or one story, presented on each page? What was happening? How did they know? Students, on the other hand, enjoyed discovering multiple meanings within the text and illustrations when invited to explore it.

There are several interesting characteristics of postmodern picturebooks. One characteristic is nonlinearity. In other words, a reader/viewer has to participate with the text in a synergistic manner where he or she moves recursively through a picturebook.

> For example, when reading *Piggybook* (Browne, 1986) a student kept returning to previous pages to see the transformation of the family into pigs to better understand how this shift happened and how it contributed to the meaning of the story. On the third reading/viewing, she said, "I get it, they were behaving badly and the mom got upset because she had to do everything so she thought they were pigs. They weren't really turning into pigs. That is what she thought they behaved like. I was surprised it took me so long to see all the clues."

A second characteristic is that postmoderm picturebooks are self-referential. By being self-referential, readers/viewers cannot just enjoy the picturebook; they are positioned to see how the book was constructed or they are asked to join the narrative. For instance, in *Chester's Back* (Watt, 2008), the author and illustrator (Watt) is threatened when Chester takes over these roles. He uses a marker to cross out Watt's name on the cover and rewrites her text throughout the book. Another example is *Do Not Open This Book* (Muntean, 2006), where the main character, a pig, argues with the reader not to open the book because the story is not complete. On each page, the pig accuses the reader of not following his or her directions.

Postmodern picturebooks are sarcastic in a playful manner. An example of a picturebook with a sarcastic tone is *Squids Will Be Squids* (Scieszka & Smith, 1998). The author and illustrator warn that years ago people were not bright and you could gossip about them as long as you changed their names like pig to donkey. In the *Squids* book Scieszka and Smith poke fun at traditional fables and the animals within.

Finally, postmodern picturebooks can be set against authority. For instance, in one of Mo Willems's pigeon books (*Don't Let the Pigeon Drive the Bus*, 2003), the pigeon argues with the reader as to why he or she should let him do something he has been told not to, like drive a bus or stay up late. In this case, the reader is positioned to make the decision for the pigeon, not an in-book character.

These picturebooks require the support of a teacher to facilitate children's understanding. Teachers need to pause and talk directly about what they are experiencing. For instance, "Why is pigeon bothering me?" or "Why didn't pig finish this book before we opened it?" Simultaneously, with discussions centered on key characteristics taking place are those focused on illustration. Illustrations in postmodern picturebooks tend to be as complex as the text and also take discussion and repeated viewings to understand. For example, in *Voices in the Park* (Browne, 1998), just one page can take extensive conversation and viewing to understand. On just one page, Browne uses a pole to separate the wealthy woman from the poorer man. He has Mary Poppins flying and her appearance requires interpretation. He changes seasons depending on the voice (character) and these changes offer room for interpretation.

Postmodern picturebooks offer students opportunities to explore books with multiple interpretations and have multiple paths for reading and viewing. These reading and viewing expectations simulate those of the Internet where readers/viewers access the screen information recursively. Sipe and McGuire (2008) note, "They present challenging and intriguing literary puzzles to solve" (p. 287). Further, students participate actively when interpreting these books and engage in sophisticated conversations as they resolve the tensions created between image and text (Wolfenbarger & Sipe, 2007).

Books Making Connections between Paper and Electronic Media

This category is provocative as authors and illustrators are highlighting the differences between reading a print-based book and anything online. In all cases, the message is that print-based books are important even if they don't tweet. The first book that was obvious in this comparison was *It's a Book* (Smith, 2010). Within this book two characters, one an expert at social networking and new literacies and the other soundly grounded in print, interact to show the uniqueness of print and electronic media. The book is written as a conversation where the tech-smart character asks, "What do you have there?" The other character responds, "It's a book." The tech-savvy character reacts with a list of questions: "How do you scroll down?" "Can you make the characters fight?" or "Can it text?" Smith continued with this topic in a similar board book, *It's a Little Book* (2011), for the youngest readers. The characters in this book are the child versions of the main characters in *It's a Book*. They are now in diapers examining the same topic with similar questions—"What is that?" The young donkey, while holding a laptop, asks if the book can be chewed, worn, or used for e-mailing.

Another book, *Goodnight iPad* (Droyd, 2011), imitates an old favorite, *Goodnight Moon* (Brown, 1991), but replaces each item in the room with electronic media. For example, the children are playing on laptops, viewing YouTube videos, and using smart phones. The text reflects today's technology involvement with quotes like "There were three little Nooks with ten thousand books" or "Goodnight LOLs and goodnight MP3s." The illustrations are changed as well and move the bunny family out of just a bedroom and into their entire home. However, if a viewer looks closely, he or she will notice the moon just outside the window and pages that become darker as the bunnies put away their gear and go to sleep, replicating details from *Goodnight Moon*.

In the book *Blackout* (Rocco, 2011), the author does not directly compare print and technology; rather, he shows what happens after the initial shock to a family experiencing a blackout. They can no longer watch television or communicate through technology. Eventually, they head outside and participate in a block party. When the power returns the family decides they will have family game night so that they are not always glued to electronics. The message in the book is direct, but young children should enjoy discussion surrounding the event. Simultaneous with the story are the illustrations that shift from full color to black and white. The use of light in this book is intriguing and children would want to talk about its effect.

Perhaps the most vivid example to explore in the shift from print to electronic is the YouTube video "A Magazine Is an iPad That Does Not Work" (*www.youtube.com/watch?v=aXV-yaFmQNk*) where a 1-year-old baby showcases how she prefers to interact with an iPad. She uses her fingers to manipulate a magazine but prefers an iPad where her finger touch changes what happens on a screen. While young students may not be the audience for this video, it is helpful to teachers as they see how young children are interacting with technology before traditional, print-based picturebooks.

Related to this video is the book *Press Here* (Tullet, 2011). Although the book does not respond like a touch screen, it appears to. For instance, a child is asked to press on a yellow dot. When the child turns the page, the yellow dot becomes two dots or it becomes part of a group of various colored dots. Each press by a child results in a change on the next page.

Authors and illustrators of books for young children are creating interesting work that acknowledges the quickly changing landscape of young children's books. For some, they are imitating the qualities of touch screens and others are just explicitly highlighting the differences.

E-Books

E-books now include children's picturebooks, older ones as well as newly published ones. Houston (2011) argues, "Children's books in digital format are essential if children's literature is going to remain a popular form of informational and leisure reading for present and future Digital Natives" (p. 39). Important to this genre is that the books include limited special features such as a narrator reading that support young children's interaction with text.

Teachers may be reluctant to use e-books because they still have an emotional attachment to paper and really enjoy turning pages. However, Roxburgh (2012) writes, "The kids learning to read on screens now will be the first generation to slough off the emotional attachment to printed books" (p. 13). Additionally, e-books are cheaper to bring to a classroom than traditional picturebooks.

Many collections of children's books are freely available through digitized libraries. The International Children's Digital Library (*http://en.childrenslibrary.org*) is the most popular. The website is attractive and has books organized by age ranges including 3 to 5. We also liked the categorization of books by short books, medium, or long, award winning, true books, and so on, making it easy for children to select. Books are also from many countries and often are in other languages like Spanish. Another popular website is StoryLine Online (*www.storylineonline.net*), where favorite stories are read by actors. For example, *Harry the Dirty Dog* (Zion, 2006) is read by Betty White.

Many other e-books are available for purchase. For instance, Golden Books, Thomas and Friends, and Sesame Street books are available. Favorites like *Skippyjon Jones* (Schachner, 2012) and *Corduroy* (Freeman, 2011) are easily downloaded. Although most of the current e-books are classics, the Caldecott winner in 2012, *A Ball for Daisy* (Raschka, 2011) is offered as an e-book.

E-books are not just fiction. Many informational books are in e-book format for young readers. Many DK readers that explore topics like earthquakes or volcanoes are available, as are books by Seymour Simon. For many teachers working with young children, they will be pleased that several of Steven Jenkins's books are in e-book format.

A real strength of e-books for teachers is that they can easily share them with a document camera and projector. All students can see the illustrations as the teacher reads the text and chats with students about the text and illustrations. E-books will

most likely replace the current use of big books that were printed in large format so that children could view the text.

App Picturebook Interpretations

Picturebook apps are a fast-growing digital area where some are better for young children than others. Bircher (2012) writes that apps must be interactive but not too much. She believes that there should be an integration of the interactive elements so that they don't disrupt the narrative. Second, all the parts of an app—text, images, music, art—should be easily accessible and enjoyable. Users should be in charge of these elements where they can turn them off or on. Quality apps make use of the "drama of the page turn even without physical pages" (p. 74). For instance, the reader/viewer must swipe the page for the turn. The application must be easy to navigate and offer young children easy-to-follow directions. The app must have a surprise and be an enjoyable experience that children want to repeat. Finally, the app must add to or extend the original book.

An excellent new app is "Freight Train" by Donald Crews. Crews was very involved with the creation of this app throughout the process. Along with the book, he included railroad songs and images from his book *Inside Freight Train* (2001) to enhance a child's experience.

Another app that young children will giggle over is "Don't Let the Pigeon Run This App" by Mo Willems. Participants can respond to queries that the bus driver asks, like "What is your favorite junk food?" "What is your name?" "What is smelly?" and so on. The participant's voice is recorded and these words become part of a pigeon story. Willems teaches children how to draw the pigeon and this artwork is saved and shows up in created stories. Participants can also listen to

stories about the pigeon. This app provides for the youngest users to more sophisticated children.

Other apps recommended for young children include: "A Present for Milo," "The Going to Bed Book," "How Rocket Learned to Read," "Pat the Bunny," "Wild about Books," "When I Grow Up," and "The Three Little Pigs: A 3-D Fairy Tale." Each of these apps fulfills the characteristics described by Bircher (2012). Other apps like "MeeGenius! Kid's Books" offer over 300 children's books that can be read to children and is free to download and "Read Me Stories" offers children's books and is also free. When considering whether to purchase an app for student use, it is important that the features do not detract from the picturebook that is at its core.

Informational Picturebooks

Informational picturebooks are a wonderful addition to a library for young children. Donovan and Smolkin (2002) observed that informational picturebooks enhance content instruction through their content and visual representations. Unfortunately, Colman (2007) noted that there is an absence of informational texts available to young children. She offered several reasons for this observation. First, teachers prefer fiction and thus, select it to use in read-alouds. Second, the terms *informational* or *nonfiction* lead most readers to consider textbooks or encyclopedias, not the full range of informational text that is available. Third, informational books tend to be more expensive to purchase. Finally, she shares myths around informational text that include it is boring and kids will not like it.

There are amazing informational picturebooks available to children, even the youngest ones. There are many board books that target information with a huge focus on animals. For children a bit older, the work of Steven Jenkins is quite remarkable. Most of his books focus on science topics such as the actual size of animals (*Actual Size*, 2004) or a focus on what can happen in a second (*Just a Second*, 2011). His website lets children see how he composes and illustrates his books (*www.stevejenkinsbooks.com*).

Another excellent author/illustrator in science is Seymour Simon. Many of his books target older students but he has a rich library of books for younger ones as well. His website highlights many of his books and he also has children's questions that he has answered (*www.seymoursimon.com*). While many informational books for young children predominantly focus on animals, Simon offers other topics, like the planets and weather events.

Certainly, all informational text is not geared to science. There are wonderful books that explore social studies topics, math, and the arts. Books focused on the social world for the youngest readers center on family where books like Bang's (2006) *In My Heart* is representative. Within this subset focused on families are multicultural books that explore other cultures like *A Night of Tamales and Roses* (Kraus, 2007).

An introductory map book is Fanelli's (1995) *My Map Book*. What is special about this picturebook is that she includes maps of her room, favorite colors, and her neighborhood making the concept of a map resonate with young children. Other picturebooks for young children focus on American heroes like Benjamin Franklin in *A Picture Book of Benjamin Franklin* (Adler, 2009). There are also books for the youngest readers that target serious concepts like racism as seen in *Rosa* (Giovanni, 2005).

There are numerous math picturebooks, many focused on counting. One that is particularly appropriate for young children and more than a counting book is *Tiger Math* (Nagda & Bickel, 2000) where the growth of a tiger is documented in photos, graphs, and charts. Niepold and Verdu have written a series that facilitates children's exposure to great visual artists. In the books *Oooh! Picasso* (2009) and *Oooh! Matisse* (2007) young children can see a Picasso sculpture come to life and explore the paintings of Matisse. A very special book that combines music and art is *Can You Hear It?* (Lach, 2006). Lach has paired paintings and music so that children can interpret art through music and music through art.

What is important for teachers to remember when exploring informational text is not to focus only on text and the information it contains; the visual aspects are equally important. For instance, informational text can include pictures, photos, paintings, sketches, diagrams, figures, legends, maps, and so on. Each element adds to the meaning being shared. Additionally, text in informational picturebooks is not read in a sequential manner, from the top to the bottom of each page. Students might elect to study a photo or a diagram and then move to text, and then recursively, they may move back to the visual source. This reading is similar to what students do when they explore websites that are filled with text and visual elements.

Contemporary picturebooks share new forms and images. There is no doubt that print and electronic forms of children's literature should be available and central to instruction in young children's classrooms. They offer opportunities for imagination and inquiry.

BRINGING CHILDREN'S LITERATURE TO THE CLASSROOM

In this section, we explored the use of postmodern picturebooks, e-books, and informational text with the youngest children both at home and in school. Their interactions with these books allow teachers to see the possibilities of new forms of text and electronic texts.

Postmodern Picturebooks

Young readers need no prompting to respond to postmodern picture books.

A preschool class of 4-year-olds listened to Melanie Watt's *You're Finally Here!* (2011), and responded to the furry protagonist's questions about where the reader has been and if the reader will stay. Similar to other postmodern picturebooks, the character speaks directly to the reader. For instance, the reader is asked, "Do you know how long I have been waiting?" (n.p.). Interestingly, the young listeners in this classroom responded to questions requiring an answer and simply listened when a rhetorical question was asked without cues from their teacher. One child commented that on some pages there was just one picture and on others four small pictures. He interpreted the pages with four images, "I think the author wants to show us a lot of things like how long he waited on this page."

In a first-grade classroom, the teacher read *Voices in the Park* (Browne, 1998) to her students. She began the lesson with a gallery walk of illustrations from the book with text removed. Students moved from illustration to illustration and made predictions and interpretations about what was happening, who was telling each part of the story, and how and what was represented in the illustrations. The teacher then read the book to the students without stopping. After her reading, students discussed what they heard and saw. One student, Micah, asked, "How could a gorilla have a chimpanzee as a baby?" Another student observed, "I think Charles is afraid of the slide. Look at the clouds over his head. The girl is happy and she is in the blue sky." These comments indicate how students were interpreting illustrations and how they contributed meaning to the picturebook.

What was interesting as we listened into these conversations was how students were willing to explore the ambiguity in the text and illustrations. They constantly asked the teacher to go back and forth between pages so they could clear up questions. For instance, Lauren wanted to view the changes in seasons and if they went with different characters. In small groups, students extended their reflections and further explored the book and had conversations about what choices the author/illustrator made to tell the story from four different perspectives. They found examples in the book that showcased each voice and each voice's identity. For instance, one student noted the change in fonts and how the fancy font represented the rich mother. Once this more formal exploration of *Voices* (Browne, 1998) was complete, children returned to view it in the library center where they often conversed about it to further their understandings.

E-Books

Our first examples share e-books in children's homes, where they are most often accessible, and then we move to their use in preschool classrooms. Our first example comes from Courtland's home during his getting-ready-for-bed routine.

Courtland, age 3, was asked to get a book that he would listen to as his mother read. He returned with his family's laptop. His mother responded, "No, a book," and he just looked at her, confused. Upon repeating herself, he responded, "Mom, there are lots of books for me to read on my computer." It had never occurred to his mother that the laptop served as a vehicle for story reading, but to him this made sense. He did not differentiate between reading a print-based book or an electronic one. Once the confusion over the type of book was solved, they settled in to reading an e-book he selected from his collection.

In another home, Easton, age 2, engaged in a reading task independently because of his familiarity with technology, the intuitiveness of it, and easy access to it. He retrieved the family iPad, unlocked the screen, called up his apps folder, selected a book, and had the iPad recite the text to him as he "turned" the pages—all without any adult assistance. For this reading, he chose *Dr. Seuss's ABC* (Dr. Seuss, 2010) and following the reading he represented his ideas about letters in a drawing as shown in Figure 7.1. His drawing showed how he was internalizing the letters and letter-like forms that he experienced with this book and other letter activities. Clearly, his focus was on learning about letters.

Moving from home to school, a preschool teacher of 4-year-olds was working one-on-one and in small groups introducing e-books to her students. Some students had obvious exposure to such technology as they easily navigated the device, while others needed some assistance to start. However, by the end of instruction, all students accessed the books, and started the narration independently, showcasing how easy it was for young children to interact with electronic books.

Eleanor, a child in this room, especially enjoyed reading the electronic version of Judy Schachner's *Skippyjon Jones* (2012). She was familiar with the print version of the book, and said it was one of her favorites. While interacting with the e-book, Eleanor compared and contrasted the electronic and print versions. She explored features, such as the tap technology and animated illustrations and said, " Wow,

FIGURE 7.1. Easton's writing.

look at this. I can make them dance. I can't do that in the book." She was especially intrigued with the narration, and how the narrator pronounced the Spanish and Spanglish words compared to her mother's pronunciation. Further, she reported, "I know how to read on this thing. My mom lets me read on her Kindle Fire." For Eleanor, reading an e-book in school was a natural connection between her at-home and in-school reading.

Informational Text

Similar to fiction, young children can read or recite favorite informational text.

> Noah read *The Ladybug and Other Insects* (de Bourgoing, Jeunesse, & Perois, 1991) by recalling facts from the book. He said, "The lady bug has six legs" while pointing to text that read, "Like all insects, the ladybug has six legs." Through informational text, Noah was becoming a reader who knows about the world around him. When observing him in the classroom library, he gravitated to books and magazines about animals or insects.

In our visits to preschool we saw interesting uses of informational text as teachers were grouping informational text sets to explore with children.

> Miss Kitt taught a unit on gardening and plant life with her 2- and 3-year-old class. She integrated several informational books that she connected with language experience activities where children dictated their thoughts about the topic. She read a multitude of books aloud repeatedly throughout her unit of study. Rather than reading a whole book in its entirety, Miss Kitt broke longer text, such as *From Seed to Plant* (Fowler, 2001), into shorter sections. She was aware that just reading a book from cover to cover would be too much for her students to take in at one time. Additionally, she wanted to model that it was OK to read informational text in parts or to focus on one image and neglect the longer text feature during a single reading.

> In a 4-year-old preschool class, we saw Miss Massey engage her students in an exploration of community helpers. She began her unit with *Whose Hat Is This?* (Cooper, 2007) and then continued with other books in this series of informational books. In *Whose Hat Is This?* (Cooper, 2007), she brought children's attention to the colorful illustrations used by the author and illustrator to introduce community helpers through the hats they wear. Through the read-aloud, she provided key vocabulary and shared familiar examples of community helpers to build students' knowledge. She shared each book in this series so that children were comfortable with the format and could concentrate on the topic of community helpers.
> The teacher added to this series by having books related in topic available to students in different centers around the room. Students interacted with the books, both print and electronic, while dressing up in community workers' costumes in

the play center. Miss Massey also used the informational read-aloud book as a mentor text for writing activities. For example, each child followed the pattern of *Whose Hat Is This?* (Cooper, 2007) when contributing pages to a class-made book about community workers.

CONCLUSION

While teachers may be reluctant in moving away from a reliance on narrative print media, young children are already comfortable shifting between print and electronic media. For instance, 70% of 4- to 6-year-olds have used a computer (Rideout, Vandewater, & Wartella, 2003). Moreover, 64% of 3- to 5-year-olds can use a mouse, 56% can use a computer independently, and 37% are competent at turning a computer on, all alone (Glaubke, 2007). Preschoolers are also using the Internet as 25% of 3-year-olds and 50% of 5-year-olds went online at home (National Center for Education Statistics, 2005). This data documents computer and Internet use of preschoolers, but did not report on the use of iPads or smart phones. It is easy to predict that young children are fully enamored with these technology innovations and engage with them on a routine basis either with their parents or independently. With the quickly moving advances in e-books and applications, we recommend that teachers bring these new forms of reading into their classrooms while balancing them with more traditional print-based books. This balance will allow teachers to continue with what is familiar as they adjust to the demands of electronic media.

In addition to electronic book forms, we recommend that teachers enjoy with their students the complexity of postmodern picturebooks where multiple interpretations are the norm. Further, teachers of young children might also reflect on their use of informational text with their students and seek a balance between fiction and informational text. Young children, as shown in our examples, love learning facts about all kinds of topics.

The importance of the genres and book forms that we highlighted in this chapter open up possibilities by describing the shifts in children's literature available to young children. Clearly, e-books and apps containing both fiction and informational text will gain in popularity as young children so readily engage with them and as teachers embrace them in their classrooms.

REFERENCES

Adler, D. (2009). *A picture book of Benjamin Franklin*. New York: Holiday House.
Bang, M. (2006). *In my heart*. New York: Little, Brown Young Readers.
Barone, D. (2011). *Children's literature in the classroom*. New York: Guilford Press.

Bircher, K. (2012). What makes a good picture book app? *Horn Book Magazine, LXXXVII*(2), 71–78.

Brown, M. (1991). *Goodnight moon.* New York: HarperFestival.

Browne, A. (1986). *Piggybook.* New York: Knopf.

Browne, A. (1998). *Voices in the park.* New York: DK Publishing.

Colman, P. (2007). A new way to look at literature: A visual model for analyzing fiction and nonfiction texts. *Language Arts, 84,* 251–268.

Cooper, S. (2007). *Whose hat is this?* New York: Picture Window Books.

Crews, D. (2001). *Inside freight train.* New York: HarperFestival.

Cronin, D., & Lewin, B. (2008). *Thump, quack, moo: A whacky adventure.* New York: Atheneum Books for Young Readers.

de Bourgoing, P., Jeunesse, G., & Perois, S. (1991). *The ladybug and other insects.* New York: Scholastic.

Donovan, C., & Smolkin, L. (2002). Considering genre, content, and visual features in the selection of trade books for science instruction. *The Reading Teacher, 55,* 501–520.

Dr. Seuss. (2010). *Dr. Seuss's ABC ebook.* San Diego, CA: Oceanhouse Media and Dr. Seuss Enterprises, LP.

Droyd, A. (2011). *Goodnight iPad.* New York: Blue Rider Press.

Fanelli, S. (1995). *My map book.* New York: HarperCollins.

Fowler, A. (2001). *From seed to plant.* New York: Children's Press.

Freeman, D. (2011). *Corduroy.* New York: Penguin.

Giovanni, N. (2005). *Rosa.* New York: Holt.

Glaubke, C. (2007). *The effects of interactive media and preschoolers' learning: A review of the research and recommendations for the future.* Oakland, CA: Children Now.

Houston, C. (2011). Digital books for digital natives. *Children and Libraries, 9*(3), 31–42.

Jenkins, S. (2004). *Actual size.* Boston: Houghton Mifflin.

Jenkins, S. (2011). *Just a second.* Boston: Houghton Mifflin.

Kraus, J. (2007). *A night of tamales and roses.* Summit, NJ: Shenanigan Books.

Kress, G. (2003). *Literacy in the new media age.* London: Routledge.

Kress, G., & van Leeuwen, T. (1996). *Reading images: The grammar of visual design.* London: Routledge.

Lach, W. (2006). *Can you hear it?* London: Abrams Books for Young Readers.

Lave, J., & Wenger, E. (1991). *Situated learning: Legitimate peripheral participation.* Cambridge, UK: Cambridge University Press.

Macaulay, D. (1990). *Black and white.* Boston: Houghton Mifflin.

Muntean, M. (2006). *Do not open this book.* New York: Scholastic.

Nagda, A., & Bickel, C. (2000). *Tiger math.* New York: Holt.

National Center for Education Statistics. (2005). *Rates of computer and Internet use by children in nursery school and students in kindergarten through twelfth grade: 2003.* Available at *http://nces.ed.gob/pubsearch/pubsinfo.asp?pubid=2005111rev.*

Niepold, M., & Verdu, J. (2007). *Oooh! Matisse.* Berkeley, CA: Tricycle Press.

Niepold, M., & Verdu, J. (2009). *Oooh! Picasso.* Berkeley, CA: Tricycle Press.

Nikolajeva, M. (2005). *Aesthetic approaches to children's literature: An introduction.* Lanham, MD: Scarecrow Press.

Page, G. (2006). *How to be a good dog*. New York: Bloomsbury Children's Books.

Raschka, C. (2011). *A ball for Daisy*. New York: Schwartz and Wade.

Reynolds, P. (2003). *The dot*. Cambridge, MA: Candlewick Press.

Rideout, V., Vandewater, E., & Wartella, E. (2003). *Zero to six: Electronic media in the lives of infants, toddlers and preschoolers*. Menlo Park, CA: Kaiser Family Foundation.

Rocco, J. (2011). *Blackout*. New York: Hyperion.

Roxburgh, S. (2012). The e-future. *Horn Book Magazine, LXXXVII*(2), 11–21.

Schachner, J. (2012). *SkippyJon Jones ebook*. New York: Dutton.

Scieszka, J., & Smith, L. (1998). *Squids will be squids*. New York: Scholastic.

Serafini, F. (2010). Reading multimodal texts: Perceptual, structural, and ideological perspectives. *Children's Literature in Education, 41*, 81–104.

Serafini, F., & Giorgis, C. (2003). *Reading aloud and beyond: Fostering the intellectual life with older readers*. Portsmouth, NH: Heinemann.

Sipe, L. (2008). Young children's visual meaning making in response to picturebooks. In J. Flood, S. B. Heath, & D. Lapp (Eds.), *Handbook of research on teaching literacy through the communicative and visual arts* (Vol. 2, pp. 381–391). New York: Erlbaum.

Sipe, L., & McGuire, C. (2008). The Stinky Cheese Man and other fairly postmodern picture nooks for children. In S. Lehr (Ed.), *Shattering the looking glass: Challenge, risk and controversy in children's literature* (pp. 271–288). Norwood, MA: Christopher-Gordon.

Smith, L. (2010). *It's a book*. New York: Roaring Brook Press.

Smith, L. (2011). *It's a little book*. New York: Roaring Brook Press.

Staines, B. (2009). *All god's critters*. New York: Simon & Schuster.

Tullet, H. (2011). *Press here*. San Francisco: Chronicle Books.

Watt, M. (2008). *Chester's back*. Toronto: Kids Can Press.

Watt, M. (2011). *You're finally here!* New York: Hyperion.

Willems, M. (2003). *Don't let the pigeon drive the bus*. New York: Hyperion.

Wolfenbarger, C., & Sipe, L. (2007). A unique visual and literary art form: Recent research on picturebooks. *Language Arts, 84*, 271–280.

Zion, G. (2006). *Harry the dirty dog*. New York: Harper.

CHAPTER 8

❖

Read All About I.T.!

INFORMATIONAL TEXT
IN THE EARLY CHILDHOOD CLASSROOM

Lynne M. Watanabe
Nell K. Duke

It's free-choice time in Ms. W's kindergarten class, and a large group of children are huddled together at the center of the classroom carpet. There are "oohs" and "aahs" coming from the boys and girls. They are laughing, talking, and looking at something together. There are other groups scattered in different areas of the classroom. A few are playing with blocks and other toys, but a scan around the room helps you to see that most children are looking at books—animal books. There are books about sharks and bugs, books about deep sea fish, and books about spiders. The kindergarteners are choosing to read these information books over other texts and activities. In fact, as children finished their assigned work they had raced to choose the information book they wanted to read first.

Recently, there has been a lot of talk about informational text in conjunction with literacy learning and instruction. However, this brings up major questions about whether, why and how informational text can and should be used in the early childhood classroom. This chapter sets out to address this topic with the following guiding questions:

GUIDING QUESTIONS

❖ Why use informational text in the early childhood (birth to 8) classroom?

❖ How can we use informational text in the early childhood (birth to 8) classroom?

This chapter includes an overview of informational text and its use for young children, a discussion of the research base in this area, and strategies for bringing this knowledge to the early literacy classroom.

OVERVIEW OF INFORMATIONAL TEXT

The term *informational text* has been used with various definitions and understandings throughout the years. The Common Core State Standards or CCSS (National Governors Association [NGA] & Council of Chief State School Officers [CCSSO], 2010) divide texts into two broad categories: literary and informational. Informational texts listed for K–5 are "biographies and autobiographies; books about history, social studies, science, and the arts; technical texts, including directions, forms, and information displayed in graphs, charts, or maps; and digital sources on a range of topics" (p. 31). Literature for K–5 includes a variety of types of stories, drama, and poetry (p. 31). According to the National Assessment of Educational Progress (NAEP) Framework (National Assessment Governing Board, 2009), invoked by the CCSS (p. 5), the ratio of informational to literary text should increase as children progress through schooling (see Table 8.1). That said, even "In K–5, the Standards follow NAEP's lead in balancing the reading of literature with the reading of informational texts" (p. 5), and the CCSS include a number of standards for even kindergarten-age children.

In the past, we have defined informational text more narrowly than the CCSS (NGA & CCSSO, 2010) and NAEP Framework (2009) suggest. We have conceptualized informational text (which we will call "informative/explanatory" for the remainder of this chapter to distinguish it from informational text in the broader usage of the CCSS) as text that has as a primary purpose conveying information about the natural and social world that includes specific features to accomplish that

TABLE 8.1. Distribution of Passages from the 2009 NAEP Framework

Grade level	Literary	Informational
4	50%	50%
8	45%	55%
12	30%	70%

Note. Figures from the National Assessment Governing Board (2008).

purpose (e.g., Duke, 2000). We view it as distinct from other text types such as procedural texts—texts that have as a primary purpose teaching someone how to do something (Purcell-Gates, Duke, & Martineau, 2007) and persuasive text—texts that strive to influence or convince someone to change his or her ideas or behavior (e.g., Duke, Caughlan, Juzwik, & Martin, 2012). We believe that these distinctions are important because different text purposes are associated with different text features, which provide different opportunities and challenges for readers and writers. For example, while informative/explanatory text requires use of timeless verbs (e.g., Polar bears *live* in cold climates, insects *have* six legs), procedural text requires the use of imperative verbs (e.g., *Measure* the water . . . *Wait* three minutes . . .); with persuasive text, the reader works to identify the claim(s) and weigh the evidence in support of them; with procedural text, the reader is not looking for a claim or evidence but rather for materials needed and steps to follow. Indeed, a recent study found that even second graders engage in different processes when reading procedural than other forms of text (Martin, 2011). For some of the features of informative/explanatory, procedural, and persuasive text, see Table 8.2.

In the remainder of this chapter, we include all of these different kinds of text, using the term *informational text* in the broader manner consistent with the CCSS (NGA & CCSSO, 2010).

TABLE 8.2. Some of the Features of Informative/Explanatory, Procedural, and Persuasive Texts

Informative/explanatory	Procedural	Persuasive
• "Opening statement or general classification" • "Description of attributes or components of the subject" • "Frequent repetition of the topic of the text" • "Generic noun constructions and timeless verb constructions" • "Denotative rather than connotative language" • "Definitions in running text and/or glossary" • "Realistic illustrations or photographs" • "Labels and/or captions" • "Boldfaced and italicized vocabulary" • "Headings/subheadings" (pp. 93–94)	• "A statement of goal and/or inquiry question" • "A materials section" • "Methods/procedures/steps" • "Letters or numbers to indicate the order of the steps" • "An explicit, clear description of materials" • "Imperative verbs" • "Units of measure" • "Graphics, and the graphics are almost always demonstrative" • "A graphic of the end product" • "Headings/subcategories" • "Materials [listed] in order of use" (p. 68)	• "Compelling opening (can include prose, graphics, or music)" • "Claim: any argument makes a claim—a statement that is supported by data and evidence" • "Evidence: everything that supports the claim" • "Warrants: how the evidence is linked to the claim" • "Appeals: tools used to get a particular audience on your side" • "Counterarguments or rebuttals: acknowledgments of possible protests or doubts regarding the claim that might be expressed" (p. 149)

Note. Based on Duke, Caughlan, Juzwik, and Martin (2012).

THE RESEARCH BASE

Research has shown that there has been and continues to be limited use of informational text in early childhood classrooms (Jeong, Gaffney, & Choi, 2010; Pentimonti, Zucker, Justice, & Kaderavek, 2010; Wright, 2011), and this includes the informational text that is displayed, included in classroom libraries, and used in written language activities. Further, children of low socioeconomic status receive even less exposure to and experience with informational text (Duke, 2000). Narrative text has been seen by many to be more appropriate and natural for young children, but research has found that young children can learn from, produce, and discuss informational text (e.g., Duke & Kays, 1998; Maduram, 2000; Oyler & Barry, 1996; Pappas, 1993; Strachan, 2012; Tower, 2002). As referred to above, the CCSS (NGA & CCSSO, 2010) makes a call for "a significant amount of reading of informational texts [to] take place in and outside of the ELA classroom" (p. 5). The CCSS explain that this is because the ability to read and write informational text is a major component of college and career readiness. They contend that not only should the amount of informational text reading be considerable (again, see Table 8.1) but so too should the amount of informational text writing (see Table 8.3 for the distribution invoked by the CCSS). Therefore, it is critical that informational texts have a major presence in the texts that we read, discuss, teach, and write with all age groups and at all levels.

Studies suggest various potential benefits for young children engaged in the reading and writing of informational text, including but not limited to (1) connecting to their interests—some children prefer informational text over other genres, (2) increasing their content knowledge, and (3) developing their language knowledge.

Children's Interest in Informational Text

As suggested by the example at the beginning of this chapter, many children have been found to prefer informational text to other genres (e.g., Chapman, Filipenko, McTavish, & Shapiro, 2007; Mohr, 2006). The majority of the first-grade boys and

TABLE 8.3. Distribution of Communicative Purposes from the 2011 NAEP Writing Framework

Grade level	Persuasion	Explanation	Conveying experience
4	30%	35%	35%
8	35%	35%	30%
12	40%	40%	20%

Note. Figures from National Assessment Governing Board (2007).

girls within one study were found to prefer informational text (Mohr, 2006). The Chapman et al. (2007) study also found that young girls and boys preferred informational texts. However, an interesting finding in this study was that both boys and girls had the perception that boys would prefer informational text and girls would prefer narrative text, even though gender differences were not actually found. When we include informational text in the early childhood classroom, we address the preferences of some children, and can address topics that even children who prefer literary text may find engaging (think, e.g., animals, sports, crafts). We may also better engage children whose opportunities to engage with informational text are so limited that they do not yet even know they prefer it.

Increasing Content Knowledge with Informational Text

Nell and colleague Anne-Lise Halvorsen share anecdotes about their young children:

> Two-year-old Spencer [Anne-Lise's son] announces that Jackie Robinson played baseball a long time ago and that at that time "black people had to sit in the back of the bus."
>
> Five-year-old Cooper [Nell's son] explains, "[Sharks] like the smell of blood. To try to get away from a shark you should punch it in the nose, eyes, gills, or maybe even fin. Hammerheads are less likely to attack you than tigers, bulls, and great whites." (Duke, Halvorsen, & Knight, 2012, p. 205)

This content knowledge did not come from personal experience (thank goodness!) but rather from being read informational texts. Fingeret (2008) found that kindergarten children's content knowledge increased after viewing and engaging in activities related to an informational documentary film. Children were able to internalize a great deal of content and talk about this content to demonstrate their understanding. Strachan (2012) found that kindergarten children made statistically significant gains in social studies content knowledge after interactive read-alouds of a set of five books on common early childhood social studies topics.

Increasing Language Knowledge with Informational Text

Children have also been found to make language gains from interactions with informational text. After hearing information books read aloud, kindergarteners included more language features and vocabulary that were specific to and appropriate for informational text (e.g., Duke & Kays, 1998; Pappas, 1993). For example, after 25 information books were read aloud to them, when pretending to read an informational text children included more key features of information book language including timeless verbs, generic nouns, repetition of the topic, book openings typical of informative/explanatory text, classificatory structures, and compare/contrast structures.

Informational Text Instruction

A research base of promising ways to use informational text with young children is developing as a result of the work described above, as well as the work of many others. Work has been done to emphasize comprehension instruction (e.g., Reutzel, Smith, & Fawson, 2005; Santoro, Chard, Howard, & Baker, 2008; Williams et al., 2007) and writing (e.g., Chapman, 1995; Kamberelis, 1999) of informational texts. For example, one promising method for informational text comprehension instruction involves enhancing the experience of reading an information book aloud by incorporating vocabulary instruction, text structure instruction, and instruction in comprehension strategies (Santoro et al., 2008). Researchers included both informational and narrative texts, and first graders participated in activities before, during, and after reading to promote comprehension. For the information books, children charted out what they initially knew and questions they had regarding the topic. Then, they listened to the book and participated in retelling the information using fact sheets and illustrations of the topic in small groups. Finally, children participated in a teacher-guided summary of the information. The read-aloud was a setting to employ comprehension strategies, attend to text structure, and develop vocabulary, and the first graders were able to make gains in comprehension and vocabulary from it.

Another study examined second and third graders' reading and writing of both informational and procedural texts (Purcell-Gates et al., 2007). This analysis found that children showed greater growth when their teachers engaged them in reading and writing more real-world informational texts for more real-world purposes (rather than simply to satisfy a teacher's assignment). These results did not differ by contextual factors such as parental education. Thus, other important factors to consider while engaging children in reading and writing informational texts are children's purpose for reading and their purpose and audience for writing. This study also involved a discourse analysis to identify common characteristics of informational and procedural texts appropriate for second- and third-grade children in science. This work has been used to inform other investigations. For example, Watanabe (2013) asked preschoolers to read and write procedural texts for a specific purpose and audience before and after a unit focused on the reading and writing of such texts. The preschoolers were found to include key procedural text features identified by Purcell-Gates et al. in their pretend reading and writing samples.

The fact that instruction can enhance young children's informational text knowledge provides further evidence of its appropriateness for young children. Further, as mentioned earlier, the CCSS (NGA & CCSSO, 2010) make a compelling call for incorporating informational text into literacy instruction early on. Informational texts are texts that children use to learn and convey content as they progress through school. They are also texts that are frequently encountered and used by adults. There are good reasons to incorporate informational text into the early childhood classroom.

BRINGING THIS KNOWLEDGE
TO THE EARLY LITERACY CLASSROOM

The following are examples of how informational text can be used in the early childhood classroom. The examples specify a grade level and/or age, but they can easily be modified for implementation in most other early childhood settings. Examples include a variety of different types of informational text, though we ask you to bear in mind our earlier discussion that there are important differences among different types of informational text.

Signs, Labels, and Captions: Green-Haired Gus Caption

Signs and labels are often part of the first writing done in early childhood. Children can participate in interactive or shared writing activities to create signs and labels for areas or items in the classroom. For example, they might label bins to indicate where things go, label shelves, bins, or baskets of books by categories, or post signs to remind one another about appropriate behaviors (e.g., "Don't forget to sit with pretzel legs!"). Children can create and post diagrams (which show the parts of a whole, typically with labels) related to topics they are studying, such as insects or weather. Captions offer another form of labeling in the classroom. Children can create captions for photographs, drawings, or other artifacts. For example, preschoolers created their own "Green-Haired Gus" plants using grass seeds, soil, and nylons. Children tracked the growth of the plants over time and made observational drawings. They also took pictures and displayed the plants as part of a party held celebrating what they had learned about and done related to plants over the course of the unit. Another class was invited to attend and pictures were compiled to record the event and share it with family members and others. These pictures could easily be added to a newsletter or website to demonstrate the success of "Green-Haired Gus" and children could work together to generate captions for each drawing they made and picture they took (see Figure 8.1).

Green-Haired Guses need water and sunlight to grow.

FIGURE 8.1. Green-Haired Gus photograph and caption.

Brochures: All about Our Classroom

Brochures are concise, selectively highlighting information in a particular way and for a specific purpose. This may involve strategies such as summarization, conservation, and sometimes, persuasion. Children can use the knowledge they have gained about their classroom, in which they are active participants, to create brochures about their classroom. Children use their expertise about the classroom and communicate it to an audience that is unfamiliar with the topic. For example, the brochures could be used when a new student moves in and for the Open House or Back-to-School Night. They could also be written for the children coming into the class next year. How fun would it be for incoming students to receive that in the mail during the summer before they start school?

Children can look at examples of brochures and discuss what they like and dislike about the examples. Then, they can work together (or in small groups or individually) to create a single brochure or set of brochures (e.g., *All about Mr. B's Classroom*; *The Marvelous Math of Room 109*). Brochures might address the classroom curriculum, schedule and routines, layout, expectations, the teacher and class members, and key achievements. They can also address the school as a whole, depending on the children's engagement and the time available.

Generating captions for photographs and illustrations is likely to support children's developing understanding of informational text. Graphics play an important role in conveying information about the natural and social world, demonstrating steps in a procedure, or influencing thoughts or emotions in a persuasive text. Captions can be provided on paper or in digital contexts such as on a class blog or website.

How-To Texts: How to Wash Your Hands

Procedural or how-to texts can be fun to read and write and are commonly encountered outside of school. They are one way to bridge school and home contexts. With children, determine a real purpose for reading or writing a how-to text. Be sure that the purpose for reading involves learning how to do something you want or need to know how to do; be sure that the purpose for writing involves teaching people how to do something that they want or need to know how to do. For example, children might be interested in reading directions for how to play a new playground game or writing directions for how to use a new app many children want to learn to use. Have children create texts by paying attention to the features and characteristics of procedural texts (e.g., a materials section, steps). This is even possible for very young children. In this example, a 4-year-old preschooler created a procedural text to tell another preschooler in a different classroom how to wash his hands (see Figure 8.2). It was important to make sure that the topic was something the child knew how to do (wash her hands) and that the text was for an actual audience that might benefit from the text (a younger preschooler).

Informative/Explanatory Books: Books for Friends and Younger Buddies

You may already engage children in writing information books—either as a class or in small groups or individually—on topics that they have studied in your classroom.

FIGURE 8.2. A preschooler's procedure text on how to wash your hands

However, a twist on this concept is to present children with the real problem of finding information books on certain topics that are of interest to younger children or peers in the school. Maybe there is a kindergarten class that is really interested in planets. Finding a quality information book on the topic and at an appropriate reading level can be difficult. Your second graders can work together to study planets and create a text or texts on this topic for the kindergarteners. Among other things, this requires pulling together what they have learned and thinking through how best to present this information. Your students may not realize how much they are talking about and considering the content and features of information books, and the kindergarteners will benefit from an age-appropriate text on a high-interest topic.

Informative/Explanatory Articles: Improve-a-Text

Often informational texts could convey information more accurately or effectively. It can be quite empowering to young children to recognize these limitations in texts authored by adults and to address them in some way. Duke, Halladay, and Roberts (2013) describe a strategy in which children are engaged in improving an informational text, for example, by adding a table of contents, index, or glossary to a book when that feature would help more effectively convey information. This strategy can be used not only with books but also with articles, as in magazines that may be delivered regularly to your classroom. For example, children may identify a word or concept in an article that would benefit from explanation (see Figure 8.3) or children may create a diagram or other graphic that would improve understanding of an article they read (see Figure 8.4). Online articles can also provide material for a variation of this technique as, unfortunately, many such articles contain errors (Zhang & Duke, 2011). Children might work with you to compose an e-mail to the author of the site correcting the information.

Travel Log: Learning about Others' Adventures

An informational genre (in CCSS nomenclature, perhaps literary by NAEP's definition) one of us (Lynne Watanabe) used in her kindergarten classroom was a travel log. Sometimes parents would tell her that they were going on a trip and their child was going to be gone for a period of time. Lynne wanted students to continue reading and writing on their trip in a way that was fun and easy for parents to support while traveling. She created a travel log for the child by putting together pieces of blank paper with a construction paper cover (see similar log in Figure 8.5). The child was to write about places visited on his or her trip using pictures and words. Lynne told the children to write about where they went (where it was, what it was like, why they went), and she stressed that this was going to be shared with the classmates

Meet the Marine Iguana

By Sherry Shahan

Marine is stay in water

Halfway between the North and South Poles live lizards that eat only from the sea.

Galápagos Islands

North America

South America

Pacific Ocean

Off the coast of South America, there is a group of islands called the Galápagos. These islands are home to animals that don't live anywhere else in the world. One of those animals is the marine iguana.

FIGURE 8.3. A child's explanation of a term in an article. Copyright © Highlights for Children, Inc., Columbus, Ohio. All rights reserved. Reprinted by permission.

who did not go on the trip. Therefore, children had to write to an audience that was familiar to them but unfamiliar with the location and activities. When the children came back, Lynne gave them a few minutes to share their travel log with the class. This provided opportunities to provide geographical and cultural descriptions, and it elicited a question-and-answer discussion among the kindergarteners. Lynne also maintained logs over school breaks and at other times during the year.

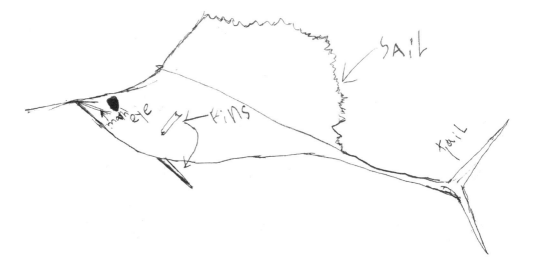

FIGURE 8.4. A child's graphical addition to an article that didn't include a diagram.

FIGURE 8.5. Travel log.

Lists: Writing Center Materials List

Many people, especially teachers, use lists in their everyday lives. Children can create and use lists within the classroom for real purposes. Whether it is a list of the books in the library, books read by the class, the day's events, or materials in a certain center, lists can be used to help children, as adults, to keep track of important information and to understand the value of this concise genre. For example, materials lists for each center area help children to know what is available, and what might be needed in the specific center. If children help to compose the materials lists, they will know what is there and what they might want that is within the center. This process helps with categorization and comparing–contrasting materials. Additionally, lists can help in cleaning up and organizing the center. In this example (see Figure 8.6), the materials included at the writing center at the beginning of the year were listed as a group writing activity. The list was typed up and added to the center. However, additional items were added during the year, and these items were then added to the list as part of another shared writing activity. Children saw the need for keeping the additional items in stock at the center and suggested adding them to the list to be sure that it was up to date. They understood the purpose of the list and they were using it for that intended purpose.

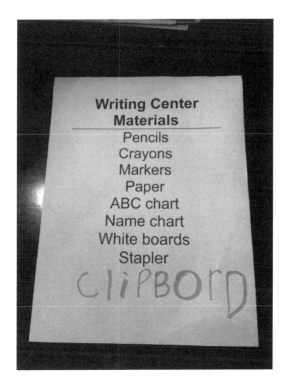

FIGURE 8.6. Writing center materials list.

Clues: Surprise Sack

Young children love games that involve clues and guessing. Many games from a variety of disciplines use clues as children participate. I Spy games and Twenty Questions are prime examples of these. Clues help children to pay attention to central and distinguishing features. They can also lead to concepts such as categorization and compare–contrast. They promote descriptive vocabulary and other language features generally attributed to informational texts such as timeless verbs and generic noun constructions (e.g., It eats aphids). One game that effectively uses clues with 5- and 6-year-olds is called Surprise Sack. Children find an item from home or school and put it in a sack of some sort. Then, they write three clues to help their classmates guess what the item is (see Figures 8.7 and 8.8). The child reads the first clue and picks a classmate to try to guess what the item is. The child then reads the second clue, selects someone for a second guess, and finally reads the third clue. If classmates guess the item, the item is pulled out of the sack and the remaining clues (if any) are shared.

Reviews/Testimonials: Book Reviews

Reviews and testimonials involve communicating your perspective in an effort to persuade someone toward certain thoughts or actions. The world uses more and more reviews and testimonials with the help of technology (e.g., book reviews on *Amazon.com*). Reviews and testimonials are texts that we encounter every day— think, for example, about how many reviews you use as an adult before you buy something, go somewhere, or eat something. Review and testimonials are an

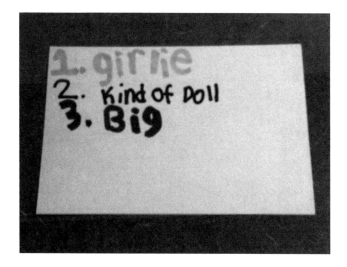

FIGURE 8.7. Three clues written to help classmates guess the doll inside the Surprise Sack.

FIGURE 8.8. Surprise Sack showing the doll inside.

age-appropriate means of using and creating persuasive texts in the early childhood classroom. Producing their own reviews and testimonials may not only support children's informational writing development but also help children become more critical consumers of them. Begin by engaging children in exploring book reviews and testimonials. They can be found on the back of books in your classroom, on websites, in advertisements, and perhaps from others in the school community (e.g., a librarian's testimonial about a new book in the library). After reading and talking about these reviews, have children produce their own reviews of a book that the children in your classroom feel passionate about (either positively or negatively) as a class, in small groups, and individually. They can be video based (as, for example, used to appear on the *Reading Rainbow* program) or written. Stress the use of evidence to support any claims. You can bring in vocabulary and concepts related to rating and evaluating quality as well.

Case Example: Wendy's Preschool Classroom

Wendy teaches preschool in a program for 4-year-olds that targets at-risk children within an urban school district. Generally, her students come to school with limited literacy knowledge and skills. The curriculum she began implementing over the school year integrates literacy, mathematics, science, and socioemotional domains (Clements, Sarama, Hemmeter, Brenneman, & Duke, 2012). Each unit involves a culminating project incorporating knowledge and skills from all four domains. Children engage in activities throughout the unit that promote learning and contribute to the culminating project and beyond.

One particular unit involves reading and writing informational texts to learn about the local environment and to compare it to a less familiar environment, a coral reef. The culminating project of this unit is to organize and implement a scavenger hunt for families and friends. During the course of the unit, children participate in read-alouds of information books emphasizing what an environment is, what it contains, and how to appreciate and take care of an environment. They make predictions and connect the information to their own experiences. They practice asking and answering questions about the environment so they can field these questions during the scavenger hunt. The children participate in small-group experiences and lessons that build on what they have read by using "hands-on" activities and creating representations of their learning (e.g., a 3D coral reef mural, writing about a nature walk). Then, the children write signs and clues during interactive writing sessions to be used for the scavenger hunt for family and friends. They consider content, their purpose, and their audience. They consult books that they have read to come up with clues that will help their audience to be successful in the scavenger hunt. Wendy's preschoolers are using informational texts every day. They are reading, writing, and talking about these texts in a variety of ways and across domains. Reading and writing informational texts for real-world purposes is emphasized, and children are learning about informational texts as they increase their content knowledge.

CONCLUSION

In this chapter, we shared a wide range of reasons to engage children in reading and writing informational text in early childhood—from meeting the expectations of standards and assessments to developing children's language and content knowledge to addressing the interests of children who prefer this type of text or are engaged by topics addressed in it. We reviewed some research suggesting how we might teach informational reading and writing with young children, and offered many suggestions for incorporating informational reading and writing into the early childhood classroom. We hope you will continue for years to come "Read All About I.T.!"

REFERENCES

Chapman, M., Filipenko, M., McTavish, M., & Shapiro, J. (2007). First graders' preferences for narrative and/or information books and perceptions of other boys' and girls' book preferences. *Canadian Journal of Education, 30*(2), 531–553.

Chapman, M. L. (1995). The sociocognitive construction of written genres in first grade. *Research in the Teaching of English, 29*, 164–192.

Clements, D. H., Sarama, J., Hemmeter, M. L., Brenneman, K., & Duke, N. K. (2012, April). *Connect4Learning: Early childhood education in the context of mathematics, science, literacy, and social-emotional development.* Paper presented at the annual meeting of the American Educational Research Association, Vancouver, BC, Canada.

Duke, N. K. (2000). 3.6 minutes per day: The scarcity of informational texts in first grade. *Reading Research Quarterly, 35*, 202–224.

Duke, N. K., Caughlan, S., Juzwik, M. M., & Martin, N. M. (2012). *Reading and writing genre with purpose in K–8 classrooms.* Portsmouth, NH: Heinemann.

Duke, N. K., Halladay, J. L., & Roberts, K. L. (2013). Reading informational text. In L. M. Morrow, T. Shanahan, & K. K. Wixson (Eds.), *Teaching with the common core standards for English language arts, PreK–2* (pp. 46–66). New York: Guilford Press.

Duke, N. K., Halvorsen, A.-L., & Knight, J. A. (2012). Building knowledge through informational text. In A. M. Pinkham, T. Keefer, & S. B. Neuman (Eds.), *Knowledge development in early childhood: Sources of learning and classroom implications* (pp. 205–219). New York: Guilford Press.

Duke, N. K., & Kays, J. (1998). "Can I say 'once upon a time'?": Kindergarten children developing knowledge of information book language. *Early Childhood Research Quarterly, 13*, 295–318.

Fingeret, L. (2008). March of the penguins: Building knowledge in the kindergarten classroom. *The Reading Teacher, 62*, 96–103.

Jeong, J., Gaffney, J. S., & Choi, J-O. (2010). Availability and use of informational text in second-, third-, and fourth-grade classrooms. *Research in the Teaching of English, 44*, 435–456.

Kamberelis, G. (1999). Genre development and learning: Children writing stories, science reports, and poems. *Research in the Teaching of English, 33*, 403–460.

Maduram, I. (2000). "Playing possum": A young child's responses to information books. *Language Arts, 77*, 391–397.

Martin, N. M. (2011). Exploring informational text comprehension: Reading biography, persuasive text, and procedural text in the elementary grades (Doctoral dissertation). Retrieved from *ProQuest Dissertations and Theses* (Order No. 3465046).

Mohr, K. A. (2006). Children's choices for recreational reading: A three-part investigation of selection preferences, rationales, and processes. *Journal of Literacy Research, 38*, 81–104.

National Assessment Governing Board. (2008). *Reading framework for the 2009 National Assessment of Educational Progress.* Retrieved from *www.nagb.org/publications/frameworks/reading09.pdf.*

National Governors Association (NGA) & Council of Chief State School Officers (CCSSO). (2010). *Common core state standards for English language arts and literacy in history/social studies, science, and technical subjects.* Available at *www.corestandards.org/the-standards.*

Oyler, C., & Barry, A. B. (1996). Intertextual connections in read-alouds of information books. *Language Arts, 73*, 324–329.

Pappas, C. C. (1993). Is narrative "primary"?: Some insights from kindergarteners' pretend readings of stories and information books. *Journal of Reading Behavior, 25*, 97–129.

Pentimonti, J. M., Zucker, T. A., Justice, L. M., & Kaderavek J. A. (2010). Informational text use in preschool classroom read-alouds. *The Reading Teacher, 63*, 656–665.

Purcell-Gates, V., Duke, N. K., & Martineau, J. A. (2007). Learning to read and write genre-specific text: Roles of authentic experience and explicit teaching. *Reading Research Quarterly, 42*, 8–45.

Reutzel, D. R., Smith, J. A., & Fawson, P. C. (2005). An examination of two approaches for teaching reading comprehension strategies in the primary years using science information texts. *Early Childhood Research Quarterly, 20*, 276–305.

Santoro, L. E., Chard, D. J., Howard, L., & Baker, S. K. (2008). Making the very most of classroom read-alouds to promote comprehension and vocabulary. *The Reading Teacher, 61*, 396–408.

Strachan, S. L. (2012). *Kindergarten students' social studies and content literacy learning from interactive read-alouds of informational texts* (working title). Unpublished manuscript, Michigan State University.

Tower, C. (2002). "It's a snake, you guys!": The power of text characteristics on children's responses to information books. *Research in the Teaching of English, 37*, 55–88.

Watanabe, L. M. (2013). *Preschoolers' reading and writing of procedural texts* (working title). Unpublished manuscript, Michigan State University.

Williams, J. P., Nubla-Kung, A. A., Pollini, S., Stafford, K. B., Garcia, A., & Snyder, A. E. (2007). Teaching cause–effect text structure through social studies content to at-risk second graders. *Journal of Learning Disabilities, 40*, 111–120.

Wright, T. S. (2011). *What classroom observations reveal about oral vocabulary instruction in kindergarten* (Doctoral dissertation). Retrieved from *ProQuest Dissertations and Theses* (Order No. 3458922).

Zhang, S., & Duke, N. K. (2011). The impact of instruction in the WWWDOT framework on students' disposition and ability to evaluate web sites as sources of information. *Elementary School Journal, 112*(1), 132–154.

PART III

RECONCEPTUALIZING DEVELOPMENTALLY APPROPRIATE PRACTICE

CHAPTER 9

❖

Phonological Awareness and Alphabet Knowledge

THE FOUNDATIONS OF EARLY READING

Marcia Invernizzi
Laura S. Tortorelli

GUIDING QUESTIONS

❖ How do phonological awareness and alphabet knowledge contribute to later reading?

❖ How can teachers design phonological awareness and alphabet instruction to meet the needs of individual students?

❖ What are best practices for integrating phonological awareness and alphabet knowledge into early literacy instruction?

The first thing Ms. Gimm's kindergarten class does when they arrive in the morning is find their name cards on a pocket chart and place them in another pocket labeled "I'm Here Today!" During circle time, Ms. Gimm goes through the list of names and comments on how many share the same first letter, J: *Jared, Jameeya, Javier,* and *Jack.* She points out the first letter, *J,* and talks about how *Jared, Jameeya,* and *Jack* all start with the /j/ sound, though *Javier* does not. She explains that in Spanish, the *J* is pronounced more like the /h/ sound made by the letter *H.* She then asks the children to clap with her as they pronounce each name. *Ja-red* has two claps. *Ja-mee-ya* and *Ja-vi-er* have three claps. *Jack* has only one clap. They clap to each name again and this time she sorts each name card under the numbers 1, 2, or 3, for the number of claps. Whose name is longer? They count and name the letters in Jack's name (4), in Jared's name (5), and in Javier's and Jameeya's names (6 and 7, respectively). They discuss how the names with more letters also have more claps when they pronounce them—they have more syllables. She calls on students to match the student name cards with their pictures, and in each case asks, "How did you know that was his or her name?" This question prompts further discussion about the /j/ sound, the letter *J*, and the number of syllables and letters.

This simple "name of the day" activity demonstrates an interplay between *phonological awareness*, the understanding that spoken language is made up of smaller sounds, and *alphabet knowledge*, knowledge of what letters look like, their names, and the speech sounds they represent. Together, phonological awareness and alphabet knowledge are the two most powerful predictors of early literacy achievement (National Early Literacy Panel [NELP], 2008). It is impossible to learn to read without both of these skills because English is an alphabetic language; its written form uses an alphabet to represent speech sounds and meaning. Phonological awareness plays an important part in early literacy development by focusing children's attention on the sounds within words, and when combined with alphabet knowledge, allows for the development of letter–sound knowledge and the acquisition of the *alphabetic principle*. The alphabetic principle is the understanding that spoken language is made up of individual sounds and that letters represent those sounds in a systematic way (Liberman, Shankweiler, & Liberman, 1990). The alphabetic principle allows children to invent phonetic spellings and begin to decode words (Ehri, 1998; National Institute of Child Health and Human Development, 2000).

WHY PHONOLOGICAL AWARENESS AND ALPHABET KNOWLEDGE MATTER

Phonological awareness and alphabet knowledge develop in a reciprocal relationship as a result of children's exposure to and participation in oral and written language structures (Burgess & Lonigan, 1998). These early literacy skills are not fundamentally different from the more conventional reading skills that follow developmentally; instead, these early skills, when highly developed and integrated, *become* reading behavior (Storch & Whitehurst, 2002; Whitehurst & Lonigan, 1998). The first few years of literacy instruction in school can be seen as a process of developing, solidifying, and integrating language and early literacy skills, such as phonological awareness and alphabet knowledge, to allow for word recognition and understanding.

Phonological awareness is an "umbrella term" for an array of insights about the sound structures of oral language, including syllables, rhymes, and *alliteration*, or strings of words all starting with the same sound (Bear, Invernizzi, Templeton, & Johnston, 2012). Phonological awareness develops sequentially, starting with larger linguistic units like words and syllables followed by smaller units like rhymes and beginning sounds (Pufpaff, 2009). *Phonemic awareness* is a subcategory of phonological awareness that refers to identifying and consciously reflecting on the smallest units of speech, individual phonemes, for example, identifying all three sounds in the word *bed*, /b/-/e/-/d/. Many people confuse phonological awareness and phonics because they both focus on the sounds that make up words. Phonological awareness refers to the sound structures of spoken words only, whereas phonics refers to the consistent correspondence between letters and sounds (Bear et al., 2012). Phonological awareness and alphabet knowledge, in particular letter–sound correspondences, provide the basis for future phonics instruction (Adams, 1990; McBride-Chang, 1999) and predict the ease of reading acquisition (NELP, 2008; Storch & Whitehurst, 2002).

Both phonological awareness and alphabet knowledge must be explicitly taught because most children will not naturally pick up these skills on their own. When we talk, we focus on the meaning of the words and sentences, not the sequence of speech sounds we are producing to create that meaning. Likewise, when we talk, we speak in syllables and phrases that are not divided up into separate words and letters as they are in print. Children may have a tacit sensitivity to speech sounds, as evidenced in their language play and silly talk, but these sounds must be brought to conscious attention and explicitly wedded with the alphabet to move into reading. Students must learn to recognize and name both upper- and lower-case letters, match letters to their sounds, and understand the relationship of letters to speech sounds and meaning in print and writing.

While phonological awareness and alphabetic knowledge are both necessary to learn to read and write, neither one alone, or even in combination, are sufficient. Children must also have ample opportunity to apply these concepts in real-language contexts that involve speaking, listening, reading, and writing. Alphabet knowledge and phonological awareness work in concert with other language skills such as vocabulary and syntax to allow children to become attentive to smaller sounds within words, remember new words, and make distinctions between words (Ehri & Roberts, 2006). As children's vocabularies grow larger, they encounter more and more similar-sounding words like *net* and *nest*, or *desk* and *disc*. To tell these words apart, it is necessary to analyze their sounds and spellings in greater detail so as not to confuse them (Metsala, 2011). For this reason, it is important to enrich children's oral vocabulary, because the larger their oral vocabulary, the more attentive they must be to a word's sound structure to tell words like *nest* and *net* apart! Strengthening a child's phonological awareness and alphabet knowledge will support his or her developing vocabulary and vice versa.

Developmental Progressions in Phonological Awareness

Phonological awareness develops gradually in response to instruction that focuses children's attention on smaller and smaller parts of oral language. Children begin to notice how stories are built from sentences, sentences from words, words from syllables, and syllables themselves from a relatively small set of basic speech sounds—phonemes (Adams, Foorman, Lundberg, & Beeler, 1998). Figure 9.1 illustrates this developmental continuum, starting at the bottom of the ladder with words within sentences (e.g., "Twinkle, twinkle, little star" is made up of four words). The next two rungs move to syllables (Twin-kle, lit-tle) and rhymes (*star–are, high–sky*) within words. The top two rungs of the ladder are the most difficult to reach because they deal with the smallest parts of language, including alliterative beginnings (onsets; *c*-ar, *c*-at, *c*-arrot) and ending (rimes; st-*ar*, c-*ar*, f-*ar*), and eventually, individual phonemes (*c-a-r, s-t-a-r*). Individual phonemes within words are the hardest sounds to isolate, because the sound of any given phoneme can vary considerably from word to word and from speaker to speaker because of *coarticulation*, the process of articulating speech sounds within an environment of other speech sounds that influence it (Liberman, Cooper, Shankweiler, & Studdert-Kennedy, 1967). That is why we cannot hear a short /i/ sound in words like *sting*, or *third*, because the /n/ and /r/ sounds following the vowel make it sound quite different than it does in words like *sit* or *hid*.

Children develop phonological awareness incrementally during the preschool and primary years. In preschool, children develop sensitivity to rhyme and alliteration by singing, chanting, clapping, and jumping to nursery rhymes and alliterative books that play with beginning sounds. By the end of kindergarten most children can divide words into syllables, identify and generate rhymes, and segment and blend beginnings (onsets) and endings (rimes) in simple words like *c-at* (*cat*) or *sh-ip*

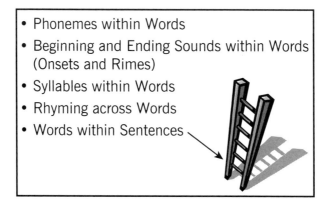

- Phonemes within Words
- Beginning and Ending Sounds within Words (Onsets and Rimes)
- Syllables within Words
- Rhyming across Words
- Words within Sentences

FIGURE 9.1. Phonological awareness ladder.

(*ship*). By the end of first grade, most children have reached the top rung of the ladder and are able to segment phonemes within words and perhaps even manipulate phonemes to generate new words. This developmental progression is best thought of a series of insights into the sound structures of language. Since insight into the larger sound structures of oral language (e.g., syllables, rhymes) do not require reading ability, phonological awareness instruction focused on these larger speech sounds are particularly suitable for young learners. Later insights into smaller units of sound such as the phoneme interact with early literacy and print-related skills and so are more appropriate for early readers.

Developmental Progressions in Alphabet Knowledge

Alphabet knowledge also develops in a recognizable progression. Most children in the United States have their first exposure to the alphabet through the "Alphabet" song, but children who know the song by heart do not necessarily recognize the individual letter names within the song, as evidenced by the fact that many young children initially think that "elemenopee" (*LMNOP*) is one letter. The "Alphabet" song can be a great starting place for alphabet instruction, for example, by "tracking" each letter on an alphabet strip while singing the song. Children often begin to learn letter names at home through educational TV, alphabet books, and toys, but letter sounds are usually learned later in school (Adams, 1990; Treiman & Kessler, 2003). The first letters that a child recognizes and refers to by name are usually the letters of his or her first name (Bloodgood, 1999; Haney, 2002; Levin & Ehri, 2009; Treiman & Broderick, 1998). Children are motivated to learn "their own" letters and the letters of the names of their close friends and family members. As a result, activities that focus on the names of children in your class provide an easy and motivating way to start alphabet instruction.

Many alphabet knowledge instructional programs take a one-letter-per-week approach (Justice, Pence, Bowles, & Wiggins, 2006), however, because some letters are more difficult for young children to learn than others, one letter per week may not be enough. In general, children learn to recognize upper-case letters first, followed by lower-case letters, and they learn lower-case letters that resemble their upper-case counterparts (*C, c*) more easily than those that do not (*E, e*; Evans, Bell, Shaw, Moretti, & Page, 2006; Huang & Invernizzi, 2012; Treiman & Kessler, 2004; Turnball, Bowles, Skibbe, Justice, & Wiggins, 2010). As a result, children will benefit from activities that include matching upper-case to lower-case letters, highlighting pairs that appear quite different. Children have an easier time learning to recognize letters that are visually distinct from other letters (*o* or *x*) than letters that are very visually similar to other letters (*n, m*, and *h*, or *b, d, p*, and *q*; Evans et al., 2006; Huang & Invernizzi, 2012; Treiman & Kessler, 2003), so working on more than one letter at a time, especially comparing, contrasting, and noting similarities and differences between letters, will help children learn more efficiently. Children also learn letters that appear frequently in print before more rare letters (Turnbull et al., 2010), so build in extra time when planning instruction for rarely occurring letters such as *q* and *w*.

Children use letter-name knowledge to help them learn the sounds of those letters (Evans et al., 2006; Kim, Petscher, Foorman, & Zhou, 2010; Treiman, Tincoff, & Richmond-Welty, 1996). Many letter names contain a clue to their sounds, for example, the letter name for *B*, "bee," contains that letter's sound, /b/. Letter names can be divided into three categories, according to how they represent their letter sounds. The first category have letter names that provide the letter sound at the beginning, like the /j/ sound at the beginning of the letter name for *J*, "jay"; this category includes *B, D, J, K, P, T, V,* and *Z*. The second category are letter names that provide the letter sound at the end, like the /f/ sound at the end of the letter name for *F*, "efff"; this category includes *F, L, M, N, R, S,* and *X*. The other letter names, including the vowels and other letters that have more than one sound, like *C* and *G*, do not provide straightforward clues to their sounds. Because of the supports that these letter names provide, the first two categories of letter sounds are easier to learn than the third, more ambiguous category, which will take more instructional time.

Writing: The Wedding of Phonological Awareness and Alphabet Knowledge

Children's writing skills will develop in tandem with their phonological awareness and alphabet knowledge. As children move up the phonological awareness ladder their insights about the sounds of oral language begin to merge with their understanding of how these sounds are represented in print, and they make their first attempts at phonetic writing, also called invented spelling. As children begin to understand the alphabetic principle, they develop *partial phonemic awareness*, which allows them to recognize and detach the beginning consonant sounds of words, and this understanding is reflected in their early writings. They recognize that the words *sun, soap,* and *Sally* all begin with an /s/ sound, and they might represent all of these words with a single *S* in writing. Until children have a solid grasp of all the letter sounds, they will sometimes make substitutions of letter names for the letter sounds, for example, spelling *Katie* as *KT* ("kay-tee"). Early writing attempts will often look odd to adults who are used to more conventional spelling patterns, but these experimentations help children further develop their early literacy skills and decoding abilities and should be encouraged.

By late kindergarten or early first grade early readers usually have developed *full phonemic awareness*—the capacity to segment *all* the sounds within a one-syllable word, including consonant blends (*s-n-ap*) and the vowels in the middle (*s-n-a-p*). Their invented spellings begin to mirror this growing phonemic awareness as all phonemes are represented, though not always correctly (e.g., *SHEP* for *ship*).

Once children learn the consistent associations between letters and speech sounds, their phonemic awareness amalgamates more completely with their growing understanding of the spelling of words. They begin to chunk spelling or orthographic patterns with those larger phonological units they learned earlier, such as rhyme, and they recognize recurring spelling patterns that represent these chunks, like the -*ake* in *take, shake,* and *flake.* When this happens, students are said to have *consolidated phonemic awareness* because their phonemic awareness is fully fused with larger spelling patterns (Ehri, 2005). At this point, phonemic awareness is fully integrated with phonics and spelling instruction. The more children practice writing, the more they will exercise their growing phonological awareness, alphabet knowledge, and spelling knowledge (Clay, 1979; Chomsky, 1971), so encourage them to write early and often!

ASSESSMENT AND DIFFERENTIATION

All children progress along a developmental continuum in phonological awareness and alphabet knowledge, but not all children progress at the same rate. Informal, formative assessments are needed to find out exactly what children know so you can design instruction to meet all children's needs. Phonological awareness assessments can be conducted using pictures and simple oral language tasks in engaging, gamelike formats. Once children attain the alphabetic principle, that is, the understanding that spoken language is made up of individual sounds and that letters represent those sounds in a systematic way, children's invented spelling and early writing can serve as a diagnostic window into their more advanced phonological insights. Alphabet knowledge can be assessed using simple letter recognition and letter–sound tasks until they reach mastery. Thereafter, children's invented spelling can once again provide a diagnostic window into the application of their alphabet knowledge in early writing.

Assessing before the Alphabetic Principle

The easiest assessments consist of hands-on interactive tasks that involve the manipulation of picture cards representing the developmental continuum of speech-sound units (e.g., syllables and rhymes, to smaller sound units, such as beginning sounds). Children match or group pictures by the targeted speech sound, or they pick the picture that does not belong with the other two. More difficult assessments ask children to orally produce a given speech sound (e.g., rhyme, beginning sound).

Assessing the development of children's phonological awareness during preschool and kindergarten helps teachers differentiate their instruction to meet children's needs.

To assess children's growing alphabet knowledge, simply ask children to name the letters or to say the letter sounds. As simple as this sounds, it is important to consider four caveats in assessing alphabet knowledge. First, randomize the letters in the presentation—children can and will use their memory of the "ABC" song if the letters are presented in order, and this is no guarantee that they will be able to recognize them out of order. Second, assess *all* of the letters. Many assessments see how many letters children can name in 1 minute, but the results of such assessment do not tell you which letters the child already knows versus which letters must be emphasized in instruction. Third, be sure to assess lower-case letters eventually— although the upper-case letters are easier to learn, the vast majority of text in books is printed using lower case. Last, in assessing letter sounds, use upper-case letters as the prompt because these are more likely to be recognized accurately.

Assessing after the Alphabetic Principle

For students who have achieved the alphabetic principle, invented spelling tasks and uncorrected writing samples can be used diagnostically to plan differentiated instruction. Many educators have developed scoring rubrics for analyzing children's invented spellings by the number of phonemes represented (Clay, 1985; Invernizzi, Justice, Landrum, & Booker, 2005; Tangel & Blachman, 1992). Figure 9.2 shows a spelling sample of the words elicited from the invented spelling task from the Phonological Awareness Literacy Screening–Kindergarten (PALS-K; Invernizzi, Swank, Juel, & Meier, 2006). It is easy to see that these spellings demonstrate partial phonemic awareness by the partial representations of individual sounds in the words *fan* (two phonemes represented), *rug* (one phoneme represented), and *sit* (two phonemes represented). Invented spelling tasks such as these can inform our understanding of students' insights into the phonemic structure of words, moving from partial to full phonemic awareness. Children's early writing samples can also reveal their degree of phonemic awareness, as in Bella's writing sample in Figure 9.3 that suggests "fuller" phonemic awareness in her spelling of BRD for *bird*, HAJS for *hatche*s, FEDS for *feeds*, and WRM for *worm*.

Alphabet knowledge assessments are constrained by the number of letters in the alphabet (Paris, 2005). There are only 52 letters (26 upper and 26 lower) to be assessed. Even when children "reach the ceiling" on alphabetic assessments, there is plenty to learn about the consistent relationships between letters and speech sounds. For children who have already achieved insight into the alphabetic principle and know all their letters and sounds, phonics–spelling assessments can further inform instruction. Similar to the invented spelling measures described above,

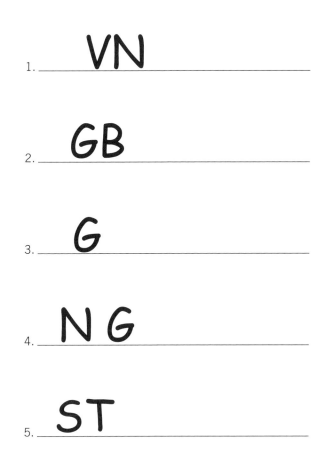

FIGURE 9.2. PALS-K Spelling Inventory scored by number of phonemes represented. 1 = fan, 2 = pet, 3 = rug, 4 = mop, 5 = sit.

informal phonics–spelling inventories provide insight into children's understanding of larger alphabetic strings, or spelling patterns, that relate to speech sounds (Bear et al., 2012; Ganske, 2000; Schlagal, 1992; Viise, 1994). Instead of scoring children's spelling productions by the number of phonemes represented, these qualitative spelling inventories score the presence or absence of specific phonics features such as consonant digraphs and blends, short vowels, long-vowel patterns, and the like. The instructional needs of students who are still grappling with basic phonics features such as consonant digraphs and blends are quite different from students who have mastered these and are negotiating consolidated chunks or spelling patterns that include silent letters.

Instructionally transparent assessments such as these have been scientifically validated by Invernizzi et al. (2006) with thousands of children screened using the Phonological Awareness Literacy Screening (PALS) assessments at the preschool

FIGURE 9.3. Bella's baby bird story. "A baby bird hatches. Mom feeds it a worm."

and primary grade levels. Other assessments tapping similar aspects of phonological awareness and alphabet knowledge are also available (see Pence, 2007, for a full review).

Designing Instruction to Meet the Needs of All Students

Assessing your students' early phonological awareness and alphabet knowledge will be a waste of time if it does not lead you to adjust your instruction in response. Depending on what you find when analyzing the results of your assessments, you can use assessment information to modify instruction in one of two ways: to adjust your instructional plan for the entire group, or to target particular skills for one or more children in the class. If your assessments indicate that most of your class cannot identify rhyming words, then beginning instruction with identifying short-vowel sounds in the middle of words will be over most of your students' heads, and you would be better off adjusting your plan of instruction to begin with easier content, including rhyme and syllable awareness. On the other hand, if your assessment results indicate that several students can identify only a few letters, while most of your class knows most of their letters and sounds, you would need to provide small-group instruction to catch up those students, so they can benefit from the writing and early phonics instruction appropriate for the rest of the class. Since each level of early literacy knowledge provides the crucial foundation for the next level, students who do not master the earlier levels of phonological awareness and alphabet knowledge may struggle counterproductively with more advanced material. That being said, complete mastery of each level of skills is not necessary or even desirable before moving onto the next level; just be sure to give children plenty of time to internalize new information before moving to the next level.

Modifying Task Difficulty

In addition to selecting the content of your instruction to match your students' developmental level, additional consideration must be given to the cognitive demands of the instructional tasks themselves. You can adjust the difficulty of particular content by changing the tasks you ask students to complete. Phonological awareness activities that ask children to identify, isolate, match, and categorize ("Which words begin with the sound /b/, as in *ball—bear, cat, bat*?") are easier than those that require children to blend and segment ("What sound do you hear at the beginning of *ball*?"). This is because blending and segmenting add an additional cognitive dimension to the task involving memory. For this reason, matching and sorting tasks that require students to recognize and identify sounds are more appropriate for younger emergent learners in preschool and early kindergarten. Phoneme blending and segmenting are more suited to children just learning to read because the letter–sound correspondences will help them remember the individual sounds. The most cognitively demanding tasks ask children to subtract, add, or substitute sounds ("What word do you get if you take the /b/ sound out of the word *ball*? *All!*"). These kinds of tasks are more appropriate for children who are already reading and can advance their decoding and spelling skills through this kind of practice. There is an interaction of phonological awareness skills with the alphabetic principle as children learn to finger-point read memorized text across the kindergarten year (Flanigan, 2007; Morris, Bloodgood, Lomax, & Perney, 2003; Uhry, 1999). Figure 9.4 provides a quick reference to the phonological awareness skills and tasks covered here, organized from least difficult to most difficult, which you can use to plan and adjust your instruction.

Similarly, when developing alphabet activities for your students, some tasks are easier than others. Simply recognizing a letter, for example, being asked to choose the letter *B* out of a selection of three letters, is among the easiest tasks. Identifying a letter by providing its name or matching upper- and lower-case letters and the same letters across font types is more difficult. Producing a letter in writing is more difficult still, but all these activities are appropriate for young children. Matching letters to their sounds, by providing the letter sounds when presented with the letter or vice versa, is more difficult, and generally appropriate for children further along

Least difficult	Words	Rhyme	Syllables	Beginning and ending sounds	Individual phonemes
Matching/Isolation/Identification/Sorting					
Blending/Segmenting					
Subtraction/Addition/Substitution					**Most Difficult**

FIGURE 9.4. Phonological awareness skills and tasks.

in the developmental continuum. Finally, spelling phonetically or decoding words in order to read are the most complex tasks, as these activities require combining knowledge of letter–sound correspondences with phonemic awareness. Figure 9.5 provides lists of the less difficult and more difficult alphabet tasks, letter names, and letter sounds to help you plan and adjust instruction.

Supporting English Language Learners

Like most teachers, you likely have at least several students in your class who speak a language other than English as their first language, or *English language learners*

	Less Difficult	**More Difficult**
Tasks	Recognition → Naming → Letter formation	Letter–sound correspondences → Alphabetic writing and decoding
Letters	Upper case	Lower case
	Similar upper and lower case (*C, c*)	Different upper and lower case (*Q, q*)
	Visually distinct letters (*x, o*)	Easily confused letters (*b, d, p, q*)
	More frequent letters	Less frequent letters
	Letters in child's name	Letters not in child's name
Letter Sounds	Letter sounds included in letter names (*b*/"bee", *f*/"eff")	Letter sounds not included in letter names (*w, y, x*)
	Letters associated with only one sound	Letters associated with more than one sound (*c, g*)
	Letter sounds in child's name	Letter sounds not in child's name

FIGURE 9.5. Alphabet knowledge content and tasks.

(ELLs). These students have a double challenge, learning to speak and read in English at the same time. However, many of the same activities that support the early literacy development of English-speaking children will benefit ELLs as well. Here are a few things to keep in mind when adapting instruction for the ELLs in your class:

◆ *The alphabetic principle transfers across languages.* Once a child understands that words are made up of smaller sounds and that letters represent those sounds, that child can apply that understanding to any alphabetic language. For example, while you may not speak Italian at all, because you are reading this chapter in English, another alphabetic language, you already know that in order to read Italian you need to learn what letter combinations represent what sounds (August et al., 2006; Lesaux & Siegel, 2003).

◆ *Phonological awareness may be more highly developed for ELLs than for monolingual children.* Children who speak more than one language often demonstrate what is known as a "bilingual advantage" in phonological awareness, in which they develop a greater sensitivity to the sounds within words and greater awareness of the differences between sounds as a result of learning to process two different languages. This advantage means that the remedial instruction that helps struggling English-speaking readers (i.e., lots of phonological awareness training) may not address the source of reading difficulties for ELLs. A one-size-fits-all approach to early reading difficulties will not serve all children equally well (Lesaux & Siegel, 2003; Lesaux, Rupp, & Siegel, 2007).

◆ *Assessment is still the key to good instruction for ELLs.* Assessment of alphabet knowledge and phonological awareness can help you make the distinction between ELLs who struggle with early literacy skills and those who only need to develop their oral proficiency in English to improve their reading skills. Whenever possible, it is best to assess these early skills in both English *and* the child's native language, so you can determine how far the child's literacy development has proceeded in each language and build on what the child knows in his or her first language (Peña & Halle, 2011).

◆ *Not all languages are alike.* It is important to familiarize yourself with the key differences between the child's first language and English for both assessment and instruction. For example, some common sounds in English, like the /v/ sound, are quite rare in other languages, and even a child with strong phonological awareness may have trouble identifying an unfamiliar sound at first. Sounds and spelling patterns that do not appear in the first language may be trickier for ELLs, and you should be prepared to offer them extra support in these areas of instruction. For example, students who speak Spanish as a first language may often substitute *ch* for the digraph *sh*, because *sh* does not appear in Spanish (Helman, 2004). In addition, the instructional traditions of other countries may differ from the United States, so a child educated in another country may not have had a chance to learn all the same content; for example, many children educated abroad know all the letter sounds but few letter names.

BEST PRACTICES FOR INTEGRATING PHONOLOGICAL AWARENESS AND ALPHABET INSTRUCTION

Like other important literacy skills, phonological awareness and alphabet knowledge can best be developed through carefully planned systematic instruction. When planning your lessons, you will want to consider the developmental progressions described above, as well as the age and current skills and knowledge of your students. In the lesson below, Ms. Gimm builds differentiated instruction in phonological awareness and alphabet knowledge into her early literacy lesson.

Case Example

Ms. Gimm routinely sings nursery rhymes and other simple jingles with her whole kindergarten class, and she coordinates her repertoire with the music teacher so the children really get to learn the lyrics "by heart." Although everyone learns the same songs (typically a new one each week), and she engages everyone in the language play each song allows, she forms small instructional groups to differentiate reading instruction according to her formative assessments. She uses the lyrics to songs like "Five Little Ducks," "I'm a Little Teapot," and other classics to integrate phonological awareness and alphabet instruction in a meaningful context.

Ms. Gimm uses a before, during, and after framework to guide her daily small-group instruction. *Before* working with the rhyme or jingle, she engages her students in a name-of-the-day activity that develops phonological awareness (described above) and alphabetic instruction, usually on the floor in front of the pocket chart and easel she will use. Depending on where that particular group of students are on the alphabet knowledge continuum, she may have them sing and track the "Alphabet" song (everyone has their own alphabet strip), work with their name by matching letter tiles to the model (upper- to upper-, lower- to lower-, or lower- to upper-case, depending), or she may have them practice forming letters on a dry-erase board in response to a particular sound her friend Pat the Puppet produces. Other activities might include a font sort, or an alphabet game such as Bingo, Concentration, or Letter Spin (Bear et al., 2012). These activities are fun and engaging and typically do not last more than 5 minutes or so.

After working with the alphabet before the lesson proper, Ms. Gimm moves into the *during* phase of the lesson. *During* the lesson Ms. Gimm and her students recite "Five Little Ducks" once more, and then play a brief phonological awareness activity. For some groups, this activity might focus on rhyming words such as *day* and *away, quack* and *back;* other groups might clap the syllables in words like *little,* or *away.* Another group might focus on the beginning sounds /f/ and /d/ found in words like *five, four, ducks,* and *day,* respectively. Whatever the sound unit, Ms. Gimm also is mindful of the task difficulty and will adjust according to each child's comfort level with the content.

Following this brief but focused language play, Ms. Gimm presents the written version of the rhyme that she has written on chart paper, one sentence per line. She models how to point to each word as they all recite the rhyme in unison (choral reading), and then they take turns reciting each line, as she again models pointing to each word (echo reading). She may have a volunteer come up to use her magic pointer to point to each word as everyone recites it in unison a third time. On subsequent days she will have students match sentence strips and then word cards to their counterparts in a pocket chart, working within a whole-to-part framework across the week (Johnston, Invernizzi, Bear, Helman, & Templeton, in press). On the final day in the weeklong sequence she will play "I'm thinking of," using beginning letter sounds as the challenge. She might ask, "I'm thinking of a word in the first sentence that starts like *food.* What word am I thinking of?" As children shout out *"Five!"* she asks, "How did you know?" prompting children to notice they both start with the /f/ sound and the letter *F.* The "I'm thinking of" features may change for other groups, depending on where children are along the developmental continuum in phonological awareness and alphabet knowledge.

Following the during part of the lesson plan Ms. Gimm moves into the *after* part of the lesson plan. *After* working with the written version of "Five Little Ducks," children work with targeted letter sounds or phonics features that were present in the text of the rhyme. For some groups of students, this may be specific letter sounds, such as the /f/ sound made by the letter *F* and the /d/ sound made by the letter *D.* For other students further along in their alphabet knowledge, the features may be more difficult letter sounds, such as the /l/ in *little* and the /w/ in *went.* Students even further along might work with consolidated chunks in the -*ack* word family as in *quack* and *back.* Whatever the feature, Ms. Gimm may ask children to sort pictures (and words if they are able) into contrasting categories, or, if they are not yet able to sort, she will ask them to identify a matching sound in a choice of three. For sorting, first she introduces the feature and models the process of categorizing. Next, she supports children's efforts as they work in buddy pairs to sort and check the accuracy of their sorts. Then, she prompts children to reflect on the reasons they placed each picture or word in a given category. These last two steps, sort and check, and reflect, are repeated by her students during the after portion of the lesson plan each day. By the third or fourth day, Ms. Gimm adds a word hunt to this sorting routine as children return to the written context of "Five Little Ducks" to find a printed word that matches the feature of interest—the words *five* and *four*, for the /f/ sound made by the letter *F*, or the words *day* and *duck* for the /d/ sound made by the letter *D*, for example. Other groups of students would "hunt" for exemplars of the features they were working with. At the end of this 5-day sequence, students are given a few word cards to match back to their counterparts in text. Again, from group to group the words may change, depending on where they are on the developmental continuum in phonological awareness and alphabet knowledge.

In this way, working with a whole-to-part lesson plan within a before, during, and after format, Ms. Gimm integrates her phonological awareness and alphabet knowledge instruction into a comprehensive lesson plan that includes listening, speaking, reading, and writing. Although everyone learns the same song, different groups of students work with different aspects of the song, depending on their formative assessments. Figure 9.6 provides a summary of the activities in this lesson.

	Phonological Awareness Activities	Alphabet Knowledge Activities
Before	Name-of-the-day activities (beginning sounds, syllables)	Sing and track the "Alphabet" song (letter naming)
		Upper and lower case matching (letter naming and identification)
		Letter dictation (letter–sound and letter formation)
		Font sorts (letter identification)
		Alphabet games (letter–sound)
During	Differentiated instruction based on "Five Little Ducks" (rhyme for some groups, beginning sounds for others)	
	Tracking and echo/choral reading of "Five Little Ducks" (words)	
	"I'm thinking of" game (beginning sounds and letters)	
After	Picture and word sorts (targeted letter sounds and spelling patterns)	
	Word hunts (letter recognition, beginning sounds, and spelling patterns)	
	Word cards (word recognition)	

FIGURE 9.6. Whole-to-part lesson plan. Based on the PALS Emergent Electronic Lesson Plan (*www.pals.virginia.edu*).

Insights from Ms. Gimm

Ms. Gimm's lesson is engaging, developmentally appropriate, and effective because she incorporates a few clear guidelines:

◆ *She designs fun, engaging, and motivating instruction.* Rather than using repetitive drills, Ms. Gimm designs engaging activities in a supportive structure that provide the repeated exposure children need to achieve mastery of these skills. As a follow-up to differentiated small-group instruction, Ms. Gimm may engage her students in other games and other fun activities. Most traditional children's games like Red Light/Green Light, Duck-Duck-Goose, Simon Says, and Memory can be adapted to focus on sounds in words and/or letters in a fun, high-energy way, and many silly songs and nursery rhymes highlight particular sounds.

◆ *She fosters word consciousness and interest in words and language.* Children naturally enjoy playing with words and sounds, including rhymes, songs, and make-believe words. Ms. Gimm uses students' pride of ownership of their own names and letters in her opening activity, and she designs the bulk of the lesson around an enjoyable silly song that rhymes. She models her own interest and curiosity about words, sounds, and letters by playing games such as "I'm thinking of."

◆ *She embeds instruction in a literacy context.* Phonological awareness and alphabet knowledge are the beginning of the lifelong journey of reading. Ms. Gimm embeds her instruction in the context of reading by presenting the song lyrics on chart paper and in a pocket chart, and by helping her children make connections between the song and the printed words. Whole-to-part lessons like this can also be designed through the use of storybooks, rhyming books, alphabet books, nursery rhymes, and jump-rope jingles (Bear, Invernizzi, Johnston, & Templeton, 2010).

◆ *She scaffolds instruction to gradually release support.* Ms. Gimm gradually releases support by moving from explanation by the teacher to recognition, identification, and finally to production by the child. *Exposure and explanation* constitute the most fundamental teaching technique and is a good place to state what is to be learned. For example, after singing the song "Five Little Ducks," Ms. Gimm might pause to explain "rhyme" as a concept. After singing it again, she might say, "I hear some rhyming words in this song. *Day* and *away* are rhyming words. Listen, *day–away.* They sound alike at the end." She actively involves her students by planning activities that require them to demonstrate their ability to *recognize and identify* as they match two objects that rhyme (e.g., *shell, bell*), match word cards to text, or sort pictures by their beginning sounds (e.g., *boy, ball, bed,* vs. *man, moon, money*). For more advanced students, Ms. Gimm plans activities that require them to *produce* their own examples of the concept. To scaffold their productions, Ms. Gimm pauses before a rhyming word in a song or story to allow children to generate the word that rhymes.

CONCLUSION

Providing your students with strong phonological awareness and alphabet instruction in an integrated context will set them up for success in learning to read and get them off to a great start in the first years of school (Vellutino & Scanlon, 2002). These critical emergent literacy skills have a facilitating effect on the development of early finger-point reading, decoding, writing, and spelling, and vice versa. This is great news for teachers and students alike, because both of these skills are easily teachable and will develop over time through carefully sequenced instruction. The best instruction, as described above, will embed these skills in authentic reading and writing contexts that are sensitive to developmental differences among children.

REFERENCES

Adams, M. (1990). *Beginning to read: Thinking and learning about print*. Urbana–Champaign: University of Illinois.

Adams, M. J., Foorman, B. R., Lundberg, I., & Beeler, T. (1998). *Phonemic awareness in young children: A classroom curriculum*. Baltimore, MD: Brookes.

August, D., Snow, C., Carlo, M., Proctor, C., Rolla de San Francisco, A., Duursma, E., et al. (2006). Literacy development in elementary school second-language learners. *Topics in Language Disorders, 26*(4), 351–364.

Bear, D. R., Invernizzi, M., Johnston, F., & Templeton, S. (2010). *Words their way: Letter and picture sorts for emergent spellers* (2nd ed.). Boston: Allyn & Bacon.

Bear, D. R., Invernizzi, M., Templeton, S., & Johnston, F. (2012). *Words their way: Word study for phonics, vocabulary, and spelling instruction* (5th ed.). Boston: Pearson.

Bloodgood, J. W. (1999). What's in a name? Children's name writing and literacy acquisition. *Reading Research Quarterly, 34*, 342–367.

Burgess, S., & Lonigan, C. (1998). Bidirectional relations of phonological sensitivity and pre-reading abilities: Evidence from a preschool sample. *Journal of Experimental Child Psychology, 70*(2), 117–141.

Chomsky, C. (1971). Write first, read later. *Childhood Education, 47*, 296–299.

Clay, M. (1985). *The early detection of reading difficulties*. Portsmouth, NH: Heinemann.

Clay, M. M. (1979). *What did I write?: Beginning writing behaviour*. Portsmouth, NH: Heinemann.

Ehri, L. C. (1998). Grapheme–phoneme knowledge is essential for learning to read words in English. In J. L. Metsala & L. C. Ehri (Eds.), *Word recognition in beginning literacy* (pp. 3–40). Mahwah, NJ: Erlbaum.

Ehri, L. C. (2005). Learning to read words: Theory, findings, and issues. *Scientific Studies of Reading, 9*, 167–188.

Ehri, L. C., & Roberts, T. (2006). The roots of learning to read and write: Acquisition of letters and phonemic awareness. In D. K. Dickenson & S. B. Neuman (Eds.), *Handbook of early literacy research* (Vol. 2, pp. 113–131). New York: Guilford Press.

Evans, M., Bell, M., Shaw, D., Moretti, S., & Page, J. (2006). Letter names, letter sounds and phonological awareness: An examination of kindergarten children across letters and of letters across children. *Reading and Writing, 19*, 959–989.

Flanigan, K. (2007). A concept of word in text: A pivotal event in early reading acquisition. *Journal of Literacy Research, 39*(1), 37–70.

Ganske, K. (2000). *Word journeys: Assessment-guided phonics, spelling, and vocabulary instruction.* New York: Guilford Press.

Haney, M. R. (2002). Name writing: A window into the emergent literacy skills of young children. *Early Childhood Education Journal, 30*, 101–105.

Helman, L. (2004). Building on the sound system of Spanish. *The Reading Teacher, 57*, 452–460.

Huang, F., & Invernizzi, M. (2012). The case for confusability and other: Factors associated with lowercase alphabet recognition. *Applied Psycholinguistics.*

Invernizzi, M., Justice, L., Landrum, T., & Booker, K. (2005). Early literacy screening: Widespread implementation in Virginia. *Journal of Literacy Research, 35*, 479–500.

Invernizzi, M., Swank, L., Juel, C., & Meier, J. (2006). *Phonological Awareness Literacy Screening–Kindergarten.* Charlottesville, VA: University Printing.

Johnston, F., Invernizzi, M., Bear, D., Helman, L., & Templeton, S. (in press). *Words their way for PreK–K.* Boston: Pearson.

Justice, L. M., Pence, K., Bowles, R. B., & Wiggins, A. (2006). An investigation of four hypotheses concerning the order by which 4-year-old children learn the alphabet letters. *Early Childhood Research Quarterly, 21*, 374–389.

Kim, Y., Petscher, Y., Foorman, B. R., Zhou, C. (2010). The contributions of phonological awareness and letter-name knowledge to letter-sound acquisition—A cross-classified multilevel model approach. *Journal of Educational Psychology, 102*(2), 313–326.

Lesaux, N., Rupp, A., & Siegel, L. (2007). Growth in reading skills of children from diverse linguistic backgrounds: Findings from a 5-year longitudinal study. *Journal of Educational Psychology, 99*(8), 821–834.

Lesaux, N., & Siegel, L. (2003). The development of reading in children who speak English as a second language. *Developmental Psychology, 39*(6), 1005–1019.

Levin, I., & Ehri, L. C. (2009). Young children's ability to read and spell their own and classmates' names: The role of letter knowledge. *Scientific Studies of Reading, 13*, 249–273.

Liberman, I., Shankweiler, D., & Liberman, A. (1990). The alphabetic principle and learning to read. *Haskins Laboratories Status Report on Speech Research, 6*, 1–13.

Liberman, I. Y., Cooper, F. S., Shankweiler, D., & Studdert-Kennedy, M. (1967). Perception of the speech code. *Psychological Review, 74*, 731–761.

McBride-Chang, C. (1999). The ABCs of ABCs: The development of letter–name and letter–sound knowledge. *Merrill–Palmer Quarterly, 45*(2), 285–308.

Metsala, J. L. (2011). Lexical reorganization and the emergence of phonological awareness. In S. B. Neuman & D. K. Dickinson (Eds.), *Handbook of early literacy research* (Vol. 3, pp. 66–84). New York: Guilford Press.

Morris, D., Bloodgood, J. W., Lomax, R. G., & Perney, J. (2003). Developmental steps in learning to read: A longitudinal study in kindergarten and first grade. *Reading Research Quarterly, 38*, 302–328.

National Early Literacy Panel (NELP). (2008). *Developing early literacy: The report of the National Early Literacy Panel.* Washington, DC: National Institute for Literacy.

National Institute of Child Health and Human Development. (2000). Report of the National Reading Panel. *Teaching children to read: An evidenced-based assessment of the scientific research literature on reading and its implications for reading instruction* (NIH Publication No. 00-4769). Washington, DC: U.S. Government Printing Office.

Paris, S. (2005). Reinterpreting the development of reading skills. *Reading Research Quarterly, 40,* 184–202.

Peña E. D., & Halle, T. G. (2011). Assessing preschool dual language learners: Traveling a multiforked road. *Child Development Perspectives, 5*(1), 28–32.

Pence, K. L. (2007). *Assessment in emergent literacy.* San Diego, CA: Plural.

Pufpaff, L. (2009). A developmental continuum of phonological sensitivity skills. *Psychology in the Schools, 46*(7), 679–691.

Schlagal, R. (1992). Patterns of orthographic development into the intermediate grades. In S. Templeton & D. Bear (Eds.), *Development of orthographic knowledge and the foundations of literacy* (pp. 31–52). Hillsdale, NJ: Erlbaum.

Storch, S., & Whitehurst, G. (2002). Oral language and code-related precursors to reading: Evidence from a longitudinal structural model. *Developmental Psychology, 38,* 934–947.

Tangel, D. M., & Blachman, B. A. (1992). Effect of phoneme awareness training on kindergarten children's invented spelling. *Journal of Reading Behavior, 24,* 233–261.

Treiman, R., & Broderick, V. (1998). What's in a name: Children's knowledge about the letters in their own names. *Journal of Experimental Child Psychology, 70,* 97–116.

Treiman, R., & Kessler, B. (2003). The role of letter names in the acquisition of literacy. In R. V. Kail (Ed.), *Advances in child development and behavior* (Vol. 31, pp. 105–135). San Diego, CA: Academic Press. Retrieved from *http://spell.psychology.wustl.edu/~bkessler/Advances/Advances.pdf.*

Treiman, R., & Kessler, B. (2004). The case of case: Children's knowledge and use of upper and lowercase letters. *Applied Psycholinguistics, 25,* 413–428.

Treiman, R., Tincoff, R., & Richmond-Welty, E. D. (1996). Letter names help children to connect print and speech. *Developmental Psychology, 32,* 505–514.

Turnbull, K. L. P., Bowles, R. P., Skibbe, L. E., Justice, L. M., & Wiggins, A. K. (2010). Theoretical explanations for preschoolers' lowercase alphabet knowledge. *Journal of Speech, Language & Hearing Research, 53,* 1757–1768.

Uhry, J. (1999). Invented spelling in kindergarten: The relationship with finger-point reading. *Reading and Writing: An Interdiscipinary Journal, 11,* 441–464.

Vellutino, F., & Scanlon, D. (2002). The interactive strategies approach to reading intervention. *Contemporary Educational Pscyhology, 27*(4), 573–635.

Viise, N. (1994). *Feature word spelling list: A diagnosis of progressing word knowledge through an assessment of spelling errors.* Unpublished doctoral dissertation, University of Virginia, Charlottesville.

Whitehurst, G. J., & Lonigan, C. J. (1998). Child development and emergent literacy. *Child Development, 69,* 848–872.

CHAPTER 10

❖

Reading to Learn from the Beginning

COMPREHENSION INSTRUCTION
IN THE PRIMARY GRADES

KATHERINE A. DOUGHERTY STAHL

GUIDING QUESTIONS

❖ What developmental tendencies must be considered when planning comprehension instruction in the early grades?

❖ What are the essential elements of a comprehensive comprehension curriculum?

OVERVIEW OF THE TOPIC

In the early grades, exemplary comprehension instruction is likely to be framed within a context that applies experiences, oral language, visual representations, writing, and reading in tandem around engaging content. It doesn't exist in a vacuum nor is it isolated from the comprehensive primary content curriculum. Figure 10.1 presents a model of the essential elements that are likely to lead to the development of readers who can reflect high levels of comprehension in oral and written response formats.

Current research and learning standards that are used to inform effective comprehension instruction indicate that it should be situated in functional learning contexts (Common Core State Standards Initiative [CCSSI], 2010; Shanahan et al., 2010). Hopefully, the radical extremes of children directing their own development as they read silently in isolation or drills on main idea identification, rote generation

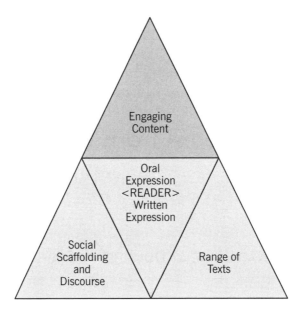

FIGURE 10.1. Essential elements of effective comprehension instruction.

of predictions, or teaching children to parrot text–self, text–text, text–world connections are practices relegated to the past. Exemplary comprehension instruction is multifaceted, contextualized, and requires intentional, responsive teaching. A level of instructional complexity is added in the primary grades because teachers need to facilitate the shift from listening comprehension to reading comprehension while balancing time for instruction in foundational reading skills (phonological awareness, decoding, and fluency). Seeing as comprehension is an in-head, invisible process, good instruction also requires explicitly teaching children to reflect their comprehension through oral language and writing (Stahl, 2009a; Stahl, Garcia, Bauer, Pearson, & Taylor, 2006).

Of key importance is the recognition by teachers that instructional adjustments must occur as children gradually become fluent, competent readers. While the preliminary instruction will be conducted with videos, teacher read-alouds, and during shared reading, the target should always be the creation of independent, thoughtful, self-regulating readers. The RAND report (RAND Reading Study Group, 2002) defines comprehension as "the process of simultaneously extracting and constructing meaning through interaction and involvement with written language" (p. 11). Teachers in the primary grades must be deliberate in building bridges between comprehension of visual media, listening comprehension, and reading comprehension. Finally, it is important to recognize that foundational skills are necessary but not sufficient to achieve high levels of reading comprehension and should not dominate the early literacy curriculum (Paris, 2005; Stahl, 2011).

THEORETICAL BACKGROUND AND RESEARCH BASE

Considering Development

The skills, abilities, and knowledge that contribute to comprehension develop across a lifetime. The development of narrative, the understanding and expression of temporal relationships, concept categorization, and the ever-increasing collection of world experiences all influence the dynamic and ongoing growth in one's ability to comprehend text (Kintsch, 1998; Nelson, 1996). As a result, young children are able to comprehend many texts before they are able to read them and in contrast, there may be texts that novice readers may decode accurately without fully comprehending.

Constrained skills theory explicates the ways that the unconstrained abilities of comprehension and vocabulary differ from highly constrained skills such as letter identification and phonics (Paris, 2005). Phonological awareness and fluency are considered moderately constrained. Highly constrained skills have a finite number of items to be learned so mastery occurs within a short time span. The developmental trajectory goes from no knowledge to mastery within a relatively short period of time depending on the size of the set of items. Variability by child lasts only for a short period. For example, in kindergarten there is a great deal of variability in letter identification by students. This variability diminishes by first grade as all students master letter-name identification. Once constrained skills are mastered, they can be transferred uniformly in all settings. The silent *e* rule works equally well whether the silent *e* word is found in a first-grade book or a medical journal. However, the ability to comprehend never reaches mastery. One can have high levels of comprehension with some texts and minimal comprehension of other texts. Each reader's prior knowledge and vocabulary have a strong influence on comprehension. Text factors such as readability, genre, and conceptual density influence one's reading comprehension. Finally, comprehension may be manipulated by adjusting the instructional context and the purpose for reading.

Historically, there has been a greater emphasis on mastering constrained skills and reading simple texts fluently in the early grades while learning how to make sense of complex narrative texts and acquiring new knowledge from informational texts, emphasized in the intermediate grades and beyond. However, the youngest readers need opportunities to be "code breakers, meaning makers, text users and text critics" (Muspratt, Luke, & Freebody, 1997, p. 95). Although we recognize that phonological awareness, decoding abilities, and reading fluency are the foundational building blocks for effective reading, today we know that comprehension instruction must occur from the very beginning, even well before the child begins to read (Dooley, 2010; Shanahan et al., 2010; Stahl, 2009b). Instruction of foundational skills to mastery levels must be a priority in the primary grades. However, evidence indicates that the correlation between foundational skills and reading comprehension diminishes over time (Paris, Carpenter, Paris, & Hamilton, 2005;

Schwanenflugel et al., 2006). As a result, schools that allow foundational skills to dominate the early literacy curriculum will pay the price in the intermediate grades when accountability stakes for comprehension are raised and spotlighted.

Adults can begin holding children accountable for comprehension well before they are able to independently read sophisticated texts. Conducting adult read-alouds embedded with and followed by rich conversation is a good starting point. Additionally, we now have evidence indicating that comprehension skills transfer across different types of media (Goldman, Varma, Sharp, & Cognition and Technology Group at Vanderbilt, 1999; Kendeou, Bohn-Gettler, White, & van den Broek, 2008; Kendeou et al., 2006). The ability to comprehend is not limited to one medium (print, video, audio). Further, narrative comprehension skills applied by young children to video and audio presentations tend to predict comprehension skills when reading printed text later in elementary school (Kendeou et al., 2006). Put another way, a preschooler who can summarize the key points of a video is also likely to be able to summarize the key ideas based on a teacher read-aloud and later, when he or she is reading a text. This implies that teachers of young children should be assertive in dedicating time to the comprehension of texts read to and with children, as well as supporting students in becoming accountable for comprehending video presentations. Teachers can direct young students' attention to narrative structure, concept organization, and causal, sequential event streams during reading, writing, video viewing, and oral language experiences.

Instructional Considerations

Although the majority of research investigating reading comprehension has been conducted in the intermediate grades and beyond, we do have a body of research that can be used to inform comprehension instruction in the early grades (Shanahan et al., 2010; Stahl, 2004). Shanahan et al. reviewed over 800 studies conducted in the primary grades over the last 20 years. After analyzing 27 studies that met rigorous research standards, they came up with a set of five recommendations for teaching comprehension in the early grades (see Table 10.1). The level of evidence for each practice ranged from strong to minimal. Recommendations with minimal evidence in the primary grades were included because of their potential for developing critical literacy and high levels of thinking. What became clear through this body of work is that these recommendations need to be used in concert with each other. It cannot be emphasized too strongly that explicit instruction, modeling, and guided practice need to lead to increasing levels of student independence (Pearson & Gallagher, 1983; see Figure 10.2). This gradual release of responsibility needs to be employed whether teaching strategies, teaching conversational moves, reading a complex text, or writing in response to reading. It is a structural thread that will be woven throughout all aspects of comprehension instruction because comprehension varies by context and mastery is elusive.

TABLE 10.1. Evidence-Based Practices for Comprehension Instruction in the Early Grades

Recommendation	Evidence
Teach students how to use comprehension strategies.	Strong
Teach students to identify and use the text's structure to comprehend, learn, and remember content.	Moderate
Guide students through focused, high-quality discussion on the meaning of text.	Minimal
Select texts purposefully to support comprehension.	Minimal
Establish an engaging and motivating context in which to teach comprehension.	Moderate

Note. Based on Shanahan et al. (2010, p. 9).

Creating Engagement

It is somewhat idealistic and unrealistic to believe that classroom teachers can follow and build instruction around individual student interests. What we can do is inspire student interest. Teachers have a great deal of power and the responsibility to create an engaging context (Guthrie et al., 2004; Morrow, Pressley, & Smith, 1995). Using disciplinary themes based on content standards generates student interest and supports reading for authentic purposes (Cervetti, Pearson, Bravo, & Barber, 2006; Purcell-Gates, Duke, & Martineau, 2007). Building conceptual knowledge serves as a scaffold for reading comprehension. In addition to providing an opportunity for deep study of a topic, repeated exposure to target vocabulary, and reading and writing for authentic purposes, units of themed study provide opportunities

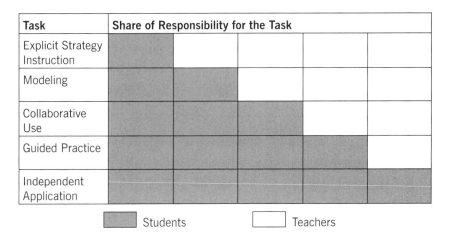

FIGURE 10.2. The gradual release of responsibility. Based on Duke and Pearson (2002), Pearson and Gallagher (1983), and Shanahan et al. (2010, p. 15).

for students to read a range of texts about a particular topic. These texts serve as anchor texts for student writing using the conventions of that discipline. They also provide the vehicle for a series of lessons on comprehension strategy instruction in functional ways. For example, a literary unit on fairytales provides a logical context for teaching narrative story structure. Reading multiple fairytales during a unit provides an opportunity to create a series of lessons moving from explicit instruction to independent practice over time (see Figure 10.2). It also allows for authentic opportunities for students to express increasing knowledge of the genre through both oral and written expression. As students gain increasing knowledge about the topic, opportunities for independent reading and writing choices abound and complement the shared experiences presented to the classroom community. State standards for literature, science, and social studies provide the fodder for developing units of study that are ripe with opportunities for engaging, comprehensive comprehension instruction.

Social Scaffolding and Discourse

Social interactions with teachers, parents, and peers help students put language to in-head processing. Whether it is hearing a teacher think aloud the strategies for figuring out a confusing bit of a textbook, hearing a peer describe a unique perspective on the events in a story, participating in a literary book club, or collaborating on a research project, social interactions extend comprehension beyond what is possible when students read text as a solitary activity. A conference can provide a brief opportunity for a teacher to check in on students individually but the time allocation in a class of 20 children doesn't allow for deep teaching or multilayered, compelling conversation during the exchange.

Comprehension Strategies

The range of genres encountered in themed units provides the vehicle for teaching comprehension strategies and text structures in service to reading comprehension. While it is important to teach each strategy individually using explicit instruction, they need to be viewed as a collective repertoire (Brown, Pressley, Van Meter, & Schuder, 1996; Palincsar & Brown, 1984; Schuder, 1993). Although instruction in a single strategy can improve comprehension (e.g., Gambrell & Jawitz, 1993; Morrow, 1985), evidence seems to indicate that good readers use multiple strategies in flexible ways (Kintsch, 1998; Pressley & Afflerbach, 1995). There is strong evidence to support the instruction of the following strategies:

◆ Targeted activation of prior knowledge leading to purposeful predictions.
◆ Identification of narrative and expository text structures.

◆ Visualizing.
◆ Questions: Answering and asking high-level questions.
◆ Taking stock: Summarizing and retelling.
◆ Generating inferences.
◆ Monitoring and applying fix-up strategies.

Instruction should begin with an explicit explanation of declarative, procedural, and conditional information about the strategy (Duffy, 1993; Paris, Lipson, & Wixson, 1983). First, one should describe the strategy to the students (declarative knowledge). Additionally, it is necessary to explain and demonstrate a procedure for applying the strategy or how to do it. Conditional knowledge includes a discussion of why the strategy is useful, when it's useful and when it is not likely to be useful.

Before expecting students to apply the strategies independently, a gradual release of responsibility needs to take place (Pearson & Gallagher, 1983; see Figure 10.2). After explicitly teaching a strategy, the teacher might model the strategy using a think-aloud. Next, individual students model the strategy within the whole-class setting. Scaffolding moves from highly supportive activities to minimally supported activities. A sequence might move along a continuum of social support such as think–pair–share within a whole-class discussion, a teacher-led small group, and a student-led small group, followed by a partner activity before a child is called on to assume independent responsibility. It is at this final stage that the conference is useful, but teaching and guided practice must precede it.

Teachers of young children can also consider strategy application in more or less supportive media, such as moving from experiences to video to little book to complex picturebook to chapter book without pictures to hypertext. Finally, representation of the ideas would also move from oral to written expression. Teachers need to be mindful that if moving to a less supportive social scaffold one may want to begin students in an easier medium and move to more challenging media as students demonstrate success.

A few cautions are warranted regarding strategy instruction. First, the primary goal of reading is comprehension, not applying reading strategies. Strategy application should be viewed as a tool to overcome hurdles to meaning making, not the goal of reading instruction. If generating predictions takes longer than text reading, strategy instruction may be dominating instruction in unhealthy ways. Second, although taught individually, students need to be able to apply multiple strategies flexibly in response to hurdles.

Reciprocal teaching (RT), a multiple-strategy protocol, has been applied successfully in the primary grades (Coley, DePinto, Craig, & Gardner, 1993; Palincsar, 1988, 1991). During RT, each child in the small-group setting takes turns acting as teacher to discuss a segment of text applying a routine for clarifying, questioning, summarizing, and predicting. RT is useful for providing temporary guided practice in strategy application before children move to more flexible, independent, in-head application. Once the routine is taught, it can be used whenever students are required to read a difficult text. Transactional strategy instruction (TSI) also has a strong research base in the primary grades (Brown & Coy-Ogan, 1993; Brown et al., 1996; Schuder, 1993). Each comprehension strategy is taught explicitly, but the text discussions incorporate all of the strategies in organic ways. TSI is long term and the strategies propel text discussions.

High-Level Discussion

Both RT and TSI conversations are structured around comprehension strategies and have been demonstrated to contribute to deep reading. However, deep reading that leads to comprehension can also be facilitated by high-level discussions that are not built around strategy application (Beck & McKeown, 2001; McKeown, Beck, & Blake, 2009; Rosenshine & Meister, 1994; Saunders & Goldenberg, 1999; Stahl, 2009b; Taylor, Pearson, Clark, & Walpole, 2000; Taylor, Peterson, Pearson, & Rodriguez, 2002). Discussions about text may be teacher-led or student-led. They may involve the whole class or a small group. In the discussions observed by Taylor and her colleagues, effective teachers asked high-level questions in whole-class settings that addressed text themes, personal connections, and required students to make inferences.

Two instructional protocols provide frames for implementing high-level discussions in response to text. Text Talk is a teacher read-aloud discussion protocol that incorporates targeted prereading discussions, high-level questioning, and elaborated vocabulary development activities to support young children's comprehension of sophisticated picturebooks (Beck & McKeown, 2001). By emphasizing questioning and deemphasizing each book's pictures, this protocol helps children begin to use each book's language as the source of meaning. Both English-only and English Learners (ELs) reaped the benefits of small-group Instructional Conversations that followed shared reading of rich literature (Saunders & Goldenberg, 1999). Students responded in writing to teacher-generated theme-based prompts and used these written journal entries to propel small student-led conversations.

Although most discussions in response to read-alouds occur in a whole-class setting, whenever manageable it is useful to provide a small-group opportunity to discuss the text. Only a limited number of students get to respond to questions that are asked in a whole-class setting. Creating an opportunity for students to discuss a compelling question about the book following the reading in a small-group setting allows for more children to share their response to the text. Shy children, ELs, and children who speak nonstandard English who may be less likely to share in a whole-class setting need safe places where they get more talk time to discuss their insights and expand their language skills (Saunders & Goldenberg, 1999; Schwanenflugel et al., 2010; Silverman & Crandell, 2010).

In order for small student-led groups to be productive, a gradual release of responsibility needs to be applied (see Figure 10.2). Stahl (2009b) determined that explicit instruction that focuses on the characteristics of a good discussion, modeling, and releasing the leadership of the small-group discussion to students must occur slowly in the primary grades. Sustained teacher commitment is required. Providing opportunities for students to observe and use a rubric to critique their peers engaging in student-led discussions in a "fishbowl" setting or in a video recording have been demonstrated to be effective forms of scaffolding. Time spent sitting "on the side" and gently coaching as students assume ownership is the only way to guarantee that student-led discussions will be interactive and rich (Maloch, 2002, 2005; Stahl, 2009b).

Text Variety

Students need to be immersed in a wide range of texts (CCSSI, 2010; Shanahan et al., 2010). The Common Core State Standards recommend achieving a balance of 50% narrative and 50% informational text by grade 4. Exposure to texts that vary by genre, topic, difficulty, and medium is needed to develop cognitively responsive, competent readers. While readers need immersion in many types of texts, the unit of study often provides enough sustained practice with one or two genres to allow children to become successful readers and writers of those types of texts. Reading, writing, and discussing specific kinds of texts should operate in tandem. Reading text is responsive, provides an exemplar, and is less demanding than generating text. Discussion is generative requiring cognitive engagement, adherence to the disciplinary discourse style, and practice using target vocabulary. Writing text is also a productive task that allows for the expression of ideas and a deeper knowledge of the genre that will feed recursively into ongoing reading development.

In addition to reading a variety of text genres, a classroom needs to provide students with opportunities to read texts within a wide range of complexity. This takes on increased importance in the primary grades because the students' decoding abilities limit what they can read independently. Comprehension instruction requires *heavy* texts, texts with rich vocabulary, universal themes, and conceptual density. Heavy texts need to be introduced in a read-aloud or shared-reading setting. Follow-up reading, discussion, and writing activities in the small-group and independent setting provide continuous exposure to difficult texts in ways that support literacy growth as opposed to frustration or boredom. Instructional protocols such as Fluency-Oriented Reading Instruction and Wide Reading (FORI) are essential practices for building bridges between listening comprehension and reading comprehension (Schwanenflugel et al., 2006, 2009). Kuhn, Phelan and Schwanenflugel describe these procedures in detail in Chapter 12.

Writing is a means of consolidating and extending our thinking about what we have read. It is also one of the most important ways that sophisticated readers convey their text comprehension to the outside world. As a result, a focus on the writing that young children do in response to text must be a priority in comprehension instruction (Cervetti et al., 2006; Guthrie et al., 2004; Purcell et al., 2007). The Standards also emphasize the importance of writing in response to text (CCSSI, 2010). As with reading, writing activities need to be varied. Short personal reactions to text, responses to theme-based prompts, and exposition based on new learning are just a few examples of shorter products that would be likely expressions that evolve from reading experiences. However, extended writing activities that relate to the overall unit theme are also important. These projects typically require the application of a writing process that includes prewriting, drafting, revising, and publishing. When students are engaged in studying a science or social studies unit, the product might be based on their own research. In literary units, the outcome might be a creative product or an extended personal narrative. An example of such a project is described in the accompanying box.

A second-grade class was involved in a monthlong literary unit on family narratives. Many of Patricia Polacco's books that addressed family themes (and other similar complex picturebooks) were used as teacher read-alouds or shared reading. After the first reading by the teacher, each book was placed in the class library and became available to students for independent choice reading. A teacher read-aloud was conducted daily. Additionally, four different texts were used as shared reading. These books were also sophisticated picturebooks with a family narrative theme. All students had their own copy of texts used for shared reading. Each story used for shared reading was the focus of a weeklong study. During each of the 4 weeks the students engaged in echo reading, choral reading, and partner reading the story. They also engaged in comprehension strategy instruction, small-group discussion, and writing short responses to the text.

During the first week of the unit the students were responsible for interviewing their parents and grandparents to identify an interesting family story that occurred before the student was born. This story might tell how their parents met, how their family came to live in their hometown, convey how a family member overcame a hardship, describe an honorable act by a family member, or recount some other significant family memory. During week 2, each child shared the story orally with a small group of peers. The peers asked questions about the details of the story. During weeks 3 and 4, the children drafted, revised, and published their family memory in writing. Additionally, each child brought a favorite family recipe to class. Each story and recipe became an entry in a class cookbook that was sent home as a Mother's Day gift.

A KINDERGARTEN EXAMPLE

Natalie teaches kindergarten in a high-poverty urban school. In the spring, she teaches an integrated 2-week science unit on light and shadow. Each morning, she conducts small instructional reading groups and developmental word study that incorporates phonological awareness, phonics, and spelling. In the afternoon, she focuses on comprehension, conceptual vocabulary, and writing processes using her current unit on light and shadow as the vehicle for instruction. The lesson below occurred a few days into the unit.

Teacher read-aloud (30 minutes): Natalie reads and discusses the story *Bear Shadow* (Asch, 1990) with the students in a whole-class format. It is a narrative describing Bear's efforts to get rid of a shadow that appears to pose an obstacle to a fishing expedition. Although it is fiction, conceptual information about the ways that sunlight influences the formation of shadows is presented in story illustrations. During some episodes Natalie has the children act out the story. She briefly defines a few vocabulary words at the point of contact (*fishing line, brook, annoyed*). Questioning occurs intermittently throughout the story to ensure that the content is understood, particularly as it relates to the disciplinary knowledge of shadow formation. Her questioning leads the children to describe how the sun's position in the sky is causing the size of the shadow to change. After reading, the children recount the sequence of episodes that portrayed Bear's attempts to get rid of Shadow. Next, they describe Bear's physical traits and character traits. Natalie writes the words for each trait on a drawing of Bear (see the accompanying photo). Following the read-aloud the students go to one of eight stations around the room (see Figure 10.3 on pages 186–187). Some of the stations are related to the story and others relate to light and shadow. Each station requires reading or writing, sometimes both. Children stay in one station for 15 minutes. Most stations will be in place throughout the unit.

CONCLUSION

Young children learn about their world through experiences and oral language. As time goes on, particularly after school entry and throughout one's lifetime, our understanding of the world is shaped by what we read. The primary grades are a crucial time for creating the bridge that leads children beyond the mechanics of reading to the glory of discovery promised by each new page that we turn or tap.

REFERENCES

Asch, F. (1990). *Bear shadow*. New York: Scholastic.

Beck, I. L., & McKeown, M. G. (2001). Text Talk: Capturing the benefits of read aloud experiences for young children. *The Reading Teacher, 55*, 10–35.

Station	Materials	Activity
Written response to story	Paper, pencils, and crayons	Students write a trait that describes their favorite character in the book (Bear or Shadow) and illustrate it.
Read around the room	Pointer; poems about light and shadow on chart paper posted around the room	Partners walk around the room reading or singing poetry posters as they point to the words. They select one poem to illustrate. (See Photo 1 on page 187.)
Computer station	Computer set to e-book: R. L. Stevenson's "My Shadow" (www.starfall.com/n/poetry/myshadow/load.htm?f)	Students echo read the poem.
Light inquiry notebook	Basket of easy-to-read informational little books about light and shadow; personal light inquiry notebook	Students read little books and add new learning, including drawings with captions, to their personal light inquiry notebook. (See Photo 2 on page 187.)
Shadow puppets	Light on mini-tripod; shadow puppet book	Create shadow puppets. (See Photo 3 on page 187.)
How do shadows change?	Lamp; wooden blocks; personal light inquiry notebook	Students change the position of the block to explore how shadows change; record observations in personal light inquiry notebook.
Categorization activity	Light table; a variety of materials to demonstrate opaque, translucent, and transparent	Students create structures on the light table with the materials. Categorize each item as opaque, translucent, and transparent on a chart.
Skeleton activity	Light table; X-rays of body parts	Assemble a human body using the X-rays. (See Photo 4 on page 187.)

FIGURE 10.3. Light and shadow stations.

Photo 1

Photo 2

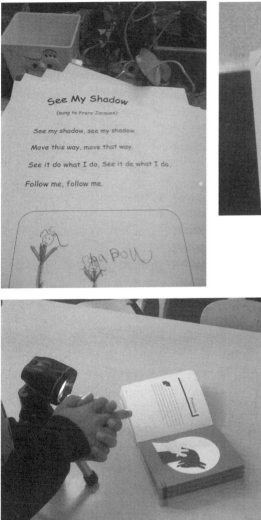

Photo 3

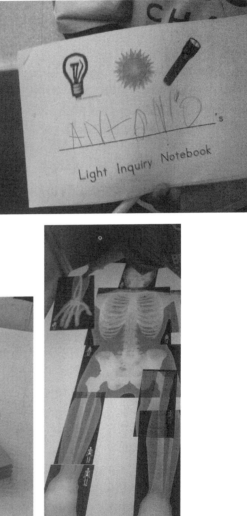

Photo 4

Brown, R., & Coy-Ogan, L. (1993). The evolution of transactional strategies instruction in one teacher's classroom. *Elementary School Journal, 94*, 221–233.

Brown, R., Pressley, M., Van Meter, P., & Schuder, T. (1996). A quasi-experimental validation of transactional strategies instruction with low-achieving second grade readers. *Journal of Educational Psychology, 88*, 18–37.

Cervetti, G., Pearson, P. D., Bravo, M., & Barber, J. (2006) Reading and writing in the service of inquiry-based science. In R. Douglas, M. P. Klentschy, & K. Worth (Eds.), *Linking science and literacy in the K–8 classroom* (pp. 221–244). Arlington, VA: National Science Teachers Association Press.

Coley, J. D., DePinto, T., Craig, S., & Gardner, R. (1993). From college to classroom: Three teachers' accounts of their adaptations of reciprocal teaching. *Elementary School Journal, 94*, 255–266.

Common Core State Standards Initiative. (2010). *Common core state standards for English language arts and literacy in history/social studies, science, and technical subjects*. Washington, DC: National Governors Association Center for Best Practices and the Council of Chief State School Officers.

Dooley, C. M. (2010). Young children's approaches to books: The emergence of comprehension. *The Reading Teacher, 64*, 120–131.

Duffy, G. (1993). Rethinking strategy instruction: Four teachers' development and their low achievers' understanding. *Elementary School Journal, 93*, 231–247.

Duke, N. K., & Pearson, P. D. (2002). Effective practices for developing reading comprehension. In A. E. Farstrup & S. Samuels (Eds.), *What research has to say about reading instruction* (pp. 205–242). Newark, DE: International Reading Association.

Gambrell, L. B., & Jawitz, P. B. (1993). Mental imagery, text illustrations, and children's story comprehension and recall. *Reading Research Quarterly, 28*, 265–273.

Goldman, S. R., Varma, K. O., Sharp, D., & Cognition and Technology Group at Vanderbilt. (1999). Children's understanding of complex stories: Issues of representation and assessment. In S. R. Goldman, A. C. Graesser, & P. van den Broek (Eds.), *Narrative comprehension, causality, and coherence: Essays in honor of Tom Trabaso* (pp. 135–159). Mahwah, NJ: Erlbaum.

Guthrie, J. T., Wigfield, A., Barbosa, P., Perencevich, K. C., Taboada, A., Davis, M. H., et al. (2004). Increasing reading comprehension and engagement through Concept-Oriented Reading Instruction. *Journal of Educational Psychology, 96*, 403–423.

Kendeou, P., Bohn-Gettler, C., White, M. J., & van den Broek, P. (2008). Children's inference generation across different media. *Journal of Research in Reading, 31*(3), 259–272.

Kendeou, P., Lynch, J. S., van den Broek, P., Espin, C. A., White, M. J., & Kremer, K. E. (2006). Developing successful readers: Building early comprehension skills through television viewing and listening. *Early Childhood Education Journal, 33*(2), 91–98.

Kintsch, W. (1998). *Comprehension: A paradigm for cognition*. Cambridge, UK: Cambridge University Press.

Maloch, B. (2002). Scaffolding student talk: One teacher's role in literature discussion groups. *Reading Research Quarterly, 37*, 94–112.

Maloch, B. (2005). Moments by which change is made: A cross-case exploration of teacher mediation and student participation in literacy events. *Journal of Literacy Research, 37,* 95–142.

McKeown, M. G., Beck, I. L., & Blake, R. G. K. (2009). Rethinking reading comprehension instruction: A comparison of instruction for strategies and content approaches. *Reading Research Quarterly, 44*(3), 218–253.

Morrow, L. M. (1985). Retelling stories: A strategy for improving young children's comprehension concept of story structure, and oral language complexity. *Elementary School Journal, 85,* 646–660.

Morrow, L. M., Pressley, M., & Smith, J. K. (1995). *The effect of a literature-based program integrated into literacy and science instruction on achievement, use, and attitudes toward literacy and science* (Reading Research Report No. 37). College Park, MD: National Reading Research Center.

Muspratt, S., Luke, A., & Freebody, P. (1997). *Constructing critical literacies.* Cresskills, NJ: Hampton.

Nelson, K. (1996). *Language in cognitive development: Emergence of the mediated mind.* Cambridge, UK: Cambridge University Press.

Palincsar, A. S. (1988, April 5–9). *Collaborating in the interest of collaborative learning.* Paper presented at the annual meeting of the American Educational Research Association, New Orleans, LA.

Palincsar, A. S. (1991). Scaffolded instruction of listening comprehension with first graders at risk for academic difficulty. In A. M. McKeough & J. L. Lupart (Eds.), *Toward the practice of theory-based instruction* (pp. 50–65). Mahwah, NJ: Erlbaum.

Palincsar, A. S., & Brown, A. L. (1984). Reciprocal teaching of comprehension-fostering and comprehension-monitoring activities. *Cognition and Instruction, 2,* 117–175.

Paris, S. G. (2005). Re-interpreting the development of reading skills. *Reading Research Quarterly, 40,* 184–202.

Paris, S. G., Carpenter, R. D., Paris, A. H., & Hamilton, E. (2005). Spurious and genuine correlates of children's reading comprehension. In S. G. Paris & S. A. Stahl (Eds.), *Children's reading comprehension and assessment* (pp. 131–160). Hillsdale, NJ: Erlbaum.

Paris, S. G., Lipson, M. Y., & Wixson, K. K. (1983). Becoming a strategic reader. *Contemporary Educational Psychology, 8,* 293–316.

Pearson, P. D., & Gallagher, M. C. (1983). The instruction of reading comprehension. *Contemporary Educational Psychology, 8,* 317–344.

Pressley, M., & Afflerbach, P. (1995). *Verbal protocols of reading: The nature of constructively responsive reading.* Mahwah, NJ: Erlbaum.

Purcell-Gates, V., Duke, N. K., & Martineau, J. A. (2007). Learning to read and write genre-specific text: Roles of authentic experience and explicit teaching. *Reading Research Quarterly, 42,* 8–45.

RAND Reading Study Group. (2002). *Reading for understanding: Toward an R&D program in reading comprehension.* Santa Monica, CA: RAND Corporation.

Rosenshine, B., & Meister, C. (1994). Reciprocal teaching: A review of the research. *Review of Educational Research, 64,* 479–530.

Saunders, W. M., & Goldenberg, C. (1999). The effects of instructional conversations and literature logs on the story comprehension and thematic understanding of English Proficient and Limited English Proficient Students. *Elementary School Journal, 99*, 279–301.

Schuder, T. (1993). The genesis of transactional strategies instruction in a reading program for at-risk students. *Elementary School Journal, 94*, 183–200.

Schwanenflugel, P. J., Hamilton, C. E., Neuwirth-Pritchett, S., Restrepo, M. A., Bradley, B. A., & Webb, M. Y. (2010). PAVEd for success: An evaluation of a comprehensive preliteracy program for four-year-old children. *Journal of Literacy Research, 42*, 227–275.

Schwanenflugel, P. J., Kuhn, M. R., Morris, R. D., Morrow, L. M., Meisinger, E. B., Woo, D. G., et al. (2009). Insights into fluency instruction: Short- and long-term effects of two reading programs. *Literacy Research and Instruction, 48*(4), 318–336.

Schwanenflugel, P. J., Meisinger, E., Wisenbaker, J. M., Kuhn, M. R., Strauss, G. P., & Morris, R. D. (2006). Becoming a fluent and automatic reader in the early elementary school years. *Reading Research Quarterly, 41*(4), 496–522.

Shanahan, T., Callison, K., Carriere, C., Duke, N. K., Pearson, P. D., Schatschneider, C., et al. (2010). *Improving reading comprehension in kindergarten through 3rd grade: A practice guide* (NCEE 2010-4038). Washington, DC: National Center for Education Evaluation and Regional Assistance, Institute of Education Sciences, U.S. Department of Education. Retrieved from *whatworks.ed.gov/publications/practiceguides*.

Silverman, R., & Crandell, J. D. (2010). Vocabulary practices in prekindergarten and kindergarten classrooms. *Reading Research Quarterly, 45*, 318–340.

Stahl, K. A. D. (2004). Proof, practice and promise: Comprehension strategy instruction in the primary grades. *The Reading Teacher, 57*, 598–609.

Stahl, K. A. D. (2009a). Assessing the comprehension of young children. In S. E. Israel & G. G. Duffy (Eds.), *Handbook of research on reading comprehension* (pp. 428–448). New York: Guilford Press.

Stahl, K. A. D. (2009b). Comprehensive synthesized comprehension instruction in primary classrooms: A story of successes and challenges. *Reading and Writing Quarterly, 25*, 334–355.

Stahl, K. A. D. (2011). Applying new visions of reading development in today's classrooms. *The Reading Teacher, 65*, 52–56.

Stahl, K. A. D., Garcia, G. E., Bauer, E. B., Pearson, P. D., & Taylor, B. M. (2006). Making the invisible visible: The development of a comprehension assessment system. In K. A. D. Stahl & M. C. McKenna (Eds.), *Reading research at work: Foundations of effective practice* (pp. 425–436). New York: Guilford Press.

Stevenson, R. L. (1921). *My shadow*. Retrieved from *www.starfall.com/n/poetry/myshadow/load.htm?f*.

Taylor, B. M., Pearson, P. D., Clark, K., & Walpole, S. (2000). Effective schools and accomplished teachers: Lessons about primary grade reading instruction in low-income schools. *Elementary School Journal, 101*, 121–166.

Taylor, B. M., Peterson, D. P., Pearson, P. D., & Rodriguez, M. C. (2002). Looking inside classrooms: Reflecting on the "how" as well as the "what" in effective reading instruction. *The Reading Teacher, 56*, 70–79.

CHAPTER 11

❖

Best Practices
in Oral Vocabulary Instruction

Susan B. Neuman
Tanya S. Wright

GUIDING QUESTIONS

❖ How can we accelerate children's oral vocabulary development in the early years of instruction?

❖ What are the most beneficial instructional principles to support oral vocabulary development?

Vocabulary occupies an important role in learning to read. As children begin to read, the words that they encounter in texts must be mapped on to the oral vocabulary they see in the text. That is, the young reader must be taught to translate the (relatively) unfamiliar print on to their oral language (Kamil, 2004). Understandably, these connections work only if the words they read make sense to them. Consequently, oral vocabulary development is critical to learning to read, especially when beginning readers make the transition from oral to written forms. By grade 4, children with below-average vocabulary levels, even if they have adequate word-identification skills, are likely to "slump" in reading comprehension, unable to profit from independent reading of most grade-level texts (Chall, Jacobs, & Baldwin, 1990).

Despite the clear importance of vocabulary, the practical problem is that right from the beginning of schooling there are profound differences in vocabulary knowledge among young learners from different socioeconomic groups (Hart & Risley, 1995; Hoff, 2003). Just consider the following statistics: By age 3, a child's interaction with his or her family has already produced significant vocabulary differences across socioeconomic lines, differences so dramatic that they represent a "30-million-word catastrophe," according to Hart and Risley (2003). Recent analyses (Rodriquez & Tamis-LeMonda, 2011) indicate that environmental factors associated with vocabulary development and emergent literacy skills are already present among children as early as 15 months of age. By first grade, unfortunately, its repercussions become all too clear (Graves, 2006): Children from higher SES groups are likely to know about twice as many words as lower SES children, putting these children at significant risk for school failure.

At the same time, recent evidence (Beck & McKeown, 2007; Coyne, McCoach, & Kapp, 2007; Marulis & Neuman, 2010) indicates that there is much we can do to improve children's oral vocabulary development. Converging evidence indicates that providing children with explicit definitions of words, discussing words in various contexts, and reviewing words on many occasions promotes oral language comprehension and development. In short, this research emphasizes that when vocabulary instruction is active and multidimensional, we can go a long way toward narrowing the achievement gap.

In this chapter, we first describe the rich knowledge base that has accumulated in recent years on vocabulary development. We then bring this knowledge to practice in early literacy classrooms. We will describe powerful instructional principles that are designed to accelerate children's learning, indicating that quality teaching practices can significantly improve children's vocabulary and comprehension skills, getting children on the road to successful reading.

THE RESEARCH BASE
FOR TEACHING ORAL VOCABULARY INSTRUCTION

There has been an explosion of interest in oral vocabulary instruction in recent years. To summarize much of this work, we conducted two syntheses of reviews: first with 67 studies and 216 effect sizes (Marulis & Neuman, 2010), and the second, targeting children at risk with 46 studies and 133 effect sizes (Marulis & Neuman, 2011). In our review of children at risk, we examined studies in a number of risk categories: poverty, language delays and language diversity, special education, and minority status. In each case, we asked whether vocabulary interventions were effective, for whom, and under what conditions.

It turns out that certain pedagogical features support oral language more than others. One key feature, for example, is the importance of explicit vocabulary instruction. A program that uses explicit instruction may include detailed definitions and examples given before, during, or after a storybook reading with a follow-up discussion designed to review these words. There are numerous ways to provide explicit instruction. For example, prior to a story, Coyne and his colleagues

(Coyne, Simmons, Kame'enui, & Stoolmiller, 2004) introduced children to "magic words" (i.e., vocabulary words that were particularly salient in the storybook). As a teacher reads the story, children are encouraged to raise their hands when hearing the magic word, helping them to become *word conscious* throughout the reading. Another example is to include clear, child-friendly definitions and explanations of target words before reading these words in the rich context of authentic children's literature. In our work with the World of Words (Neuman, Newman, & Dwyer, 2011), we use video to introduce children to a target word, an exemplar of a category such as "parts of the body." We then engage children in choral response activities that highlight the word in new contexts.

Similarly, Beck and McKeown (2007) describe "rich instruction" in which words are explicitly introduced first in context, "In the story it says that robbers had lots of good things to eat, and so they had a *'feast,'* " followed by a definition of the word's meaning (e.g., "A *feast* is a big special meal with lots of delicious foods."). Although varying in their approach, each of these programs provides explicit definitions or descriptions of target words.

Studies have shown that programs that engage children in explicit instruction have greater effects than those that rely on words taught implicitly in the context of reading (Marulis & Neuman, 2010). For example, implicit instruction might involve hearing the word embedded in an activity, such as a storybook reading activity without intentional stopping or deliberate teaching of word meanings. At the same time, here is something to remember that is critically important. Programs that use *both* explicit and implicit instruction are more effective than those that use explicit instruction alone. For example, Coyne and his colleagues (Coyne, McCoach, Loftus, Zipoli, Ruby, et al., 2010) followed storybook reading with open-ended questions containing target words. Students were also given prompts to extend or expand their responses to encourage them to demonstrate their understanding of target words. This program was more effective than explicit instruction alone. Similarly, in addition to questions and prompts, Silverman (2007) gave children opportunities to act out the meaning of words, and/or to use visual aids to illustrate their meaning. In the WOW (Neuman, Dwyer, Koh, & Wright, 2007), we involve children in an activity called "time for a challenge," asking them to sort challenging words into categories and to describe their reasons for doing so. Each of these programs engages children in using words in multiple contexts, giving them time to review and practice what they had learned. In this respect, the most successful programs use an instructional regime of explicit selection of words, opportunities to give meaning, practice, review, and strategies to determine children's progress in word learning.

One of the continuing challenges is to determine which words need to be taught, especially given that at most, only 500 words per year can be explicitly instructed (Jenkins, Stein, & Wysocki, 1984). The usual approach has been to select words from storybooks that are likely to be judged as unfamiliar to children. However, researchers have recently proposed more specific considerations for choosing words. Biemiller (2001), for example, has advocated for focusing on the breadth of word knowledge, helping children learn words that are already partially familiar. Given that children are likely to learn these words rapidly, he argues that such an approach can increase vocabulary size dramatically. Beck and McKeown (2007), on the other hand, posit that words for vocabulary instruction should be selected from the portion of the word stock that comprises sophisticated words of high utility for mature language users and that are characteristic of written language. These words, which are described in their heuristic as Tier Two words, are domain general, representing more refined labels for concepts with which children are already familiar. The word *elegant*, for example, might be a refinement of the concept of *good-looking*. While Biemiller's approach focuses on breadth, Beck, McKeown, and Kucan (2002) focus on depth of word knowledge.

In contrast to both of these approaches, we have argued in our work (Neuman et al., 2011) for a third method for selecting words. Focusing on state standards in four content areas (e.g., math, science, arts, social studies) as well as the Common Core State Standards (CCSS; Common Core State Standards—ELA, 2010) we suggest that words be selected based on their utility for learning in content areas. For example, words like *habitat, desert*, and *jungle* are all associated with learning about wild animals—a key learning topic in science. In addition, when we teach these words in semantic relationships through richly organized categories we provide a mechanism for generalization and inference generation. For example, here is a typical word list from a core reading program: *platypus, around, lost, found*, and *groceries* (Wright & Neuman, 2013). In contrast, when we teach about "parts of the body," our list includes *elbow, shoulders, organs*, and *heart*. Further, words supporting the learning of science in this case, such as *compare–contrast, inquiry, question*, and so forth are critical for engaging in problem-solving learning. If vocabulary instruction is to enhance children's word knowledge, it needs to produce knowledge of high utility for additional learning.

Finally, our syntheses of research highlighted the importance of assessment. Authors of previous consensus reports (National Reading Panel Report, 2000; National Research Council, 2001) have recognized the difficulty in the measurement of vocabulary. One of these difficulties is that researchers must distinguish between many different aspects of vocabulary knowledge. Receptive vocabulary reflects the cognitive processing involved in comprehending oral, symbolic, or written language, whereas productive vocabulary reflects an understanding of the words when speaking to others. It is generally believed that receptive vocabulary is much larger than productive vocabulary (National Reading Panel Report, 2000). Another difficulty with the measurement of vocabulary is that interventions teach only a relatively small number of words, yet standardized assessments are designed to evaluate a broader cross-section of vocabulary.

These difficulties are especially problematic when it comes to measuring vocabulary improvements. Like others (Elleman, Lindo, Morphy, & Compton, 2009), we have found evidence that teacher-developed measures are more sensitive in detecting improvements in vocabulary development than standardized measures. Teacher-created measures tend to reflect more immediate, curriculum-based learning outcomes than the more distal measures of language development. Since these teacher-created measures may be more closely tied to what you teach, they may answer a basic question: Have children learned what I have taught? However, without standardized measures for confirmatory evidence, teacher-created measures, on their own, may provide an inflated portrait of the vocabulary gains made in studies. Standardized assessments, therefore, tend to reflect the most conservative end of the spectrum of vocabulary acquisition for young children, with the growth on teacher-created measures reflecting the other end of the spectrum.

In summary, recent studies provide strong, research-based guidance for instruction in oral vocabulary in early literacy development. Teachers can make dramatic improvements in reading instruction when we apply what is known from this evidence. In addition, these studies also reveal the importance of pedagogical approaches that entail active engagement with word learning, multiple repetitions in multiple settings, and the use of ancillary tools such as multimedia presentations. These are all features that can easily be incorporated in daily instruction.

BRINGING ORAL VOCABULARY INSTRUCTION INTO THE EARLY LITERACY CLASSROOM

Brianna and Mia are on their knees on their rest mats in their prekindergarten classroom with their hands surrounding their heads. Once in a while they peek over their arms to look at each other and giggle. Their teacher, Sarah, comes over to investigate.

SARAH: Girls, this is a very unusual way to nap. What's going on?

BRIANNA: (*giggling*) We're a nocturtle.

SARAH: Oh. What's a nocturtle?

BRIANNA: We're being a turtle that stays awake all night long.

MIA: We can't do rest time 'cause we're being a nocturtle.

SARAH: (*laughing as well*) So you're nocturnal turtles?

BOTH GIRLS: (*giggling hysterically now*) YEAH! We're a nocturtle.

SARAH: Well, that is pretty funny and it makes me wonder if there are nocturnal turtles, so after rest time I think we really need to look that up on the computer.

In Sarah's prekindergarten classroom, the children have been learning about different types of animals—nocturnal animals, insects, marine mammals, and even pets. For each of these topics, Sarah selects key concepts and vocabulary that she wants the children to learn and then structures a variety of opportunities for young children to build this knowledge through read-alouds, discussions, and play. She uses an instructional framework to guide her teaching (Neuman & Dwyer, 2009), which includes thoughtful word selection, explicit instruction, practice, review, and progress monitoring. This well-planned sequence of instruction, based on the evidence of research, ensures that all of her children build word and world knowledge in her classroom. As this scenario demonstrates, these 4-year-olds are pretty confident in engaging with sophisticated concepts and vocabulary. You can also sense their excitement in applying new words and ideas to their daily experiences.

In the following sections, we review this instructional framework, highlighting an approach that is consistent with the research base and the CCSS. Today's children will need to learn not only the academic vocabulary but the content-specific words and the concepts that underlie them sufficiently well early on so that they can be prepared to read more complex text.

Word Selection

In our work, we focus specifically on content-rich vocabulary instruction. That is, we believe that children must learn words that are tied to meaningful concepts about the world around them. This vocabulary will be necessary for them to comprehend complex text, and to have discussions related to their learning. Therefore, we emphasize words that will be essential in children's further work. For example, children will need to learn words such as *investigate, observe, predict, inquire,* and *examine,* all words that are associated with learning in content areas.

Here are things to keep in mind when you begin to select words for explicit instruction.

Teach Word Meanings and Concepts Together

In our work with teachers, we use a system of word selection that is focused on building children's content knowledge. The goal is to expand children's vocabulary and "schemata" (i.e., knowledge networks) by teaching sets of conceptually related words in the context of meaningful knowledge-building experiences.

To do this, we begin with the concepts and ideas that we want children to learn and then choose the vocabulary to support children in understanding and discussing these ideas. For example, if we want children to understand that each part of a plant has a particular function, we need to teach the vocabulary to label each part (e.g., *root*), as well as to describe its function (e.g., *absorb, support*). Teaching words in the context of learning new ideas is engaging for children because the focus is not on words for their own sake, but on developing coherent and meaningful knowledge and understanding.

A good place to start is to examine the themes you teach each year. Are there topics that you already teach (e.g., emotions, bugs, weather, marine mammals) that can be supplemented with more challenging words? Next, go to the library and find lots of books—both literature and informational texts—related to this topic. Think about ideas and concepts that you want children to learn and then select challenging words that children will need to understand and discuss this topic. For example, if children already discuss weather during circle time using the words *rainy, sunny, cloudy,* and *snowy,* you can add new words that articulate these words in greater detail—such as *muggy, overcast, precipitation, climate,* and *forecast*—in order to deepen children's knowledge and vocabulary for this topic.

Make Sure the Words You Teach Are Challenging

In our research we have found that commonly used curricula often spend a good percentage of the time focused on teaching common word meanings that children are likely to already know—words they may learn from everyday conversations rather than on more challenging words and concepts (Wright & Neuman, 2013). While briefly explaining common words (e.g., *baby, flower, sunny*) when they arise in daily conversation may be useful for English language learners and for children with very limited vocabularies, your efforts should be used for more systematic and planned instruction of the more content-rich academic words to support listening and reading comprehension. For example, children are unlikely to encounter the words *sapling* or *life cycle* in their everyday conversations. However, these words are essential for developing an in-depth understanding of plants—a common science topic in early childhood classrooms. Children who can use and explain the word *sapling* probably know a lot about plants, and this knowledge and vocabulary work together to support their comprehension of texts and discussions related to this topic.

Day-to-day words can be taught through teachable moments, and may only require a brief explanation. Challenging, content-rich words, such as *fragrant, pollen, seedling,* and *moisture,* on the other hand, will need more attention because they are not typical of common speech. These challenging words will be new to most young children, and therefore good candidates for more systematic instruction.

Teach Many Words

Often core curricula—your basal reading texts—also underestimate the number of vocabulary words children will need in order to be successful. In our research, we found some teach as little as two to five new words per week. Particularly for children who arrive at school with more limited vocabulary, even five words a week is too slow a rate and will hardly make a dent in the 80,000 words that children will need by the end of high school. While we obviously cannot teach all of these words in school, it is important to remember that young children, who cannot yet read independently, *need* adults in order to learn new words. Unlike older children who can learn new words by reading, the only way for young children to be exposed to a new word is if an adult says it or reads it aloud. So teachers will need to use and explain many new words if we want children to develop a rich vocabulary base for comprehending complex text.

In WOW, we teach 10 new target words related to a particular topic (e.g., *insects, marine mammals*) in a 2-week period, along with over 20 or so supporting words—which we describe as words needed to support children's learning of target words (see Figure 11.1, for example). Children can retain these words when there is sufficient practice, and when they are tied to meaningful learning. Consequently, as you select words to teach in your classroom, remember that you (and other adults in the children's environment) are the primary source for their vocabulary development. If you teach large sets of conceptually related words, children will learn them, and will be able to use this knowledge and vocabulary as a foundation for future learning.

Explicit Instruction

After selecting a set of conceptually related and challenging vocabulary, the next step is to provide explicit instruction for each of them. Word meanings should be explained and discussed multiple times, then used repeatedly in the context of the topic of study. Consider several of the approaches listed below to help children learn the meanings for new vocabulary words.

Topic	Main Concepts	Vocabulary
Parts of the Body	1. Our bodies have many parts. 2. Body parts are attached to our bodies. They do not come off. 3. Every body part has a job, and each helps us to do something. 4. Some body parts help us to move. 5. Some body parts are part of our five senses. 6. Body parts come in different numbers.	***eyebrows, forehead, torso, organs, shoulders, lungs, stomach, abdomen, heart, elbow, spine*** *oxygen, carbon dioxide, breathe, blood, hair, tears, attached, job, move, walk, run, jump, dance, rotate, hold things/hands, throw, catch, wave, feel, touch, smell, taste, hear, see, senses, unique, bend, nod, clap, snap*

FIGURE 11.1. An example of words taught in a topic in the World of Words (WOW) curriculum. Words in **bold italics** are target words; words in *italics* are supporting words.

Use Child-Friendly Definitions

Connecting new words to something children already know a good deal about is an effective strategy for learning. A child-friendly definition goes a long way. For example, when we explain *life cycle* to prekindergarten children who are learning about plants, we say:

> "Just like people, plants have a *life cycle*, which means they start out young and they can grow old. Many of our trees are hundreds of years old but they were all young once. Just think of that! Many trees can grow much older than we can. They grow and change during their *life cycle*. Let's think of other examples of things that have a *life cycle*.

Use Pictures

For words that are labels (*object, animal, place, simple actions*), a picture can be worth a thousand words. For example, if children are learning about *evergreen* trees, teachers can show pictures of trees that have leaves during the winter and compare these to trees that do not keep their leaves in the winter. Or, to learn about why a spider is not a type of *insect*, children might need to look closely at its body and legs. A photograph or picture allows children to take time to examine these differences. Pictures can be an efficient way to provide additional meaning beyond a verbal description or explanation.

We create picture cards for many of our most difficult words. We use them to highlight certain features of the object or animal, and to compare and contrast one thing with another. For example, we will ask children to describe how a sunflower is like a bush; then we will ask children how these plants are different from one another. Having pictures helps children to recall their vocabulary words. Each week's word cards are then prominently displayed in a pocket chart so that children can refer them during their independent work time.

Use Media

In our WOW curriculum, we use brief clips (1 to 2 minutes) from *Sesame Street* to show what children may not have the opportunity to experience in their everyday lives. For example, when we are studying plants, we watch videos about a field of sunflowers or the life cycle of an apple tree. Few early childhood classrooms are likely to have access to these real experiences particularly for some topics (e.g., marine mammals), so media can serve to build and reinforce words and concepts. Media also allows children to look at what would normally be slow processes in real time (e.g., a seed growing into a plant) in more exaggerated terms, enhancing the experiences that could only otherwise be simulated in the classroom. New media, in addition, can be an excellent source of content building and vocabulary. Children love to use e-books and the "point and drag" of iPads. For many of these topics that children study in their classrooms, teachers can find brief videos that support children's learning of complex words and concepts. Following these vivid demonstrations, conversations and discussions are bound to be lively.

Build Categorical Knowledge

In addition to an explanation or definition, we want children to begin to structure their new knowledge in ways that make it more accessible for learning. For example, when we introduce the word *evergreen*, we ask children to describe the properties that make it similar to other types of plants (e.g., is a living thing, needs sunlight and water to grow). In this respect, we are beginning to build knowledge networks. If you learn a new word, such as *ficus*, and know it is a plant, then you can generalize beyond that simple definition, to know that it will need water and sunlight to grow. When you help children understand categories of common objects or things, you begin to build a more coherent framework for children by making them aware of the relationships among vocabulary being taught. Teaching categories, therefore, is a natural vocabulary builder. It consolidates children's thinking about words, and provides a strategy for understanding new ones.

Relate Words to Key Concepts or "Big Ideas"

You can also help children deepen their word knowledge by explicitly linking new vocabulary to the concepts or big ideas that are being taught. For example, in our topics we often focus on such "big ideas" as "habitat," "protection," "life cycle"— big ideas that cut across different topics, and support words that are related to one another at their conceptual level. When we talk about habitat in our work on the human body we may focus on our home as a habitat. When we talk about marine mammals, they, too, of course have a habitat. These big ideas help to link your curriculum in fundamental ways: Children are no longer just moving from one topic to another. Rather, they are building a rich storehouse of words, categories, and concepts along the way.

Practice and Review

Children need many opportunities to practice and review words in multiple contexts—maybe even more than we once thought. A particular benefit of linking vocabulary to a topic or area of investigation is that opportunities for practice and review arise naturally. This is because there is a coherent unit of study that requires continual use of the same set of words over a sustained period of time. Children encounter their new vocabulary, and teachers can explain and review word meanings frequently. We typically use a variety of methods to provided distributed practice and review of vocabulary words over the course of a unit of study.

Interactive Read-Alouds

While shared book reading has often been considered a type of vocabulary instruction in and of itself, recent evidence suggests that reading a book alone, without more explicit instruction, may not be a powerful enough intervention to bridge vocabulary gaps (Marulis & Neuman, 2010). Therefore, we use books to reinforce vocabulary and concepts, rather than to do the teaching for us. As teachers read and discuss a variety of texts related to a topic of interest, these read-alouds will naturally reinforce learning as the same words and ideas reappear. Often, children can use their new vocabulary to ask sophisticated questions and deepen their knowledge. For example, after reading *Bread and Jam for Frances* by Russell Hoban (1993), children in a classroom studying healthy foods could have a wonderful discussion about whether eating only bread and jam is a *nutritious diet*. While these vocabulary words were not in the text of the book, it contains relevant concepts and therefore serves as a meaningful and engaging context for children to practice and review key vocabulary for this topic.

Information books typically contain more complex vocabulary than many narrative stories (Price, van Kleeck, & Huberty, 2009). In fact, the CCSS recommend more deliberate attention to information text early on. Although this goal is worthy, we would certainly not want to diminish the use of wonderful literature that children love. In our program, we have successfully used text sets that combine both fiction and information books on a topic. For example, in a recent unit on marine mammals, we began the topic study with a wonderful predictable book that engaged children in choral responses using their new vocabulary words. We then moved on to storybooks about whales, and then information books about mammals. Giving children a rich diet of books on a similar topic using multiple genres helps to support vocabulary development.

Every Pupil Response Techniques

Young children often have a difficult time paying attention when they are asked to sit and listen for a prolonged period as friends have a turn to speak. Although individual opportunities to respond are important, we have also found that young children respond enthusiastically to every pupil response techniques during whole-class discussions. You can use these techniques to ensure that all children have an opportunity to say each new word (i.e., to help them form a phonological representation of the word) and to use new words in meaningful contexts. In particular, we use choral response as well as hand signals (i.e., thumbs up or put your hands in the air) to enable all children to participate. In a typical conversation, the teacher might say, "Can you put your hands high in the air if a plant that I name grows high above the ground and put your hands on the floor if the plant I name grows low to the ground?" Or after introducing a definition and picture for the word *sapling*, the teacher might ask:

> TEACHER: Can everyone tell me, what do we call a young tree?
>
> WHOLE CLASS: *Sapling.*
>
> TEACHER: Is a sapling a type of animal?
>
> WHOLE CLASS: No!!!!
>
> TEACHER: You're right. I was being so silly. Is a sapling a type of plant?
>
> WHOLE CLASS: Yes!!
>
> TEACHER: Does a sapling need to eat food like meat and carrots and pasta to grow bigger?
>
> WHOLE CLASS: No!
>
> TEACHER: Does a sapling need sunlight and water to grow bigger?
>
> WHOLE CLASS: Yes.
>
> TEACHER: That's right. A sapling is a baby tree so it is a plant. Plants need sunlight and water to grow.

Young children love to show off what they know, and they find conversations like this where the teacher is wrong to be hysterically funny! Try using brief and silly oral language games to help children practice applying new words and concepts.

"Brains On" Small-Group Activities

Another way to reinforce vocabulary and conceptual learning is to engage children in small-group activities that expand upon and reinforce information they have gained during whole-class discussions. We think of these activities as "brains on" not just "hands on" because they are carefully planned to reinforce words and concepts rather than to focus only on a craft, a project, or skill practice. For example, children pantomime growing from a seed to a plant while the teacher narrates using the new vocabulary that children have learned:

"The spring rains sprinkle on our soil. Now the warm sun is shining and you are getting warm in the soil. Your roots start to grow downward and your shoots start reaching upward. You are germinating. Your new stem pokes through the soil. Your new leaves start unfurling and you grow. The sun keeps shining, the air blows around your stem and leaves, the rain moistens your soil, and you grow and grow and GROW!"

After the teacher describes this process, each child can take a turn to describe the life cycle of a plant as the teacher and a small group of children act out this process. Consider adding small-group activities that necessitate applying new concepts and vocabulary during investigations and play.

Picture Sorts with Explanations

Picture sorts help children to consider the relationships among words and concepts they are learning. Children name the pictures and sort them into different categories. In addition to just sorting, we always ask children to articulate their reasoning and decision making in order to scaffold their use of vocabulary and key concepts: "Why do you think a moth is an insect?" As children's knowledge and vocabulary develop, we purposefully include more challenging pictures that require children to think deeply about their sorting decisions: "Is a pinecone a plant?" Our goal is for children to deepen their knowledge and build vocabulary to the point that they can apply these ideas in novel situations.

Discovery Centers

We use discovery centers as the name for topic-focused centers where children can explore ideas related to their learning. Discovery centers are set up so that children can independently use materials and teachers can engage children in conversations about their work. For example, if the class is learning about a science topic, the teacher can review scientific inquiry words such as *problem* and *hypotheses*, while asking children about their work. In one classroom, as children used tweezers and magnifying glasses to sort different types of seeds, their teacher discussed their work by using and explaining the words *compare, measure*, and *classify*: "How are you *comparing* all of the different seeds?"

Developmental Writing

In small groups and during independent work in discovery centers, children should be encouraged to draw and write about their learning. The youngest children draw pictures and then dictate words to their teachers while older PreK students can label their drawings with a few words or letters. For example, before learning about insects, children might talk about their drawings simply by saying, "It's a bug." As their vocabulary develops, teachers can encourage children to describe their drawings by using new vocabulary. Children have the vocabulary and knowledge to describe their work in more detail and demonstrate their learning: "I made a katydid and here is the head and thorax and abdomen and I made all of the 1, 2, 3, 4, 5, 6 legs and it's green like a leaf for camouflage. Uh oh. I forgot antennae. [Grabs a crayon.] I'm going to put that on too."

Progress Monitoring

A key question for all teachers is whether children are learning what has been taught. In our work, we have found that some of the best ways to monitor learning occur in the course of teaching. In particular, as we watch and listen to children during the practice and review activities above, we can tell if they've learned new vocabulary and concepts. For example, when children engage in a picture sort or developmental writing and explain their thinking or drawing, teachers can listen to the words and ideas they use. In fact, we have used a picture-sort methodology to more formally serve as our end-of-unit assessments for research purposes. You can also see whether children are learning by watching for children who are unable to respond correctly and use new vocabulary during "every pupil response" conversations, small-group activities, and during read-alouds.

We recommend that teachers keep brief anecdotal notes after a whole-class or small-group lesson to track children who may or may not be participating fully. Another option is to keep a list of the vocabulary words that you are trying to teach and put a child's initials next to each word when you see or hear evidence that the child can use it. If certain vocabulary words have very few initials next to them, that might be a sign that most children in the classroom need more explicit instruction and practice opportunities for this word. On the other hand, if one child's initials rarely appear across the list of words, this child might need more individualized opportunities to practice and review new vocabulary with you.

Other strategies can also be useful. For example, we use developmental writing as a way of monitoring children's progress. We ask children to "drite" (i.e., draw and write) about the habitat of a marine mammal. Their driting and the conversation that surrounds their work can provide an excellent window into their thinking about the topic.

Progress monitoring is essential because it provides you with a road map for better tailoring your instruction to children's needs. It should not be used for external accountability. Rather, it should be designed to give you information so that you can more accurately calibrate the pace of instruction and whether there is sufficient review and practice for your young learners. Regular assessments can support more fine-tuned teaching, and ensure that your children are learning.

CONCLUSION

Vocabulary development is foundational for learning to read. It is the entry to concepts and comprehension. We cannot leave it to chance. Rather, we must engage children in planned, sequential instruction, giving them the opportunity to discuss, describe, and develop word knowledge and concepts they will need to be successful when they begin to read complex text.

There is now a robust literature, highlighting principles that are essential in teaching vocabulary in early childhood classes. These principles suggest that we need to be more intentional in our teaching of oral vocabulary through more systematic instruction. This includes a careful selection of words children will need to know—content-rich vocabulary—explicit instructional strategies to actively engage children in learning, followed by a systematic sequence of practice, review, and progress monitoring. Together with quality teaching the so-called fourth-grade slump will be a thing of the past.

REFERENCES

Beck, I., & McKeown, M. (2007). Increasing young low-income children's oral vocabulary repertoires through rich and focused instruction. *Elementary School Journal, 107*, 251–271.

Beck, I., McKeown, M., & Kucan, L. (2002). *Bringing words to life*. New York: Guilford Press.

Biemiller, A. (2001). Teaching vocabulary: Early, direct, and sequential. *American Educator, 25*(1), 24–28, 47.

Chall, J., Jacobs, V., & Baldwin, L. (1990). *The reading crisis: Why poor children fall behind*. Cambridge, MA: Harvard University Press.

Common Core State Standards—ELA. (2010). Washington, DC: National Governors Association for Best Practices & Chief Council of State School Officers.

Coyne, M., McCoach, B., & Kapp, S. (2007). Vocabulary intervention for kindergarten students: Comparing extended instruction and incidental exposure. *Learning Disabilities Quarterly, 30*, 74–88.

Coyne, M., McCoach, D., Loftus, S., Zipoli, R., Ruby, M., Creveceour, Y., et al. (2010). Direct and extended vocabulary instruction in kindergarten: Investigating transfer effects. *Journal of Research on Educational Effectiveness, 3*, 93–120.

Coyne, M., Simmons, D., Kame'enui, E., & Stoolmiller, M. (2004). Teaching vocabulary during shared storybook readings: An examination of differential effects. *Exceptionality, 12*(3), 145–162.

Elleman, A., Lindo, E., Morphy, P., & Compton, D. (2009). The impact of vocabulary instruction on passage-level comprehension of school-age children: A meta-analysis. *Journal of Educational Effectiveness, 2,* 1–44.

Graves, M. (2006). *The vocabulary book.* New York: Teachers College Press.

Hart, B., & Risley, T. (1995). *Meaningful differences.* Baltimore, MD: Brookes.

Hart, B., & Risley, T. (2003). The early catastrophe. *American Educator, 27,* 4, 6–9.

Hoban, R. (1993). *Bread and jam for Frances.* New York: HarperTrophy.

Hoff, E. (2003). The specificity of environment influence: Socioeconomic status affects early vocabulary development via maternal speech. *Child Development, 74,* 1368–1378.

Jenkins, J., Stein, M., & Wysocki, K. (1984). Learning words through reading. *American Educational Research Journal, 21,* 767–787.

Kamil, M. (2004). Vocabulary and comprehension instruction: Summary and implications from the National Reading Panel findings. In P. McCardle & V. Chhabra (Eds.), *The voice of evidence in reading research* (pp. 213–235). Baltimore, MD: Brookes.

Marulis, L., & Neuman, S. B. (2011). How vocabulary interventions affect young children at risk: A meta-analytic review. *Society for Research on Educational Effectiveness.*

Marulis, L. M., & Neuman, S. B. (2010). The effects of vocabulary training on word learning: A meta-analysis. *Review of Educational Research, 80*(3), 300–335.

National Reading Panel Report. (2000). *Teaching children to read.* Washington, DC: National Institute of Child Health and Development.

National Research Council. (Ed.). (2001). *Knowing what students know: The science and design of educational assessment.* Washington, DC: National Academy Press.

Neuman, S. B., & Dwyer, J. (2009). Missing in action: Vocabulary instruction in pre-K. *The Reading Teacher, 62,* 384–392.

Neuman, S. B., Dwyer, J., Koh, S., & Wright, T. (2007). *The World of Words: A vocabulary intervention for preschool children.* Ann Arbor: University of Michigan.

Neuman, S. B., Newman, E., & Dwyer, J. (2011). Educational effects of a vocabulary intervention on preschoolers' word knowledge and conceptual development: A cluster randomized trial. *Reading Research Quarterly, 46,* 249–272.

Price, L., van Kleeck, A., & Huberty, C. (2009). Talk during book sharing between parents and preschool children: A comparison between storybook and expository conditions. *Reading Research Quarterly, 44,* 171–194.

Rodriquez, E., & Tamis-LeMonda, C. (2011). Trajectories of the home learning environment across the first 5 years: Associations with children's vocabulary and literacy skills at prekindergarten. *Child Development, 82*(4), 1058–1075.

Silverman, R. (2007). A comparison of three methods of vocabulary instruction during read-alouds in kindergarten. *Elementary School Journal, 108,* 97–113.

Wright, T., & Neuman, S. B. (2013). Vocabulary instruction in commonly used core reading curricula. *Elementary School Journal, 113*(3).

CHAPTER 12

❖❖❖

Real Books, Real Reading

EFFECTIVE FLUENCY INSTRUCTION FOR STRIVING READERS

MELANIE R. KUHN
KRISTINA ZUKAUSKAS PHELAN
PAULA J. SCHWANENFLUGEL

GUIDING QUESTION

❖ How can we create fluency instruction that will allow striving readers to expand their vocabulary, conceptual knowledge, and comprehension through the use of challenging, engaging texts?

OVERVIEW OF READING FLUENCY

Fluency is a central component of skilled reading. And, in order to create effective instruction, we feel it is critical to discuss what fluency is. However, given its current implementation in many classrooms, we feel it is just as important to discuss what fluency is not. When it comes to defining fluency, we would argue that

> fluency combines accuracy, automaticity, and oral reading prosody, which, taken together, facilitate the reader's construction of meaning. It is demonstrated during oral reading through ease of word recognition, appropriate pacing, phrasing, and intonation. It is a factor in both oral and silent reading that can limit or support comprehension. (Kuhn, Schwanenflugel, & Meisinger, 2010, p. 240)

This definition emphasizes the three components of fluent reading, accurate decoding, automatic word recognition, and the use of prosodic elements. We consider the inclusion of prosody to be critical because this element helps learners read with expression or appropriate intonation, proper phrasing, and pacing that reflects meaning. Additionally, this definition recognizes that an important relationship exists between comprehension and fluency. This is not to say that fluency guarantees comprehension, but rather that it is one of the many factors that work together to ensure readers are able to construct meaning from text.

What is important here is the recognition that this definition runs counter to a common "working definition" that has developed around fluency in many educational environments, often in relation to prevalent assessments (e.g., AIMsweb and DIBELS; Kuhn et al., 2010; Samuels, 2007). This definition focuses on two of the three elements of reading fluency: accuracy and automaticity. Unfortunately, this not only results in an emphasis on reading rate, it does so at the expense of appropriate pacing and intonation. Similarly, while these assessments include a measure of comprehension through text recall, we do not believe this provides an adequate emphasis on student understanding. In fact, we would argue that this emphasis on accuracy and automaticity has actually confounded the relationship between fluency and skilled reading, so that teaching students to read rapidly has become an end in itself rather than a means to an end (Applegate, Applegate, & Modla, 2009; Samuels, 2007).

In order to create effective fluency instruction, we need to implement instructional approaches that emphasize all of the elements of fluent reading as well as their connection to comprehension. This involves considering both the ways in which fluency contributes to students' understanding of text and those strategies that assist students in developing their reading fluency. We do this by briefly looking at the theory and research that has developed around the concept of fluent reading and its instruction.

IMPORTANT THEORETICAL BACKGROUND AND RESEARCH BASE

As was noted above, fluent reading incorporates three elements: accuracy, automaticity, and prosody. It is important to consider, first, how these elements contribute to comprehension and, second, what research indicates we can do to promote fluency development within the classroom.

Considering the Contribution of Automaticity to Comprehension

It is the case that skilled readers not only recognize the vast majority of words they encounter accurately, they also do so effortlessly or automatically (e.g., Adams, 1990). This means that, rather than expending their attention on word recognition, they are able to focus on the meaning of a text. Beginning readers, on the other hand, are in the process of developing their word-recognition skills. As a result, they need to focus a great deal of their attention on word recognition (e.g., Samuels, 2004), which means they have limited attention left for comprehension. Underlying this argument is the understanding that developing automaticity in beginning readers is important because it allows them to shift their attention away from word identification and toward the construction of meaning. In terms of automaticity, the question is, how can we best help students achieve this goal?

A consensus exists that automaticity can best be developed through practice. However, it is essential that this practice consist not only of word recognition in isolation but also through the scaffolded reading of a wide variety of connected texts (e.g., Kuhn et al., 2010; Rasinski, Reutzel, Chard, & Linan-Thompson, 2011). The process of repeatedly encountering words in text allows learners to integrate those words into their sight vocabulary, or words that are recognized immediately. Further, it is important to note that automaticity can be developed either through the repeated reading of a given text, through the wide reading of a range of texts,

or through a mix of repeated and wide reading; this understanding has important implications for instruction that is discussed below.

Considering the Contribution of Prosody to Comprehension

Although automaticity clearly has a central role in the development of reading fluency, fluency consists of more than simply reading words quickly and accurately. It also involves prosodic reading, or those elements of language such as suitable phasing and changes in intonation that fit the meaning of the text (e.g., Rasinski et al., 2011; Schwanenflugel & Benjamin, 2012). These elements ensure that oral reading takes on the qualities of fluent speech. More importantly, however, prosody contributes to comprehension above and beyond the contribution made by automatic word recognition (Benjamin & Schwanenflugel, 2010), possibly because it contributes to shades of meaning and a richer understanding of what is written (Kuhn et al., 2010). Further, prosody contributes to learners' engagement with text, improving its comprehension, and helping to bring text to life (Mira & Schwanenflugel, 2012).

Again, it is important to think about the third aspect of fluency in terms of classroom practice. For us, this means that if fluency instruction is to be truly effective, it cannot simply emphasize rate and accuracy. It also needs to focus on prosodic reading—as well as constantly linking the reading of any text back to comprehension. Just as teaching word recognition is not an end in itself, but a means of unlocking what is written, fluency instruction should not be an end in itself. We should not be teaching students to read rapidly; instead, we should be teaching them to read thoughtfully (Kuhn et al., 2010; Samuels, 2007). This means they need to read at an appropriate pace, one that allows them to make sense of what they are reading, and with appropriate intonation, or in such a way that they are deepening their understanding of the text. Fortunately, such instruction can be achieved through a range of strategies that support learners as they become fluent readers.

Considering Research on Fluency Instruction

Much research has been undertaken on ways of developing fluent reading; the list is extensive and includes repeated readings (Samuels, 1979), the neurological impress method (Heckelman, 1966, 1969), reading while listening (Chomsky, 1976), the Oral Recitation Lesson (Hoffman & Crone, 1985), Fluency-Oriented Reading Instruction (FORI; Kuhn & Schwanenflugel, 2008), and Fluency-Oriented Oral Reading (FOOR; Kuhn, 2009), among others. This has left us with a solid range of instructional approaches that can help students make the transition from stilted and monotonous reading to reading that is smooth and expressive. However, before we discuss particular strategies and how they have been implemented in one primary school, we want to discuss some concepts that we feel are common across many effective approaches.

We feel that there are several principles common to effective fluency instruction, (e.g., Rasinski, 2003) and that these commonalities will be apparent in the discussion of classroom scenarios below. The first involves modeling of expressive reading. When comparing children who listen to prosodic readings with children who listen to one that is monotone, those listening to the expressive readings showed greater comprehension (Mira & Schwanenflugel, 2012). It seems likely that when a teacher reads a text expressively, it not only provides learners with a sense of what good reading should sound like, it also instills a love for the written word among students. Although reading aloud is a fairly common practice in the primary grades, it becomes less frequent as students get older. However, there is a substantial body of literature that lends itself to being read aloud well beyond the second grade, including poems, plays, highly descriptive narrative passages, and gripping pieces of nonfiction. The identification and reading of such a text, even when brief, can create a shared experience for a group of learners. At the same time, it provides students with the chance to hear what fluent reading sounds like, something critically important for striving readers. Finally, the inclusion of a range of genre as part of this practice increases the chances that your students will find something that interests them and may entice them to continue reading a selection on their own.

Before leaving this first principle, we wish to reinforce the notion that such modeling should be brief. This is important because the ultimate goal of a literacy curriculum is to create opportunities for students to develop their own reading skills, not just to listen to a skilled reader, no matter how engaging. And while reading aloud may seem like an effective way of covering challenging material, it is far better to provide students with the necessary scaffolding to read such texts themselves. This leads to the second principle, the integration of sufficient support and assistance as part of effective fluency instruction. Ultimately, we consider scaffolding to be critical to the learning process because, without it, the likelihood that students, especially striving readers, will develop the ability to read challenging material is significantly decreased. In terms of fluency instruction, it can be as simple as the use of echo or choral reading as is seen in some of the approaches outlined in the next section.

The third principle incorporates the use of instruction that is explicit and accompanied by clear and specific feedback. All of the approaches below provide students with guidance in their literacy development and target both areas of strength and areas that would benefit from additional support. In conjunction with these principles, we feel it is important to present one additional suggestion. We feel it is equally important to provide learners with multiple, and extensive, opportunities to practice the reading of challenging, connected text as part of effective fluency instruction. We firmly believe that if students are to make the transition to fluent reading, they need a substantial amount of practice to consolidate what they are learning, allowing them practice in coordinating word, sentence, and text elements to derive meaning. Importantly, this understanding has been demonstrated through research that looked at teacher implementation of an effective fluency approach, FORI (Kuhn & Schwanenflugel, 2008). What became clear through classroom observation was that student gains in reading ability were dependent on the amount of time spent engaged in the actual reading of connected text. In other words, teachers who spent greater amounts of instructional time involving students in reading through the use of strategies such as echo, choral, or partner reading made greater gains than teachers who did not.

Importantly, the strategies that we discuss below incorporate the ideas outlined in this section. They are designed to integrate effective oral reading instruction into small-group literacy lessons specifically targeted for striving readers. As such, they substantially increase the likelihood that all students will become fluent readers.

BRINGING OUR KNOWLEDGE OF FLUENCY INSTRUCTION TO THE EARLY LITERACY CLASSROOM

One of us (Kristina Zukauskas Phelan) is a reading specialist at a K–3 public school with approximately 680 students in suburban New Jersey. Her role as an interventionist is to teach all areas of reading in a pullout program, and she works with small groups of students (six or fewer) who need extra support in reading, meeting with her groups either three or five times a week for 45 minutes per session. As part of this instruction, she works with her striving learners on their fluency development. We present three of the strategies she has found to be particularly effective in helping her second- and third-grade students become more fluent readers.

One of the most important choices teachers make involves determining which strategies should be used to help students maximize their reading growth; this is especially important given the limited instructional time available to us. When deciding upon a particular fluency strategy for an individual learner or group of learners, Kristina uses the following three criteria:

1. Has research found it to be effective in promoting fluency?
2. Does the strategy tap into children's intrinsic motivation to want to learn how to read? Does it get them excited about reading?
3. Is it easy to implement?

The three strategies that we describe here meet these criteria and have been found to be effective in boosting both the fluency and the overall reading ability of striving readers. By integrating these strategies into her teaching, Kristina has been able to create a supportive and challenging learning environment for all of her students; this is particularly important given their diverse needs as striving readers. For each of the three strategies, we present background information, the rationale for using the strategy in a specific context, a discussion of the implementation, a lesson summary, and a brief reflection on the strategy's effectiveness.

Strategy 1: The Oral Recitation Lesson

Background

Jim Hoffman and Susan Crone (1985) developed the Oral Recitation Lesson as an alternative to round-robin reading and as a way to help students with challenging material. The authors used the approach with second graders who were experiencing difficulties reading their second-grade basals with the hope that this strategy would provide the learners with greater support. There are three cornerstones of this strategy: teacher modeling, comprehension instruction early in the procedure, and student practice.

The Oral Recitation Lesson is a two-phase, multistep strategy conducted over several days. In the first phase, students listen to the teacher read a story, undertake comprehension work, echo read the story with the teacher, and practice reading a section of the text that they can perform for their peers. In the second phase, students repeatedly practice previously read material until they reach a targeted rate and number of miscues.

Rationale for Use

It is often the case that groups of students have a mixed range of skills. Recently, Kristina worked with a group of five third-grade boys who had a broad range of academic challenges. One student was a very poor decoder but had fairly good comprehension skills. Another boy had very strong decoding skills but poor comprehension skills, while the other students had a mix of reading difficulties. She chose the Oral Recitation Lesson for use with this group because she wanted to improve their fluency and help them develop their comprehension skills while exposing them to grade-level text, material that was challenging for these learners. The Oral Recitation Lesson allowed her to accomplish these goals with students who demonstrated this broad range of abilities.

Implementation

Using the Oral Recitation Lesson enabled Kristina to help her striving readers develop their fluency and comprehension skills while reading interesting, grade-level material. As was noted in our initial criteria, her results parallel what others have found in their research (Hoffman & Crone, 1985; Reutzel & Hollingsworth, 1993; Reutzel, Hollingsworth, & Eldredge, 1994): Kristina's students were able to read challenging texts with fluency because they had heard her read the text, they discussed and understood it, they practiced it by rereading it, and in most cases, they performed a portion of the text aloud. Next, throughout the lessons, Kristina found student engagement to be high. This was clearly demonstrated by learners' animated discussions and the connections that they made to the text. Importantly,

LESSON SUMMARY: THE ORAL RECITATION LESSON

The Oral Recitation Lesson is comprised of two phases, and each phase consists of several components, which occur over several days.

Phase 1: Direct Instruction

This phase was created to develop expressive reading and increase comprehension of grade-level texts.

◆ Choose a challenging text that will be interesting to your students.

◆ Read the text aloud while students read along in their copies. (This gives them the chance to hear what the text is supposed to sound like when read by a fluent reader.)

◆ After this initial reading, discuss the selection in order to expand their understanding. In the original intervention, students constructed a story map identifying the setting, characters, main events, conflict, and resolution. This information was then used to create a written summary of the story. Other comprehension activities can also be integrated to expand student understanding.

◆ Next, students engage in fluency strategies, such as echo or choral reading of the selection, in order to develop prosody as well as automaticity with the reading.

◆ In the final component of this phase, students select a section of the text to practice. Once the students are comfortable reading their selections, they may read their portion of the text aloud to their peers if they choose.

Phase 2: Indirect Instruction

This phase was designed to give struggling students extra practice with previously read stories in order to achieve mastery (to create motivation, students should select the section they would like to practice).

◆ Students practice their selected passages for 10 minutes a day until they are able to read it with at least 98% accuracy and at a rate of 75 correct words per minute or higher.

◆ Students reread using whisper or mumble reading and can bring home their passages for extra practice.

her struggling readers were very excited to read third-grade chapter books like their higher-achieving peers and pleaded with her to buy each of them their own copies of the books they read—and when they read books from a series, they wanted to read all of the sequels. Finally, given the clear outline developed for implementation and the fact that the strategy was designed for small-group instruction, Kristina found it easily implemented in her classroom.

Reflections

The Oral Recitation Lesson is a great strategy to use when you are working with students with a range of reading levels. Kristina found that all of her students demonstrated comprehension of the stories, and each student benefited in different ways from this strategy. The repeated reading practice helped the poor decoders get extra practice reading grade-level text while the stronger readers started making inferences and asking higher-level questions with each subsequent read.

Strategy 2: Fluency-Oriented Oral Reading/Wide Fluency-Oriented Oral Reading

Background

As we discussed in the section on research, Melanie Kuhn (2009), another of the chapter's authors, designed FOOR and Wide Fluency-Oriented Oral Reading (Wide FOOR) to explore the effects of repeated versus wide reading. In her research, she worked with small groups of second graders for 15 to 20 minutes, three times per week. One group received FOOR, which consisted of echo or choral reading the same challenging text three times in 1 week. The second group, Wide FOOR, echo or choral read three different challenging texts per week. A third group listened to the same stories that were read by students in the Wide FOOR, while a fourth group did not receive any extra intervention. Results showed both the FOOR and Wide FOOR groups outperformed the other groups on measures of word recognition in isolation, prosody, and correct words per minute. Students in the Wide FOOR group also made greater growth in comprehension than those in other groups, although it is important to note that there was no explicit comprehension instruction beyond a general discussion during reading.

Rationale for Use

Each year, Kristina works with one or two groups of second graders who are at least a year behind in terms of their reading level. Many of these students are shy, and it

is also the case that one or more students in each group are English language learners. To improve the fluency skills of these students, it is important to use a strategy that will boost their confidence through peer support and interaction. Further, since these learners are all a year or more below grade level, it is important to expose them to grade-level texts in order to help develop their vocabulary and comprehension skills. FOOR and Wide FOOR accomplish these goals in a flexible, supportive format.

Implementation

Connecting her literacy instruction back to our criteria, Kristina finds this procedure boosts her students' fluency; her success with the procedure reflects the success found in the initial research on the intervention (Kuhn, 2009). Next, FOOR and Wide FOOR are effective ways to motivate students to embrace challenging books. Students are able to read these more challenging books because they are getting high levels of support. In Kristina's experience, students love to echo read and often request that they use it in class. They feel supported, and many students become bolder and more confident in their oral reading skills. They have also developed their own echo-reading traditions. Sometimes students will take turns being the teacher, and they always chorally read the last page of the text. Although motivation was not directly addressed in the original FOOR study, a whole-class approach modeled after Wide FORI, found it led to greater confidence in students' concept of themselves as readers (Schwanenflugel et al., 2009). Finally, FOOR and Wide FOOR are simple strategies to implement; all you need is multiple copies of an interesting text.

LESSON SUMMARY: FOOR AND WIDE FOOR

Day 1 (FOOR and Wide FOOR)

◆ Introduce a sufficiently challenging text (one that is at approximately an 85% accuracy level for most of the students). Briefly discuss what the story may be about based on the title and cover. (Because the focus of this activity is to develop fluency, comprehension is developed as you read the text instead of through separate instructional activities.)

◆ Echo read the text (you may wish to switch to choral reading as word recognition improves). Ideally, the text should be long enough that you can spend 15 to 20 minutes reading, per session, without repetition. However, if there is time, you may want to do a second echo or choral reading of the text or a part of the text.

◆ During the reading, stop occasionally to have students predict what may happen next and clarify new words. At the end, you can have a discussion of the story.

Days 2 and 3 (Wide FOOR)

◆ For Wide FOOR, on the second and third days, repeat the procedure from the first day with a second and third text. The text may be any sufficiently challenging reading material including selections from a literature anthology or basal reader, trade books collected from the school and classroom libraries, children's magazines, books from a guided reading program, or material found on websites.

Day 2 (FOOR)

◆ For FOOR, on the second day of the procedure, students partner read the selection from the first day. Have one student read the odd pages and the partner read the even pages. If there is time, have students switch pages and read through the material a second time.

Day 3 (FOOR)

◆ On the third day, chorally read the selection one final time. If your students need additional support, you may decide to echo read the text a second time instead. After this final reread, you can also have students volunteer to read a part of the selection or you may want to complete a running record to see how their reading of the text has progressed.

Reflections

Kristina uses these strategies all year long with her second graders. However, she uses Wide FOOR more often because it exposes her students to a greater number of texts and, as a result, a broader vocabulary and more content. She also finds that her students respond better to having a new text for each session. Novelty is a great motivator by itself. It is worth noting that even when using Wide FOOR, she has students reread the day's selection with a partner if there is time. However, when there isn't time she will sometimes begin the next class session with a reread of the previous day's text. Additionally, because Kristina is responsible for teaching all areas of reading, she likes to weave in other strategies while using the echo-, choral-, and partner-reading formats. For example, she finds that using reciprocal teaching (Palincsar & Brown, 1984) for comprehension instruction in conjunction with Wide FOOR works really well. She also likes to highlight the new and challenging vocabulary through a variety of postreading vocabulary strategies.

Strategy 3: Repeated Readings

Background

Repeated readings is a strategy that was developed to improve automatic word recognition among disfluent readers (Samuels, 1979). The premise of the strategy is that students can develop word-recognition skills by repeatedly reading a given passage and that these gains would transfer to the reading of new texts; claims that have been substantiated in multiple studies (e.g., Dowhower, 1989). The procedure involves having an individual student repeatedly read a short, challenging, and

interesting text and recording both the reader's rate and his or her miscues for each reading. One highly motivating aspect of this procedure involves students' ability to track their progress as their reading rate increases and their number of miscues decreases (e.g., Kuhn, 2009). So as not to overemphasize rate at the expense of comprehension, it is important to ask students to focus on meaning as well as rate as part of the procedure.

Rationale for Use

There are times when Kristina finds one or more of her students have particular difficulties with word recognition and, as a result, their oral reading is extremely slow and disfluent. To improve their rate and overall fluency, she works with them individually using the repeated readings procedure. Darnell (pseudonym) is an example of a student who benefited from this strategy. He was one of Kristina's third-grade students and, when he started with her, he was reading at a beginning first-grade level. His biggest deficit involved his lack of automatic word recognition; on the other hand, his comprehension skills were fairly strong. As a result, when it came to reading, Darnell had low motivation and, according to his classroom teacher, very little initiative. Since his word-recognition skills were much lower than the others in his group, Kristina needed to work with him individually. Repeated readings was the ideal approach for this situation.

Implementation

Connecting Kristina's instruction of the repeated readings strategy to our criteria, Darnell's results confirm the success seen in research in terms of fluency growth, motivation, and ease of implementation. Darnell found this strategy fun and challenging, and he was always motivated to read more quickly on his additional readings. Figure 12.1 shows how Darnell did when reading a particular passage five times. You can see that Darnell made steady improvement in his reading, going from 62 correct words per minute (CWPM) on his initial read to over 100 by his fifth read. Likewise, his miscues steadily decreased. These gains helped Darnell see his development as a reader and served to decrease the gap between his ability to read text fluently and his ability to comprehend it.

Reflections

This strategy provides a great way to document students' growth, although it is important to note that students need to be beyond the primer stage to benefit from the strategy. And while this is not a difficult strategy to implement, finding 10 to 15 minutes to work individually with a student can be a challenge. Using this

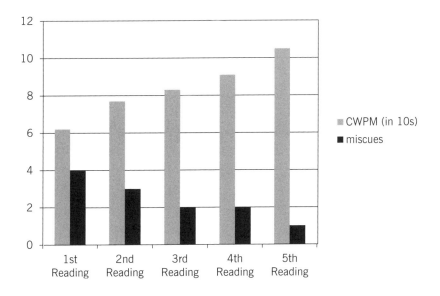

FIGURE 12.1. Student progress: Repeated readings. CWPM, correct words per minute.

LESSON SUMMARY: REPEATED READINGS

◆ Choose an interesting passage that is slightly above your student's reading level (approximately 100 to 200 words).

◆ Have the child read the passage aloud, timing the reading. Record the number of words read, miscues, and total time for the initial read. Transfer this information on to a chart or a graph like the one in Figure 12.1. The first reading should have an accuracy rate of 85 to 90%, otherwise the passage is likely to be either too easy or too difficult for the student.

◆ Discuss the student's reading and review his or her miscues. Decide upon a goal for the final rate in terms of CWPM. Explain to the student that over the course of the rereadings, the two of you will be discussing the story so that he or she doesn't overly focus on rate or miscues.

◆ Have the student reread the passage between three and five times until he or she reaches approximately 100 CWPM with two or fewer miscues (if he or she is unable to get to 100 CWPM by the fifth read, the passage is likely to be too difficult and you need to go down a level). The student does not need to get down to zero miscues because 98% is considered independent; further, students will often repeat the same miscue and extensive repetition risks their learning the word as the miscue.

◆ Select another passage at the same level until the child can read the text fluently upon the initial encounter, and then move to passages at a more difficult reading level.

strategy during independent reading time is one way to achieve this goal; given that repeated readings is a powerful strategy for those students who need a big boost in their automatic word-recognition skills, it is well worth the effort required to find the time.

CONCLUSION

Each year, teachers must meet the diverse needs of a new group of students. Learning how to implement these flexible, research-based fluency strategies will allow you to begin to address your students' reading weaknesses. All kids deserve challenging and engaging books, our striving readers especially, and these strategies will help you to give them access. Effective fluency strategies combine sufficiently challenging texts with modeling and/or repetition. The three strategies described here are motivating, easy to implement, and research based, and will help you to improve your students' reading skills.

REFERENCES

Adams, M. J. (1990). *Beginning to read: Thinking and learning about print*. Cambridge, MA: M.I.T. Press.

Applegate, M. D., Applegate, A. J., & Modla, V. B. (2009). "She's my best reader; she just can't comprehend": Studying the relationship between fluency and comprehension. *The Reading Teacher, 62*(6), 512–521.

Benjamin, R. G., & Schwanenflugel, P. J. (2010). Text complexity and oral reading prosody in young readers. *Reading Research Quarterly, 45*(4), 388–404.

Chomsky, C. (1976). After decoding: What? *Language Arts, 53*, 288–296.

Dowhower, S. L. (1989). Repeated reading: Research into practice. *The Reading Teacher, 42*, 502–507.

Heckelman, R. G. (1966). A neurological-impress method of remedial-reading instruction. *Academic Therapy Quarterly, 4*, 277–282.

Heckelman, R. G. (1969). N. I. M. revisited. *Academic Therapy, 21*, 411–420.

Hoffman, J. V., & Crone, S. (1985), The oral recitation lesson: A research-derived strategy for reading basal texts. In J. A. Niles & R. V. Lalik (Eds.), *Issues in literacy: A research perspective, thirty-fourth yearbook of the National Reading Conference* (pp. 76–83). Rochester, NY: National Reading Conference.

Kuhn, M. R. (2009). *The hows and whys of fluency instruction*. Boston: Allyn & Bacon.

Kuhn, M. R., & Schwanenflugel, P. J. (Eds.). (2008). *Fluency in the classroom*. New York: Guilford Press.

Kuhn, M. R., Schwanenflugel, P. J., & Meisinger, E. B. (2010). Aligning theory and assessment of reading fluency: Automaticity, prosody, and definitions of fluency. Invited review of the literature. *Reading Research Quarterly, 45*, 232–253.

Mira, W. A., & Schwanenflugel, P. J. (2012). *The impact of reading expressiveness on the listening comprehension of storybooks by prekindergarten children.* Unpublished manuscript, University of Georgia, Athens.

Palincsar, A., & Brown, A. (1984). Reciprocal teaching of comprehension-fostering and comprehension-monitoring activities. *Cognition and Instruction, 1*(2), 117–175.

Rasinski, T. V. (2003). *The fluent reader: Oral reading strategies for building word recognition, fluency, and comprehension.* New York: Scholastic.

Rasinski, T. V., Reutzel, R., Chard, D., & Linan-Thompson, S. (2011). Reading fluency. In M. L. Kamil, P. D. Pearson, E. B. Moje, & P. Afflerbach (Eds.), *Handbook of reading research* (Vol. 4, pp. 286–319). Mahwah, NJ: Erlbaum.

Reutzel, D. R., & Hollingsworth, P. M. (1993). Effects of fluency training on second graders' reading comprehension. *Journal of Educational Research, 86*, 325–331.

Reutzel, D. R., Hollingsworth, P. M., & Eldredge, J. L. (1994). Oral reading instruction: The impact on student reading development. *Reading Research Quarterly, 29*, 40–62.

Samuels, S. J. (1979). The method of repeated readings. *The Reading Teacher, 32*, 403–408.

Samuels, S. J. (2004). Toward a theory of automatic information processing in reading, revisited. In R. B. Ruddell & N. J. Unrau (Eds.), *Theoretical models and processes* (pp. 1127–1148). Newark, DE: International Reading Association.

Samuels, S. J. (2007). The DIBELS tests: Is speed of barking at print what we mean by reading fluency? *Reading Research Quarterly, 42*(4), 563–566.

Schwanenflugel, P. J., & Benjamin, R. G. (2012). Reading expressiveness: The neglected aspect of reading fluency. In T. Rasinski, C. Blachowicz, & C. Lems (Eds.), *Fluency instruction* (2nd ed., pp. 35–54). New York: Guilford Press.

Schwanenflugel, P. J., Kuhn, M. R., Morris, R. D., Morrow, L. M., Meisinger, E. B., Woo, D. G., et al. (2009). Insights into fluency instruction: Short- and long-term effects of two reading programs. *Literacy Research and Instruction, 48*, 318–336.

CHAPTER 13

❖

Best Practices
in Early Writing Instruction

DEBORAH WELLS ROWE
TANYA R. FLUSHMAN

Young children are irrepressible mark makers. It is the rare parent who cannot tell a story about finding their preschooler's writing in unexpected places. Parents of our students have reported their young writers independently and neatly filling every page of the family checkbook with looping lines of personal cursive, or leaving a signature of unconventional letterlike forms on the wall. Several decades of early literacy research have established that children are forming foundational under-standings about print in these first forays into writing (e.g., Rowe, 2009; Yaden, Rowe, & MacGillivray, 2000; Tolchinsky, 2006). The early writing behaviors that precede and develop into conventional literacy have been termed *emergent literacy* (Teale & Sulzby, 1986). While children's emergent writing is often unconventional in form, it is not random. Instead, young children's writing is shaped by their current understandings about print. As with oral language, children construct hypotheses about print and test them as they take part in everyday literacy events (Rowe, 1994). For young writers, conventional understandings about print are a by-product of repeated opportunities for participation (Cambourne, 2009; Rowe, 2008) in events where literacy is used for meaningful social purposes.

GUIDING QUESTIONS

In this chapter, we describe classroom environments and interactions that capital-ize on children's natural inclination to explore writing when it is used for authentic purposes. Our goal is to provide research-based insights about how teachers can support young children as writers in the classroom. Support for these ideas comes from a series of classroom-based research studies we have conducted in preschool and early grades classrooms (Flushman, 2012; Rowe, 1994, 1998, 2008; Rowe, Fitch, & Bass, 2003; Rowe & Neitzel, 2010), as well as the work of other early literacy researchers. Our insights about instruction for young writers have been further developed through a 4-year collaboration with 13 public school prekindergarten teachers and their literacy coaches as part of the Enhanced Language and Literacy Success Project (Rowe & Dickinson, 2008), funded by a U.S. Department of Education Early Reading First grant.

Specifically, we address the following questions:

❖ What kinds of writing can we expect from 2- to 6-year-olds?

❖ What kinds of curricular environments support young writers?

❖ What kinds of teacher interactions support young writers?

EMERGENT WRITING: PATTERNS IN FORMS AND MEANINGS

Learning to write is much more than learning how to form letters. As young writers construct and test hypotheses about the way print looks and the ways marks represent speech, they also learn about the kinds of messages print carries and its purposes. When children write in supportive classroom environments, they simultaneously learn about the content, processes, and purposes of writing (Rowe, 1994).

Writing Forms

Table 13.1 presents an overview of the print forms 2- to 6-year-olds used in the Write Start! Project (Rowe & Neitzel, 2010; Rowe & Wilson, 2009) when they were asked to write a caption for a photo showing them playing at school. Descriptive categories were generated through qualitative analysis of the children's writing in the fall and spring of each school year. These patterns, ordered from least to most sophisticated in Table 13.1, confirm earlier findings (e.g., Hildreth, 1936; Sulzby, 1985) that children's writing forms become more conventional in appearance over time. Each category also provides clues to children's current hypotheses about print.

For example, when asked to write, some children make no marks or choose to draw (Categories 1.1 and 1.2). While these responses tell us little about the child's writing, they speak volumes about the child's willingness to "have a go" at writing. Other youngsters demonstrate a willingness to participate as writers by producing scribbles (Category 1.3) usually focusing more on the physical/motor activity

TABLE 13.1. Emergent Writing Forms Produced by 2- to 6-Year-Olds in the Write Start! Writing Assessment (Rowe & Wilson, 2009)

Category	Label	Description	Example
1.1	No marks	Child makes no marks.	
1.2	Drawing only	Child draws a picture instead of writing; marks are clearly identifiable as a picture.	
1.3	Scribbles	Child purposefully makes marks; large mass of undifferentiated scribbles; uses forearm movements to create large scribbles.	
1.4	Scribble units	Child makes small patches of scribbles separated from one another with space; usually created with wrist and hand movements.	
1.5	Individual stroke units	Child makes many repeated lines, circles, or curve strokes, usually of the same type.	
1.6a	Personal manuscript	Child makes letterlike forms; combinations of strokes within the same unit; not recognizable as a conventional letter.	
	or		
1.6b	Personal cursive	Child makes horizontal runs of loops, or zig zags.	
1.7	Conventional letters plus inventions	Child writes at least one recognizable letter, but it may be upside down or backward; the remaining marks may be letterlike forms, scribbles, and so on.	
1.8	Conventional letters (no letter–sound correspondence)	Child uses upper- or lower-case, may be mixed; reversals are OK; recognizable by others as letters; no letter–sound correspondence.	
1.9	Conventional letters, memorized words	Child uses conventional letters and words, but writes something memorized like his or her name or "I love you."	Child writes name.

(continued)

TABLE 13.1. *(continued)*

Category	Label	Description	Example
1.10	Invented spelling: First-letter sound	Child uses first-letter sound of word or syllable; may not use conventional letter: *c* for *seal*; may contain other random letters; must have evidence that child is intentionally generating a spelling with letter–sound correspondence.	I was sliding the slide.
1.11	Invented spelling: First- and last-letter sounds	Child uses first- and last-letter sounds of word or syllables; many sounds left out.	"rainbow"
1.12	Invented spelling: Most sounds represented	Child attempts to sound out most sounds in the syllable or word; letter choices may not be correct.	"ship"

of mark making, than the resulting visual array. Children who produce scribble units (Category 1.4) show awareness that print is composed of units separated by white space. Stroke units (Category 1.5) demonstrate understanding of units as well as more sophisticated ideas about the kinds of strokes that make up English manuscript letters. Personal manuscript (Category 1.6a; Harste, Woodward, & Burke, 1984) is visually even more printlike, in that children now notice that print strings involve variation in letter shapes and combine more than one kind of stroke in each unit. In our data, personal cursive (Category 1.6b; Harste et al., 1984) often occurs at about the same time as personal manuscript, but represents a visual focus on the connected and linear features of print, and perhaps on cursive forms of writing.

Beginning with Category 1.7, children show the direct influence of adult instruction in forming letters, often those that make up their names (Treiman, Kessler, & Bourassa, 2001). At first, children focus on visual features of letters, rather than the ways letters are related to sounds. Children mix conventional letters with stroke units or letterlike forms (Category 1.7) and later when they can more easily write letters, their texts contain only conventional letters (Category 1.8), but without letter–sound correspondence. Some children use well-practiced conventional forms and spellings to write memorized words or short messages (Category 1.9).

Starting with Category 1.10, children's hypotheses shift from a purely visual focus, to one that recognizes the connection between visual and sound-based features of print. When children begin to select letters to represent sounds in words, they actively apply the alphabetic principle. This is a watershed event in early writing, in that it marks an entirely new understanding about print processes. From this point, children's hypotheses about spelling words (Gentry, 2000) move from the outside edges of the word by including first and last sounds (Category 1.11), to spellings that also include internal sounds of syllables and words (Category 1.12).

As children form new hypotheses about print forms, they do not drop all previous forms from their repertoire (Sulzby, 1991), but instead use less or more sophisticated forms depending on task demands and their interest (Kress, 1997) at the moment. Still, data from the Write Start! Project confirm that when samples of children's writing produced in response to a standard task are analyzed across time, they become increasingly more conventional.

Marise's responses to the Write Start! photo-labeling task show a typical progression. At 2 years, 11 months of age (Figure 13.1), Marise uses a combination of personal cursivelike zigzags that are joined into a mass of scribbles. At age 3 years, 11 months (Figure 13.2), he combines circular stroke units with shaky letters, mostly

FIGURE 13.1. Marise's photo label: 2 years, 11 months.

FIGURE 13.2. Marise's photo label at 3 years, 11 months.

selected from his name. As he begins prekindergarten at 4 years, 11 months (Figure 13.3), he purposefully chooses the letter *I* to stand for the first word of his message, "I am writing on the little board," but selects the remaining letters randomly. By the end of prekindergarten, at 5 years, 7 months of age (Figure 13.4), he confidently produces a message using invented spellings that represent the initial sound of each word.

Writing Meanings

There has been considerably less research focusing on the *meanings* children assign to their marks. In the Write Start! photo-labeling task, we asked 2- to 6-year-olds to read their marks, as a way of understanding how they assigned meaning to their marks. Table 13.2 presents categories describing the kinds of messages children produced when asked to read their written photo labels (Rowe & Wilson, 2009).

Initially, even with adult modeling and support, some children refused to read their marks (Category 2.1). Other children solved the problem of assigning meaning to their marks by producing talk, but without any discernable links to the photo (Category 2.2). A third approach to assigning meaning to the marks was to read a conventional message previously associated with print but not associated with the photo-labeling task. Beginning with the fourth category (Category 2.4), children

MArIse

I IPO
A O MB

I am writing on the little board.

FIGURE 13.3. Marise's photo label at 4 years, 11 months.

MArIse

IWPOeuTMB

I was playing on the monkey bars.

FIGURE 13.4. Marise's photo label at 5 years, 7 months.

showed awareness that the message should in some way relate to the writing event under way. The final two categories (Categories 2.5 and 2.6) showed awareness that the caption should relate either generally or specifically to the items pictured in the photo.

These categories represent differential willingness to assign meaning to marks and most importantly, qualitatively different approaches to deciding what one's marks might say. In short, these data suggest that 2- to 6-year-olds are not only developing and testing hypotheses about print forms but also about their roles as writers, how messages are related to print, and the kinds of messages one might expect to find expressed through writing in different situations.

TABLE 13.2. Types of Messages Produced by 2- to 6-Year-Olds in the Write Start! Photo-Labeling Task (Rowe & Wilson, 2009)

Category	Written label	Description	Example
2.1	No understandable oral message	No message assigned to marks.	Silence. Unintelligible mumble. Gesture only.
2.2	Message unrelated to photo-labeling task	Child reads a message, but it is not related to photo content, or to the writing materials, processes, or functions of the photo-labeling task.	"I love my Mommy." [Photo shows the child working a puzzle.]
2.3	Message unrelated to photo-labeling task/other conventional message	Child reads message not related to photo or task. Only "standard" messages like those in the example would score here; otherwise, score as 1.	"I Love You." "A, B, C, D" Names of family/friends [not pictured]
2.4	Global relation to writing materials, functions, or processes	Child reads message that describes characteristics of writing materials, the function of the product, or processes used in writing marks; often sounds like oral language directed at the adult rather than a written label.	"It's red." "It's for you. I'm gonna take it home." "I went around and around." [to describe movement of pen]
2.5	Global relation to photo content	Child reads message that is related to items pictured in photo; often sounds like oral language directed at assessor rather than a written label.	"It's about dinosaurs." [Photo shows the child playing with dinosaur toys and blocks.]
2.6	Photo label: word, phrase, or sentence	Child reads message as word, phrase, or sentence that serves as a label for items or actions in photo.	"Bike" [Photo shows the child on the playground riding a bike.] "I am playing with KeMiyah." [Photo shows the child playing with KeMiyah.]

Form–Meaning Relationships

As a final observation about early writing development, we note that our data (Flushman, 2012) show that conventional writing form is not always related to sophisticated messages in the ways that most adults expect; that is, the ability to legibly write alphabet letters does not always mean the child holds sophisticated notions about how one assigns meaning to print or the kinds of messages that are appropriate for a particular writing situation. Conversely, children producing sophisticated messages do not always use sophisticated writing forms to represent them. Some children, like Marise at age 2 (Figure 13.1), write and read their marks with a sophisticated understanding of the expected match between task and message, while producing highly unconventional print forms. Conversely, some children use relatively sophisticated marks, but approach the meaning-making aspect of writing less conventionally. In Figure 13.5, Nurrava's text is composed of several lines of letters and personal manuscript divided by spaces and produced with conventional directional patterns. When asked to read her marks, Nurrava produced a lengthy, stream-of-consciousness personal narrative with content that was related to neither the photo

FIGURE 13.5. Nurrava's photo caption: "I wanta go to my . . . gonna see my house, then Mommy is in the house, then cry and now I'm crying. . . . "

nor the immediate writing event. Her understanding of visual features of print were more sophisticated than her understanding of social purposes for writing.

For young writers, control of conventional form does not equal control of written language (Harste et al., 1984). Writing not only requires knowledge of print forms, but also of writing processes, messages, and social purposes for writing. Children explore each of these aspects of writing, but not necessarily in a logical or predetermined sequence. Data from the Write Start! Project support Clay's (1979) finding that there is not one expected sequence for forming and testing hypotheses about how print works, nor does every child form exactly the same hypotheses.

Summing Up: Kidwatching as the Foundation for Early Writing Instruction

An understanding of young writers' approaches to producing print forms and messages is foundational to implementing the best practices in early writing instruction that we describe in the next sections. First, teachers need to be good "kid watchers" (Goodman, 1996) who use children's unconventional writing performances not as evidence of "errors" but instead as indicators of children's current hypotheses about print (Goodman & Goodman, 2004). Second, because children's print hypotheses are multifaceted, teachers need to consider each child's writing profile. They need to consistently ask themselves "What does this child know about print forms, processes, meanings, and purposes?" Third, early childhood teachers need to take a "strengths" approach to teaching writing. Recognizing that children's hypotheses about print are not always equally sophisticated in all respects, teachers can consciously use children's most sophisticated understandings about writing as resources to support exploration of other features of print. Fourth, teachers need to expect and value variation in children's approaches to writing. Children's interests (Kress, 1997; Rowe & Neitzel, 2010; Rowsell & Pahl, 2007) influence what they notice about print and the ways they take part in writing events.

DESIGNING ENVIRONMENTS THAT SUPPORT YOUNG WRITERS

Our goal in designing instructional environments for young writers has been to capitalize on children's natural curiosity about writing and to build into our curriculum the same conditions that have supported their learning outside of school. A number of emergent literacy researchers (Cambourne, 2009; Goodman, 1990; Harste et al., 1984) have argued that children begin to learn about print in the same ways they learn oral language. Cambourne's analysis of the conditions of "natural learning" suggests that supportive environments for learning to write have the following characteristics:

1. Immersion: Learners are saturated in print.
2. Demonstration: Learners see writing in use.
3. Expectation: Learners are expected to be capable of participating as writers.
4. Response: Learners get feedback from knowledgeable others.
5. Responsibility: Learners make choices about what demonstrations to engage with and what kinds of texts they write.
6. Approximation: Learners have freedom to make mistakes as they learn to write.
7. Use: Learners have opportunities to use the writing skills they are learning.

Based on social and cultural views of early literacy learning (e.g., Barton & Hamilton, 2000; Gee, 2003; Rogoff, Mistry, Goncu, & Mosier, 1993; Rowe, 2010), we extend Cambourne's ideas by adding that children's hypotheses about writing are collaboratively constructed as they engage in writing with other members of their communities. Literacy learning is a collective process rather than an individual one. Learners not only get feedback (i.e., response) from others but also provide responses that help to shape the local writing practices of their homes, communities, and classrooms.

Based on these perspectives and our analyses of children's participation in emergent writing classrooms, we have created our own "top 10" list of essential curricular supports for emergent writers (see Figure 13.6). We consider each of these features to be essential to creating environments where young children are enthusiastically engaged as writers.

Essential Supports for Emergent Writers

Young Writers

1. Participation: Children write for a variety of purposes.
2. Approximation: Emergent forms of writing are expected and valued.

Learning-to-Write Events

3. Authenticity: Writing is used for functional purposes.
4. Openness: Children of all skill levels can participate successfully in writing activities.
5. Collaboration: Children work with adults and peers during writing.

Teachers

6. Demonstration: Teachers write in front of children; texts are strategically accessed as demonstrations.
7. Direct teaching: Teachers teach formal and informal writing lessons.

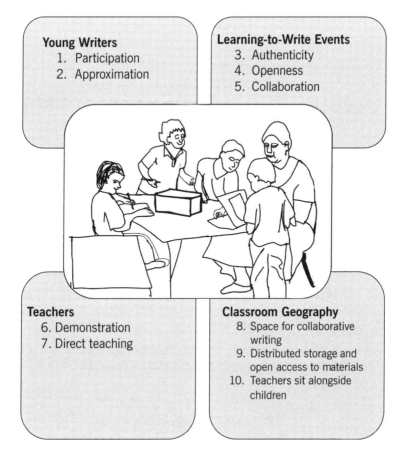

Young Writers
1. Participation
2. Approximation

Learning-to-Write Events
3. Authenticity
4. Openness
5. Collaboration

Teachers
6. Demonstration
7. Direct teaching

Classroom Geography
8. Space for collaborative writing
9. Distributed storage and open access to materials
10. Teachers sit alongside children

FIGURE 13.6. Curricular supports for emergent writers.

Classroom Geography

8. Materials: There is distributed storage and open access to books and writing materials.
9. Space: Classrooms have spaces for collaborative writing.
10. Bodies: Teachers sit alongside of children as they write.

In our work with teachers, we have used this framework and the questions it generates to design instructional environments where children's participation in writing is central. To give readers a feel for the ways these features work together in classroom writing events, we turn to Classroom Narrative 1, the Frog Log event, where two prekindergarten boys, Bronte and Jaron, worked with Rowe to write about a frog they were observing at the science table. Bronte was a confident writer. He often came to the writing table to compose his own texts using a combination of conventional letters and invented spellings. Jaron rarely chose to write on his own, despite many teacher invitations. He complied with teacher requests to write by dashing off a few quickly formed marks, usually scribble units, stroke units, or a few letters from his name. After reading his text to the teacher, he quickly moved to other preferred activities, rarely staying with a writing activity for more than a few minutes.

The Frog Log event occurred in April, when both boys had had many opportunities to take part in classroom writing events. While the writing occurred during the learning centers period, Bronte's and Jaron's interest in the frog began earlier when they had an opportunity to look at the frog and take part in a lively discussion of how to observe a live animal without scaring it, what frogs eat, and so on.

In Classroom Narrative 1, we pick up the action at the classroom science table. Column 1 presents the transcript of Jaron's interactions with Ms. Debbie (Rowe) as they drew and wrote about the frog. For easier reference, numbers have been inserted in the narrative to mark participants' turns and to show the sequence of events as transcribed from the video. Some turns have been omitted because of space considerations. Following the narrative, we discuss 10 essential curricular supports for young writers, referring to column 2 for examples. Then, we discuss features of teacher talk and actions as highlighted in column 3.

CLASSROOM NARRATIVE 1:
COMPOSING JARON'S FROG LOG

Transcript	Curricular supports	Teacher talk and actions
Jaron and Bronte have joined Ms. Debbie at the science table. All three are peering through the sides of a plastic box containing a frog their teacher has found in her yard at home.	Space for collaborative writing Teacher sits alongside children	
(1) "Do you see 'im?" Jaron asks.		Find common ground
(2) "I don't right now," replies Ms. Debbie.		
(3) Jaron points to the side of the box. "I see him. I see him. I see him on the *dirt*. Right here on the dirt."		
(4) Ms. Debbie peers into the box.		
(5) Bronte arrives and joins the inspection of the frog, leaning over Ms. Debbie's shoulder.		
(6) "He won't come out 'cause he scared!" Jaron insists.		

(20) Ms. Debbie draws a picture of a frog on her paper. "Let's make his big ol' eyes. I'm not that good at drawing." [Figure 13.7]	Authenticity Openness Demonstration	
(21) Jaron leans over to see what she is drawing. "That his tongue," he comments with excitement.		
(22) Ms. Debbie continues drawing as the boys look on. She narrates each addition to the picture. "There are his legs. Let's make him have a big long tongue."		
(23) As she finishes drawing, she puts the picture and her pencil on the table between Bronte and Jaron. "Now draw some bugs he's eating," she suggests.	Openness Collaboration Participation as artist	Invite (to draw) Suggest
(24) Jaron grabs the pencil before Bronte can reach it. "I do it! I do it!" He begins to add to Ms. Debbie's drawing. [Figure 13.7]		
(28) When Jaron finishes drawing he holds his paper up, facing Ms. Debbie and Bronte. "There the dragonfly," he announces.	Approximation	Share
(29) Ms. Debbie reaches across the table to point to the mark representing a dragonfly. "Yeah . . . frogs love dragonflies when they come by."		
(30) "Make it say, 'The frog eats dragonflies,'" Ms. Debbie suggests. She says each word slowly as if she is dictating.	Participation as writer	Invite (to write) Suggest
(31) Jaron takes up the task enthusiastically. "Yes!"		
(31) He puts his paper back on the table and bends over it with concentration. He says his message aloud, emphasizing each word. "Frog eat bug. Frog eat bugs." As he voices each word, he draws a series of the small horizontal lines like the ones his teacher uses to support the children in writing each word of their messages. Still bent close to the page, he returns to the left side of the line and records a mark on each word line as he says his message: "Frog eat bugs. Frog eat bugs." [Figure 13.7]		
(32) He hands his paper to Ms. Debbie: "The frog ate the bugs."	Approximation	
(33) "Oh! That's great!" she says. She holds the page so Bronte can see, also. "That's great!" She points to the small mark at top center. "There's the *dragonfly.* That's great, Jaron!"		
(34) "Thank you," he replies.		
(35) "Excellent!" she says.		

FIGURE 13.7. Jaron's Frog Log.

(36) Ms. Debbie pages through an informational text. "I'm looking through this book. . . . Let's see . . . I don't know if there're any frogs in this book or not. This is about the rain forest . . . "	Demonstration Distributed storage Open access	
(37) Jaron takes the book Ms. Debbie hands him. He begins to look, talking to himself. "Let's see if it has frogs."	Participation as reader	Invite (to read)
(38) Ms. Debbie takes out another book and begins to look. "Let's see if we can find any pictures of frogs."	Demonstration	
(39) "I see a frog!" He holds the book up for Ms. Debbie and Bronte to see, pointing to the picture.	Participation as reader	
(40) "That's an orange one," Ms. Debbie observes. "That's different from the one we've got."		
(41) Jaron holds his open book up again: "What is this?"		
(42) Ms. Debbie points to the print and reads. "That says, 'the tree sloth.' That's a tree sloth," she says.	Direct teaching	Support
(43) Jaron takes the book back and turns some more pages. "I'm looking for some more frogs."	Participation as reader	
(102) The clean-up signal sounds. Ms. Debbie hands Jaron his paper. "Go read that to Ms. Amy and tell her what you noticed about the frog."		Share
(103) Jaron finds his teacher across the room, and pushes the paper into her hands: "Here!"		

(104) "Oh, Jaron! Did you write this?" she asks.	Approximation	Invite to read
(105) He reads, gesturing to the paper. "It says, 'Frog eat bugs.'"	Participation as reader and writer	
(106) "That's wonderful! Will you share this at group?" she asks.	Approximation	Share
(107) Jaron breaks in to a big smile.		↓
(108) "Go put it on my chair. You can read it at group."		

◆ *Participation: Is the pen in the child's hand?* If children learn to write by forming and testing hypotheses about print, then it follows that they need reasons, opportunities, and support for participating as writers. The Frog Log event is typical of classrooms where we have worked, in that expert teachers of early writers engage in some direct teaching, some teacher–child coauthoring, and lots of demonstration, but all of these teaching activities occur in an environment guided by one mantra: "Put the pen in the child's hand."

In the Frog Log event, beginning at Turn 20, Rowe uses her own text as a means of drawing the boys into writing. In practice, we have learned that most children are willing to take up roles as coauthors when asked to help with our texts. Few children refuse to write when we lay the pencil and our page in their space and wait expectantly for them to write (e.g., Turn 23).

The central importance of engaging young children as writers is based on the observation that learners who perceive themselves as potential "do-ers" of a target activity engage with instruction with an eye toward application in their own practice (Cambourne, 1988, 2009). For example, Jaron observed Ms. Debbie's drawing and writing and used these demonstrations as the starting point for his own text. When adults invite young children to participate as writers, they fundamentally change their opportunities for literacy learning. The child who actively takes up the role of writer has compelling reasons to form and test personal hypotheses about print and many more chances to do so.

In the emergent writing classroom, our goal is for children to unequivocally see themselves as writers, and to view their texts as legitimate and useful. To this end, we invite even the youngest children to write for meaningful purposes—regardless of their ability to produce conventional texts (Turn 30). We talk to them "as if" they are writers (Turn 104). We ask them to read their marks. We recognize their expertise (Turn 33), and refer other children to them as experts on specific aspects of the writing process.

◆ *Approximation: Do teacher responses show that children's unconventional writing is valued?* Young children are unlikely to be able to participate with any regularity in writing, if they or their teachers expect them to produce fully conventional texts. Jaron's text, seen in Figure 13.7, makes this point. Up to this point in the year,

Jaron had been a reluctant participant in writing events, and the forms he used to represent his message were usually scribble units, stroke units, or personal manuscript along with the *J* that begins his first name. If conventional letters had been a requirement for participating in the Frog Log event, Jaron would almost certainly have been unsuccessful.

In our early writing classrooms, teachers accept and praise all attempts at writing, however unconventional (e.g., Turns 33, 106). We explicitly talk with children about the importance of writing approximations (Cambourne, 1988), what we call "kid writing." When children ask us if a word is spelled correctly, we provide the information they need about "adult writing," but praise their willingness to get their meanings down in their own way first. Along with the children, we notice and celebrate the ways their writing is becoming more conventional. Accepting approximations allows children to participate as writers no matter the sophistication of their print knowledge. The social press to communicate more effectively keeps children moving forward toward convention.

♦ *Authenticity: Is writing used in a functional way?* Children need authentic (Edelsky & Smith, 1984) and socially meaningful reasons for writing. To this end, we carefully examine all curricular areas to see how writing would naturally be used. As teachers make careful plans for writing invitations, they also continually look for writing opportunities that grow from children's interests and activities. The Frog Log event is a good example. Rowe based her writing invitation on the boys' intense interest in observing and talking about the frog. In our classrooms, our goal is to invite children to write for a variety of purposes that make "human sense" (Donaldson, 1978) as part of everyday classroom life.

♦ *Openness: Can children of all skill levels and interests participate successfully?* Curricular activities are open when they invite a variety of ways of responding and when children with a variety of skill levels can successfully participate. The openness of a writing activity comes, in part, from the willingness of teachers to accept a variety of writing approximations. In the Frog Log event, while Jaron responded with scribble units (Figure 13.7), his friend Bronte independently created spellings using letter–sound correspondence (Figure 13.8). When teachers issue open-ended invitations for children to use their current version of "kid writing," they can observe what children understand about print, and individualize their teaching so it is matched to the child's level. Designing for openness is essential given the variety of skill levels in any classroom and also the variety of ways that young writers approach text production at any point in the year.

♦ *Collaboration: Are there opportunities for teachers and children to work together or side by side on their writing?* In our classrooms, even though children are encouraged to "hold the pen," they are rarely required to work independently. Instead,

FIGURE 13.8. Bronte's Frog Log.

the kind of collaborative composing and observation of other writers seen in the Frog Log event is the norm (Turn 23). Rather than encouraging children to "do your own work," we encourage them to use others' demonstrations as springboards for their own writing projects. Opportunities to write collaboratively with teachers and peers provide both demonstrations and easy access to the support children need to move forward with their texts. Writing with a more experienced peer or adult provides the kind of scaffolding children need to work at the far end of their zone of proximal development (Vygotsky, 1978).

◆ *Demonstration: Do children see "live" demonstrations of writing? Do they have access to published or class-authored texts of the kinds they are writing?* Demonstrations are acts and artifacts that show children how writing is done, why it is done, and what print "says" in different situations (Smith, 2004). Young writers need many opportunities to see adults writing and also to explore the demonstrations provided by familiar texts (Cambourne, 2009; Harste et al., 1984; Smith, 2004). In our Enhanced Language and Literacy Success prekindergarten classrooms, teachers provide live demonstrations of writing through daily large-group interactive writing where they write in enlarged print in front of children. As in the Frog Log event, they also coauthor texts with children or write their own texts alongside them during the learning center/workshop period (e.g., Turn 20). As teachers write their own texts, they have natural opportunities to think out loud to make their writing and reading processes more understandable to young writers (Turns 20–22). Children have access to teachers' and peers' texts as well as published texts, and children are encouraged to consult them as demonstrations for how, what, and why they might write in the activities that are under way (Turns 36–40).

◆ *Direct teaching: What lessons on writing content, processes, or purposes do children need as touchstones for their writing?* While children learn by participating in writing, teachers play an important role by explicitly explaining the use of key features of print such as letter names and shapes, letter–sound correspondence, purposes for writing in different situations, and so on. Teachers teach formal lessons that serve to highlight writing content, processes, and purposes, and provide touchstone experiences that both teachers and children refer to as they write their own texts. Direct teaching of literacy skills and strategies also occurs informally as part of composing events, where teachers individualize instruction to match children's interests and needs for support in the texts they are constructing. An example comes from Ms. Debbie's interaction with Bronte in another segment of the Frog Log event presented in Classroom Narrative 2.

CLASSROOM NARRATIVE 2: BRONTE'S FROG LOG

Transcript	Curricular supports	Teacher talk and actions
(7) As Ms. Debbie draws a picture of the box with the frog inside. [Figure 13.8] (8) Bronte leans over her page watching as she draws and writes.	Demonstration	Find common ground
(9) Ms. Debbie narrates as she begins to draw. "This is the box . . . I think he's down here." She draws the frog under the dirt. "I'm not a real good frog drawer. He's got a body and big legs." She peers into the box again, then returns to drawing. "I think he's down under the dirt."		
(10) Bronte points to the dirt in the box. "There he go."		
(11) Ms. Debbie begins to draw a line for each word of her message, saying each word separately. "This says, 'The . . . frog . . . is . . . hiding.' There's my period." She rereads the planned message, touching each line: "The frog is hiding."	Demonstration	
(12) Bronte points to the frog. "Yeah, I see him. I see 'im right there!"		
(13) Bronte, Jaron, and Ms. Debbie bend forward with heads crowded together looking for the frog.		
(14) Ms. Debbie sits up and begins to write again, reading her message aloud as she records the words. "The . . . " She pauses to make eye contact with Bronte, then continues. "This is the frog word. Fuhh . . . " She stretches out the initial *F* sound, then continues to read as she writes: "frog is . . . "	Direct teaching	
(15) She stops writing and hands the pencil to Bronte. "Write *hiding* for me!"	Collaboration	Invite to write Suggest

(16) Bronte takes the pencil. *"H?"* he asks.	Participation as Writer	
(17) She confirms his choice. *"H*, huh huh," she says drawing out the initial sound. Ms. Debbie taps the page indicating Bronte should write the letter on the line.		Support
(18) Bronte leans over the paper to write, then announces the letters, *"H, I."*		
(19) *"H, I.* You're right!" she says. "This is what scientists do. They write down and draw pictures of what they're seeing, and when they come back if it's changed, they draw another picture."	Direct teaching	

In this portion of the Frog Log event, Rowe not only provides demonstrations of writing for Bronte but also teaches two quick mini-lessons on sounding out words (Turn 11) and the function of science logs (Turn 19). This teaching is tailored to Bronte's interests and current hypotheses about writing and is linked to the familiar context of the Frog Log event they are constructing together.

Designing Spaces for Writing

The physical arrangement of classroom furniture, space, materials, and people sends powerful messages about the kinds of writing activities that are expected. Our research (Rowe, 2008, 2010) shows that classroom geography is as much a part of supportive conditions of learning to write as are teaching interactions. In our research classrooms, we follow three broad guidelines when designing spaces for writing.

◆ *Materials: Are writing materials present and easily accessible to children throughout the classroom?* First, in emergent writing classrooms, we store writing materials and texts throughout the classroom on open shelving. Decentralized storage and open access to writing materials physically send the message that writing is an expected part of children's activities throughout the classroom. As in the Frog Log event, when children and teachers only have to reach over to a nearby shelf to get writing materials or books (Turns 36–43), they are more likely to follow through on ideas for writing or reading that emerge as part of ongoing activities. Having books and other texts available for consultation gives children easy access to demonstrations they need to support their writing.

◆ *Space: Are spaces available for collaborative writing?* Second, we make sure that space and furniture is arranged so that it comfortably accommodates small groups of children and a teacher working together on their writing. The drawing in Figure 13.6 was created from a photo taken in one of our research classrooms and shows a typical arrangement where the teacher sits at a table writing with a small group of children. In addition to a designated writing center, many teachers store materials in totes that can be moved to the multipurpose spaces used for writing during the learning centers/workshop time. In general, we consider whether each ecological area of the classroom can comfortably accommodate two to three children and an adult. In the Enhanced Language and Literacy Success Project, we have found that when writing spaces are too small, teachers rarely spend time in these areas, and possibilities for collaborative writing decrease. If collaboration with teachers and peers is an important feature of supportive learning-to-write events, then the arrangement of space needs to send that message.

◆ *Bodies: Do teachers sit alongside children as they write?* Third, if teachers value collaborative composing, they need to consider the messages their physical positioning sends about expected teacher–child interactions. We encourage teachers to arrange both space and time so they can sit down with small groups of children and compose alongside them. Figures 13.6 and 13.9 illustrate how changing the arrangement of space and bodies can alter the potentials for activity, interaction, and learning. The image seen in Figure 13.9 was created from a photo taken during the first year of the Write Start! Project and shows typical arrangements of space, materials, and people during writing in one of our research classrooms. Figure 13.6 shows the kind of arrangement the teacher used for writing with her students in the second year of the project. This is a writing space purposefully planned to provide very different possibilities for interaction and composing. The close, side-by-side, eye-to-eye

FIGURE 13.9. Spaces for observing and directing writers.

seating arrangement provided opportunities for two-way conversation, observation of both peers' and teachers' demonstrations, and shared access to the page for collaborative composing.

Summing Up: Essential Features of Emergent Writing Classrooms

In every classroom, every year, teachers and children build a local culture that includes values and expectations about what it means to learn to write. This includes understandings of children's and teachers' roles, the kinds of learning-to-write activities that are a usual part of classroom life, and the ways teachers and children are expected to use materials and arrange their bodies in classroom spaces. The features listed on our Top 10 list (Figure 13.6) provide a good starting point for reflection and planning when the goal is to build a classroom that supports children's engagement as emergent writers. In the next section, we focus on patterns of teacher talk and actions that engage young children as writers in these kinds of curricular environments.

THE FISSIS MODEL AS A GUIDE FOR TEACHER TALK AND INTERACTION

In working with preschool and early grades teachers, many have shared that they are unsure what to do once they are sitting with the children during writing time. While teachers typically have considerable experience teaching children about the alphabet or correcting unconventional letter forms, many have less experience supporting children in composing messages using emergent writing. To provide research-based answers to this question, we analyzed patterns of interaction of the expert teachers in our research classrooms (Flushman, 2012; Rowe, 2008; Rowe et al., 2003). We found that though teachers' styles of talk differed somewhat, and the content of talk varied widely depending on the nature of the event under way, teacher interactions with young writers tended to include the six interactive moves (abbreviated with the acronym FISSIS) seen in Figure 13.10. As we discuss how the FISSIS model can guide teaching interactions, we refer to column 3 in Classroom Narratives 1 and 2 where adult interactive moves are labeled for the Frog Log event.

Find Common Ground

To engage children in writing, the first step is building the common ground needed to construct a shared purpose for writing. Teachers need to understand the child's current activities in order to support his or her participation as a writer. For example, in Classroom Narratives 1 and 2 (Turns 1–22), Ms. Debbie, Jaron, and Bronte's

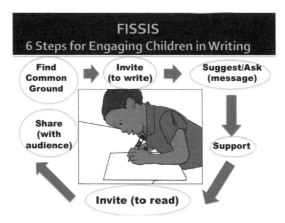

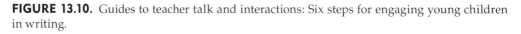

FIGURE 13.10. Guides to teacher talk and interactions: Six steps for engaging young children in writing.

talk about frogs became the common ground for the writing and drawing that followed. Writing is a rich opportunity for conversation that can help teachers understand how writing connects to the child's interests. Conversations about emergent writers' texts are especially important, since their products may not be conventional enough to be understood without the author's explanations.

Invite Children to Write and Suggest Messages

Because young children will not always know how print can be used functionally, an important role for teachers is issuing invitations for specific types of writing, and suggesting possible content for children's texts. Rowe's writing invitation and suggestions for text content in Classroom Narratives 1 and 2 are typical (Turns 15, 23, 30). Because emergent writing teachers plan for openness, their invitations for writing projects and suggestions for text content are offered tentatively, and children usually have the opportunity to take up and build on their suggestions as Jaron and Bronte did, or to respond with their own ideas. If children are already moving forward with their own text ideas, teachers ask what they are writing about, instead of offering adult suggestions.

Provide Support

When teachers are present as children write, children often seek them out for help in recording their messages. Sometimes teachers also offer unsolicited help (Rowe, 2008). Teachers match instructional supports to the child's specific needs at the moment and, more generally, to the child's level of skill and understanding about print. The phonics lesson Rowe taught at Turn 14 of the Frog Log event was a good fit for Bronte's skills, while her focus on Jaron's message was appropriate as a way to fan the spark of interest shown by this reluctant writer (Turn 33). The goal in supporting young writers is to offer just enough help to nudge them to the next level in their understandings. Teacher support can come in the form of coauthoring, demonstrating, suggesting writing strategies, direct teaching, or directing children to resources they can use to solve their authoring problems.

Invite Children to Read Their Messages

When we work with emergent writers, we ask them to read their marks whether they have produced scribbles or invented spellings. "What did you write?" is one of the most powerful questions that emergent writing teachers can ask (Rowe, 2008). In the span of four words, children are addressed as writers and their writing approximations are legitimized as readable texts. As children become experienced participants in emergent writing classrooms, the teacher's question is often unnecessary. When teachers consistently show interest and approval for children's texts, as Rowe and Jaron's teacher did at Turns 28 and 104 in Classroom Narrative 1, children are eager to seek them out as audiences, and often read their texts spontaneously as Jaron did at Turns 32 and 105.

Share Writing with an Audience

When writing is used for authentic purposes, sharing it with an audience is an important step. In emergent writing classrooms, the audience is often the group of peers and teachers who are present as the text is created. As children talk about their writing, the content is negotiated and their positions as writers are validated (Rowe, 2008). Teachers may also provide opportunities for young writers to share their texts with the large group from the author's chair (Graves, 1994), as Jaron's teacher did in the Frog Log event (Turn 108). Writers need audiences to encourage, motivate, and challenge them to think about writing in new ways.

Summing Up: Teachers' Interactions with Young Writers

As is evident from a quick scan of the third column in Classroom Narratives 1 and 2, in practice, teacher–child interactions do not always cycle through every step of the FISSIS model as presented in Figure 13.10, and teachers sometimes move recursively back and forth between steps several times in a single writing event. As children become more engaged as writers, they often initiate some of the steps, making teacher action unnecessary. Overall, the FISSIS model centers on two teacher actions that are essential to emergent writing classrooms: Invite the child to write! Invite the child to read his or her marks.

CONCLUSION

While research on emergent writing has been available for several decades (e.g., Goodman, 1980; Harste et al., 1984; Teale & Sulzby, 1986), it has been slow to affect classroom practice. This may, in part, be because educational attention has been so strongly focused on beginning reading. However, recent research converges on the conclusion that early writing experiences are an important way children learn skills needed for conventional reading and writing (National Early Literacy Panel, 2008).

Reading and writing are two sides of the same coin. Children who experience supported opportunities to try out writing in their classrooms have increased opportunities to learn foundational skills needed for later reading and writing. If young children are not supported as writers, they are missing powerful opportunities for literacy learning. The best practices in early writing instruction are those that encourage children to participate as writers, to use their current understandings to get their messages down, and to use their texts for purposes that are meaningful as part of everyday classroom activities.

REFERENCES

Barton, D., & Hamilton, M. (2000). Literacy practices. In D. Barton, M. Hamilton, & R. Ivanic (Eds.), *Situated literacies. Reading and writing in context* (pp. 7–15). London: Routledge.

Cambourne, B. (1988). *The whole story. Natural learning and the acquisiton of literacy in the classroom.* New York: Scholastic.

Cambourne, B. (2009). Revisiting the concept of "natural learning." In J. V. Hoffman & Y. Goodman (Eds.), *Changing literacies for changing times. An historical perspective on the future of reading research, public policy, and classroom practices.* New York: Routledge.

Clay, M. M. (1979). *Reading: The patterning of complex behavior.* Auckland, New Zealand: Heinemann.

Donaldson, M. (1978). *Children's minds.* New York: Norton.

Edelsky, C., & Smith, K. (1984). Is that writing—or are those marks just a figment of your curriculum? *Language Arts, 67*(1), 192–205.

Flushman, T. R. (2012). *Nonfiction writing in prekindergarten. Understandings of informational text features and use of science journals.* Unpublished doctoral dissertation, Vanderbilt University, Nashville, TN.

Gee, J. P. (2003). A sociocultural perspective on early literacy development. In S. B. Neuman & D. Dickinson (Eds.), *Handbook of early literacy research* (pp. 30–42). New York: Guilford Press.

Gentry, J. R. (2000). A retrospective on invented spelling and a look forward. *The Reading Teacher, 54*(3), 318–332.

Goodman, Y. (1980). The roots of literacy. In M. P. Douglas (Ed.), *Claremont Reading Conference, 44th Yearbook* (pp. 1–32). Claremont, CA: Claremont Colleges.

Goodman, Y. (Ed.). (1990). *How children construct literacy: Piagetian perspectives.* Newark, DE: International Reading Association.

Goodman, Y. (1996). Kid watching: An alternative to testing. In S. Wilde (Ed.), *Notes from a kidwatcher. Selected writing of Yetta M. Goodman* (pp. 211–218). Portsmouth, NH: Heinemann.

Goodman, Y., & Goodman, K. S. (2004). To err is human: Learning about language processes by analyzing miscues. In R. B. Ruddell & N. J. Unrau (Eds.), *Theoretical models and processes of reading* (5th ed., pp. 620–639). Newark, DE: International Reading Association.

Graves, D. (1994). *A fresh look at writing.* Portsmouth, NH: Heinemann.

Harste, J. C., Woodward, V. A., & Burke, C. L. (1984). *Language stories and literacy lessons.* Portsmouth, NH: Heinemann.

Hildreth, G. (1936). Developmental sequences in name writing. *Child Development, 7,* 291–303.

Kress, G. (1997). *Before writing: Rethinking the paths to literacy.* London: Routledge.

National Early Literacy Panel. (2008). *Developing early literacy. Report of the National Early Literacy Panel. A scientific synthesis of early literacy development and implications for intervention.* Jessup, MD: National Institute for Literacy.

Rogoff, B., Mistry, J., Goncu, A., & Mosier, C. (1993). Guided participation in cultural activity by toddlers and caregivers. *Monographs of the Society for Research in Child Development, 58*(8, Serial 236).

Rowe, D. W. (1994). *Preschoolers as authors: Literacy learning in the social world of the classroom.* Cresskill, NJ: Hampton Press.

Rowe, D. W. (1998). The literate potentials of book-related dramatic play. *Reading Research Quarterly, 33,* 10–35.

Rowe, D. W. (2008). The social construction of intentionality: Two-year-olds' and adults' participation at a preschool writing center. *Research in the Teaching of English, 42*(4), 387–434.

Rowe, D. W. (2009). Early written communication. In R. Beard, D. Myhill, J. Riley, & M. Nystrand (Eds.), *SAGE handbook of writing development* (pp. 213–231). Los Angeles: Sage.

Rowe, D. W. (2010). Directions for studying early literacy as social practice. *Language Arts, 88*(2), 134–143.

Rowe, D. W., & Dickinson, D. K. (2008). *Enhanced language & literacy success.* Nashville, TN: U.S. Department of Education.

Rowe, D. W., Fitch, J. F., & Bass, A. (2003). Toy stories as opportunities for imagination and reflection in writers' workshop. *Language Arts, 80*(5), 363–374.

Rowe, D. W., & Neitzel, C. (2010). Interest and agency in two- and three-year-olds' participation in emergent writing. *Reading Research Quarterly, 45*(2), 169–195.

Rowe, D. W., & Wilson, S. (2009). *Write Start! Writing assessment.* Nashville: Vanderbilt University.

Rowsell, J., & Pahl, K. (2007). Sedimented identities in texts: Instances of practice. *Reading Research Quarterly, 42*(3), 388–404.

Smith, F. (2004). *Understanding reading* (6th ed.). Mahwah, NJ: Erlbaum.

Sulzby, E. (1985). Kindergarteners as writers and readers. In M. Farr (Ed.), *Advances in writing research. Children's early writing* (Vol. 1, pp. 127–200). Norwood, NJ: Ablex.

Sulzby, E. (1991). The development of the young child and the emergence of literacy. In J.

Flood, J. Jensen, & J. Squire (Eds.), *Handbook of research on teaching the English language arts* (pp. 273–285). New York: Macmillan.

Teale, W., & Sulzby, E. (1986). Introduction. Emergent literacy as a perspective for examining how young children become writers and readers. In W. Teale & E. Sulzby (Eds.), *Emergent literacy* (pp. vii–xxv). Norwood, NJ: Ablex.

Tolchinsky, L. (2006). The emergence of writing. In C. A. MacArthur, S. Graham, & J. Fitzgerald (Eds.), *Handbook of writing research* (pp. 83–95). New York: Guilford Press.

Treiman, R., Kessler, B., & Bourassa, D. (2001). Children's own names influence their spelling. *Applied Psycholinguistics, 22,* 555–570.

Vygotsky, L. S. (1978). *Mind in society.* Cambridge, MA: Harvard University Press.

Yaden, D., Rowe, D. W., & MacGillivray, L. (2000). Emergent literacy. A matter (polyphony) of perspectives. In M. Kamil, P. Mosenthal, P. D. Pearson, & R. Barr (Eds.), *Handbook of reading research* (Vol. III, pp. 425–454). Mahwah, NJ: Erlbaum.

CHAPTER 14

❖

Strengthening Play
in Early Literacy Teaching Practice

KATHLEEN A. ROSKOS
JAMES CHRISTIE

GUIDING QUESTIONS

❖ What are the design features of a literacy-enriched play environment?

❖ What kinds of play activity support early literacy development and learning?

❖ How can teachers assess children's play maturity to strengthen play in early literacy experience and learning?

That play and literacy share common ground is a milestone in the scientific journey of emergent literacy in early childhood. Not all that long ago, the idea that some kinds of play might support literacy readiness was not prevalent, although in theory it seemed promising (Pellegrini & Galda, 1993). Only recently has a body of play–literacy research, rooted in strong theory, shown the potentially significant influences of play activity on young children's literacy development (Roskos & Christie, 2012).

Building bridges between play–literacy research (what we know) and practice (what we do), however, remains a challenge in early literacy education. Implementation of any new research evidence into classroom practice is difficult. Linking play and literacy is especially so because it involves the interweaving of environment, curriculum, instruction, and assessment, not to mention deeply rooted belief systems of educators. In this chapter we discuss the knowledge base that informs the development of a coordinated framework for strengthening play activity in early literacy teaching practice. We examine important elements of literacy-enriched play environment design, revisit the potential of topic/theme-centered play areas for literacy and learning, describe power techniques for linking play–literacy skills, and explore an assessment tool for observing play competencies that support literacy development. We close with a few comments on the role of play in an era of common core state standards, which set rigorous early literacy goals for young children upon entry into the primary grades. More than ever, play is vital in laying the foundations for the problem solving, persistence, and motivation that learning to read and write demands in a global world.

LITERACY-ENRICHED PLAY ENVIRONMENT DESIGN

That literacy-enriched play environments increase young children's literacy behaviors is one of the more robust findings in play–literacy research (Morrow & Schickedanz, 2006; Roskos & Christie, 2012; Roskos, Christie, Widman, & Holding, 2010). The physical presence of print and literacy objects/tools in play areas prompts spontaneous literacy interactions among children. In addition, the social presence of adults and peers, who model and support reading and writing, increases the amount and quality of literacy interactions in play settings. As a result, children experience increased exposure to print and literacy, which has implications for their overall literacy development (Mol & Bus, 2011).

To date, however, implementation of this strategy is not universal in all early childhood classrooms, reflecting perhaps a need for stronger play environment design content in teachers' professional education. Much of the *know-how* relevant to literacy-enriched play environment design consists of generalization guidance, although a few details related to amounts (e.g., time, space), complexity of materials, adult presence, and meaningfulness of play–literacy activity for young children have been documented. Table 14.1 summarizes the basics of literacy-enriched play environment design that early childhood educators should know and be able to apply in preschool and pre-kindergarten settings with confidence.

TOPIC-ORIENTED DRAMATIC PLAY

Topic- or theme-based dramatic play is a deeply rooted practice in early childhood, usually rather loosely structured to encourage children's exploration of ideas, relationships, and objects, and to promote the discovery of how things work and what they can do. Who among us, for example, has not helped children *play store* or *restaurant* or *hospital* in connection with broader curriculum goals?

TABLE 14.1. Basics of Literacy-Enriched Play Environment Design

Design feature	Generalization	Detail
Physical environment		
Space	Allocate about two-thirds of the available classroom space to play areas.	A literacy center should accommodate four to five children comfortably.
Signage	Use sturdy materials with complementary graphics to provide information children need to accomplish work and play goals.	• Print should be bold with sufficient white space and consistent type style. • Print should be functional, not merely decorative.
Materials	Include enough books of different genres and difficulty levels (five to eight per child), writing supplies for exploring writing and book making, and materials for active involvement in storytelling (e.g., puppets).	• Books should span three to four grade levels representing different genres; multiple copies of some books for joint reading; access to age-appropriate e-books. • Play objects should be of sufficient complexity to exercise cognitive and motor skills.
Storage	Locate storage units close to their point of use; physically arrange materials to show how they go together; use picture and print to describe the organization.	Avoid top-heavy shelving, base extenders that may cause tripping, and sharp corners at children's eye level.
Appeal	Create a welcoming, coordinated, interesting, and uncluttered space for literacy experiences.	Use displays, light, and color to attract and hold children's attention and interest in different play areas.
Social environment		
Predictability	Establish language and literacy routines that support the flow of activity across the day.	• Ensure adult presence to enhance play activity. • Use sign-in charts, play-management boards, and a variety of instructional formats to create a sense of order. • Allow ample time for play (60–75 minutes recommended).
Mood	Use welcoming entries, displays, and objects that create a sense of identity, and homelike elements to project mood.	Use color to create settings "in sync" with the immediate culture of the larger community; choose colors that communicate cultural references. Certain furnishings, for example, can serve this function such as decorated chairs, art objects, or wall hangings.
Participation	Encourage small-group adult–child and child–child interactions in small, intimate spaces for conversation, explanations, and sharing information.	• Provide regular opportunities for small-group play. • Create private niches for book browsing, shared reading, talking, and writing.

This time-honored teaching practice is also one that can be "tweaked" to enrich children's learning of disciplinary content in science, social studies, mathematics, and the language arts. Although evidence of any direct impact of play activity on children's academic learning is slim (Smith, 2010), there is some emerging indirect evidence suggesting that topic-oriented dramatic play when well aligned to language and literacy curriculum goals may support acquisition of academic concepts, facts, and vocabulary. In one Head Start Early Reading First project (Akron Ready Steps, Akron, OH), for example, children in classrooms with a high degree of alignment between specific topic studies of the *Creative Curriculum* (e.g., buildings; 2006) and dramatic play centers demonstrated significantly higher gains on curriculum-based measures of topic-oriented vocabulary than their peers. Certainly there were other influential variables at work here, such as a rigorous early literacy instructional approach. Still—the explicit play–literacy link may have helped to tilt the learning environment in favor of academic language use.

This said—and acknowledging the need for more research as to efficacy—how does the teaching practice work to potentially strengthen early literacy learning? Figure 14.1 illustrates the topic-oriented dramatic play alignment process. The play process begins with large and small group instruction where children are taught academic content that fits with a topic (e.g., for the topic "building and construction," content such as tools, construction equipment, and building materials would be appropriate). The instruction primes the upcoming dramatic play by tapping prior knowledge, sorting out confusions, and introducing relevant vocabulary and facts. Next, consider some dramatic play possibilities with the children (e.g., a fix-it shop or a construction site). After choosing the topic/theme, create signage for the play area, including a topic/theme name, storage areas, directions for object use, labels, and so on. Add props and discuss roles for play in the setting. After play is under way, use role-related language to model for the children. Once the children are familiar with the setting, introduce a problem or task that sparks children's thinking, stimulates language use, and encourages collaboration.

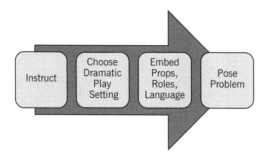

FIGURE 14.1. Topic-oriented dramatic play alignment to curriculum process.

For example, during a 6-week topic study of winter, kindergarten children were taught how to read thermometers and how to record this information, using the symbol for degrees. To connect this content with dramatic play, the teachers supplied the discovery play center (science labs) with various types of thermometers, note pads and pencils for recording data, materials for an experiment measuring the temperature of water under different conditions (warm water, tap water, water with ice), lab coats for dress-up, and printed directions related to the experiment. Children loved being scientists and did not shift to "off-task" activities, such as visiting with friends or other forms of play. The combination of dramatic play-setting cues (the "lab"), objects (scientific tools), task (measuring), and role-related talk around a common goal (to measure water temperature) engaged and focused children's attention and language to the content.

PLAY-CONTINGENT LITERACY INSTRUCTION

Two lines of play–literacy research have produced instructional techniques that weld together play activity with specific reading skills: thematic fantasy play with story comprehension and play planning with developmental spelling. The more studied of the two is the thematic fantasy play (TFP) paradigm, originally developed by Saltz and Johnson (1974). It involves the reenactment of tales or stories with a repetitive plot and a small number of characters. Studies show that children with TFP training outperformed their non-TFP-trained peers in both *specific* story comprehension (understanding of the story that was reenacted) and *generalized* story comprehension (understanding of other stories; Pellegrini, 1984; Saltz & Johnson, 1974; Silvern, Taylor, Williamson, Surbeck, & Kelley, 1986), which suggests that the play may have catalyzed comprehension.

Story drama is an instructional technique that effectively translates TFP research to practice for young children. Originally developed as a way to develop improvisational skills in a drama curriculum (James, 1967), it can be adapted to adhere to the TFP training for purposes of developing children's story comprehension skills. The basic steps follow:

1. Choose a story suitable for reenactment; fairytales, fables, predictable books work well.
2. Read and discuss the story with the children; highlight the setting and characters, the problem, the plot events and the resolution.
3. Select a number of events that are described in the story; read them and ask the children to practice movement to show what is happening; add a few props if necessary.

4. Establish the setting of the story by designating parts of the classroom as locations.
5. Divide the class into groups that represent characters in the story; characters can be represented by three to four children; put the characters into position in location and review how and where they should move to correspond with the story.
6. Read the story at a pace so each group can do its part.

After a few story drama experiences, children can attempt to coordinate a dramalike retell of a familiar story on their own to further practice comprehension skills. The teacher directs the retelling by prompting, but children are in charge of acting out *and* telling the story. Additionally, a variation of story drama can become a regular extension of shared-book lessons and read-alouds where children use stick puppets of story characters (cutouts) to reenact stories.

Play planning is an instructional technique associated with the Tools of the Mind (TOM) curriculum developed by Bodrova and Leong (2007). The primary purpose of play planning in the TOM curriculum is to develop children's self-regulation abilities by having them draw/write play plans and follow through with support in extended play activity. A unique feature of the technique is referred to as *scaffolded writing*, where children are guided to make increasingly more accurate representations of words (phoneme–grapheme matches) and thus advance their spelling knowledge. Results on the efficacy of play planning for developing self-regulation and word-level early literacy skills (e.g., developmental spelling) are mixed. Diamond, Barnett, Thomas, and Munro (2008) observed that play planning improved kindergarteners' executive functioning (inhibitory control, working memory, cognitive flexibility), which in turn boosted their early literacy skills, namely phonological awareness and alphabet knowledge. Lonigan and Phillips (2012), however, found that the technique worked better to advance self-regulation and early literacy skills when combined with a strong skills-focused literacy curriculum than when applied in TOM alone or other less rigorous early literacy curricula.

Implementation of the play planning technique is complex, and participation in professional development and training prior to applying it is highly recommended (Leong & Hensen, 2005). It is designed for use with older preschoolers and kindergarten-age children. Effective implementation requires considerable knowledge of children's developmental writing and instructional expertise in coaching the acquisition of difficult early literacy skills in young children. Teachers need the assistance of a trained teacher aid or another adult when using the technique during playtime. With these conditions in place, a graduated approach that progresses across much of the program year works best from our experience as outlined below. Teachers need to be mindful that children will vary in their abilities to participate, and make adjustments accordingly.

Phase 1: Play Management System

Establish a play management system that includes five core play areas—discovery, blocks, art, dramatic play, and library corner. Color code the play areas and use a play management board that displays the areas and the number of children it can hold. Use the board as a visible reminder for play management during a 60- to 75-minute play period (see Figure 14.2). Have on hand clipboards and markers for play planning.

Phase 2: Choose–Say–Go

Describe the five core play areas and the color coding to the children. Explain that they will choose where to go to play and tell what they plan to do there. Model the language for *choosing* and *saying*—for example: "I am going to blocks to make a house." Point out that when one play area is full, a child must choose another for that day. Monitor children's choices over time, so that they experience the full range of play areas. Then implement the *choose–say–go* routine for several weeks until most children can participate readily. Each child comes up to the play board, chooses a play area and says its name, then takes a clip, wristband, or necklace as a reminder and goes to the play area (see Figure 14.3).

FIGURE 14.2. Example of a play management board.

FIGURE 14.3. Preparing for choose–say–go.

Phase 3: Choose–Say–Draw–Go

Introduce the play plan form to the children. Explain that they will tell and then write their name and draw their plan in the space above the line as best as they can. Tell them that you and/or a teaching assistant will put a line and the name of the area where they plan to play below their drawing. Model, like this:

> "This time before you go to play, you will draw a picture of what you plan to play, like this . . . I am pretending that I am going to *blocks* to make a house. First . . . I put my name up here . . . like this. Next . . . I draw myself and my friend in the blocks here . . . like this. Then I put a line and the name of where I am going—blocks. Now I'd like you to try to do that today . . . and I will help you."

Gather those children ready for this step on the floor or at a table to draw their plans with your support (see Figure 14.4). The teacher assistant monitors the remaining children in their chosen play areas. Continue for several weeks until the majority of children can draw a plan. Note: Some children will only come this far in play planning in the program year.

Phase 4: Choose–Say–Draw–Write–Go

At this point, introduce scaffolded writing for those children who appear ready. These are children who can write their name, identify and form some alphabet letters, and know a few letter–sound matches. Scaffolded writing will progress from making lines for words to spelling attempts for some words to spelling attempts for all words. Begin by explaining to the children that now they will try to draw *and* write their play plan. Show them how to make lines for words and how to write

FIGURE 14.4. Play plan form for choose–say–draw–go.

words on each line using the stem *I am going to. . . . Model by saying something like this:*

> "This time I am going to draw and write what I am going to play. First I put my name. Then I draw what I am going to play. And then I try to write down what I am going to play. I make a line for each word, like this . . . then I write the words on the lines, like this . . . Now I want you to try to make a play plan like mine. Let's start where you make lines for words, then we'll try to write words later."

As before, gather those children who are ready around you and *scaffold* their drawing and writing (see Figure 14.5). The teacher assistant monitors the remaining children, and can also provide support as needed.

Once children demonstrate they can make a line for each word that they hear in the sentence describing their plan, encourage them to try to make words on the lines to *write* their plan. With practice, children progress from putting a single letter to signify a word (which may or may not be a phoneme–grapheme match) to letter-name spellings that typically represent the first and/or last letter of a word. Children will progress at various rates in their writing development with some making lines by the end of the program year to some producing prephonemic strings of letters to a few using invented spellings to produce their plan.

Play planning, as we briefly outlined above, is an intensive instructional technique that occurs over an extended length of time and requires substantial supportive conditions (e.g., teacher knowledge and training, logistics) for effective implementation. Still, the results can be quite stunning and worth the effort as illustrated in the play plans of the 4-year-olds in Figure 14.6.

FIGURE 14.5. Play plan form for choose–say–draw–write–go.

FIGURE 14.6. Examples of play plans.

ASSESSMENT OF PLAY MATURITY

Numerous efforts at federal and state levels are under way to improve child and program assessment in early childhood settings for purposes of monitoring school readiness, guiding instruction and practice, and screening for developmental delays (Cooper & Costa, 2012). Increasingly early childhood programs (e.g., Head Start) are urged to establish assessment systems that align with statewide early learning content standards and rigorously support child development across learning domains (Snow & Van Hemel, 2008). Systematic observation of essential skills for school readiness is key to promoting continuous improvement at child and program levels.

Play, however, is often sidelined in observations of children's school readiness where efforts primarily focus on collecting evidence of children's language, literacy, and mathematics knowledge and skills. This is unfortunate because theoretically play, particularly pretend play in the preschool developmental period, provides a lens on cognitive growth (Piaget, 1962; Vygotsky, 1966). It both reflects current levels of representational thinking (as per Piaget) and creates a zone of proximal development that reveals what children can do cognitively with supports (as per Vygotsky). The educational expectation, based on theory and play research, is that children develop *mature play* behaviors in early childhood that support intellectual growth, as well as social skills for participation and collaboration (See Table 14.2). This is a reasonable expectation, and one that should be systematically assessed to ensure children's effective use of play as a learning resource and to gauge program quality in the provision of play activity for school readiness.

We strongly encourage teachers to incorporate observations of mature play into their assessment practices. While we certainly recognize the growing demand for classroom-based assessment in many learning domains and how that significantly impacts teachers' professional work, we also advocate for a small yet balanced set

TABLE 14.2. Elements of Mature Play

Element	Example
Creation of an imaginary situation	Playing *hospital*.
Object substitution	A wand for an X-ray machine.
Role taking	Doctor, nurse, receptionist.
Implicit rules	Doctor writes prescriptions.
Language use	Comments on actions (words, sounds).
	Directs another player.
	Narrates action.
	Anticipates own actions ("I'm going to . . . ").
	Plans cycle of actions.
	Pre-plans a play scenario with peers.
Sustained amount of time	Maintains pretend play for > 45 minutes.

of formative assessment activities that observe young children's development and growth in instructional and play contexts. The informal Play Maturity Observation Checklist in Figure 14.7 provides an assessment tool for screening and monitoring children's pretend play in the classroom setting.

Teachers should plan to screen for the play maturity of all children in a preschool or prekindergarten classroom three times per year, and to monitor more regularly those who lack age-appropriate play maturity indicators. With advance planning and scheduling, this should be able to be done in most classrooms. Focus on three to five children for about 5 minutes each in the dramatic play area over a 1- to 2-week period. At most this would require 25 minutes of observation each day and allow for observation of the majority of a class in 1 week. From these results, identify those children showing signs of lower levels of play maturity for their age, and progress monitor their play activity more regularly, perhaps once a week during playtime for about 5 minutes.

Ms. Spars's midyear screening data of her preschool class (3- to 4-year-olds) provide an example (see Figure 14.8). She is quite pleased because most of the children are demonstrating complex pretend play behaviors indicative of mature play. Evalissa and Tre'Ante, however, need considerable support in moving from simple to sequences of pretend play, requiring more experience with role taking, creating props, and using toys to make up play stories. A few others (Jason, Lucas, and Meah) need more experience with complex pretend play behaviors, learning how to extend the length of their play, negotiate roles with peers, and use language to contribute to play scenarios. Ms. Spars can use this information to model more mature play behaviors in dramatic play, encourage more active participation for some in play scenarios, provide opportunities for practice with toys and props for others,

Child:		Date:	
Observer:			

Minute	Simple (18–24 months)	Sequenced (23–36 months)	Complex*(> 3 years)
1:00	☐ Performs single actions (brushes doll's hair). ☐ Performs same action on two different items (feeds self and doll). ☐ Substitutes toy object for real thing if similar properties. ☐ Mimics adult actions (pretends to read).	☐ Performs a sequence based on familiar to less familiar events. ☐ Assumes a familiar role; may talk while plays. ☐ Substitutes dissimilar objects; creates imaginary props. ☐ Gives toys roles in play.	☐ Develops imaginary themes. ☐ Takes on make-believe roles. ☐ Cooperates with others for an extended time period (>10 minutes). ☐ Creates imaginary objects and places. ☐ Uses language to create make-believe. ☐ *Assigns roles.* ☐ *Plans scenes.* ☐ *Establishes identity of objects and places.* ☐ *Substitutes talk for action.* ☐ *Develops a "story line."* ☐ *Negotiates problems without adult help.*
2:00	☐ Performs single actions. ☐ Performs same action on two different items. ☐ Substitutes toy object for real thing if similar properties. ☐ Mimics adult actions.	☐ Performs a sequence based on familiar to less familiar events. ☐ Assumes a familiar role; may talk while plays. ☐ Substitutes dissimilar objects; creates imaginary props. ☐ Gives toys roles in play.	☐ Develops imaginary themes. ☐ Takes on make-believe roles. ☐ Cooperates with others for an extended time period (>10 minutes). ☐ Creates imaginary objects and places. ☐ Uses language to create make-believe. ☐ *Assigns roles.* ☐ *Plans scenes.* ☐ *Establishes identity of objects and places.* ☐ *Substitutes talk for action.* ☐ *Develops a "story line."* ☐ *Negotiates problems without adult help.*
3:00	☐ Performs single actions. ☐ Performs same action on two different items. ☐ Substitutes toy object for real thing if similar properties. ☐ Mimics adult actions.	☐ Performs a sequence based on familiar to less familiar events. ☐ Assumes a familiar role; may talk while plays. ☐ Substitutes dissimilar objects; creates imaginary props. ☐ Gives toys roles in play.	☐ Develops imaginary themes. ☐ Takes on make-believe roles. ☐ Cooperates with others for an extended time period (>10 minutes). ☐ Creates imaginary objects and places. ☐ Uses language to create make-believe. ☐ *Assigns roles.* ☐ *Plans scenes.* ☐ *Establishes identity of objects and places.* ☐ *Substitutes talk for action.* ☐ *Develops a "story line."* ☐ *Negotiates problems without adult help.*

(continued)

FIGURE 14.7. Play Maturity Observation Checklist.

Minute	Simple (18–24 months)	Sequenced (23–36 months)	Complex*(> 3 years)
4:00	☐ Performs single actions. ☐ Performs same action on two different items. ☐ Substitutes toy object for real thing if similar properties. ☐ Mimics adult actions.	☐ Performs a sequence based on familiar to less familiar events. ☐ Assumes a familiar role; may talk while plays. ☐ Substitutes dissimilar objects; creates imaginary props. ☐ Gives toys roles in play.	☐ Develops imaginary themes. ☐ Takes on make-believe roles. ☐ Cooperates with others for an extended time period (>10 minutes). ☐ Creates imaginary objects and places. ☐ Uses language to create make-believe. ☐ *Assigns roles.* ☐ *Plans scenes.* ☐ *Establishes identity of objects and places.* ☐ *Substitutes talk for action.* ☐ *Develops a "story line."* ☐ *Negotiates problems without adult help.*
5:00	☐ Performs single actions. ☐ Performs same action on two different items. ☐ Substitutes toy object for real thing if similar properties. ☐ Mimics adult actions.	☐ Performs a sequence based on familiar to less familiar events. ☐ Assumes a familiar role; may talk while plays. ☐ Substitutes dissimilar objects; creates imaginary props. ☐ Gives toys roles in play.	☐ Develops imaginary themes. ☐ Takes on make-believe roles. ☐ Cooperates with others for an extended time period (>10 minutes). ☐ Creates imaginary objects and places. ☐ Uses language to create make-believe. ☐ *Assigns roles.* ☐ *Plans scenes.* ☐ *Establishes identity of objects and places.* ☐ *Substitutes talk for action.* ☐ *Develops a "story line."* ☐ *Negotiates problems without adult help.*
Total			

FIGURE 14.7. *(continued)*

and pair less mature with more mature players in a variety of play areas. She can also use the assessment information to monitor her overall program, ensuring sufficient time for play (not shortchanging it for other pressing priorities), generating fresh ideas that appeal to children's changing interests, and providing a variety of materials that engage children across a range of abilities in dramatic play.

PLAY'S VITAL ROLE

Our own certainty that play is important in early childhood—that it nurtures children's bodies and minds—is not enough to ensure its vital role in the 21st-century early childhood classroom. In these times of accountability, not only our professional

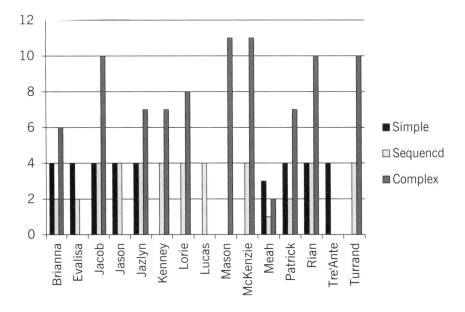

FIGURE 14.8. Midyear screening results of play maturity.

certainties but also hard evidence are the foundation of strong early literacy programs. We have, in hand, a small but solid body of research that shows play's potential in supporting early literacy development and learning. This research describes what we know with a fair degree of confidence about the benefits of a literacy-enriched play environment for early literacy experience, the advantages of alignment between topics of study and dramatic play areas for increasing access to academic content and language, the power of play-contingent techniques for learning difficult early literacy skills (e.g., phoneme–grapheme matching), and the assessment of play maturity that informs the early childhood instructional program. We have, in brief, evidence-based knowledge that can strengthen practice in more thorough, specific, accurate, and authentic ways.

CONCLUSION

What we need (and rather urgently) is to bridge the gap between what we know about play's vital role and what we do about it. This is a matter of implementation around which there is much talk, but little science (Fixen, Naoom, Blasé, Friedman, & Wallace, 2005). How to effectively and efficiently move evidence-based practices into real-world practice remains problematic. This, however, should not prevent us from using our own imaginations to gently embed play's vital role in young children's early literacy learning at preschool.

REFERENCES

Bodrova, E., & Leong, D. (2007). *Tools of the mind* (2nd ed.). Upper Saddle River, NJ: Pearson/ Merrill/Prentice Hall.

Cooper, D., & Costa, K. (2012, June). *Increasing the effectiveness and efficiency of existing public investments in early childhood education.* Washington, DC: Center for American Progress. Available at *www.americanprogress.org.*

Creative Curriculum. (2006). Washington, DC: Teaching Strategies.

Diamond, A., Barnett, W. S., Thomas, J., & Munro, S. (2008). Preschool program improves cognitive control. *Science, 318,* 1387–1388.

Fixsen, D. L., Naoom, S. F., Blasé, K. A., Friedman, R. M., & Wallace, F. (2005). *Implementation research: A synthesis of the literature.* Tampa, FL: Louis de la Parte Florida Mental Health Institute Publication 231.

James, R. (1967). *Infant drama.* London: Nelson.

Leong, D. J., & Hensen, R. (2005). *Tools of the mind preschool curriculum research project manual* (2nd ed.). Denver, CO: Center for Improving Early Learning, Metropolitan College of Denver.

Lonigan, C. J., & Phillips, B. M. (2012). *Comparing skills-focused and self-regulation focused preschool curricula: Impacts on academic and self-regulatory skills.* Paper presented at the spring conference of the Society for Research in Effective Education, Washington, DC.

Mol, S. E., & Bus, A. G. (2011, January 10). To read or not to read: A meta-analysis of print exposure from infancy to early adulthood. *Psychological Bulletin, 137,* 267–296.

Morrow, L., & Schickedanz, J. (2006). The relationship between socio dramatic play and literacy development. In D. Dickinson & S. Neuman (Eds.), *Handbook of early literacy research* (pp. 269–280). New York: Guilford Press.

Pellegrini, A. D. (1984). Identifying causal elements in the thematic–fantasy play paradigm. *American Educational Research Journal, 21,* 691701.

Pellegrini, A. D., & Galda, L. (1993). Ten years after: A reexamination of symbolic play and literacy research. *Reading Research Quarterly, 28,* 163–175.

Piaget, J. (1962). *Play, dreams and imitation in childhood.* New York: Norton.

Roskos, K., & Christie, J. (2012). The play–literacy nexus and the importance of evidence-based techniques in the classroom. *American Journal of Play, 4*(2), 204–224.

Roskos, K., Christie, J., Widman, S., & Holding, A. (2010). Three decades in: Priming for meta-analysis in play–literacy research. *Journal of Early Childhood Literacy, 10,* 55–96.

Saltz, E., & Johnson, J. (1974). Training for thematic–fantasy play in culturally disadvantaged children: Preliminary results. *Journal of Educational Psychology, 66,* 623–630.

Silvern, S. B., Taylor, J. B., Williamson, P. A., Surbeck, E., & Kelley, M. (1986). Young children's story recall as a product of play, story familiarity, and adult intervention. *Merrill–Palmer Quarterly, 32,* 73–86.

Smith, P. K. (2010). *Children and play.* Chichester, West Sussex, UK: Wiley-Blackwell.

Snow, C. E., & Van Hemel, S. B. (Eds.). (2008). *Early childhood assessment: What, why, and how.* Washington, DC: National Academies Press. Available at *www.nap.edu/catalog. php?record_id=12446.*

Vygotsky, L. (1966). Play and its role in the mental development of the child. *Soviet Psychology, 12*(6), 62–76.

PART IV

INTERVENTION
AND ASSESSMENT

CHAPTER 15

❖❖❖

"How Am I Doing?"

STUDENTS' PERCEPTIONS OF LITERACY AND THEMSELVES

MARLA H. MALLETTE
PETER P. AFFLERBACH
CHRISTINE E. WIGGS

The first order of reality in the classroom is the student's point of view.
—PALEY (1986, p. 127)

It was Hunter's first day at a new school. Records from his previous school indicated he was a struggling reader, and Hunter was sent to the Title I classroom to determine placement at his new school. Although the Title I teacher gauged students' literacy development with multiple assessments, the school required a curriculum-based measure, a timed reading to determine the number of words read correctly in 1 minute.

> TEACHER: Hi, Hunter! (*Takes out a reading passage and places it in front of Hunter; Then reads the instructions as written in the examiner's copy.*). When I say "Begin," start reading aloud at the top of this page. (*Points.*). Read across the page. (*Demonstrates by pointing.*) Try to read each word. If you come to a word you don't know, I'll tell it to you. Be sure to do your best reading. Do you have any questions?
>
> HUNTER: Do you want me to read for speed or accuracy?

We use Hunter's question to anticipate a major point of this chapter: In order to gain a more complete understanding of best practices in early literacy, it is necessary to consider "the perceptions and views of the major participants in learning, the learners themselves" (Wray & Medwell, 2006, p. 205). Although the above scenario offers just an initial glimpse into Hunter's perceptions of reading (and reading assessment), it is a powerful reminder that our students construct meaning from their educational experiences. How students perceive themselves and interpret classroom instruction may be similar to what teachers perceive and interpret, or it may not.

GUIDING QUESTIONS

❖ Why is it important for teachers to understand children's perceptions—*what children think* and *how children feel*—about literacy instruction and literacy learning?

❖ In what ways can this important information be related to the learners' perspective and guide literacy instruction?

Students' perceptions of literacy, influenced by their instruction, learning, and abilities, tend to be fluid, vary across contexts, and are shaped by their experiences (Erikson & Schultz, 1992; Pollart, Thiessen, & Filer, 1997). For example, when Bondy (1990) examined how first-grade students understood the purposes of reading, she found that their perceptions differed by their abilities. In a single classroom, children in the high reading group perceived reading as learning, social, and pleasurable; children in the low reading group described reading as saying words and completing schoolwork. The first-grade teacher did not believe she approached reading instruction differently between the two groups; however, when she examined her instruction, the differences became apparent. Students in the low reading group received considerable instruction focused at the word level. In contrast, students in the high reading group read intact texts. Researchers (see, e.g., Allington, 1983; Dahl & Freppon, 1995; Medwell, 1991) examining primary-grade students' perspectives on literacy have reached similar conclusions; the focus of instruction and students' experiences shape their perceptions.

It follows that an instructional implication is for teachers to carefully examine the focus of their instruction and the experiences they help provide to children of all abilities. Yet, without gaining the perspectives of their students, this examination is incomplete and based on assumptions. For example, Wray and Medwell (2006) found that the students' perspectives of participation and enjoyment in literacy hour (a literacy initiative in classrooms in the United Kingdom) were different from those held by teachers. Teachers were confident that their students enjoyed the literacy hour; however, data from interviews and surveys indicated that 30–40% of the students did not. There were also discrepancies between the students' self-report data (i.e., surveys and interviews) and the observational data collected by the researcher: Wrey and Medwell found that a higher percentage of students said they enjoyed the literacy hour than the percentage of students they observed as engaged in literacy during this time. It is possible that researchers and students differ in how they conceptualize enjoyment; students might not view engagement as an essential aspect of enjoyment. The data illustrate that students' perceptions of their experiences may differ considerably from teachers' (and researchers') perceptions.

PERCEPTIONS OF LITERACY: THOUGHTS AND EMOTIONS

In regard to students' perceptions of literacy learning and instruction, it is important to determine both how they *feel about literacy* and how they *think about literacy*, as attitude, motivation, and self-perception can have a powerful influence on learning (Alexander & Filler, 1976; Alvermann & Guthrie, 1993; Athey, 1985). All three constructs—attitude, motivation, and self-perception—can be examined by teachers and researchers to gain insight into students' thoughts and feelings. We focus on these three constructs in the sections that follow. Each has an established and rich research base, theoretical grounding, and instruments and procedures that are appropriate for helping us build a more complete understanding of early literacy learners.

As we explore students' attitudes, motivations, and self-perceptions we highlight the perspectives of three third-grade students: Their voices give us pause to consider the power and possible influence of their thoughts and feelings on their literacy development. The three students—Andrew, Aubrey Nicole, and Devin—are in the same third-grade classroom. The students attend a school that uses a response to intervention (RTI) plan with curriculum-based measures that are administered every 2 weeks for progress monitoring. Within the RTI plan, struggling readers are identified by comparative grade-level data; in other words, the lowest 20% of students within each grade. Andrew, Aubrey Nicole, and Devin are among that group and classified as struggling readers. Christine E. Wiggs (chapter coauthor) is the Title I teacher at their school, and the students visit Mrs. Wiggs's classroom each day for 30 minutes of reading instruction, which is in addition to their classroom instruction.

Attitude

Reading attitude can be broadly defined as "a system of feelings related to reading which causes the learner to approach or avoid a reading situation" (Alexander & Filler, 1976, p. 1). All teachers recognize the power of students' reading attitudes to influence reading development. Students with positive attitudes toward reading are most likely to look forward to reading, accept and meet reading challenges, and persevere when reading becomes complex (Skinner, Kindermann, & Furrer, 2009). In an effort to better assess and describe the development of reading attitudes in students, McKenna (1994; McKenna & Kear, 1990) examined three influential factors contributing to students' attitudes: (1) beliefs about the outcomes of reading in light of the judged desirability of those outcomes; (2) beliefs about the expectations of others (i.e., teachers, parents, peers) in light of one's motivation to conform to those expectations; and (3) the outcomes of specific incidents and experiences of reading. McKenna suggested that intention, attitude, and subjective norms influence student readers' decisions to read. Students' ability to be metacognitive (i.e., understanding their reading challenges and strengths) and their knowledge of their standing as readers in relation to subjective norms, as well as their intent and attitude, combine to determine whether the reading process will continue. Therefore, reading attitudes develop over time as a result of normative beliefs, beliefs about the outcomes of reading, and specific reading experiences.

A widely used measure of students' reading attitude is the Elementary Reading Attitude Survey (ERAS; McKenna & Kear, 1990). The ERAS consists of 40 questions that measure students' attitudes toward reading. The ERAS features a pictorial Likert scale of the face of comic strip character Garfield: Garfield's frowns represent students' negative attitudes toward reading, whereas his smiles reflect positive attitudes. The ERAS is divided into two subscales: (1) attitude toward academic reading and (2) attitude toward recreational reading, with 20 questions for each. The validation of the instrument is impressive, based on data from a national sample of over 18,000 students between grades 1 and 6. Through their data analysis, McKenna and Kear established the instrument's reliability and validity, and created grade-level norms. The ERAS has straightforward administration, providing educators with a valid and reliable measure of students' reading attitudes.

The ERAS can be administered with a whole class, a small group, or individually. As Mrs. Wiggs was interested in determining the nature of students' reading attitudes, she administered the ERAS to her whole class (i.e., Title I class of six to eight students). She then calculated their scores and determined percentile ranks. The information provided is a valuable source for better understanding her students' attitudes toward reading. The many cognitive measures that are guaranteed by curriculum-based measurement are complemented by the information that dwells on students' affect. Examination of Andrew's, Aubrey Nicole's, and Devin's' ERAS scores reflects that each has a unique attitude toward reading.

Student	Percentile rank: Total score	Percentile rank: Academic	Percentile rank: Recreational
Andrew	34th	52nd	21st
Aubrey Nicole	15th	5th	45th
Devin	73rd	41st	96th

The above table demonstrates that although all three students were considered struggling readers, their attitudes toward reading were quite different. Within these differences, each student expressed striking differences between his or her attitude toward academic reading and recreational reading, creating three unique reading attitude profiles. The differences in their attitudes illustrate that (1) attitude toward reading is multifaceted, (2) it is necessary to consider the full scale and the two subscales, and (3) not all struggling readers have negative attitudes about reading.

The results from the ERAS provided Mrs. Wiggs with valuable information about her students' reading attitudes. However, Mrs. Wiggs wanted to better understand reading attitudes from the students' perspectives. She analyzed their ERAS responses to determine what questions or types of questions elicited stronger responses and then, based on her analysis, she selected questions for follow-up conversation. Mrs. Wiggs found that for recreational reading, Devin marked the *happiest Garfield* on every question except for one (i.e., how he felt about reading instead of playing, for which he marked the second-highest rating, *slightly smiling Garfield*). Mrs. Wiggs chose several statements for which Devin marked the *happiest Garfield* to further explain. When asked why he felt good *about reading on a rainy Saturday,* Devin explained, "It is a rainy day and I read a book and I make hot chocolate and stuff." He also explained that he liked *getting books for presents* because "my mom gives me rock books and volcanoes and stuff because I like volcanoes a lot."

Although Devin's attitude was very positive toward recreational reading, Mrs. Wiggs's analysis of the academic subscale on the ERAS indicated that he did not like reading aloud in the classroom, taking reading tests, reading stories from his reading book, or reading in class. Mrs. Wiggs asked Devin about his rating for how he felt when it was time for reading in class. Devin explained that he put the *grumpier Garfield* "'cause you have to read out loud and I don't like that," and "I feel shy to read out loud." In contrast to the happiness Devin noted about reading books at home, he did not like the stories from his reading book. Devin explained, "I have to read the same thing over and over again." He also felt "not so happy" when his classroom teacher asked him questions about what he read because, "if I get them wrong I have to read the story again." The discussions of items on the ERAS helps to understand Devin's perspective on reading in and out of school, and describes a student who enjoys reading in certain contexts. Unfortunately, reading in school is not one of them.

Ms. Wiggs also used discussions of ERAS items to gain a fuller understanding of Aubrey Nicole's perspectives on reading. Like Devin, Aubrey Nicole revealed negative feelings about academic reading. When asked, "How do you feel when a teacher asks you questions about what you read?" she responded, "Mad, cause she [her classroom teacher] expects you to get the answer right there, and there's some words I don't really know . . . from the story." When Mrs. Wiggs asked her about marking the grumpiest Garfield (representing how she felt about reading workbook pages and worksheets), Aubrey Nicole stated, "I don't like to read that much on homework and stuff." Aubrey Nicole indicated that if she felt the books were difficult for her, she did not like trying to learn from them because, "I have to remember it all." In contrast, she also explained, "Yeah, I like those books," referring to below-grade-level shorter texts she reads in Title I, "'cause they're a little shorter, and the pages are shorter and the words are not as hard . . . but at least a little shorter than the ones I got in class." When asked why she chose the grumpy Garfield for how she felt when it was time for reading in class, Aubrey Nicole said, "I don't really like reading time because the words are so hard."

The ERAS provides reliable and valid comparative information regarding students' attitudes toward reading. Following the ERAS with questions that allow students to explain their answers, teachers can gain further insight into their students' attitudes toward reading. As demonstrated by these students, mixed attitudes about reading emanate from different experiences with reading. Clarification of the types of reading and reading situations in which her students have improved attitude helps Ms. Wiggs plan appropriately. If we value students' perspectives on reading, and we pay attention to the variation in how different students (or the same students in different settings) approach reading, we gain valuable information that can be used to inform instruction.

Motivation

Reading motivation can make the difference between learning that is shallow and superficial versus learning that is engaged, internalized, and lasting (Gambrell, Palmer, Codling, & Mazzoni, 1996; Guthrie, Wigfield, & You, 2012). Motivation to read can be an influential factor in the growth and development of students' reading abilities. Reading motivation, along with prior achievement and experiences, are strong predictors of future reading and academic achievements (Anderman, Anderman, & Griesinger, 1999; Guay, Marsh, & Boivin, 2003). When students are motivated to read, they will generate their own learning opportunities and invest in their growth as readers (Guthrie, 1996). Reading motivation mediates teachers' reading instruction, and contributes to reading growth.

The Motivation to Read Profile (MRP; Gambrell et al., 1996) is an instrument that combines quantitative and qualitative approaches for assessing students' self-concept and task value, two essential components of motivation theory. The MRP is divided into two sections: (1) the Reading Survey and (2) the Conversational Interview. On the Reading Survey, there are 20 items (i.e., 10 for self-concept as a reader and 10 for value of reading) that are rated on a 4-point response scale. The Conversational Interview is divided into three sections that include questions that (1) probe motivational factors related to the reading of narrative text, (2) elicit information about informational text reading, and (3) examine factors related to reading motivation.

The validation process for the MRP was both extensive and multifaceted. The Reading Survey was modified and revised based on data from multiple levels of field-testing. Analysis of the final version demonstrated that the Reading Survey was both valid and reliable. The Conversational Interview also underwent extensive field-testing. An analysis of student protocol data during the piloting of the MRP revealed the most insightful information about the students' reading motivation, and 14 items were chosen for the final version (Gambrell et al., 1996).

Mrs. Wiggs administered the MRP individually with Devin, Andrew, and Aubrey Nicole. Building on her experiences with the ERAS, and considering the insights she gained from asking the students to explain and/or discuss their responses, she decided to use a think-aloud approach. That is, Mrs. Wiggs asked the students to further explain their responses *while* they were answering the questions.

While administering the MRP with Andrew, Mrs. Wiggs noticed that he was choosing mainly neutral responses (e.g., *sometimes* or *OK*). For example, on the MRP item *When I come to a word I don't know, I can _____*, Andrew had to select one of the following four options: (1) *almost always figure it out*, (2) *sometimes figure it out*, (3) *almost never figure it out*, or (4) *never figure it out*. He selected *sometimes figure it out*. When Mrs. Wiggs asked Andrew why he chose *sometimes*, Andrew explained, "Because the words that I don't know that much, she [his classroom teacher] doesn't explain, I have to sound it out, but it doesn't make sense, and so I figure it out *hey I can undo it a little bit*, but sometimes they are not doable." Andrew's response of *sometimes* is quite thoughtful within his process to figure out unknown words. He seems to feel he's on his own to figure out words, which he first tries to sound out, but when that does not work for him, he uses a second approach of trying to chunk the word or break it apart into smaller words. As Andrew indicates, *sometimes* these strategies don't work, "they are not doable." Here, we can view Andrew's response to the MRP as an opportunity to further understand his motivations. They are clearly complex and dependent on the reading situation. Using student responses to questions from the MRP allows us to probe further about the nuances of student reading motivation.

Describing his comprehension, Andrew indicated that when reading by himself, he felt that he understood *some* of what he read. He explained, "Sometimes things don't make sense to me in a story." He then provided an example about a story where an evil person started singing, but Andrew confided that he didn't "get it." He did not understand why the character was singing or what was going on in the story. Andrew selected *OK* in response to what kind of reader he thought he was. He explained, "I feel that I am a good reader, but sometimes my friends say 'you're OK.' . . . Some of them say 'you need to work a little bit on those words' that I don't know." Andrew then said that he "feels OK" with this because "I do have to work on them."

When asked to describe an area that he would like to be better at in reading, Andrew said, "read medium so you don't mess up; if I go medium I know the words already . . . but if I hit the fast mark, then I mess up on words and lose my spot, I skip lines when I read fast . . . I am like that is jumping." Andrew's perspective on growing as a reader captures his introspective comments on his struggles as a reader, but also illustrates how students' goals can differ from those of school. Andrew's reading rate is tested every 2 weeks and he receives Title I instruction because he has not met a benchmark for words read correctly in 1 minute. Andrew understands that a fast (or faster than his own) reading rate is one way his school determines good readers. And yet, Andrew's idea for improving his own reading is simply not to have to read fast. Most important, he understands that reading is related to meaning.

Self-Perception

Readers' self-perceptions involve evaluations and judgments of themselves and their abilities to succeed at reading, which differ from their thoughts and feelings directed toward the task of reading process. Like motivation and attitude, self-perception must be examined cautiously, as young children's attributions for their reading performances (i.e., the reasons individuals use to understand or explain past successes or failures in task completion) are developing throughout the primary grades. Young children may attribute their reading performance to luck or task difficulty, or effort or ability (Hiebert, Winograd, & Danner, 1984; McCrudden, Perkins, & Putney, 2009; Wilson & Trainin, 2007). Over time, these attributions are central to students' theories of self: They influence how students approach reading, what they expect from reading, how (or whether) they persevere when reading is difficult, and if they take credit for a reading job well done. It is essential to understand the self-perceptions of young children as these perceptions are shaped by their literacy experiences.

The Early Literacy Motivation Survey (ELMS; Wilson & Trainin, 2007) was created as a developmentally appropriate measure for students in kindergarten through second grade. For example, the instrument uses scenarios and short tasks to contextualize the questions for young children and also includes a visual aid with happy and sad faces to use in their responses to the questions. The ELMS examines students' perceived competence, self-efficacy, and attributions. In field-testing this instrument to determine reliability, Wilson and Trainin found moderate internal consistency within each of three subscales. In studying the literacy self-perceptions of first-grade students, they also found statistically significant differences in the students' self-perceptions among reading, spelling, and writing tasks. Wilson and Trainin speculated that these differences were related to teacher feedback (e.g., first-grade students receive more specific task feedback in reading than in writing).

The Reader Self-Perception Scale (RSPS; Henk & Melnick, 1995) is a highly valid and reliable instrument for measuring self-perception that is grounded in self-efficacy theory (Bandura, 1977, 1982); as such it is not developmentally appropriate for children below third grade. However, the RSPS provides a solid theoretical framework for thinking about the self-perception of young readers. The RSPS is divided into four subscales: (1) Progress (how one's perception of present reading performance compares with past performance), (2) Observational Comparison (how a child perceives his or her reading performance compared with the performance of classmates), (3) Social Feedback (direct or indirect input about reading from teachers, classmates, and people in the child's family), and (4) Physiological States (internal feelings that the child experiences during reading). Perhaps one of the most important considerations of young children's literacy self-perceptions is that although their attributions for success or failure might be unrealistic (e.g., they may attribute a good performance to luck rather than effort), their perceptions are continuously shaped, formed, and/or changed through their literacy experiences (Pitkanen & Nunes, 2000). Students' perceptions of teacher and peer perspectives further act to influence how they "are" as readers.

Mrs. Wiggs administered the RSPS in a manner similar to the MRP. That is, she asked each student to elaborate on some responses by thinking aloud while choosing responses. The chart provides an overview of the scores for Andrew, Aubrey Nicole, and Devin. As with the ERAS, examining the four sections of the RSPS accentuates each student's unique self-perception profile. In addition, when considering all three measures, we see that Devin is the only one of the three to have scores below the low cutoff scores in all four areas, which is quite different from his positive attitude as indicated on the ERAS and how he values reading, as indicated by the MRP.

Student	Progress			Observational Comparison			Social Feedback			Physiological States		
	H (44+)	A (39)	**L (34)**	H (26+)	A (21)	**L (16)**	H (38+)	A (33)	**L (27)**	H (37+)	A (31)	**L (25)**
Andrew		*32*			18			31			*23*	
Aubrey Nicole		*32*			*10*			28			*17*	
Devin		24			8			17			*17*	

Note. H, high; A, average; L, low.

Statement 1 on the RSPS, *I think I am a good reader*, is not a part of one of the four areas; rather it is a general self-perception statement. Devin first circled *4* for *agree*, then erased it and circled *1*, indicating that he *strongly disagreed*. When explaining why he changed his mind, he said, "Every time I read to someone I think they feel like I am not a good reader . . . they stare at me in a weird way."

In the area of *Progress*, Devin chose *agree*, when making progress was related to his decoding skills. He explained that "words are easier." However, when progress was about his comprehension, Devin did not perceive that he was making gains. Devin marked *strongly disagree* for the statement *I understand what I read better than I could before*. When Mrs. Wiggs asked him to explain, Devin said, "'cause I don't know, I just don't understand." Devin also chose *strongly disagree* for the statement *When I read, I don't have to try as hard as I used to*, and said, "I disagree because I try hard to read." Devin's responses illustrate the value of the RSPS in providing detailed information about how student readers perceive themselves.

In the area of *Observational Comparison*, Devin's ratings indicate that when comparing himself to others, his self-perception was quite low. Devin chose *strongly disagree* on every statement but one, for which he chose *undecided*. Devin strongly disagreed that he could read faster than other kids, and when asked why, he said, "I can't read faster than other kids." He also strongly disagreed that he *understood what he read as well as other kids*, and explained, "'cause they can understand and I don't . . . because every time I read when I am done I forget about it because I forget fast . . . 'cause at the end, well I don't know, 'cause at the end I am done reading it and I don't remember it." When discussing why he strongly disagreed that he *read better than other kids in his class*, he said, "'cause they like read faster than me because I read slow." In explaining why he strongly disagreed that *I read more than other kids*, Devin said, "I have littler books, they have big books that they check out from the library." Ms. Wiggs appreciates that these responses reflect both Devin's self-perceptions and his theory of successful reading.

In the area of *Social Feedback*, Devin marked *disagree* or *strongly disagree* on statements about his perceptions of what his teacher and classmates thought of his reading. When Mrs. Wiggs asked him why he marked *strongly disagree* for the statement *My teacher thinks that my reading is fine*, he explained, "I don't think that she [his classroom teacher] thinks . . . because every time I read to myself I don't understand it." Devin also marked that he strongly disagreed that his classmates thought he read pretty well and explained by saying, "They stare at me in a different way now and I don't think they like how I read because I read slow." However, when the statements were about his family's perceptions of his reading (if they like to listen to him read) Devin chose *undecided*. He explained that "my brother and sister do, but I am not sure about my mom and dad."

In the area of *Physiological States*, which explores readers' inward feelings about reading, Devin agreed with the statements *Reading makes me feel good* and *Reading makes me feel happy inside*. However, he was clear in qualifying these choices by specifying he felt good inside when he read "at home . . . because it is not so loud," and "when I read I feel happy and then when people stare at me I don't feel happy . . . when I read out loud I get shy, when I read in my head I don't." Devin indicated that he only felt good inside "when I read alone." Based on this information, Ms. Wiggs better understands that Devin can feel happiness related to reading, but that this positive feeling depends on the reading context.

Andrew's scores on the RSPS were between low and average for both *Observational Comparison* and *Social Feedback*. When Andrew compared himself to his classmates, his ratings indicated that does not perceive himself to be a better reader than his peers, as he rated these items with either *disagree* or *undecided*. For the statement *I read faster than other kids*, he marked that he disagreed and explained, "Because kids read faster than me, I take my time with words." Similarly, for the statement *When I read, I can figure out words better than other kids* he first marked *D*, then changed it to *U* and explained, "Not sure because some words are kinda long and I have to sound them out." Andrew also chose a *U* for the statement *I seem to know more words than other kids when I read*, and clarified his response, "No because some kids know and some kids don't know, and I am like between, like the middle one that knows some of the words." Andrew's perception in comparing himself to his peers as "in the middle" was also reflected by his marking *agree* with statements that included *as well as*. Andrew choose *agree* for the statement *I understand what I read as well as other kids do*. He said, "I agree because some kids know the same words as me and we are like jinx because we know the same words."

In the area of *Social Feedback*, Andrew chose *agree* on items that were about his perception of his family and his teacher; however, he mostly marked *undecided* on items related to perceptions of his peers. In explaining his choice of *undecided* on *My classmates like to listen to me read*, Andrew said, "Some of my classmates I know like to listen to me read, but I don't think the other classmates want to listen to me read . . . because most of them are like, want to listen to me read, and they are like 'see you later Andrew,' and I go to the next person and ask if they want to listen to me read, and only my friends want to listen to me read."

In the areas of *Progress* and *Physiological States*, Andrew's scores were below the low cutoff and for many statements Andrew marked *undecided*. However, Andrew had clear explanations as to why he was undecided. When asked why he chose *undecided* for *I am getting better at reading*, he explained, "Because, I don't know yet, because there are big words that I am still learning." When asked why he chose *undecided* for *I feel good inside when I read*, Andrew said, "I am not sure, I don't feel it, because sometimes I am like this is interesting and sometimes I am like this is boring." The only *strongly disagree* that Andrew marked for the entire scale was in response to the statement *I like to read aloud*. Andrew explained how he felt when asked to read aloud: "Nervousy, don't want to. I read aloud like once yesterday, and I was like nervous, and I was like 'do not shake Andrew, do not stop on words.' Sometimes I had to stop on words to rethink them again, I get all nervous and sweaty . . . [laughing] but I keep my sweat to myself."

STUDENT PERCEPTIONS AND TEACHING REALITIES

Often, our ideas about students' reading progress are in relation to classroom norms—students' work toward, and attainment of, instructional goals. Students who are experiencing challenge and difficulties in meeting such goals receive extra attention, often in the form of more instruction that assumes specific student needs. Frequently, these needs are perceived by schools to be cognitive strategy and skill. This may well be the case, in part. However, students' lives are both cognitive and affective. When classrooms focus exclusively (or almost exclusively) on cognitive strategy or skill, other critical aspects of reading development and successful reading may be missed. A risk in such situations is that we miss the powerful student perceptions—the way students view themselves and reading—that underlie classroom achievement. An exemplary strategy and skill instructional program may prove ineffective if we are unable to coordinate it with a detailed understanding of students' perceptions.

We describe the ERAS, MRP, and RSPS as measures of important aspects of students' affective reading development, and points of departure for teachers who want to determine in detail the nature of their students' perceptions, achievements, and challenges. Mrs. Wiggs values the results of the instruments she uses, in part because they indicate places to examine through further questioning and discussion with her students. They provide insights upon which ongoing, detailed understandings of her student readers can be constructed. Devin, Aubrey Nicole, and Andrew describe their perceptions of reading and their variations as readers. In doing so, they become multidimensional readers—individuals who report happiness, frustration, avoidance, or enthusiasm—depending on the reading situation. Being able to "read" her students through both cognitive and affective lenses helps Mrs. Wiggs more fully address their needs.

CONCLUSION

Underlying our attention to students' perceptions, the use of instruments such as the ERAS, MRP, and RSPS, and effective, related instruction are teacher time and effort. Administering, scoring, and interpreting a single instrument related to students' affect demands teacher expertise. As well, they demand the commitment of time, which is at a premium in all classrooms. It is our hope that the demonstrated importance of investigating and determining students' perceptions related to reading is a strong incentive: to explain to others this importance, to lobby for inclusion of attention to affect in reading instruction, and to remember that students' perceptions are always present. Knowing that student perceptions operate in a powerful manner, we do well to know them and to work in relation to them.

REFERENCES

Alexander J. E., & Filler, R. C. (1976). *Attitudes and reading.* Newark, DE: International Reading Association.

Allington, R. L. (1983). The reading instruction provided readers of differing reading abilities. *Elementary School Journal, 83,* 548–559.

Alvermann, D. E., & Guthrie, J. T. (1993). Themes and directions of the National Reading Research Center. *Perspectives in Reading Research, 1,* 1–11.

Anderman, E. M., Anderman, L. H., & Griesinger, T. (1999). The relation of present and possible academic selves during early adolescence to grade point average and achievement goals. *Elementary School Journal, 100,* 3–17.

Athey, I. (1985). Reading research in the affective domain. In H. Singer & R. B. Ruddell (Eds.), *Theoretical models and processes of reading* (3rd ed., pp. 527–557). Newark, DE: International Reading Association.

Bandura, A. (1977). Self-efficacy: Toward a unifying theory of behavioral change. *Psychological Review, 84,* 191–215.

Bandura, A. (1982). Self-efficacy mechanism and human agency. *American Psychologist, 37,* 122–147.

Bondy, E. (1990). Seeing it their way: What children's definitions of reading tell us about improving teacher education. *Journal of Teacher Education, 41*(5), 33–45.

Dahl, K. L., & Freppon, P. A. (1995). A comparison of inner-city children's interpretations of reading and writing instruction in the early grades in skills-based and whole language classrooms. *Reading Research Quarterly, 30,* 50–74.

Erikson, F., & Schultz, J. (1992). Students' experience of the curriculum. In P. W. Jackson (Ed.), *Handbook of research on curriculum* (pp. 465–485). New York: Macmillan.

Gambrell, L. B., Palmer, B. M., Codling, R. M., & Mazzoni, S. A. (1996). Assessing motivation to read. *The Reading Teacher, 49,* 518–533.

Guay, F., Marsh, H. W., & Boivin, M. (2003). Academic self-concept and academic achievement: Developmental perspectives on their causal ordering. *Journal of Educational Psychology, 95,* 124–136.

Guthrie, J. T. (1996). Educational contexts for engagement in literacy. *The Reading Teacher, 49,* 432–445.

Guthrie, J. T., Wigfield, A., & You, W. (2012). Instructional contexts for engagement and achievement in reading. In S. L. Christensen, A. L. Reschly, & C. Wylie (Eds.), *Handbook of research on student engagement* (pp. 601–634). New York: Springer Science.

Henk, W. A., & Melnick, S. A. (1995). The reader self-perception scale (RSPS): A new tool for measuring how children feel about themselves as readers. *The Reading Teacher, 48,* 470–482.

Hiebert, E. H., Winograd, P. N., & Danner, F. W. (1984). Children's attributions for failure and success in different aspects of reading. *Journal of Educational Psychology, 76,* 1139–1148.

McCrudden, M. T., Perkins, P. G., & Putney, L. G. (2009). Self-efficacy and interest in the use of reading strategies. *Journal of Research in Childhood Education, 20,* 119–131.

McKenna, M. C. (1994). Toward a model of reading attitude acquisition. In E. H. Cramer &

M. Castle (Eds.), *Fostering the life-long love of reading: The affective domain in reading education* (pp. 18–40). Newark, DE: International Reading Association.

McKenna, M. C., & Kear, D. J. (1990). Measuring attitude toward reading: A new tool for teachers. *The Reading Teacher, 43,* 626–639.

Medwell, J. (1991). What do children think about reading: Does it matter? In C. Harrison & E. Ashworth (Eds.), *Celebrating literacy: Defending literacy* (pp. 104–114). Oxford, UK: Blackwell.

Paley, V. (1986). On listening to what children say. *Harvard Educational Review, 56,* 122–131.

Pitkanen J., & Nunes, T. (2000). *Teachers' representations of intelligence and their consequences for pupils.* Paper presented at the XVIth Biennial Meeting of ISSBD. Beijing, China.

Pollart, A., Thiessen, D., & Filer, A. (Eds). (1997). *Children and their curriculum: The perspectives of primary and elementary school children.* London: Falmer.

Skinner, E. A., Kindermann, T. A., & Furrer, C. J. (2009). A motivational perspective on engagement and disaffection: Conceptualization and assessment of children's behavioral and emotional participation in academic activities in the classroom. *Educational and Psychological Measurement, 69,* 493–525.

Wilson, K. M., & Trainin, G. (2007). First-grade students' motivation and achievement for reading, writing, and spelling. *Reading Psychology, 28,* 257–282.

Wray, D. J., & Medwell, J. (2006). Pupils' perspectives on literacy teaching. *Education 3-13, 34,* 201–210.

CHAPTER 16

❖◆❖

The Interactive Strategies Approach to Early Literacy Intervention

Donna M. Scanlon
Kimberly L. Anderson
Frank R. Vellutino

GUIDING QUESTIONS

❖ What is the Interactive Strategies Approach (ISA) to early intervention?

❖ What is the research evidence in support of this approach to early intervention?

❖ How is the ISA different from other approaches?

❖ What are the goals and premises of the ISA?

❖ What are the elements of an ISA intervention lesson and what do they look like?

OVERVIEW OF THE TOPIC

The Interactive Strategies Approach (ISA) to early literacy instruction and intervention (Scanlon, Anderson, & Sweeney, 2010; Vellutino & Scanlon, 2002) was originally developed across a series of three large-scale longitudinal studies (Scanlon, Gelzheiser, Vellutino, Schatschneider, & Sweeney, 2008; Scanlon, Vellutino, Small, Fanuele, & Sweeney, 2005; Vellutino et al., 1996) that demonstrated that teachers who participate in professional development focused on the approach are able to reduce the number of children who experience early literacy difficulties. This was true when the teachers were working in classroom, small-group, and one-to-one pull-out situations. In this chapter, we describe the approach with a focus on small group and one-to-one lessons that both classroom and intervention teachers provide.

WHAT IS THE ISA?

> The ISA is an *approach* to early literacy instruction, not a program. It is not tied to particular instructional materials, nor does it provide highly scripted instructional interactions. Rather, the ISA offers a way to conceptualize early literacy development and to support children as they learn to read and write. We view teachers as professionals who use their knowledge of their students' skills in combination with knowledge of their curriculum and the process of literacy development more generally to plan and deliver effective literacy instruction. (Scanlon, Anderson, & Sweeney, 2010, p. 4)

In teaching teachers about the ISA, our primary goal is to help them "more thoroughly understand early literacy development and to effectively respond to, plan for, and teach the children who find reading challenging" (Scanlon, Anderson, & Sweeney, 2010, p. 4). To meet this goal, across multiple iterations of the ISA, we drew on the body of research related to early literacy development, literacy learning difficulties, and effective practices, and our experience in working with struggling readers and observing and collaborating with primary-grade teachers who were particularly successful in accelerating the progress of their struggling literacy learners.

THEORETICAL BACKGROUND AND RESEARCH BASE

The ISA is based on the premise that the process of constructing meaning from text is dependent upon relatively effortless identification of a high percentage of the words in the text, syntactic and semantic knowledge about how words relate to one another and the concepts they represent, content-relevant background knowledge, and motivational and intentional factors that result in active engagement with text. At the earliest stages of literacy acquisition, the development of the foundational skills that enable readers to read words is a prominent focus of instruction. Related to this aspect of development, the ISA draws on several guiding assumptions derived from reading research (Ehri, 2005; Frith, 1985; Henderson, 1990; McClelland & Rumelhart, 1981; Plaut, McClelland, Seidenberg, & Patterson, 1996; Seidenberg & McClelland, 1989; Share, 1995) that indicate that, to learn to read printed words in an alphabetic writing system, children must develop knowledge of the various types of information embodied in words (visual, orthographic, phonological, semantic, and syntactic), learn about print concepts and conventions, learn to make effective use of the alphabetic code, develop multiple and complementary strategies for identifying unfamiliar words encountered while reading, and engage in extensive amounts of reading in order to learn the huge number of words that proficient readers can identify at sight. Finally, because young children are diverse in terms of their background knowledge, language skills, experiences with print, and interest in and motivation for learning to read, a major premise of the ISA is that reading instruction must be tailored and responsive to the children's identified needs.

In our first intervention study (Vellutino et al., 1996), children identified as having severe reading difficulties in mid-first grade were randomly assigned to either a control group or to a one-to-one tutoring condition with tutors trained in an early version of the ISA. Children in the intervention group significantly outperformed the children in the control group and many of them reached or exceeded grade-level expectations in reading. However, 15% of the children in the ISA tutoring group continued to score below the 15th percentile. Further, it was clear that intensive one-to-one intervention was not sustainable on a large scale. Therefore, a second study was undertaken with the dual goals of (1) reducing the number of children who needed intensive intervention in first grade, and (2) improving the outcomes for the children who continued to struggle despite receiving one-to-one tutoring.

In this second intervention study (Scanlon et al., 2005), we evaluated the effects of beginning intervention efforts in kindergarten for children identified as being at increased risk for reading difficulties based on assessment of early literacy skills at kindergarten entry. At-risk children from within participating classrooms were randomly assigned to intervention and control conditions. Intervention involved 30 minutes of small-group instruction (usually three children per group) provided twice per week by a certified teacher trained in the ISA. The first important finding from this study was that kindergarten intervention was effective in reducing the number of children who qualified for intervention in first grade, especially in schools that provided no support services for the kindergartners in the control group.

In the next phase of the study, children from the kindergarten intervention and control groups who qualified for intervention in first grade were randomly assigned to one of three treatment conditions: a control group where the children received the support services that were normally available to them in school, or one of two one-to-one tutoring conditions that were variants of the ISA. One variant (Phonological Skills Emphasis) placed greater emphasis on the development of phonological skills, while the other (Text Emphasis) placed greater emphasis on engaging and supporting children in reading books that provided some but not too much challenge. Children in both tutoring conditions outperformed children in the control group and averages for the tutored groups did not differ significantly. However, there were important distributional differences between these conditions. First, we found that, as compared to the Phonological Skills Emphasis condition, a higher proportion of the children in the Text Emphasis condition scored above the 50th percentile on a measure of early literacy skills. And, somewhat counterintuitively, a higher proportion of the children in the Text Emphasis condition scored below the 15th percentile as compared to the Phonological Skills Emphasis condition.

Why would the tutoring approach that emphasized text reading yield both more strong readers (those above the 50th percentile) and more weak readers (those below the 15th percentile)? Our interpretation of this pattern was that the Text Emphasis condition met the needs of the children who acquired phonological skills with relative ease but did not effectively meet the needs of the children who had difficulty acquiring these skills. Conversely, the Phonological Skills Emphasis condition more effectively met the needs of children who were slower to acquire these skills but did not meet the needs of those children who acquired these skills more readily. For the latter children, engagement in more reading would quite likely have accelerated their growth as readers. This pattern of outcomes supports one of the most important premises of the ISA: Reading instruction must be tailored and responsive to the children's identified needs.

Another major finding from this study was that, across all three first-grade conditions, children who had participated in the ISA intervention in kindergarten were less likely to score below the 15th percentile at the end of first grade and more likely to score above the 50th percentile than were children who were in the control group in kindergarten. Together, these findings clearly suggested that addressing the needs of children who appear to be at risk for literacy learning difficulties as early as their risk status can be identified can have long-term benefits and at a relatively low instructional cost. The kindergarten intervention program involved approximately 25 hours of small-group instruction distributed across the school year (two 30-minute, small-group sessions per week from mid-October through mid-May).

The third major intervention study (Scanlon et al., 2008) explored, among other things, the potential utility of providing kindergarten and first-grade classroom teachers with ISA-based professional development as a means of helping them to become more effective in addressing the needs of the struggling literacy learners in their classrooms.[1] Three cohorts of entering kindergartners from high-needs school districts were studied from the time they entered kindergarten until the end of second or third grade. The first cohort served as the Baseline group. No attempt was made to influence the instruction the students in this group received as they moved through the primary grades. The second cohort served as the Implementation group. For this group, the kindergarten classroom teachers participated in

---

[1]Due to space constraints, we report only limited aspects of this rather complex study.

professional development in the summer before and the year during which they taught these children. First-grade teachers participated in the professional development program the following year (which was the year in which they taught the Implementation cohort). The third group of kindergartners served as the Maintenance cohort; teachers taught this group in the year after the professional development.

In each cohort, an average of approximately 50% of the children in each classroom qualified as being at risk for literacy difficulties at the beginning of kindergarten (we were working in low-income neighborhoods in the Albany, New York, area). By the end of kindergarten, we found that only 25–30% of the children qualified as at risk in the Baseline cohort, which suggests that the teachers were reasonably effective in meeting the needs of their at-risk learners. However, for the Implementation and Maintenance cohorts, the number of at-risk children was reduced even further to about 15%. We also found that teachers made changes in their instruction that were consistent with the professional development that was provided. When the children from the Scanlon et al. 2008 study were followed into first grade, those who remained at risk after the kindergarten year (approximately 20% by the end of the summer) showed substantial gains during their first-grade year and, on average, scored at approximately the 50th percentile by the end of first grade (Scanlon, Anderson, & Gelzheiser, 2010).

Together, the three major studies using the ISA indicate that the approach is effective in helping to accelerate the progress of at-risk and struggling literacy learners when implemented in one-to-one, small-group, and classroom contexts, and when used by both interventionists and classroom teachers. While all three of these studies were initiated before the legislation that drives current Response-to-Intervention (RTI) approaches, it is important to note that the evidence derived from these studies, especially the Vellutino et al. (1996) study, is often credited with contributing to the paradigm shift, which suggests that literacy learning difficulties are largely attributable to experiential factors rather than to innate differences in literacy learning abilities.

BRINGING THE KNOWLEDGE
TO THE EARLY LITERACY CLASSROOM

Case Example

When Mrs. Jones, an experienced and highly regarded first-grade teacher, first learned about RTI she wondered what impact it would have on her and the instruction she offered her weakest readers. What would she need to do differently? What role would other professionals play? In support of the school's RTI initiative, professional development based on the ISA was offered to kindergarten through second-grade-classroom teachers and specialists. This strongly influenced Mrs. Jones's thinking.

In the remainder of the chapter, we describe the goals and premises of the ISA and describe important elements of the professional development offered to teachers who became involved in the ISA. We focus especially on small-group and one-to-one instruction that provides maximum opportunity to differentiate instruction so as to meet the diverse needs of children who are at various points in their literacy development. However, given the constraints of a chapter-length treatment, our discussion of important goals and premises is, often, rather cursory. A more comprehensive discussion of the ISA can be found in Scanlon, Anderson, and Sweeney (2010).

We begin our work with teachers by engaging them in conversations about the complexity of the reading process and about the need to be attentive to this complexity in planning and delivering instruction that will help to accelerate literacy learning among children who are at risk. We use a series of "perspective-taking" activities to help teachers experience some of the common stumbling blocks for early literacy learners and to flesh out the characteristics of proficient readers. Focusing on what proficient readers know and are able to do draws attention to comprehension and knowledge development, which are the ultimate goals of literacy instruction. These goals are sometimes overlooked in attempts to meet the needs of children who struggle because those who are identified as being in need of intervention for early literacy learning difficulties are typically identified on the basis of limitations in foundational skills such as phonemic awareness, alphabet knowledge and phonics, and/or word learning, and these areas become the focus of intervention efforts. However, in focusing intervention efforts so narrowly, there is a risk of conveying to children that reading is only about saying the words accurately and quickly. This is obviously not anyone's intention. By forefronting comprehension and knowledge development, we hope to help teachers keep from inadvertently sending such a message.[2] Thus, we argue that we need to teach for the purposes of (1) developing the knowledge base upon which comprehension depends, and (2) encouraging children to actively engage in meaning construction when listening to and reading texts. In the early primary grades, these purposes are served primarily, but not exclusively, through the use of interactive read-alouds, especially of information-rich books and, ideally, books that are thematically related.

With comprehension and knowledge development as the points of departure, we discuss the many contributors to a child's ability to comprehend and learn from

---

[2] Those familiar with earlier iterations of the ISA may be surprised by the emphasis placed on comprehension and knowledge. This emphasis emerged in our 2008 study (which was begun in 2002) when we began to work in high-needs school districts where limitations in background knowledge are likely to be much more prevalent.

text, most of which are addressed in the instructional goals around which the ISA is organized (see Figure 16.1). Teachers often report that they feel that this conversation gets pretty complex. And that is, in fact, one of the major points: Reading is a complex process. If teachers are to help children who find reading challenging, they need to understand the complexity of the process along with the potential sources of confusion so that they can plan and deliver optimal instruction.

We organize *professional development* for teachers around instructional goals for children, rather than around components of instruction (such as read-aloud,

---

- **Motivation to Read and Write.** The child will develop the belief that reading and writing are enjoyable and informative activities that are not beyond his or her capabilities.

- **Alphabetics**
  - **Print Concepts and Conventions.** The child will understand that the purpose of print is to communicate. Further, the child will understand some of the most basic print conventions, such as the left-to-right and top-to-bottom sequencing of print, where to begin reading a book, the concepts of letter and word, and so on.
  - **Phoneme Awareness.** The child will have a conceptual grasp of the fact that words are made up of somewhat separable sound segments. Further, the child will be able to say individual sounds in simple words spoken by the instructor and to blend separate sounds to form whole words.
  - **Letter Identification.** The child will be able to name, rapidly and accurately, all 26 letters of the alphabet, both upper- and lower-case versions.
  - **Letter–Sound Association.** The child will be able to associate the sounds of the majority of consonants with their printed representations.
  - **Alphabetic Principle.** The child will understand that the letters in printed words represent the sounds in spoken words and will understand how to use the alphabetic code to read and spell words.
  - **Larger Alphabetic Units and Multisyllabic Words.** The child will develop the ability to use a variety of larger orthographic units (word families, prefixes, suffixes, and so on) to read and spell words.

- **Word Learning**
  - **Strategic Word Learning.** The child will develop flexibility and independence in applying a variety of strategies to facilitate the identification of unfamiliar words encountered in text.
  - **High Frequency Words.** The child will be able to quickly and accurately identify a large number of high frequency words.

- **Meaning Construction**
  - **Vocabulary and Oral Language Development.** The child will learn the meanings of new words encountered in instructional interactions and be able to use those words conversationally. Further, the child's ability to understand and use more complex grammatical structures will improve.
  - **Comprehension and Knowledge Development.** The child will develop comprehension skills and strategies that will enhance his or her ability to construct the meaning and learn from texts heard or read.

FIGURE 16.1. Instructional goals of the ISA. Adapted from Scanlon, Anderson, and Sweeney (2010). Copyright by the International Reading Association. Adapted by permission.

supported reading groups, writing/composition, etc.), because we want teachers to plan and deliver instruction that is goal oriented rather than activity oriented. However, *instruction* is, of course, organized around specific instructional components that enable teachers to address the goals. And, clearly, some language arts components are better suited to addressing particular instructional goals than are others. For example, as noted, read-alouds in the primary grades provide important opportunities to address the comprehension and knowledge development goal while small-group supported reading (often referred to as guided reading groups) is less effective in this regard owing largely to the characteristics of the texts that children are able to read in the early primary grades.

As the focus of this chapter is on intervention rather than on language arts instruction more generally, we describe how the goals listed in Figure 16.1 might be addressed in small-group or one-to-one intervention lessons. These lessons would typically consist of five or six segments that include rereading of familiar texts, phonological and alphabetic skills (treated separately for children at the earliest stages of development and brought together later), reading of a new book(s), high-frequency word practice, and writing. Figure 16.2 presents a brief outline of the lesson segments that are described in some detail below. Before describing them, however, it is necessary to discuss some of the important premises that underlie and drive these lessons. First, in all interactions around text, we want to ensure that children perceive reading and writing as meaning-making enterprises. Therefore, while there will be, of necessity, substantial focus on the development of foundational skills (such as learning about the workings of the alphabetic code), teachers also need to bring meaning construction into focus whenever continuous text is in use. Second, supported reading lessons are intended to be both comprehensive, in that they address all of the goals listed in Figure 16.1, and responsive, in that they take account of what the children already know and are able to do and teach them what they are ready to learn next. Third, instruction should have the goal of developing strategic, self-regulated, independent learners. By this we mean that,

---

- Rereading texts from previous lessons
- Phonological skills—including
  - Phonemic awareness
  - Phonics
- Reading new books
- High-frequency word practice
- Writing

FIGURE 16.2. Components of an ISA intervention lesson.

ultimately, children should be expected to take responsibility for their own learning by independently recognizing when problems in reading arise and knowing what to do to solve those problems. To this end, for children at the early stages of literacy development, we encourage teachers to provide resources such as word lists and strategy charts that children can reference on an as-needed basis when they encounter difficulties. Fourth, to the greatest extent possible, we encourage teachers to strive for coherence and congruence in the classroom language arts program and in small-group or one-to-one intervention settings. For example, in RTI contexts, we have often observed that children are exposed to distinctly different instructional programs as they move through the different tiers of intervention. Such "program switching" seems likely to confuse children rather than accelerate their progress. Instead, we encourage teachers who share responsibility for teaching the same children to coordinate their efforts and to strive for consistency in the way they address foundational literacy skills and strategies and to use common supports (such as alphabet charts).

Below we provide a generalized description of a supported reading lesson. We describe each segment in some detail and connect it to the goal structure in Figure 16.1. Such lessons may be provided by the classroom teacher during small-group time and by intervention teachers. Children who are receiving more intensive tiers of intervention would participate in lessons provided by both the classroom and an intervention teacher as accelerated progress is most likely to occur when children are given more opportunities to respond and receive guidance.

SUPPORTED READING LESSON SEGMENTS

Rereading Familiar Texts

This segment of the lesson is intended to build fluency and confidence and thus addresses both the word learning and the motivation goals. In this segment, children read one or two books that were read in previous lessons. Often, the teacher offers some choice about what book to read and would, if deemed necessary, prepare the children to read the book by reminding them of elements that they found challenging on the previous reading. The teacher might also remind the children of word-identification strategies (discussed later) that they are not yet using independently. The rereading segment also addresses the comprehension and knowledge subgoals because, on a reread, the need to attend to the word-solving process will be reduced and, therefore, more of the readers' attention can be focused on the meaning construction/knowledge building. Even with early emergent texts, there are opportunities to add to one's knowledge base, particularly if a "knowledgeable other," through conversation about the text, helps to extend the children's thinking. Depending on the nature of the text, vocabulary and language skills may also be enhanced during a reread as the child re-experiences words and syntactic structures that may have been novel on the first read.

Rereading helps to reinforce a variety of alphabetics skills as well. At early stages of reading development, rereading even a memorized text can help to reinforce important print concepts such as what constitutes a word versus a letter and the conventional left-to-right and top-to-bottom processing of print. At later points, children's successful identification of words can add to their understandings of the alphabetic code. For example, encountering a word in a word family that was previously taught and practiced will serve to reinforce that phonic element, making it more readily accessible on subsequent encounters.

One of the biggest advantages of rereading is in the service of word learning. When words that a child may have needed to "solve" on the first encounter with the text are revisited upon rereading, the status of those words in the child's sight vocabulary is "bumped up" so to speak. That is, the children will (typically) need to do less thinking about the word in order to accurately identify it both because the context is more familiar and because a representation of the word is likely to have been stored more thoroughly in memory, especially if they looked all the way through the word upon their first attempt to identify it.

With regard to motivation, young children tend to be very motivated by the ability to read "like a storyteller," which is much more likely to occur on second and subsequent reads of a text. This clearly has the potential to build a sense of confidence and competence, which is likely to help the children to sustain their efforts when encountering more challenging texts in the future.

Phonological Skills Instruction

This segment of the lesson focuses on addressing the alphabetics skills goal, which is comprised of multiple subgoals. It also supports word learning, particularly the Strategic Word Learning subgoal in that skill with the alphabetic code is a critical contributor to the child's ability to effectively puzzle through, identify, and ultimately learn unfamiliar words encountered during reading. Depending on the children's skills, this segment of the lesson may include explicit instruction to promote phonemic awareness and an understanding of important print conventions, but would always include instruction on some element of the alphabetic code that can be applied in reading the text they will read in the next segment. The teacher might, for example, teach and provide practice with the short and long sounds of a vowel or a word family that the children will encounter in a new book. Often the teacher does not include the specific words that will appear in the book. Instead, he or she uses words that have the same phonic elements and reserves the words from the book that contain those elements for the children to solve when they read the book. Thus, the children have a fairly immediate opportunity to apply emerging phonics skills to authentic word-solving challenges.

Once a new phonics element has been introduced, three types of instructional activities are used to build familiarity with the new element(s) and to revisit previously taught elements. The first involves word building, in which the children use movable letters to build words dictated by the teacher. The second involves the teacher building words with the same elements and the children reading them. Finally, the children write words dictated by the teacher. We follow this word-building–reading–writing sequence to encourage the children to both carefully attend to the phonics elements and to gain a sense of mastery over the particular elements. Word building, we argue, is the easiest of the tasks, and therefore comes up first. During word building, the children are provided with a small set of letters to manipulate and the specific manipulation entails the portion of a word that the children are ready to learn about. Thus, for example, children who are beginning to learn about consonant sounds might first be asked to simply manipulate the beginning letters and sounds (change *sat* to *fat* to *mat*). They would then read and write the same words, which requires that they recall the component sounds (in reading the words) and the letters that represent those sounds (in writing). With increasing skill, children would be asked to attend to and manipulate both beginning and ending sounds (change *fat* to *fan* to *can* to *cat*, etc.). Later still, when the children are readily able to attend to beginning and ending sounds, the teacher draws their attention to the vowels. Because every vowel letter commonly represents at least two vowel sounds (the long and short sounds), and because the pronunciation of vowel sounds is substantially less reliable than the pronunciation of consonant sounds, the long and the short sounds of each vowel are taught and practiced together. This builds flexibility with the vowel sounds, which will be helpful to the children as they encounter irregularly spelled words (such as *live* and *hold*) in their reading. Teachers sometimes initially express concern that this approach will present too much challenge for children because we are asking them to learn two different pronunciations for a given letter simultaneously. We counter that, by the time we begin to teach the sounds of a particular vowel, the children already know the vowel's name and so in initial instruction, all we are really asking them to do is to learn one additional association (the short sound) for a particular vowel. And, before introducing the new sound, we remind the children that they already know one possible sound for the vowel, because it is just the same as the vowel's name. Once the two vowel sounds have been discussed, we introduce a picture representing a key word to remind the children of the short vowel sound (e.g., *apple* for the short sound of *a*) and, from thereon, leave that key word available as a resource that the children are encouraged to refer to during their reading and writing. The silent-*e* generalization is also explained (or reviewed) and practiced in the context of the word-building, word-reading, word-writing activities described above. In this context, changes revolve around the two sounds of the vowel. Thus, for example, in the word-building activity, the children might be asked to build the following words by changing one letter at a time: *mat, mate, fate, fat, fad, fade, made, mad*, and so on.

In addition to helping children learn to work through words in the letter-by-letter fashion described above, it is also important that they learn to recognize and use larger orthographic units such as the rime portions of word families and commonly occurring prefixes and suffixes. To this end, depending on the children's skills and the upcoming book, one or more word families might be taught and/or the children might be shown how to use frequently occurring prefixes and suffixes (e.g., *re, ed, ing*) as an assist in word solving. For word families, teachers introduce a family drawn from the new book for the day and incorporate previously taught word families into the practice activities both to reinforce the children's knowledge of those elements and to encourage them to treat the rime that is at the center of a word family (e.g., *ight, all*) as a useful orthographic unit. We have noted that, if only one rime is used in practice activities, some children will do little thinking about the word family itself, but will, instead, attend mostly to the changes made at the beginning of the word (changing *night* to *sight* to *fight*). Making changes to both the beginnings of words and to the rimes (changing *might* to *mall* to *fall* to *fight*) requires children to attend more carefully to the rime portion and, as a result, they are more likely to become sufficiently familiar with the rime to use it generatively in their reading and writing. To reinforce the utility of the word families, teachers maintain a display containing the rime portions of the word families that have been taught. Children are encouraged to refer to this display when attempting to read and spell words that might belong to a particular family.

The phonological skills segment is also the place where we help children to develop skills in decoding unfamiliar words that are comprised of more than one syllable. We provide several decoding suggestions that can be used individually and in combination and, as we do with monosyllabic words, emphasize the importance of flexibility (particularly with the vowel sounds) and the use of meaning-based cues to confirm the accuracy of decoding attempts.

Reading a New Book

Virtually all of the ISA instructional goals are addressed in this segment and it would be beyond the scope of this chapter to explicitly discuss each one. Therefore, we focus on the word learning and meaning construction goals (see Figure 16.1). And, given that our approach to developing strategic word-solving skills is viewed by many to be a unique aspect of the ISA, we discuss the strategic word learning subgoal in some detail.

Figure 16.3 presents the word-identification strategies that are taught in the ISA. The strategies are explicitly taught, generally one at a time. Explanations and think-alouds are provided as the strategies are introduced and as often as needed thereafter to help children understand how to effectively use the strategies to puzzle through and identify unfamiliar words. The children are provided with guided

To figure out a word:

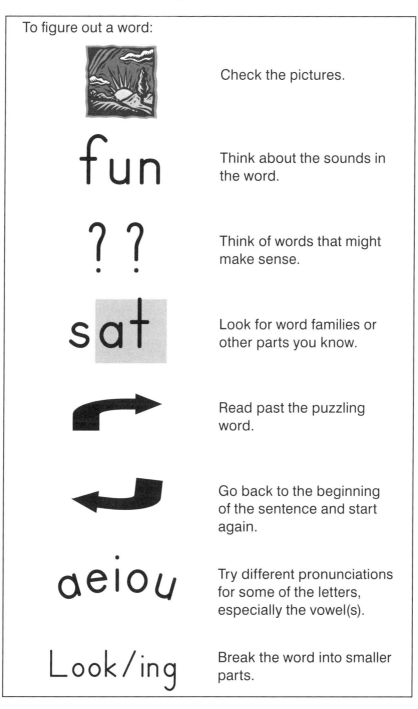

Check the pictures.

Think about the sounds in the word.

Think of words that might make sense.

Look for word families or other parts you know.

Read past the puzzling word.

Go back to the beginning of the sentence and start again.

Try different pronunciations for some of the letters, especially the vowel(s).

Break the word into smaller parts.

FIGURE 16.3. ISA strategy list. From Scanlon, Anderson, and Sweeney (2010). Copyright by the International Reading Association. Reprinted by permission.

practice in applying the strategies with an eventual press for independence in word solving following a gradual release of responsibility model (Pearson & Gallagher, 1983). Teachers are reminded to provide only as much support as children need to effectively solve unfamiliar words. The strategy list includes a combination of meaning-based and code-based strategies that children are encouraged to use in an interactive and confirmatory way. And, as perusal of the list will indicate, the phonics skills that are taught in the previous segment are intended to support the children's abilities to apply the code-based strategies they are learning.

To emphasize the need for children to become strategic word solvers, we emphasize that most words that eventually become part of a reader's sight vocabulary are not explicitly taught but, rather, are learned through effective word solving in context. Therefore, effective word-solving strategies serve as a self-teaching mechanism (Share, 1995) that enables children to learn more words and more about words with each encounter with text.

The new book segment is a critical component and can be thought of as comprising three parts: before, during, and after reading. Below we discuss each part in some detail.

Before Reading

Teachers are encouraged to select books that will present children with some but not too much challenge as such books will provide children with the opportunity to apply their developing word-identification strategies and to receive guidance in their application. Reading texts that are either too challenging or too easy will limit the children's opportunities to be actively strategic. In the case of text that is too challenging (meaning there are too many words that the children will not be able to figure out), strategic word solving will be hampered because the children will not be able to develop the context upon which the use of meaning-based strategies depends. For text that is too easy, children will have little need to be strategic, as most words are known to them.[3] We encourage teachers to use the leveling system with which they are familiar to select books for their children and to be mindful of the things that are not captured by leveling systems that can make a book more or less challenging for particular children. These include topical/background knowledge and interest in and motivation for learning about particular topics and, especially at the early stages of reading development, the specific words and phonics elements that appear in the text.

---

[3]Certainly we do not advocate against having children read texts that are quite easy for them at various points in the school day. Rather, we argue that, to make optimal use of the teacher's valuable instructional time, closely supervised small-group and one-to-one lessons should provide opportunities to offer the kind of guidance that will move the children forward on the path to becoming independent word solvers.

TEXT LEVELING

With regard to leveling systems, it is important to note that most do not take instructional sequences into account. Thus, in our 2005 and 2008 intervention studies, we provided teachers with a series of sequenced books (the Ready Readers, currently published by Pearson) that are designed to build high-frequency sight vocabulary and phonics skills across books through periodically re-presenting words and/or phonics elements in subsequent books that occurred frequently in earlier books in the series. When using such a series, a text that might qualify as being too challenging, based on one or more of the commonly used leveling systems, might actually be manageable for the children because of their familiarity with the specific high-frequency words and phonics elements encountered in previous texts. Thus, we caution teachers to be sensitive to the fact that the value of leveling systems can vary depending on the "diet" of books that children read. We do not encourage teachers to rely solely on lists of leveled texts but rather to consider what foundational skills their students currently have.

Having selected a specific text, teachers are encouraged to thoughtfully prepare children to read the text, as the extent of the preparation provided impacts the degree to which reading the new text will help to accomplish the instructional goals—especially the word-solving/word-learning goal. Thus, if a teacher provides an extensive book introduction, including a thorough picture walk, wherein the pictures on each page are jointly considered and discussed and, perhaps, some of the language from the book is used in the conversation, the children may have little need of being strategic in word identification when they begin to read the book because many of the words (and phrases) will have come up in the preparatory conversation and so will be "primed" and, therefore, require little interrogation of the print. This is all well and good, of course, if the goal is to help children be fairly fluent on the first reading of a book. The potential downside, however, is that because the children will not need to look at the unfamiliar words thoroughly to puzzle them out, they may not store the words in memory with enough detail to make subsequent identification of these words, in other contexts, more certain and more automatic. This potential interference with sight word learning is problematic, given that automatic identification of most of the words in a text is an important contributor to reading comprehension.[4] Therefore, we encourage teachers to offer rich book introductions only if they feel that their students do not have the back-

---

[4] There is an important distinction between *sight vocabulary*, which we define as printed words that can be identified "at sight" and *vocabulary*, which is defined as words for which children know the word meanings. In the current context we focus on sight vocabulary. However, the importance of knowing the meanings of words encountered in text should not be underestimated as it is one of the best predictors of reading comprehension once children have become fairly proficient with word identification.

ground knowledge, skills, and strategies that would be needed to read a given text. In most contexts, however, we expect teachers to offer a brief book introduction, to have already taught and provided practice with one or more decoding elements that will be useful in solving unfamiliar words in a given book, and, if need be, to explicitly teach one or more words that appear in the book, words that the children are unlikely to be able to puzzle through given their current skills and strategies. Cautions regarding rich book introductions extend to *meaning construction* as well, as children will not have the need to "make sense" of what they read if the entire text has been discussed in detail, prior to reading it.

Just before having the children begin to read the new book, the teacher would also teach and/or revisit one or more of the word-identification strategies. As our ultimate goal is that children will internalize the strategies and use them independently, teachers engage children in extensive amounts of strategy talk to support this goal. For example, if most of the strategies have been taught but the children do not yet use them independently and reliably, the teacher might ask the children to name (and discuss) the things they can do to figure out a puzzling word. Alternatively, the teacher might use a small bit of contrived text to help children practice (and talk about the use of) particular strategies. For instance, the teacher might present the sentence "The boys like racing cars," knowing that the word *racing* is likely to be challenging. She would then engage the group in a collaborative word-solving effort as illustrated below:

TEACHER: (*pointing to the word* racing *after reading the first three words*) Hmmm. If I don't know that word what could I do?

CHILD 1: Break it into parts. . . . I see *ing*.

TEACHER: That will help. I'll just cover that *ing* part with my finger for now so we can concentrate on the part that we don't recognize.

CHILD 2: Rake, raking!

TEACHER: Could be! Let's read past it to see if *raking* makes sense . . .

ENTIRE GROUP: The boys like raking cars . . . Noooo!

TEACHER: What else could we try?

CHILD 2: I know! RACING! The boys like racing cars! The *C* makes its other sound!

TEACHER: Does the word *racing* make sense in the sentence?

ENTIRE GROUP: Yes!

TEACHER: I agree. And, I am glad that you remembered that strategy of trying different pronunciations for some of the letters!

This particular exchange might occur in preparation for a book where there are several words with *ing* endings and perhaps words in which alternative pronunciations of some of the letters might need to be tried. Note that, in this example, the teacher responded to the suggestion that the puzzling word was *racing* by giving the children the final responsibility for determining that the word had been accurately identified ("Does the word *racing* make sense in the sentence?"). The teacher's response is important in that it clearly conveys the need to confirm that the hypothesized pronunciation of the word both fits the context and is consistent with the letters in the printed word. Children who struggle with reading are often willing to "accept," as correct, words that fit only one set of constraints (the context or the code). As a result, they misidentify many words and, as a more debilitating result, fail to build their sight vocabulary at the pace that is necessary to meet grade-level expectations and to become proficient readers.

During Reading

After all of this preparation (which took much longer to describe than it would actually take to accomplish), the children would read the book, typically using whisper reading at a volume just loud enough for the teacher to hear and monitor individual readers. Sometimes the children might read in pairs, coaching one another in the word-identification process by suggesting word-identification strategies that might help in solving particular words.

As the children read, the teacher scaffolds their word-solving attempts, being careful to provide enough support so that the child is successful but not so much as to encourage heavy dependence on the teacher. Taking into consideration the characteristics of the unfamiliar word, the supportiveness of the context, and the particular child's background knowledge, strategies, and phonics skills, the teacher

PUZZLING WORDS

An important norm that must be established is that children should not call out a word that another child is attempting to puzzle through, since doing so effectively robs the child doing the puzzling of the pleasure of solving it. Indeed, we use the word *puzzling* in reference to word solving for just this reason. We want children to perceive word solving as an engaging and "do-able" process from which one derives pleasure and a sense of accomplishment. We believe this perception influences children's independent reading, as they will be more likely to engage in strategic word solving in circumstances where they might otherwise skip unknown words and, thereby, miss both the opportunity to understand the text and to build their sight vocabulary.

continually makes decisions regarding how much support to offer. Also, as children read, the teacher encourages open discussion of the text. Because children at the beginning stages of reading often need to devote many of their cognitive resources to the process of reading the words, some will neglect the meaning of the text. Therefore, the teacher plays an important role in ensuring that children view reading as a meaning-making enterprise.

After Reading

The focus on meaning continues as the children complete the book and share their thinking on such things as what they learned in the text, whether their initial thinking about what might happen matched the author's thinking, how they would have felt/reacted in similar situations, and so on. Teachers are encouraged to try to ensure that meaning-focused conversations are not simply "comprehension checks," but genuine conversations that convey to children that their thoughts matter and that different people may think about the same text in different ways. The intention is to lay the foundation for the kind of critical thinking about texts that will be expected as the children progress in school.[5]

After reading, teachers also engage children in reflecting on the word-solving strategies they used and how well they worked. The purpose, here again, is to encourage children to view word solving as a strategic and useful process that is both doable and enjoyable.

High-Frequency Words

Given that approximately 50% of the words in just about any text are comprised of 100 or so frequently occurring words (words like *the, of, was, to*), and approximately 70% of most texts comprise the 300 or so most frequently occurring words, high-frequency word learning is critical in building reading proficiency. Thus, ensuring that children can readily identify these high-frequency words provides them stronger entrée into all texts. In an intervention lesson, new high-frequency words are taught in preparation for the new book (as noted in the "Before Reading" section above). In the high-frequency words segment, the focus is on practicing and helping the children to become automatic in identifying the accumulating set of high-frequency words that have been taught. This is a fairly short and playful segment in which gamelike activities are used that involve both word reading and written spelling with the latter activity designed to draw children's attention to the internal

---

[5]The kinds of texts that are typically read by children in the early primary grades do not always provide many opportunities for promoting the kinds of critical thinking we are suggesting here. In fact, read-alouds provide a much stronger vehicle for addressing this long-term goal. However, given the focus on the supported reading lesson in this chapter we do not address this in any detail.

BOOKS TO SUPPORT HIGH-FREQUENCY WORD LEARNING

We have noted that some children seem to experience inordinate difficulty in establishing an initial set of high-frequency words in memory. We believe that this may be partially due to an overreliance on the use of highly predictable texts. With such texts, once a predictable pattern is learned (which it often can be after only a page or two), children may pay little attention to the printed words, relying instead on pictures and repetitive refrains. For such children, we have found it useful to employ books where the language pattern changes somewhat from one page to the next. For example, instead of a book following the pattern "The dog can sit. The cat can sit. The mouse can sit. The elephant can sit," we would opt for one that varies the pattern, as in the following example: "The dog can sit. Can the cat sit? Can the mouse sit? The elephant can sit!"* The changing pattern demands closer attention to the individual words and seems to help establish early high-frequency sight vocabulary. Such books would be used in the reading and rereading segments of the lesson and the high-frequency words included in the books would be included in the practice activities in this segment.

---

*Note that while such texts are not easy to come by, they are easy to create by modifying existing predictable texts through slight changes in wording on every other page or so. Removable labels can be used for this purpose.

structures of the words and, therefore, to help them form stronger representations of those words in memory. For each small group or one-to-one intervention student, teachers develop a "Words We/I Know" chart that includes the words that the teacher believes the children can identify with some confidence. This chart is used as a resource that children are taught to refer to so that they can spell these known words conventionally in their writing. This is intended to promote automaticity in both identifying and conventionally spelling newly learned words.

Writing

This segment of the reading lesson addresses multiple goals and can occur at different points in the lesson. However, in general, the writing done in the intervention setting does not have composition as one of its major goals. Rather, in order to move the lesson along, teachers will often construct or co-construct the message that will be captured in the writing. In support of comprehension and knowledge development (meaning construction), the writing segment often follows either the reread or the new read and provides an opportunity for children to react in some way to the text that was read. Engaging the children in writing also clearly helps to support the development of all of the alphabetics subgoals listed in Figure 16.1. For example, in encouraging beginning readers to write, teachers would explicitly draw the children's attention to such things as the directionality of print, the concepts of word and letter, the function of common punctuation marks, and so on. They would model how to stretch out spoken words so that their individual phonemes can be isolated (phonemic awareness) and how to use letter–sound key words as an assist in determining which letters to use to represent particular sounds. In guiding students' writing attempts, teachers might remind them of certain phonics generalizations that have been taught (such as the silent-*e* generalization) and/or remind them of a word family that would be useful. With regard to the word learning goal, writing provides a context for children to practice conventional spellings and to attend to the internal structures of the words by relying on handy resources. For example, if the child is writing about something in the book that was just read, he or she would be encouraged to refer to the book for the conventional spellings of words. Or, if he or she was using one of the high-frequency words on the group's "Words We Know" chart, the child would check his or her spelling there. This would involve locating the proper area of the chart and then reading through the words until the desired word is found and copied.

OMISSIONS AND CONCLUDING THOUGHTS

In this brief description of the ISA intervention, we have emphasized the goals and premises of the approach that distinguish it from other approaches to early literacy intervention, including the importance of providing instruction that is explicitly goal oriented and that helps the children see the links between foundational skills and strategy instruction on the one hand and authentic reading and writing on the other. We placed particular emphasis on helping children to develop word-solving skills that would enable them to acquire new sight words and learn more about those words and words in general with each encounter with text. Word solving and word learning are emphasized in the ISA because the ability to effortlessly identify the words in a text frees readers' cognitive resources so that they can be devoted to the most important aspect of reading—comprehending and learning from texts. We also place a great deal of emphasis on helping children to become strategic and independent readers, both through the use of a gradual release of responsibility approach (Pearson & Gallagher, 1983) and through the provision of resources, such as strategy charts and key words, that children can readily refer to in order to remind themselves of some of the details of the complex process that reading entails.

Due to space constraints, we have, of necessity, glossed over very important aspects of the ISA. For example, at the level of the various contexts in which interventions occur, we only briefly noted that it is important that teachers who share responsibility for teaching the same children strive for consistency and congruence across instructional settings. Otherwise, there is a risk that children who are already struggling will receive conflicting messages (at least in their minds) about what the reading process entails and, as a result, become further confused. We discuss this topic in greater detail in Scanlon, Anderson, and Sweeney (2010). At the classroom level, we noted and briefly discussed the idea that a focus on the development of comprehension skills and the knowledge base upon which comprehension depends can be addressed through interactive read-alouds. We also noted that the texts that are accessible to beginning and struggling readers do not provide sufficient opportunity to address the comprehension and knowledge-building goal, but this aspect of reading development clearly cannot be ignored. We want children to view reading as an enjoyable and informative activity that is not beyond their capabilities (see the *motivation* goal). Reading and discussing books with children helps to address the first part of this goal. Providing small-group and one-to-one intervention addresses the second. These important topics are also discussed in greater detail in Scanlon, Anderson, and Sweeney (2010).

Case Example Follow-Up

Involvement in the ISA professional development changed Mrs. Jones's thinking about how to support children's reading development, especially for her most struggling readers. She learned that good instruction is the most important component of an RTI process and that, when she and the intervention teachers worked together to provide children with a coherent and consistent instructional approach, they made better progress. She and her colleagues were particularly impressed by the role that explicit teaching of word-identification strategies played in helping children become independent readers. As a result of the professional development, Mrs. Jones was also more attuned and attentive to the varying needs of her students during whole-class instruction and was better able to differentiate instruction during small-group supported reading lessons. For those students who required additional support, she was able to work more collaboratively with the reading specialist to address the students' learning needs.

REFERENCES

Ehri, L. C. (2005). Learning to read words: Theory, findings, and issues. *Scientific Studies of Reading, 9*(2), 167–188.

Frith, U. (1985). Beneath the surface of developmental dyslexia. In K. E. Patterson, J. C. Marshall, & M. Coltheart (Eds.), *Surface dyslexia* (pp. 301–330). London: Erlbaum.

Henderson, E. H. (1990*). Teaching spelling.* Boston: Houghton Mifflin.

McClelland, J. L., & Rumelhart, D. E. (1981). An interactive activation model of context effects in letter perception. Part 1. An account of basic findings. *Psychological Review, 88,* 375–407.

Pearson, P. D., & Gallagher, M. C. (1983). The instruction of reading comprehension. *Contemporary Educational Psychology, 8*, 317–334.

Plaut, D. C., McClelland, J. L., Seidenberg, M. S., & Patterson, K. (1996). Understanding normal and impaired word reading: Computational principles in quasi-regular domains. *Psychological Review, 103*, 56–11.

Scanlon, D. M., Anderson, K. L., & Gelzheiser, L. M. (2010, December). *Impact of professional development for teachers on children's early literacy development.* Paper presented at the annual convention of the Literacy Research Association, Fort Worth, TX.

Scanlon, D. M., Anderson, K. L., & Sweeney, J. M (2010). *Early intervention for reading difficulties: The Interactive Strategies Approach.* New York: Guilford Press.

Scanlon, D. M., Gelzheiser, L. M., Vellutino, F. R., Schatschneider, C., & Sweeney, J. M. (2008). Reducing the incidence of early reading difficulties: Professional development for classroom teachers vs. direct interventions for children. *Learning and Individual Differences, 18*, 346–359.

Scanlon, D. M., Vellutino, F. R., Small, S. G., Fanuele, D. P., & Sweeney, J. M. (2005). Severe reading difficulties—Can they be prevented?: A comparison of prevention and intervention approaches. *Exceptionality, 13(4)*, 209–227.

Seidenberg, M. S., & McClelland, J. M. (1989). A distributed, developmental model of word recognition. *Psychological Review, 96*, 523–568.

Share, D. L. (1995). Phonological recoding and self teaching: Sin qua non of reading acquisition. *Cognition, 55*, 151–218.

Vellutino, F. R., & Scanlon, D. M. (2002). The Interactive Strategies Approach to reading intervention. *Contemporary Educational Psychology, 27*, 573–635.

Vellutino, F. R., Scanlon, D. M., Sipay, E. R., Small, S. G., Pratt, A., Chen, R., et al. (1996). Cognitive profiles of difficult-to-remediate and readily remediated poor readers: Early intervention as a vehicle for distinguishing between cognitive and experiential deficits as basic causes of specific reading disability. *Journal of Educational Psychology, 88*, 601–638.

CHAPTER 17

❖

An Evidence-Based Approach to Response to Intervention

MONICA T. BILLEN
RICHARD L. ALLINGTON

I knew Taylor[1] was an intriguing child the second he walked into my (Monica Billen) classroom. While most children had a backpack and a lunch box, Taylor had a tool belt and a toolbox. He was about half the size of the surrounding third graders but his smile was easily twice as big. As the children began exploring their new classroom, Taylor came straight to me, smiled, and said, "So, you're my new teacher? I think I like you." Taylor proved to be an interesting child throughout the rest of the day; he sang songs from *The Lion King* while everyone was gathered on the carpet and shaped his pink eraser into a lion shape while the class was painting at art. Taylor's favorite pasttime, as I heard from his second-grade teacher, was to unhinge all of the doors from the school bathroom. He loved animals, was quite savvy with a screwdriver, and loved talking about his future as a mechanic.

After the first day of school had concluded, the school administrator paid a visit to my classroom. She informed me that she was quite worried about Taylor's reading abilities and had organized a reading group for him to attend during our in-class reading period. I inquired more about the tutoring that he would receive and learned he would be working with a paraprofessional completing a scripted reading program. I saw several problems with my administrator's proposition, yet as a new teacher, I didn't feel as if I had an option to disagree. Looking back at this particular situation, I now know the many troubles that came with the administrator's plan.

---

[1]Taylor is a fictitious character created by Monica Billen. He represents a composite of a few students she encountered while teaching in an elementary school.

GUIDING QUESTION

Throughout this chapter, we discuss six evidence-based elements that should be the focus when planning a response-to-intervention (RTI) initiative. The key question we attempt to address:

❖ What should educators focus on when implementing RTI?

OVERVIEW OF THE TOPIC

RTI is the most recent strategy for identifying a child with a learning disability (Scanlon, 2010). RTI requires educators to provide effective reading instruction *before* the child is referred for special education services (Barnett, Daly, Jones, & Lentz, 2004). In other words, RTI is a practice that involves high-quality instruction and intervention for students to help educators make important educational decisions (Batsche et al., 2005).

THEORETICAL BACKGROUND

The notion of instructing children before designating them as learning disabled (LD) has been considered for quite some time. Scanlon (2010) and Vellutino (2010) both date RTI research back to the 1980s when Marie Clay introduced this early intervention notion by creating the Reading Recovery program in New Zealand. Reading Recovery is a first-grade intervention effort that provides at-risk students with tutorial instruction provided by a teacher who has participated in the yearlong professional development activities that are central to becoming a Reading Recovery teacher. Recently, the federal What Works Clearinghouse (2007) identified Reading Recovery as the only reading program with "strong evidence" that it improves reading achievement. The vast majority of the 153 reading programs reviewed had not a single reliable research study indicating it improved reading proficiency! Of the 25 programs that did have reliable research, the majority (20) had evidence they improved some aspect of reading performance (decoding, rate of reading, etc.) but no research indicating improved text reading as an outcome.

Federal policymakers are concerned that the numbers of children identified as LD have increased dramatically since the label was established in 1977. Today the number of students identified as LD comprise the majority of all persons identified as persons with disabilities in the United States. Some have posited that the way in which we have identified students as LD has resulted in overclassification (Vaughn, Linan-Thompson, & Hickman, 2003). Prior to the introduction of RTI, students had been classified as LD based on a discrepancy between the child's IQ and the child's academic performance. In hopes of more accurately classifying children and frustration with the discrepancy model, RTI was introduced as an alternative option to classification (Lyon et al., 2001).

The RTI process was outlined in the reauthorization of Individuals with Disabilities Education Act (IDEA) in 2004. The reauthorized IDEA attempts to ensure that schools have (1) provided early identification and intervention for struggling readers, (2) created a method of locating students with disabilities, (3) provided effective and intensive instruction, (4) monitored students' progress, (5) created a problem-solving team, and (6) made enough reading growth to meet annual yearly progress (Lose, 2007). Beginning in 2006, schools were allowed to begin using the RTI process to determine which students might be classified as LD. Once the RTI process was adopted schools could no longer use the traditional IQ-discrepancy model for such purposes. In essence then, RTI is based on the assumption that ensuring all children have access to intensive and expert reading instruction will reduce the numbers of children identified as LD. Thus, as Johnston (2011) has noted, the RTI framework has both a prevention aspect focused on reducing the numbers of children identified as having a learning disability or dyslexia and a new process for identifying the children who may be LD or dyslexic. As he argues:

> In other words, we have the knowledge necessary to eliminate most children's difficulties acquiring literacy—eliminating any legitimate value in classifying them as learning disabled or dyslexic. This is the promise of response to intervention (RTI), a provision in the 2004 revision of the federal Individuals with Disabilities Education Act (IDEA) legislation. (Rules and Regulations for the Reauthorization of IDEA, 2006, p. 512)

What Is RTI?

RTI is an overarching process for decision making, the federal rules do not provide any particular strict set of procedures to be followed (Christ, Burns, & Ysseldyke, 2005), and so schools have implemented the RTI process quite differently (Barnes & Harlacher, 2008). There have been several different descriptions of what, exactly, RTI is and how it should be implemented. Some describe the model as a two-tiered intervention (Fuchs & Fuchs, 2005), while others describe it as four tiers (Ikeda et al., 2002) and most commonly, a three-tiered approach (Johnston, 2010).

In order for students to be identified as LD, a tiered instructional approach is often implemented, most commonly, a three-tiered approach. In Tier 1, struggling students are provided with and monitored during high-quality classroom reading instruction. If a child shows inadequate growth while participating in effective classroom instruction, then Tier 2 instruction is developed and added to the child's school day experiences along with continued classroom reading lessons. Tier 2 instruction, which usually includes small-group work, is more intense than Tier 1 instruction but not as intense as Tier 3 instruction. If a student does not show adequate growth with Tier 2 instruction, the student is recommended for Tier 3 instruction and, generally, one-on-one instruction (Scanlon, 2010). In most RTI models Tier 3 is added along with Tier 2 and Tier 1 reading lessons. Johnston (2011) described RTI as dependent on instruction, he posited that this added appropriate reading instruction is foundational in preventing struggling readers from being classified as LD students. In other words, if the RTI effort is successful, then struggling readers will have their reading development accelerated and lose their struggling status and become achieving readers.

A basic intent of the RTI process is an expected decrease in the numbers of students identified as LD. Lyon and his colleagues (2001) suggest a dramatic decrease can be expected based on the evidence available to date. By dramatic they mean a 70–80% decrease in the numbers of children identified as LD. This view is well summarized by Vellutino and Fletcher (2005), who wrote:

> Finally, there is now considerable evidence, from recent intervention studies, that reading difficulties in most beginning readers may not be directly caused by biologically based cognitive deficits intrinsic to the child, but may in fact be related to the opportunities provided for children learning to read. (p. 378)

They summarize that research shows dramatic decreases in children experiencing reading difficulties when primary-grade children struggling with learning to read are provided with intensive and expert reading instruction.

As Lyon and colleagues (2001) had noted earlier, the federal definition of a child with a learning disability required that the school ensured that a child's reading difficulties did not stem from inadequate reading instruction. But they also noted:

> All definitions of LD exclude children from consideration if their learning problems are primarily a product of inadequate instruction. Of all the different assumptions in the concept of LD, this one is the least examined yet perhaps the most important. (p. 268)

Lyon and his colleagues (2001) noted many of the same studies reviewed in the paper by Vellutino and Fletcher (2005) and suggest that the then current standard for identifying children as LD would be improved if schools actually documented that they had provided intensive and expert reading lessons prior to attempting to classify a child as LD. Thus, their recommendation for implementing the RTI process.

RTI Instruction

Every RTI model incorporates an intervention. Although instruction has been noted as a vital component of RTI, surprisingly little convergent research has been conducted to better understand successful instruction across tiers. In addition, many models of RTI encourage teachers to implement a commercial reading program with *fidelity* (Brown-Chidsey & Steege, 2005), based on little knowledge of how successful the program may actually be. Likewise, a reliance on a commercial program ignores the research that an effective teacher of reading is much more effective than use of a commercial program, even with fidelity (Allington, 2002; Nye, Konstantopoulos, & Hedges, 2004). There is no actual research to back up the claim that commercial reading intervention programs that are implemented with fidelity improve students' reading abilities (Scanlon, 2010; What Works Clearinghouse, 2007).

Reading Intervention

What lies at the foundation of an RTI intervention is the notion that all children can learn when given appropriate instruction (Allington, 2009). Although we do not have enough research to know how well RTI programs influence children's learning, we do know, from a variety of reading research studies, that appropriate reading instruction positively affects children's reading achievement (Scanlon, 2010).

Center, Wheldall, Freeman, Outhred, and McNaught (1995) evaluated the effectiveness of the Reading Recovery program. In general, the program assumes that reading involves effective strategy use, reading and writing are reciprocal, and students must engage in reading very frequently (Wasik & Slavin, 1993). Center and colleagues evaluated Reading Recovery by randomly assigning students to either be in a Reading Recovery experience or a control group. The researchers found that after 15 weeks the Reading Recovery group was superior to control students on all tests measuring reading achievement. This finding on the potential of the Reading Recovery program to resolve early difficulties in learning to read was replicated by Schwartz (2005) and Pinnell, Lyons, Deford, Bryk, and Seltzer (1994).

Similarly, Mathes and colleagues (2005) studied the effects of combining high-quality classroom instruction and intense supplemental interventions. The study involved struggling readers in first grade and a small-group expert intervention was provided for students at risk for reading difficulties. The participants received one of two reading interventions. The interventions differed primarily on whether phonics instruction was explicit or embedded. They found no significant differences in the outcomes for the two curricula. Results indicated that students who participated in supplemental instruction scored higher on reading measures than students who only received enhanced classroom instruction, yet the enhanced reading classroom instruction did promote reading growth for many students. This study indicates that enhanced classroom instruction can encourage reading growth, and when paired with supplemental interventions, almost every first-grade student can be reading on grade level by the end of the year.

Scanlon, Gelzheiser, Vellutino, Schatschneider, and Sweeney (2008) studied two tiers of reading intervention with kindergarten children. Tier 1 was the implementation of professional development for classroom teachers, while Tier 2 provided a supplemental reading tutorial intervention for children. Schools in the study were randomly assigned to one of three groups: (1) Tier 1 implementation with professional development, (2) implementation of Tier 2 with daily one-to-one expert tutorial support, or (3) implementation of both Tier 1 and Tier 2 interventions. The researchers found that all three treatments were quite effective as fewer students were considered at risk at the end of the school year regardless of which type of school they attended. However, they were surprised that providing classroom teachers with effective professional development focused on teaching early struggling readers was as effective as providing the Tier 2 tutorial support for struggling readers! Put another way, this study suggests that most of the children now assigned the label of being LD might better be considered children who simply had largely inexpert primary-grade teachers. High-quality reading lessons, regardless of who offered the lessons, effectively resulted in almost every child reading on grade level by the end of first grade.

In hopes of better understanding reading intervention effects, Torgesen and colleagues (2001) studied 60 older children ages 8 to 10 with severe reading disabilities. The children received intensive one-on-one expert reading instruction for a total of 67.5 hours in two 50-minute daily intervention periods for 8 weeks. The students were randomly assigned to two different programs. One program was a skills-intensive approach where children received mostly phonics instruction (80% of lesson time) with a small amount of time (5%) spent on text reading, while the other group received mostly text reading (80% of lesson time) with a small amount of time (20%) spent on phonics instruction. There were no differences in outcomes for the two groups. The intervention proved to be helpful as 40% of the children, a year after the intervention, no longer needed special education services. Both instructional interventions studied produced large improvements and were stable in a 2-year follow-up investigation. Torgeson et al. note that many students currently served in special education programs could have their reading development accelerated but that will require a substantial shift toward far greater use of expert and intensive reading instruction.

Through this body of research and other studies (Hiebert, Colt, Catto, & Gury, 1992; O'Connor, 2000; Pinnell et al., 1994; Scanlon, Vellutino, Small, Fanuele, & Sweeney, 2005; Vaughn, Linan-Thompson, Kouzekanani, et al., 2003; Vellutino, Sipay, Small, Pratt, Chen, & Denckla, 1996), it is clear that when implementing an appropriately expert and intensive intervention, all children's reading abilities can improve. In the next section, we discuss elements of reading instruction that research suggests are crucial aspects of any intervention program.

THE CLASSROOM: A CASE EXAMPLE

If Taylor walked into one of our classrooms today, followed by the after-school visit of the administrator, we would do things differently. Throughout the next few pages, we discuss what should have happened for Taylor, a struggling reader. We suggest six research-based principles to guide teachers through implementing necessary elements of RTI: (1) expert teachers provide instruction, (2) match text to readers, (3) dramatically expand reading activity, (4) use small groups or (5) tutoring, and (6) coordinate intervention with classroom curriculum.

Expert Teachers Provide the Instruction

Though the administrator most likely had good intentions for Taylor and his reading achievement, the first mistake in the intervention plan was taking Taylor away from his teacher and his classroom reading lessons to work with a paraprofessional. Though the paraprofessional may have made sense from an economic standpoint, it makes little sense when you consider the expertise that he or she may have had. The idea of sending a struggling child to an inexpert paraprofessional who has had very little, if any, effective educational experience in teaching children to read seemed curious.

The effect that paraprofessionals have on the academic achievement of students has been highlighted in recent research. Some have noted "teacher aides have little, if any, positive effect on students' academic achievement" (Gerber, Finn, Achilles, & Boyd-Zaharias, 2001, p. 123). These authors argued that paraprofessionals are doing a lot more teaching than they have in the past, yet are ill equipped to take on the teaching responsibility. Similarly, Gray et al. (2007) found that although teachers had somewhat pleasing remarks and positive opinions about teacher assistants, the teacher assistants in their study did not produce a positive impact on students' reading performance.

On the other hand, expert teachers have been found to have a significant effect on the reading development of children. When we say expert, we align ourselves with Pearson (2003), who stated:

> We want teachers who use their deep knowledge of subject matter along with knowledge of children's histories, routines, and dispositions to create just the right curricular mix for each and all—we want them to use their inquiry skills to alter those approaches when the evidence that passes their eye says they are not working. (p. 15)

An expert teacher has a deep knowledge base and is able to shift and adapt his or her teaching on the fly—or when an opportunity or situation arises. This is quite different from a teacher following a commercial intervention program with *fidelity*.

Research has shown the importance and vitality of an influential teacher. Nye et al. (2004) studied teacher effects in a 4-year experiment. The researchers randomly assigned teachers and students and estimated the effect that teachers have on students. They reported that the teacher was the single most important variable in explaining student reading achievement. Nye et al. wrote that "the variance due to differences among teachers [within a school] is substantial in comparison to the variance between schools" (p. 247). In other words, while policymakers have long attended to differences in achievement earned by different schools, little attention, to date, has been paid to the differences in the quality of instruction offered by different teachers working in the same building. But it is those within-building teacher differences that matter when it comes to thinking about struggling readers.

Bembry, Jordan, Gomez, Anderson, and Mendro (1998) studied teacher effectiveness in a longitudinal study. The authors found that the greater the number of highly effective teachers a student had, the better that student's reading achievement was. For example, a student who had one highly effective teacher would have a lower reading proficiency than a student who had several highly effective teachers during the elementary school years. The authors posited, "It is clear that teachers have large effects on student achievement, that effects have strong additive components over time, and that teacher effects are large enough to dwarf effects associated with most other educational interventions" (p. 19).

In a national sample of first-grade teachers, Stuhlman and Pianta (2009) found four types of distinct first-grade classrooms when observing reading instruction: high-quality (23%), mediocre-quality (28%), low-quality (17%), and positive emotional climate/lower academic demand (31%) classrooms. In the latter classrooms the teachers exhibited much caring behavior toward their students but were largely inexpert in terms of providing high-quality reading lessons. Children from low-income families were twice as likely to be placed in a low-quality classroom as placed in a high-quality classroom. The impacts of being assigned anyone but a high-quality teacher were most readily observed among at-risk children. In other words, few teachers could provide reading instruction of sufficient quality to allow at-risk students an opportunity to become on-level readers.

Match Texts to Readers

When Taylor entered my classroom with his books in a tool belt and his sandwich and chips in a toolbox, it was quite obvious he had specific interests. Taylor had specific interests and specific needs that were not met through a scripted lesson-by-lesson reading program that the paraprofessional implemented with *fidelity*. In fact, after a closer examination of the texts that Taylor was reading that he had no interest in, the texts, which focused on decoding, were far beyond his reading level. It is important, if we want children to excel at reading, to find texts that he or she can read successfully.

When we say that children should read books that he or she can read, we mean books that can be read with a high level of accuracy, fluency, and comprehension. The notion of text difficulty was examined more than 60 years ago when Emmett Betts (1946, 1949) developed guidelines for text difficulty. *Independent* level texts are books that are quite simple for an individual child—a book that a child can read without any help. *Instructional*-level texts are texts that a student can read satisfactorily, with teacher help before, during, and after reading as is usually offered during a guided reading lesson. Betts argued that *frustrational*-level texts are texts where a child struggles with words, ideas, and fluency even when a teacher is present—and should be avoided. More specifically, in 1949, Betts recommended that individual text difficulty can be broken down by a student's oral reading accuracy rate: *independent*: 99–100%; *instructional*: 95–98%; *frustrational*: less than 95%.

Of course, it seems obvious that in order to learn a new skill, one must practice the skill. It doesn't seem likely that if a child was learning to ride a bike at an early stage, that an adult would hand the child a unicycle and a tightrope and hope the child learns the needed balance and pedaling to pedal across the tightrope. Likewise, a sixth-grade struggling reader should not be given a sixth-grade-level text if he or she is reading at a third-grade level. O'Connor and colleagues (2002) studied text difficulty and found that about 80% of interventions used grade-level texts to instruct the struggling readers, even if the child was not reading on grade level. In further study, the researchers found that students made greater gains when texts were matched to their current reading level. The researchers concluded "The proposition that poor readers will make stronger comprehension gains by reading in grade level texts with appropriate support (e.g., assisted reading) was not borne out here" (p. 483).

Similarly, Ehri, Dreyer, Flugman, and Gross (2007) provided a tutoring-based reading intervention for young struggling readers. They reported that the best predictor of reading progress was the number of texts read with 98% accuracy or better. In other words, tutoring a child with more difficult text did not work out as well as giving that child books that he or she could actually read accurately, fluently, and with understanding. Not surprisingly, Taylor's experience reading books that were too difficult for him did not improve his reading proficiency.

We are unsure why in so many cases struggling readers are provided texts to read that are so difficult for them. Our advice is that success builds success. It seems essential that struggling readers have a steady diet of texts that they can read accurately, fluently, and with understanding. Perhaps one reason so few struggling readers ever become achieving readers is that far too often the texts they are provided are simply too difficult.

Dramatically Expand Reading Activity

Taylor was known around the elementary campus for asking his teacher to use the restroom, sneaking his screwdriver in his pocket, and proceeding to the restroom where he unhinged all of the stall doors and placed them in a pile. It is no doubt that Taylor was quite talented with tools—and this did not occur overnight. Taylor had years of apprenticeship and practice as he observed his father, uncle, and grandfather with their tools and had helped on many occasions. In a sense, Taylor had manifested the common quotation "Practice makes perfect" to be true—for both his mechanical abilities and his reading abilities. Although his reading abilities proved the opposite, because no practice makes a struggling reader. What is fascinating though, with this notion in mind, Taylor did not receive more reading instruction. He was pulled out during the classroom reading lessons—thus, he was not expanding his reading activity.

In general, teachers are advised to provide at least 90 minutes of reading instruction per day. Unfortunately, in too many classrooms the 90-minute block is instruction that does not fit the needs of a struggling reader. That is, the struggling reader is placed in a grade-level core reading program as the classroom teacher offers "grade-level" reading lessons. When a child is pulled out during that time for a reading intervention—the child is still only receiving 90 minutes of reading instruction. If 90 minutes a day is providing a half year of growth, it does not seem logical to expect a child to jump up to reading on grade level without providing additional minutes of effective reading instruction (Allington, 2009). In addition, federal regulations require that intervention programs provide "supplemental" reading instruction and do not "supplant" the classroom reading lessons that every child is supposed to be receiving. In Taylor's case, these federal regulations were violated every day when he left the classroom for his intervention while classmates continued on with the reading lesson he was now absent from. Because Taylor was not offered a "supplemental" reading intervention and was getting no added reading instruction, he did not make accelerated reading growth.

There is also a good deal of research that indicates that expanding reading activity increases reading achievement. Kuhn and colleagues (2006) discussed advantages of having students engaged in extensive reading. The researchers studied 24 second-grade classrooms in New Jersey and Georgia. They compared a repeated reading intervention design with an additional design that allowed them to spend most of their instructional time engaged in independent reading. The children who were mostly engaged in extensive independent reading developed fluency faster than the repeated readings group and, additionally, the extensive reading group acquired more vocabulary and improved their reading comprehension to a greater extent than the children in the repeated readings group. The authors concluded that extensive reading of appropriate texts is an effective approach for struggling readers.

Use Very Small Groups for Tutoring

While the example of Taylor's experience did have many downfalls, there was one thing that was done somewhat right. Taylor had the opportunity to work with a very small-group during reading time and sometimes even received one-on-one tutoring. In fact, the administrator who worked to get Taylor this small group time praised the notion that Taylor would be receiving more instruction that was appropriate for his individual needs.

It does seem quite understandable that a teacher may be able to better meet the needs of children when the numbers of children in the group are smaller Think back to the bike analogy discussed earlier in this chapter. When imagining a child learning to ride a bicycle, one might picture one parent to one child—possibly holding the back of the bike, steadying it. Now imagine for a moment that a teacher has 25 children in a parking lot, all learning to ride a bike. It seems plausible that a teacher may have greater success teaching a child to ride a bike when fewer students are around. It is also quite possible that a teacher may adequately teach a handful of struggling bike riders at the same time who struggle with similar bike-riding issues. Similarly, with reading instruction, teachers may be able to meet the needs of struggling readers with one-on-one instruction or in small groups. Though this seems like an easy concept to grasp, Puma et al. (1997) found that typical Title I programs had groups of five to nine students and very few schools provided one-to-one tutoring or small-group lessons. In addition, Taylor was working with a paraprofessional, not an expert teacher.

Similarly, some special education group sizes were found to be around the same size as the Title I groups (Vaughn, Linan-Thompson, Kouzekanani, et al., 2003). In this study, the researchers investigated 10 elementary schools in an urban area where 70% of the students qualified for free or reduced lunch. The study sought to better understand how grouping conditions affect children's reading growth. The possible groups studied were 1:1 (i.e., one teacher to one student), 1:3, and 1:10. The researchers concluded: "Based on effect sizes, both 1:1 and 1:3 were highly effective intervention group sizes for supplemental reading instruction" (p. 301). Also, the 1:10 (i.e., one teacher to 10 students) was not superior to the smaller groupings on any measure investigated. On the other hand, Schwartz, Schmitt and Lose (2012) criticized this study on several grounds and conducted a study that demonstrated when the intervention was not done with a commercial reading program but rather tailored to the needs of each struggling reader 1:1 expert, reading intervention produced superior growth. They provide a trend analysis that demonstrates that reading growth increased as intervention group size decreased.

The next question may be, then, should small-group sessions be one-to-one tutoring or small group? This is a question addressed before in a previous publication (Allington, 2009) wherein the topic of the *number* of students served and the *proportion* was deliberated. Or in other words, is it better to work with fewer students (1:1) resulting in fewer students accelerating their literacy development greatly? Or is it better for teachers to work with more students (1:3) and have more students accelerate at a slower pace? We would assert that the answer to these questions is both. Small-group instruction (approximately three students) should be provided for struggling readers and if the small-group instruction is not sufficiently advancing the child's reading abilities, then one-to-one tutoring can and should be employed. Of course, group size is only effective to the point wherein the professional employs effective reading intervention. In Taylor's case, he did have small-group reading intervention—but that intervention contained only one element of several that were needed to ameliorate his difficulties and so was unsuccessful.

Coordinate Intervention with Classroom Curriculum

One effective strategy for reading intervention is coordinating the students' intervention with the students' classroom curriculum. As Taylor left the classroom every day to work with a paraprofessional, there seemed to be a continental divide between the curriculum Taylor was experiencing in the classroom and the intervention he was receiving with his paraprofessional tutor. The teacher and the paraprofessional were on two completely different pages, literally and figuratively. This resulted in Taylor coming back to the classroom, in the middle of reading time, and losing precious reading time as he tried to bridge the gap between what his tutor was telling him and what his teacher was telling him to do. It would have been much more beneficial and time efficient if Taylor's instruction had been coordinated with the classroom literacy curriculum. Of course, it is quite difficult to coordinate with a paraprofessional when he or she is not contracted to stay much longer than a few hours per day and leaves the campus before the teacher is done teaching for the day. In order for intervention and classroom curriculum to coordinate there must be some type of communication between the adults who are working with the child.

In fact, communication among educators has been noted as a characterization of an effective school (Mosenthal, Lipson, Torncello, Russ, & Mekkelsen, 2004). In this study, the researchers investigated six schools that did well on statewide reading tests. All K–4 teachers and educators were interviewed and observed. The researchers indicated that the successful schools, among other things, encouraged the faculty to engage in ongoing communication. Also highlighted in this study is the importance of consistency in literacy instruction.

Yet, there has been concern for quite some time on the fragmentation among students' literacy experiences (Allington & McGill-Franzen, 1989). Over 25 years ago, Johnston, Allington, and Afflerbach (1985) examined this very notion by interviewing both classroom teachers and intervention teachers. The researchers found that the students were enduring far more experiences of curriculum conflict than curricular coordination. As you may have already guessed, curriculum conflict is when the classroom teacher and the intervention teacher had competing philosophies and emphasized different strategies, while with curricular coordination just the opposite is true—when both teachers agreed upon teaching similar strategies. Interestingly enough, two-thirds of the intervention teachers in this two-state study could not identify the reading materials that their students were using in the classroom and almost none of the classroom teachers could identify the intervention curriculum their student was experiencing. In other words, few teachers worked in schools where there was a plan for the coordination of the reading lessons offered in classrooms and in intervention programs.

Borman, Wong, Hedges, and D'Agostino (2003) used national data from the federal Title I reading program to examine the effect of curricular coordination and found that increases in coordination was

> associated with an increase of 4.7 to 7.1 normal curve equivalents in classroom mean reading achievement . . . and with a reduction of the Title 1 achievement gap by 0.2 to 0.3 standard deviation units. In other words, when Title 1 and regular teachers implement a curriculum that is similar or the same, they may increase the achievement levels of all students, and may reduce a substantial proportion of Title 1 students' achievement deficits. (p. 112)

However, they also noted that only a small subset of these programs coordinated classroom and Title I reading lessons.

There has also been recent concern about the frequency of shifting and switching among intervention programs (Brown-Chidsey & Steege, 2005). It seems as though continuously changing the focus of reading instruction throughout a students' year would prove to be quite confusing for anyone, especially a struggling reader. Scanlon (2010) argued:

> To provide a child with a program focused on developing phonics skills, for example, find that the program does not help to accelerate the child's growth, and then to place the child in a program that has a very different focus, say fluency, is apt to further confuse the child who is already confused about the reading process. (p. 142)

Although it is doubtful that educators are secretly trying to exacerbate struggling readers difficulties by creating a lack of coordination between the multiple sets of reading lessons that struggling readers experience daily, we, as a profession, must be more aware of and critical of our choices in providing reading lessons to struggling readers.

In fact, 75 years ago Gates (1937) noted the need for coordination of intervention instruction with classroom lessons:

> The success of the specialist in diagnosis and remedial work depends in no small measure upon his ability to work with, through, and for the teacher, and not independently of her. The danger is that the classroom teacher may feel that diagnosis and remedial instruction of extreme cases are matters too intricate for her to understand. In effect, therefore, she may wash her hands of the problem if a specialist is available; or if one is not she may say that the case is hopeless unless an expert is provided. (p. 413)

He argued that involving the classroom teacher was necessary if only to prevent that teacher from concluding that the instruction they could offer was likely not needed. We agree with Gates but would also assert that the research is clear that when classroom and intervention reading lessons are drawn from the same curriculum framework with instruction focused on similar skills and strategies, then progress is more likely than when we provide a fragmented curriculum and instructional experience, as has been too often the practice in schools (Valli, Croninger, & Walters, 2007).

Focus on Meaning and Metacognition

Taylor knew everything there was to know about tools; what each tool was used for, the various names tools could be referred to, and even how tools should be cared for. There was no doubt that Taylor knew precisely the purpose of tools: why one has tools and how one would use tools. This knowledge, most likely, came from years of experience of using the tools himself, and having discussions about the tools with his family members. Very dissimilarly, Taylor had very few experiences with books and reading and even fewer successful experiences. Because of his lack of successful literacy experiences, Taylor did not understand the purpose of reading or why text was created or read. He did not understand the components of a story. In fact, he even struggled with foundational concepts of print. Without a foundational knowledge about the purpose of text, it seems odd for instruction to jump straight to decoding and phonics as Taylor's intervention did. Can Taylor learn to decode if he does not even understand how to hold a book or even why a person would hold a book? We would not teach a child exactly how to hold a screwdriver without first telling him or her what a screwdriver is and why it might be important. Similarly, we should not jump to assume that the first thing struggling readers need is decoding intervention. In Taylor's case, he could not make sense of decoding because he didn't have the foundational literacy knowledge needed. Taylor's instruction should have had a large focus on meaning.

Of course, every student is quite different—as in, every student has a different literacy history and every student has different strengths and weaknesses. Some students may already understand the purpose of text—but, it is important to note that all students should be reading for meaning and metacognition. Often times, programs for struggling readers focus on decoding strategies and miss the importance of focusing on meaning and metacognition.

In a seminal study completed in the 1990s, Knapp and colleagues (Knapp, 1995; Knapp & Shields, 1991; Knapp, Shields, & Turnbull, 1992) investigated the kind of reading instruction that promoted the most gains in reading achievement. In this study, the researchers examined 140 classrooms in high-poverty schools located in three different states. Through this research, some characteristics of meaning–emphasis reading instruction were identified: (1) students had lots of opportunities to read, (2) reading instruction focused on meaning and ways in which to construct meaning, (3) instruction provided students with opportunities to discuss what was read, and (4) instruction integrated reading and writing with other subject areas. The researchers found that high-poverty schools that implemented meaning–emphasis reading lessons did better on standardized tests than schools that focused on skills instruction. Schools where children had plenty of opportunities to read, opportunities to engage in meaning-oriented lessons, discussion, and reading and writing across subject areas, developed into better readers than children who were in schools more focused on individual skill development.

This study and others (Buly & Valencia, 2002; Puma et al., 1997) highlight the importance of involving reading instruction that focuses on meaning in the classroom and intervention program. The old notion—if a child can correctly call out the words on the page, he or she can understand the text—is no longer relevant. Teachers should be helping students construct meaning. But of course you may be wondering how does a teacher help students construct meaning?

Duke and Pearson (2002) sought to answer this very question in their article about effective practices for promoting comprehension. The authors noted that there must be several elements of instruction in place in order for students to develop their comprehension skills. These elements include (1) a lot of experience reading, (2) experience reading real texts, (3) experience reading a variety of genres, (4) experience in a vocabulary-rich classroom, (5) experience writing text, and (6) experience engaging in high-quality talk about text.

With these elements in place, Duke and Pearson (2002) also report that the research suggests that teachers encourage comprehension strategies development through a scaffolding approach with five steps: (1) give an explicit description of the strategy, (2) model the strategy, (3) collaborative use of the strategy, (4) guided practice with the strategy, and (5) student independent use of the strategy. This scaffolding approach may be familiar to many teachers but it is largely absent from commercial core reading programs (Dewitz, Jones, & Leahy, 2009).

With the elements described and the scaffolding model incorporated into reading instruction, struggling readers may begin to develop strategies that good readers have shown to possess. One important skill that good readers do is monitor their understanding of the text—they display using *metacognitive* techniques (Duke & Pearson, 2002). In fact, some have posited that the most important metacognitive task is monitoring whether the text one is reading is making sense (Pressley, 2002). Other metacognitive tasks include using several different ways to decode unknown words, using background knowledge to problem solve while reading, understanding how to summarize information, visualizing images of settings, and using fix-up strategies when text gets difficult.

One last, and very important element of metacognition is the individuals' self-esteem. If teachers are teaching in such a way that discourages students from feeling successful, or if students feel as if their efforts are not getting them anywhere, it is unlikely that students will continue to try to understand text and monitor their understanding. The drive to understand text should be internally motivated, or as Carr, Borkowski, and Maxwell (1991) put it, "If the impetus for achievement is external to children (e.g., a belief in luck or in the necessity of help from others), it is unlikely that they will develop feelings of self-esteem and a repertoire of high-level meta-cognitive skills (especially executive skills) necessary for good performance" (p. 117). Johnston (2004) also argued that the talk that teachers provide their students is always linked to what students are paying attention to. Language is both representational and constitutive. It invites identities, for better or worse. Johnston noted that saying, "You're so smart" is quite different from saying, "You're so thoughtful." The ways teacher talk position them and the children in their classrooms. That positioning can situate a teacher as the giver of information as in the traditional transmission classroom. Or it can position the teacher as a co-collaborator as in the inquiry classroom. It positions students as dependent or independent. As classroom collaborators or as classroom competitors. Too often, we worry that teacher talk contributes to struggling readers' lack of a focus on meaning.

CONCLUSION

It is true that Taylor is an extremely bright child with a possible bright future ahead, but it is hard to argue that the public school system, in which he was a part, was doing everything in its power to accelerate his reading development. In general, RTI models should focus on the expert instruction that children are supposed to be receiving. We do not have good evidence that implementing scripted programs with *fidelity* is an effective way to instruct struggling readers. But, we do know that implementing responsive reading instruction by an expert teacher can encourage reading growth.

Though we cannot go back in time and metamorphose Taylor's experiences with a scripted reading program and a paraprofessional that resulted in hardly any reading growth, educators can provide more meaningful and individual instruction for future struggling readers by considering the six suggestions discussed in this chapter. Struggling readers should be taught by expert teachers in a small-group environment where the student has *plentiful* opportunities to engage with appropriate texts with a focus on meaning and metacognition that coordinates with the student's classroom instruction.

Struggling readers are waiting. They are waiting for the sort of intensive extra instructional support that research has so powerfully demonstrated as effective. They are waiting for expert reading instruction tailored to their instructional needs and well coordinated with their classroom lessons. They are waiting for us, the adults in their schools, to provide the sorts of interventions they need. How much longer must they wait?

REFERENCES

Allington, R. L. (2002). What I've learned about effective reading instruction from a decade of studying exemplary elementary classroom teachers. *Phi Delta Kappan, 83*(10), 740–747.

Allington, R. L. (2009). *What really matters in response to interventions: Research-based designs.* Boston: PearsonAllynBacon.

Allington, R. L., & McGill-Franzen, A. (1989). School response to reading failure: Chapter I and special education students in grades 2, 4, and 8. *Elementary School Journal, 89,* 529–542.

Barnes, A. C., & Harlacher, J. E. (2008). Clearing the confusion: Response-to-intervention as a set of principles. *Education and Treatment of Children, 31*(3), 417–431.

Barnett, D. W., Daly, E. J., III, Jones, K. M., & Lentz, F. E., Jr. (2004). Response to intervention empirically based special service decisions from single-case designs of increasing and decreasing intensity. *Journal of Special Education, 38*(2), 66–79.

Batsche, G., Elliot, J., Graden, J. L., Grimes, J., Kovaleski, J. F., & Prasse, D. (2005). *Response to intervention: Policy considerations and implementation.* Alexandria, VA: National Association of State Directors of Special Education.

Bembry, K. L., Jordan, H. R., Gomez, E., Anderson, M., & Mendro, R. L. (1998). *Policy implications of long-term teacher effects on student achievement.* Paper presented at the meeting of the American Educational Research Association, San Diego, CA.

Betts, E. A. (1946). *Foundations of reading instruction.* New York: American Book.

Betts, E. A. (1949). Adjusting instruction to individual needs. In N. B. Henry (Ed.), *The forty-eighth yearbook of the National Society for the Study of Education: Part II. Reading in the elementary school* (pp. 266–283). Chicago: University of Chicago Press.

Borman, G. D., Wong, K. K., Hedges, L. V., & D'Agostino, J. V. (2003). Coordinating categorical and regular programs: Effects on Title 1 students' educational opportunities and outcomes. In G. D. Borman, S. C. Stringfield, & R. E. Slavin (Eds.), *Title 1: Compensatory education at the crossroads* (pp. 79–116). Mahwah, NJ: Erlbaum.

Brown-Chidsey, R., & Steege, M. W. (2005). *Response to intervention: Principles and strategies for effective practice.* New York: Guilford Press.

Buly, M. R., & Valencia, S. W. (2002). Below the bar: Profiles of students who fail state reading assessments. *Educational Evaluation and Policy Analysis, 24*(3), 219–239.

Carr, M., Borkowski, J. G., & Maxwell, S. E. (1991). Motivational components of underachievement. *Developmental Psychology, 27*(1), 108–118.

Center, Y., Wheldall, K., Freeman, L., Outhred, L., & McNaught, M. (1995). An evaluation of Reading Recovery. *Reading Research Quarterly, 30*(2), 240–263.

Christ, T. J., Burns, M. K., & Ysseldyke, J. E. (2005). Conceptual confusion within response-to-intervention vernacular: Clarifying meaningful differences. *Communique, 34*, 6–8.

Dewitz, P., Jones, J., & Leahy, S. (2009). Comprehension strategy instruction in core reading programs. *Reading Research Quarterly, 44*(2), 102–126.

Duke, N., & Pearson, P. D. (2002). Effective practices for developing reading comprehension. In A. E. Farstrup & S. J. Samuels (Eds.), *What research says about reading instruction* (3rd ed., pp. 205–242). Newark, DE: International Reading Association.

Ehri, L. C., Dreyer, L. G., Flugman, B., & Gross, A. (2007). Reading rescue: An effective tutoring intervention model for language minority students who are struggling readers in first grade. *American Educational Research Journal, 44*(2), 414–448.

Fuchs, D., & Fuchs, L. S. (2005). Responsiveness-to-intervention: A blueprint for practitioners, policymakers, and parents. *Teaching Exceptional Children, 38*(1), 57–61.

Gates, A. I. (1937). Diagnosis and treatment of extreme cases of reading disability. In W. S. Gray (Ed.), *The teaching of reading* (Vol. 36, No. 1, pp. 409–417). Chicago: National Society for the Study of Education.

Gerber, S. B., Finn, J. D., Achilles, C. M., & Boyd-Zaharias, J. (2001). Teacher aides and students' academic achievement. *Educational Evaluation and Policy Analysis, 23*(2), 123–143.

Gray, C., McCloy, S., Dunbar, C., Dunn, J., Mitchell, D., & Ferguson, J. (2007). Added value or a familiar face: The impact of learning assistants on young readers. *Journal of Early Childhood Research, 5*(3), 285–300.

Hiebert, E. H., Colt, J. M., Catto, S. L., & Gury, E. C. (1992). Reading and writing of first-grade students in a restructured chapter 1 program. *American Educational Research Journal, 29*(3), 545–572.

Ikeda, M. J., Grimes, J., Tilly, W. D., Allison, R., Kurns, S., & Stumme, J. (2002). Implementing an intervention-based approach to service delivery: A case example. In M. R. Shinn, H. M. Walker, & G. Stoner (Eds.), *Interventions for academic and behavior problems II: Preventative and remedial approaches* (pp. 53–69). Bethesda, MD: National Association of School Psychologists.

Individuals with Disabilities Education Improvement Act of 2004, P.L. 108–446, 20 U.S.C. § *et seq.*

Johnston, P. (2010). A framework for response to intervention in literacy. In P. H. Johnston (Ed.) *RTI in Literacy—Responsive and comprehensive* (pp. 1–9). Newark, DE: International Reading Association.

Johnston, P. (2011). Response to intervention in literacy: Problems and possibilities. *Elementary School Journal, 111*(4), 511–534.

Johnston, P., Allington, R. L., & Afflerbach, P. (1985). The congruence of classroom and remedial reading instruction. *Elementary School Journal, 85*, 465–478.

Johnston, P. J. (2004). *Choice words: How our language affects children's learning.* Portland, ME: Stenhouse.

Knapp, M. S. (1995). *Teaching for meaning in high-poverty classrooms.* New York: Teachers College Press.

Knapp, M. S., & Shields, P. M. (Eds.). (1991). *Better schooling for the children of poverty: Alternatives to conventional wisdom.* Berkely, CA: McCutchan.

Knapp, M. S., Shields, P. M., & Turnbull, B. J. (1992). *Academic challenge for the children of poverty: Summary report.* Washington, DC: U.S. Department of Education, Office of Policy and Planning.

Kuhn, M. R., Schwanenflugel, P., Morris, R. D., Morrow, L. M., Woo, D., Meisinger, B., et al. (2006). Teaching children to become fluent and automatic readers. *Journal of Literacy Research, 38*(4), 357–388.

Lose, M. K. (2007). A child's response to intervention requires a responsive teacher of reading. *The Reading Teacher, 61*(3), 276–279.

Lyon, G. R., Fletcher, J. M., Shaywitz, S. E., Shaywitz, B. A., Torgesen, J. K., Wood, F. B., et al. (2001). Rethinking learning disabilities. In C. E. Finn, Jr., A. J. Rotherham, & C. R. Hokanson, Jr. (Eds.), *Rethinking special education for a new century* (pp. 259–297). Washington, DC: Thomas B. Fordham Foundation and the Progressive Policy Institute.

Mathes, P. G., Denton, C. A., Fletcher, J. M., Anthony, J. L., Francis, D. J., & Schatschneider, C. (2005). The effects of theoretically different instruction and student characteristics on the skills of struggling readers. *Reading Research Quarterly, 40*(2), 148–182.

Mosenthal, J., Lipson, M., Torncello, S., Russ, B., & Mekkelsen, J. (2004). Contexts and practices of six schools successful in obtaining reading achievement. *Elementary School Journal, 104*(5), 343–367.

Nye, B., Konstantopoulos, S., & Hedges, L. V. (2004). How large are teacher effects? *Educational Evaluation and Policy Analysis, 26*(3), 237–257.

O'Connor, R. E. (2000). Increasing the intensity of intervention in kindergarten through third grade. *Journal of Learning Disabilities, 38*(6), 532–538.

O'Connor, R. E., Bell, K. M., Harty, K. R., Larkin, L. K., Sackor, S. M., & Zigmond N. (2002). Teaching reading to poor readers in the intermediate grades: A comparison of text difficulty. *Journal of Educational Psychology, 94*(3), 474–485.

Pearson, P. D. (2003). The role of professional knowledge in reading reform. *Language Arts, 81*(1), 14–15.

Pinnell, G. S., Lyons, C. A., Deford, D. E., Bryk, A. S., & Seltzer, M. (1994). Comparing instructional models for the literacy education of high-risk first graders. *Reading Research Quarterly, 29*(1), 8–39.

Pressley, M. (2002). Effective beginning reading instruction. *Journal of Literacy Research, 34*(2), 165–188.

Puma, M. J., Karweit, N., Price, C., Ricciuti, A., Thompson, W., & Vaden-Kiernan, M. (1997). *Prospects: Final report on student outcomes.* Washington DC: U.S. Department of Education, Office of Planning and Evaluation Services.

Rules and Regulations for the Reauthorization of IDEA: Assistance to States for the Education of Children with Disabilities, Title 34, Part 300 C.F.R. Revised, 46743 Fed. Reg. 71.156 (August 14, 2006).

Scanlon, D.M. (2010). Response to intervention as an assessment approach. In A. McGill-Franzen & R. L. Allington (Eds.), *The handbook of reading disability research* (pp. 139–148). New York: Routledge.

Scanlon, D. M., Gelzheiser, L. M., Vellutino, F. R., Schatschneider, C., & Sweeney, J. M. (2008). Reducing the incidence of early reading difficulties: Professional development for classroom teachers vs. direct interventions for children. *Learning and Individual Differences, 18*, 346–359.

Scanlon, D. M., Vellutino, F. R., Small, S. G., Fanuele, D. P., & Sweeney, J. M. (2005). Severe reading difficulties—Can they be prevented? A comparision of prevention and intervention approaches. *Exceptionality, 13*(4), 209–227.

Schwartz, R. M. (2005). Literacy learning of at-risk first-grade students in the Reading Recovery early intervention. *Journal of Educational Psychology, 97*(2), 257–267.

Schwartz, R. M., Schmitt, M. C., & Lose, M. K. (2012). Effects of teacher-student ratio in response to intervention approaches. *Elementary School Journal, 112*(4), 547–567.

Stuhlman, M. W., & Pianta, R. C. (2009). Profiles of educational quality in first grade. *Elementary School Journal, 109*(4), 323–342.

Torgesen, J. K., Alexander, A. W., Wagner, R. K., Rashotte, C. A., Voeller, K., & Conway, T. (2001). Intensive remedial instruction for students with severe reading disabilities: Immediate and long-term outcomes from two instructional approaches. *Journal of Learning Disabilities, 34*, 33–58.

Valli, L., Croninger, R. G., & Walters, K. (2007). Who (else) is the teacher?: Cautionary notes on teacher accountability systems. *American Journal of Education, 113*(4), 635–662.

Vaughn, S., Linan-Thompson, S., & Hickman, P. (2003). Response to instruction as a means of identifying students with reading/learning disabilities. *Exceptional Children, 69*(4), 391–409.

Vaughn, S., Linan-Thompson, S., Kouzekanani, K., Bryant, D. P., Dickson, S., & Blozis, S. A. (2003). Reading instruction grouping for students with reading difficulties. *Remedial and Special Education, 24*(5), 301–315.

Vellutino, F. R. (2010). Learning to be learning disabled: Marie Clay's seminal contribution to the response to intervention approach to identifying specific reading disability. *Journal of Reading Recovery, 10*(1), 5–23.

Vellutino, F. R., & Fletcher, J. M. (2005). Developmental dyslexia. In M. Snowling & C. Hulme (Eds.), *The science of reading: A handbook* (pp. 362–378). Malden, MA: Blackwell.

Vellutino, F. R., Sipay, E. R., Small, S. G., Pratt, A., Chen, R., & Denckla, M. B. (1996). Cognitive profiled of difficult-to-remediate and readily remediated poor readers: Early intervention as a vehicle for distinguishing between cognitive and experiential deficits as basic causes of specific reading disability. *Journal of Educational Psychology, 88*(4), 601–638.

Wasik, B. A., & Slavin, R. E. (1993). Preventing early reading failure with one-to-one tutoring: A review of five programs. *Reading Research Quarterly, 28*, 179–200.

What Works Clearinghouse. (2007). *Beginning reading.* Available at *http://ies.ed.gov/ncee/wwc/FindWhatWorks.aspx?o=6&n=Reading/Writing&r=1.*

Index